Cambridge Human Geography

UNIONS AND COMMUNITIES
UNDER SIEGE

Cambridge Human Geography

UNIONS
AND COMMUNITIES
UNDER SIEGE

*American communities and the crisis
of organized labor*

GORDON L. CLARK

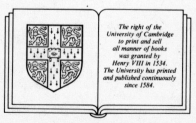

The right of the
University of Cambridge
to print and sell
all manner of books
was granted by
Henry VIII in 1534.
The University has printed
and published continuously
since 1584.

CAMBRIDGE UNIVERSITY PRESS

Cambridge

New York   New Rochelle   Melbourne   Sydney

Published by the Press Syndicate of the University of Cambridge
The Pitt Building, Trumpington Street, Cambridge CB2 IRP
32 East 57th Street, New York, NY 10022, USA
10 Stamford Road, Oakleigh, Melbourne 3166, Australia

First published 1989

Printed in Great Britain at the University Press, Cambridge

British Library cataloguing in publication data

Clark, Gordon L.
Unions and communities under siege:
American communities and the crisis of
organized labor. – (Cambridge human geography).
1. United States. Trade Unions, 1970–1988.
Social aspects
I. Title
331.88′0973

Library of Congress cataloguing in publication data

Clark, Gordon L.
Unions and communities under seige: American communities and the
crisis of organized labor / Gordon L. Clark.
p.   cm. – (Cambridge human geography)
Bibliography.
Includes index.
ISBN 0 521 36516 3
1. Industrial relations – United States.   2. Labor laws and
legislation United States.   3. Trade unions – United States –
Jurisdictional disputes – Case studies.   4. Community development –
United States. I. Title. II. Series.
HD8072.5.C63 1989
331.88′0973 – dc1988–28248   CIP

ISBN 0 521 36516 3

*For my grandfather Percy Victor Clark
(1895–1978), a railway worker and unionist of
another time and place.*

A better relationship between labor and management is the high purpose of this act. By assuring the employees the right of collective bargaining it fosters the development of the employment contract on a fair and equitable basis. By providing an orderly procedure for determining who is entitled to represent the employees, it aims to remove one of the chief causes of wasteful economic strife. By preventing practices which tend to destroy the independence of labor, it seeks, for every worker within its scope, that freedom of choice and action which is justly his. (President Franklin D. Roosevelt, 79 Cong. Rec. 10720, 5 July 1935)

[The NLRA] creates a democracy within industry which gives to our industrial workers the same general idea of freedom which the founding fathers conferred upon citizens of the United States. (Mead [D–New York], 79 Cong. Rec. 9710, 19 June 1935)

Mr. Speaker, eternal vigilance is the price American workingmen must pay for economic freedom. The strong right hand of labor must always be on the alert to stave off the armed forces of aggrandizement, and unfortunately, labor must be equally as vigilant to safeguard its interest from the mistakes of those who pose as well-meaning friends.

The amendment (Wagner–Connery disputes bill) strikes a damaging blow against national unions which labor through its own efforts has created and degenerates into an extension of the Government–union idea, one union for each plant. (Gildea [D–Pennsylvania], 79 Cong. Rec. 9731-32, 19 June 1935)

Contents

PART V   PROSPECTS FOR ORGANIZED LABOR

Tables

Figure

Preface

The essential argument of this book is that the current crisis of organized labor ought to be considered in terms of the local context of labor–management relations; that is, the communities in which men and women live and work. This argument, and the overall logic of the book, are premised upon two suppositions. First, whether by design or necessity, the structure of New Deal national labor legislation has sustained and maintained distinctive local labor–management practices. Second, as the economies of American communities (and the world) have become highly interdependent, reflecting the evolution of corporate structure and trade between economies, unions have found it difficult achieving a similar scale of integration. Indeed, the crisis of the union movement can be traced, in part, to unions' dependence upon inter-community solidarity, a fragile democratic ideal which is often overwhelmed by economic imperatives operating at higher scales in other places.

In evaluating others' analytical frameworks which have been used to study the recent performance of American labor unions, I have been surprised at the neglect or disinterest shown by scholars of the intersection between unions and communities. Too often, the diversity of local experience is rationalized in terms of a supposedly all-embracing national labor–management relations system, despite bitter disputes between labor and management which seem to have the community as an essential ingredient. And, too often, it is imagined that unions are just like corporations; national and international institutions, structured as hierarchical top–down command organizations reflecting the imperatives of the market. In a very special way, the Wagner Act of 1935 conceived unions to be federations of local democracies. Even if unions are not as idealized, legislative imperatives place a premium on local decision making and create the potential for divided loyalties within unions and between communities.

It is hard to remember a more divisive strike than the recent one involving members of the United Food and Commercial Workers union at the Hormel plant in Austin, Minnesota. Not only was the whole community divided for and against the company and the union, but the union itself was internally divided between the Local and its International executive. Ultimately, the

International union and the company prevailed over the Local, at great emotional and financial cost to the local community. Although of unusual intensity, the Hormel strike reminds us that the locus of many labor–management disputes is in particular localities, distinguished from one another by their own histories of unionization and solidarity. I would assert that these kinds of disputes are more common than often recognized. Not only do they have drastic implications for the economic prosperity of affected communities, but the internal coherence of unions and the integrity of institutions like the National Labor Relations Board are at risk as they attempt to rationalize local disputes in terms of their wider interests.

Three particular themes or perspectives appear and reappear throughout the book: the role of the community in labor–management relations; the roles of institutions like the National Labor Relations Board and the courts (state and federal) in adjudicating local labor–management disputes; and the significance of economic and geographical restructuring for the roles and future of industrial unions. In all parts of the book, these themes appear as major ingredients of the story, though the emphasis may vary. For example, part II illustrates these themes through two case studies: chapter 3 analyzes a plant closing in Allentown, Pennsylvania; and chapter 4 analyzes an arbitrator's adjudication of a dispute involving the United Auto Workers and the American Motors Corporation over an economic restructuring package which required job rationing between communities on the basis of corporate seniority. While some chapters tend to focus upon one theme, reference is always made to the other themes. For example, in chapter 8 the adjudicative integrity of the National Labor Relations Board is analyzed with reference to disputes over the location and relocation of work.

The book is quite complex, not only in subject matter and material but also in its methods and techniques of analysis. In the relevant chapters, these issues are discussed in depth. Stripping complexity from a problem is sometimes thought to be the *raison d'être* of social science. In this instance, a goal of the book is to give the complexity of local labor–management relations their due. In fact, I would suggest that the geographical complexity of labor–management relations is a vital research question even though labor relations specialists have tended to ignore the intersection of these themes in much of their work. This is despite the fact that their intersection is a distinctive aspect of the US labor–management relations system.

It should be apparent from the significance I attach to the intersection of these themes that the book trespasses (in Albert Hirschman's use of the word) across many fields of academic inquiry. At a minimum the disciplines of economics, geography, and law are represented, as are specialists' fields within these disciplines. I am not about to apologize for crossing disciplinary boundaries, nor do I spend much time defending my interdisciplinary perspective. After all, disciplinary boundaries seem more than the products of the management and defense of academics' institutional interests than the necessary limits of scholarly curiosity.

Of course, I recognize that integrating the community and the institutions of adjudication with the patterns of American unionism involves a great deal of judgment, especially with regard to the relevant literature and conceptual foundations. In the main, I have attempted to make a contribution to each field of study while maintaining the integrity of my overall interest in the intersection between themes. The accumulating crisis of the American labor movement demands a broad appreciation of the various processes at work; the aesthetics of any one discipline seems less relevant in this context.

I wish to demonstrate the significance of the intersection between communities, unions, and institutions, in understanding the prospects for major American industrial unions. No one test is produced to demonstrate the scope of their interconnections. Rather, I depend on the breadth of the book, the various legal cases, local case studies, and statistical analyses, to indicate the varying levels of significance of their intersection. Consequently, the book should be understood as a set of studies, sustained by many different examples and methods of analysis. My hope is to show by the end that the geography of American labor relations and the economy are vitally important if we are to understand the current predicament of organized labor.

Part I is devoted to an evaluation of the temporal and spatial patterns of declining unionization, and the literature that has attempted to make sense of these patterns. I argue against those who imagine the problem to be simply one of institutional ineptitude, or "old age," or something related to a strand of American ideology which would characterize society as a non-class society. The argument is made for a community-oriented perspective, set within a more general conception of the structure of American labor–management relations. Chapter 1 is relatively short and focused upon the recent geographical patterns of unionization in the United States. Chapter 2 makes the transition between the first and second parts of the book. It is a critical review of the relevant literature on union growth and decline, and the nature of unions as institutions.

The two chapters of part II develop the issues raised in the first part of the book through a set of two case studies. Chapter 3 is based upon a case study of a dispute between the United Auto Workers and Mack Trucks Corporation. This case allows me to explore many of the issues and themes relating to economic and geographical restructuring that appear throughout the book. Chapter 4 takes these issues further and considers an instance of a local union at war with its International; a case involving the United Auto Workers and the American Motors Corporation. My approach in these chapters is interpretive as opposed to fundamentally definitive. And, the interpretive perspective is constant through textual inquiries into the evolution of labor legislation, case studies, analyses of decisions by the National Labor Relations Board, and statistical analyses of unions' performance in representation elections.

In part III, the theoretical perspectives on union growth and decline are utilized to understand the electoral performance of two industrial unions, the International Brotherhood of Electrical Workers and the United Auto Workers, in representation elections over the period 1970 to 1986. The latter union is especially important to the book. Many of the case studies draw upon issues and disputes that involve the union. Its importance to the US labor movement is well known, as is its historical role in the creation of industrial unionism. Unlike some other industrial unions of similar size, it has welcomed academic study. Thus, the book uses many examples relating to its recent activities. In part III, I report the results of statistical analyses of electoral performance, focusing upon overall patterns (chapter 5), unions' electoral strategies given the geographical diversity of electoral units (chapter 6), and the role of the National Labor Relations Board in facilitating and affecting unions' electoral performance (chapter 7).

After a consideration of the role of the National Labor Relations Board in representation elections, part IV is devoted to understanding the substantive goals of the Board. This involves a brief discussion of the logic of federal labor law, from the Wagner Act to Taft–Hartley and, in detail, the adjudicative practices of the Board. Chapter 8 considers the role and stature of the National Labor Relations Board, both in terms of its political legitimacy and its adjudicative integrity. Also considered are possible local innovations in labor–management relations like the Saturn Project, and how these innovations relate to recent decisions of the Reagan-appointee dominated National Labor Relations Board (chapter 9). This chapter also provides a transition to the topic of the final part of the book: the future of the labor movement.

With an understanding of the recent performance of industrial unions and an interpretation of the roles of the National Labor Relations Board, part V speculates upon the likely future of organized labor. Chapter 10 analyzes the prospects for labor law reform, emphasizing the role that political coalitions – north and south, Republican and Democrat – have played in previous attempts at reform. In chapter 11 I consider likely state court-based innovations in local labor–management relations, emphasizing recent developments in employment-at-will and the notion of employment contracts in

nonunion environments. Chapter 12 concludes the book with a reconsideration of my arguments for a geographical perspective on the crisis of
organized labor. So many issues are involved that it would be foolish to
proclaim *the* future of American communities and organized labor. Industrial unions may in fact not survive, and their communities may dissolve
under the pressure of wholesale economic and geographical restructuring.

A number of chapters in this book were originally written as scholarly
papers and first appeared in academic journals. Where appropriate, these
papers have been updated and revised so as to reflect the thrust of the book.
A few chapters tend to be more self-contained than others, referencing
research issues and methods in the literature rather than immediately
adjacent chapters. Still, in writing each paper I was quite conscious of how it
was related to the others. And in revising each, I have attempted to build in
the links not previously apparent. The linkage I have in mind is most
obvious between the chapters on unions' performance in representation
elections; these chapters were originally planned as a sequential set of
papers. Perhaps less obvious, but no less planned, are the links between the
chapters on the role of the National Labor Relations Board, even if not
originally written in sequential form.

A danger with this kind of strategy is that technical aspects of separate
chapters may overwhelm the substantive themes of the book. I hope this is
not the case. Though there may be issues that only interest experts, each
chapter was deliberately written in a relatively open style, emphasizing
broad conceptual issues like the role of community in representation
elections rather than technical niceties like estimating predictive models of
unions' electoral performance. In any event, the contribution of a chapter or
part of the book must be judged in relation to the issues addressed therein as
well as its connections to the logic of the whole project. Readers may find
differences between chapters in structure, object, and method. These
differences are the result of my goal of providing a comprehensive overview
of the relationships between unions and communities, economic and
geographical restructuring, and the role of institutions in adjudicating the
structure of the economic landscape.

Acknowledgments

This book was written under the auspices of Carnegie Mellon University's Center for Labor Studies. Ben Fischer, Director of the Center, contributed greatly to the book with his enthusiasm for critical debate about the crucial issues facing labor unions. My understanding of labor–management relations, unions, and the evolution of the American labor movement broadened immeasurably because of many conversations with Ben over the past couple of years. Few commentators on the labor relations scene have Ben's wisdom and perspicacity, and few are as generous with their knowledge.

Ben Fischer and Everett Kassalow read and gave constructive comments and advice on practically all parts of the book. Many others have read portions of it as chapters and papers in a variety of forums. Where appropriate I have acknowledged their help in notes to each chapter. Readers' reactions were very useful both as criticism and as encouragement in taking the project from conception to completion. I would also like to thank seminar participants at the University of California, Los Angeles, and the Hubert Humphrey Institute of the University of Minnesota. Their interest in my opinions and their arguments in response prompted the formative stages of the project.

Empirical models of union performance in representation elections developed and presented here are based upon a series of papers which were co-authored with Kris Johnston. The overall conception of the project was a joint enterprise, as was the development of each paper. I am very grateful for her collaboration. John Anderson, Michael Childs, and Vivian Wang collected and organized the initial data set upon which these papers were based. Subsequently, both Andreas Olligschlaeger and Jae-Hong Kim provided the expertise to up-date the data set. Steve Garber and Neil Wrigley gave very useful advice about the empirical estimation procedures used in these chapters.

Many of the chapters are based on the experience of two unions, the International Brotherhood of Electrical Workers and the International Union, United Automobile, Aerospace & Agricultural Implement Workers of America. The United Auto Workers union was particularly responsive in providing material on a number of issues. In this respect, I would like to thank Leonard Page and Howard Young especially. Charles McDonald of the AFL–CIO and Joseph Moore of the National Labor Relations Board also contributed useful insights and information on the current status of American unions. My knowledge of organized labor and the environment now facing the union movement was very much helped by Shirley Clark and her colleagues of the United Steelworkers of America.

Writing and researching this book was made possible by the Center for Labor Studies and an earlier commitment of financial support by Martin Baral. Martin's generosity was instrumental in beginning work on the topics covered in this book. He has also provided support in previous projects leading up to this book. It is a pleasure to be able to thank him formally for his support of my research – past and present.

Finally, I would like to thank John Ashby of Pion Ltd. for permission to reproduce portions of papers originally published as "The geography of US union elections" (parts I through V) in *Environment and Planning A* 19 (1987). Clark University provided permission to publish portions of "Restructuring the US economy" which initially appeared in *Economic Geography* 62 (1986), and Butterworths gave permission for republication of "A question of integrity: the National Labor Relations Board and the relocation of work," which appeared in *Political Geography Quarterly* 7 (1988).

None of the above should be held responsible for any of the arguments or opinions expressed in this book. Rightly or wrongly, these are the sole responsibility of the author.

PART I

Economy and community

I

Crisis of organized labor

In an era predicted by some to be the mature, growth-consolidation phase of industrial unionism (Lester 1958), the United States labor movement is fighting for its survival. Industrial labor unions, the traditional centers of union power in the economy and in the labor movement, are particularly threatened. Some of these unions have lost as much as 40 percent of their membership base over the last decade. Not only have they suffered from economic restructuring, but these unions are winning proportionally fewer and fewer representation elections, contesting fewer elections, and winning only in smaller and smaller electoral units. Internally and externally industrial unions are under siege.

One startling aspect of recent patterns of union decline is that the survival of industrial unions is under threat even in their home domain: northern industrial towns and cities. Diversification strategies like the United Auto Workers' southern strategy have become practically impossible to affect. Declining membership is the norm, and growth of membership a distant memory. In contrast, over the past decade service workers' unions seem to have been able to extend their representation of American workers, though even this trend has slowed in recent years. With structural changes in the economy, large-scale displacement of industrial employment, and a relatively poor performance of industrial unions in representation elections, the flow of members to the American labor movement has slowed to barely a trickle.

These patterns require explanation. Likewise, our inherited intellectual frameworks designed for understanding the patterns and complexities of the American labor movement require revision. It is clear that standard frameworks are inadequate. This much has been recognized in numerous reviews of the academic literature, wherein commentators complain that dominant models of unionization have failed to comprehend the complexity of processes and the diversity of patterns of American unionization. Sometimes it is suggested that their failure is a product of ad hoc theorizing (a point made by Fiorito and Greer 1982); other times it is suggested that their failure is methodological and empirical (see Hirsch and Addison's 1986 extended review). I hope to help in the intellectual reconstruction process,

3

particularly with regard to raising the significance of the geographical dimensions of American unionism.

This chapter has two interlocking components. One is a description of the patterns of declining American unionism. Here, the focus is upon the stocks and flows of unionization – union membership and union success rates in representation elections by industry, union, and region. The second is an argument for a geographical perspective on American unionism; in terms of understanding the decline of organized labor, and understanding location decision making.

Declining unionism in America

That the US labor movement is fighting for its survival has been recognized by many commentators. The AFL–CIO's Committee on the Future of Work (1985) responded by proposing alternatives to traditional union policies, emphasizing how changes in the structure of work are likely to bring into being new forms of unions and union objectives. Academics sympathetic to the objectives of the labor movement but otherwise doubtful of unions' ability to fashion and implement new policies have become involved in publicly defending and advancing unions as desirable economic agents in advancing labor productivity and competitiveness (see Freeman 1985, and Freeman and Medoff 1984). Still, compared to other advanced industrial countries, the American labor movement is a shell of its past. While unions in other countries, especially the United Kingdom, France, and West Germany, are also under some pressure from conservative governments, the American labor movement is faced with extinction.[1]

Recognition of the crisis of declining levels of unionization, let alone development of policies to deal with the crisis, has been a source of considerable debate amongst union leaders. There appears to be no consensus for a single cause of this crisis, within the union movement and/or amongst academic commentators. Some would blame the Reagan administration for the most recent downturn in rates of unionization. Coincident with, or because of the Reagan administration, there was a precipitous decline in union strength during the 1980s. In just over eight years, unions' share of the work force dropped from about 25 percent in 1978 to 21.9 percent in 1982, to about 17.5 percent in 1986 (table 1.1). All indications are that there has been a further drop in unions' share of employment in the last couple of years.[2]

Weiler (1983, 1984a,b) identified supposed anti-union attitudes of Reagan-appointed members of the National Labor Relations Board (NLRB), delays in the representation election process, and an adjudication process

Table 1.1. *US union membership, for
selected years 1953–86*

Year	Total (000)	Percent (empl.)
1953	16,310	32.5
1960	15,516	28.6
1970	20,990	29.6
1974	22,165	28.3
1978	21,757	25.1
1982	19,571	21.9
1986	16,975	17.5

Sources: Troy and Sheflin (1985, table
3.41, pp. 3–10) and unpublished
data from the US Department of
Labor (Washington DC)

quite unable to deal with the explosion of management unfair labor
practices, as vital reasons for unions' most recent decline. By some accounts,
the Reagan NLRB has sought to strip unions of their traditional contract
privileges, and limit their discretion in management decisions, leading one
labor law scholar to suggest that the current Board is the most anti-labor
Board on record (Murphy 1987). These issues have prompted renewed calls
for federal labor law reform and reform of the NLRB, its procedures, and
the right-to-work (RTW) option provided to states by the Taft–Hartley
amendments of 1947. Other commentators are less concerned about possible
biases of adjudication, and contend that poor performance in representation
elections is due to unions' incompetence. This is Getman's (1986) opinion,
informed by a detailed case study of a union's internal organization of the
organizing process at Yale University.

There is general agreement that unions' poor performance in representation elections is a vital part of any explanation of the overall patterns of
decline. But more often than not, studies of unions' electoral performance
have failed to consider the role of localities in understanding aggregate
patterns of decline. There is also general agreement that regulation of local
labor–management relations by the NLRB has something to do with these
trends. But, few would agree with Goldfield (1987) that anti-union sentiment
within regulatory agencies like the NLRB and the courts is the essential basis
for understanding the crisis of organized labor. In fact, for all the rhetoric
there are very few studies of the interaction between regulative environ-
ment(s) – NLRB, RTW, and local – and union success rates in representation elections.

Another kind of explanation of union decline centers upon the changing structure of the US economy (see Dickens and Leonard 1985). In historically highly unionized industrial sectors like autos, chemicals, rubber, and steel there are literally fewer jobs than ten years ago. Deindustrialization has taken its toll of workers and communities, and the once dominant industry-concentrated unions like the United Auto Workers and the United Steel-workers of America. Manufacturing has for many years been steadily declining in relative significance as an employer. Recently, though, this process seems to have accelerated as manufacturing has not only lost relative position but absolute numbers of employment. According to Farber (1987), economic crises in traditional industries have meant fewer union jobs and, perhaps just as importantly, less loyalty (as indicated by declining union success rates in representation elections) of workers to their unions.[3]

By this logic, the changing structure of the US economy has drastically affected the stock of available union jobs, and has also reduced the flow of new members to these unions. Implied by this argument is a certain geographical fixity of the process of declining unionism. To the extent that deindustrialization is spatially concentrated as measured by employment losses and the like, declining unionization is also spatially concentrated. But as I argue in chapters 3 and 4, the fragility of union support could be interpreted as the product of corporate (re)location strategies designed to fragment and avoid unions. In this interpretation, not only has the home domain of organized labor been affected by economic restructuring and its attendant job losses, but corporations may have designed geographical restructuring programs as deliberate anti-union strategies.

At this point, I am not about to adjudicate between explanations of declining unionization – explicating their relative significance is, after all, an objective of the book. The decline of organized labor is a very complicated issue, made so by the economic and geographical diversity of the US economy. However, it should be immediately obvious from the discussion here that I favor an explanation of declining unionism which integrates issues of national and local economic restructuring with the regulation of labor–management relations, and the process of local representation elections. Their precise relationships with one another will, of course, vary in particular instances.

Labor relations and location

Location is a vital element in understanding union performance and the anti-union strategies of corporations. At an obvious level, the connection between location and labor relations was created by the structure of federal and state labor relations laws. But at a deeper level, the connection is strategic in the sense that unions and employers use this inherited geography in their bargaining with one another as their behavior is structured by the geography of labor relations. For the reader to appreciate the significance of this argument it is important to understand the background to these issues, especially the rudiments of location theory.

Weber's (1929) industrial location theory, developed with reference to Von Thunen's (1964) original masterpiece on land rent, integrated labor costs with transportation costs to generate maps of industrial production.[4] Most industrial location theories give labor costs a central role in allocating production across the landscape, especially neoclassical economic theories.[5] Labor costs were defined by Weber as those costs of production directly attributed to "the expenditures of human labor" (Weber 1929:95). While he accepted that labor was not a commodity like other production inputs, he nevertheless suggested that in economic terms, "the energies expended in labor ... are in a capitalistic economy of today the wages and salaries which are paid out per unit of product" (95). Weber's economic landscape was formed through the techniques of marginal economic analysis, and with reference to the inherited economic system (capitalism).

Weber apparently aimed to go beyond abstract theory. He claimed to have a "realistic" theory (12) of the "location of industries" (1) (see Gregory 1981, p. 536 for an interpretation of the "realistic" roots of Weber's theory). But, at the same time, he aimed to provide a "pure" theory of location. In particular, he analyzed the rules of location relevant to labor costs, transportation costs, and agglomeration economies. He excluded reference to "any differences of political organization and to the influence of trade and tariff policies; and ... to differences of race, climate, and environment" (13). While he considered these issues relevant to the organization of the international economy, to the extent that they were also important within nations he would also have excluded them from consideration.

Like Von Thunen, who used a featureless isolated state, Weber sought to develop his theory within a featureless institutional and physical environment. This does not mean that he thought these issues unimportant: quite the contrary. He argued that his pure theory of industrial location was just a first step; a general theory would necessarily introduce these issues afterwards.

Since publication of *Theory of the location of industries*, location theorists have been preoccupied with Weber's first step. This has meant a very narrow conception of the location problem, a limited repertoire of analytical techniques, a limited definition of labor costs, and the exclusion of some of the most important factors (like institutional regulations) affecting the location of economic activities within and between nations. Essentially, few steps have been made to account for the issues which Weber thought so crucial, but which he deliberately left out of his pure theory of industrial location. It is little wonder that conventional location theory has so few adherents nowadays, despite attempts to generalize Weber's original theory (Smith 1981). Weber's expansive conception of the industrial location problem has not been taken seriously enough.

Still, there have been some recent developments in location theory which might be interpreted in the spirit of Weber's expansive conception of the location problem. Here, I refer to the growing literature on the structure of local social relations of production, their role in firms' location decisions, and their implications for the reproduction of spatial economic differentiation. Of course, the underlying rationale of this literature is quite different from Weber's pure theory of industrial location. Instead of using standard neoclassical theoretical tools, the analytical logic is premised upon a commitment to historical materialism. The cost of labor is broadly interpreted, including reference to issues like the flexibility of local work practices with respect to technological innovation, and the allocation of the social wage between capital, the local community, and the state.

For example, Richard Walker (1985) argued that technological change and regional growth and decline is mediated, indeed sustained, through local employment relations. To the extent that regions are dominated by different forms of employment relations there will be consequent differences in the pace, type, and nature of technological change. It is apparent that the institutional environment of production is the crucial factor in allocating capital between places.[6] In an empirical analysis of this proposition, Clark, Gertler, and Whiteman (1986, ch. 3), differences in state-level regulations regarding workers' rights of union representation and open-shop employment were argued to be fundamentally important in understanding the locational imperatives of firms' investment decisions, and the consequent map of economic growth and decline.

Similarly, Warde (1985) and Cooke (1985), following Massey's (1984) lead, argued that differences in local work practices provide multi-locational firms with opportunities to dominate certain geographical labor markets, and thereby escape entrapment by sections of organized labor who would otherwise constrain firms' abilities to accumulate capital. Johnston's (1986) paper on the role of the National Labor Relations Board in regulating relocation decisions has shown that the institutional structure of local labor relations can have a deciding role in firms' location decisions. In Johnston's example, the right of a firm to relocate production during the course of a contract was interpreted by the NLRB in terms of a legal relationship between capital and labor. The fact that the local social relations of production are regulated by government and interpreted by the courts emphasizes the important role of institutions in structuring the map(s) of production.

There are, of course, a variety of approaches used by those writing on this theme. Generally, though, it is assumed that understanding the structure of local labor relations is a necessary step if a more general, and historically realistic, theory of location is to be developed. As Scott (1985:479) suggested, "the characteristics of social life and reproduction in the spatial context are decisively structured by the division of labor . . . [and] the forms of social life and reproduction that emerge at specific places feed back upon locational processes and the organization of production." Instead of labor costs being interpreted narrowly as simply wages and salaries, the whole ensemble of local class relations is the object of inquiry. In this sense, the literature on the spatial division of labor is premised upon the political and environmental factors so quickly excluded by Weber from his theory of location.[7]

In this setting, the geography of unionization is very important for a couple of reasons. Not only does it go to the heart of current problems faced by the union movement, but it also has a crucial role to play in the strategies and behavior of corporations with respect to unions. Not only is the overall national level of unionization important, but so too is the spatial differentiation of unionization. In the remaining sections of this chapter these dimensions are described over space and time.

Patterns of unionization

In the early 1950s, unions' share of national nonagricultural employment peaked at about 39.0 percent. Since then the level of national unionization has significantly declined. From 1954 to 1980, unions' share of working men and women fell from 39.2 percent to 23.6 percent (Dickens and Leonard 1985). Periodically, unionization levels have stabilized, even slightly increased (table 1.1). Through most of the 1960s and 1970s, unionization was around 28.0 percent, with slight ups (1960, 1970, 1978) and downs (1974, 1982) associated with macroeconomic conditions. Kokkelenberg and Sockell (1985) contend that unionization was relatively constant over the period 1973 to 1981. At the most general level, the evidence seems to support their claims, although it appears that there was a steady erosion of union support beginning in the late 1970s. However, since 1980, there appears to have been a precipitous decline in unionization.

At one time, the major industrial unions were the national leaders. Indeed, in the early 1950s, the Steelworkers Union was the nation's largest

Table 1.2. *Membership (000) and affiliation of the ten
largest US unions, 1983*

Union (affl.)	Membership
Teamsters (AFL–CIO)	1,523
National Education Assn. (Ind.)	1,444
Food and Commercial Wks. (AFL–CIO)	993
AFSCME (AFL–CIO)	959
United Auto Workers (AFL–CIO)	904
IBEW (AFL–CIO)	820
United Steelworkers (AFL–CIO)	707
Carpenters (AFL–CIO)	609
Service Employees Union (AFL–CIO)	589
Communication Workers (AFL–CIO)	573

Source: Gifford (1986, appendix A), and Troy and Sheflin (1985,
table 3.33, pp. 3–6)

union, with over one million members. By 1983 (table 1.2), however, it was
at the lower end of the top ten unions. Twenty-five years ago, the top ten list
would have been dominated by other unions like the Machinists Union.
Now, the service unions are much more important. Current membership
patterns by union are indicative of more general trends of employment
growth in non-manufacturing industries, and the recent economic and
manufacturing crisis which stripped many of the industrial unions of a third
or more of their members.

As Table 1.2 indicates, in 1983 American unionization was spread
between a variety of sectors. Beginning with the Teamsters Union, an
independent diversified union with strong representation in the transportation industry,[8] the next three unions were professional (National Education Association), service oriented (Food and Commercial Workers
Union), and white-collar oriented (AFSCME, a union representing state and
local government employees). Then, the UAW (United Auto Workers) and
the IBEW (International Brotherhood of Electrical Workers) followed – two
quite different unions, the former industrial production-oriented, the latter
craft-oriented with strong representation in a range of industries and firms
including electrical and construction. The Steelworkers Union ranked about
seventh, a more diversified union with proportionally more members from
the clerical and service sectors. After these three industrial unions came
another service workers' union (Service Employees Union), and the Commu-
nication Workers, who are closely related to the telecommunications sector,
and especially AT&T.

Table 1.3. *Percent of US unionized employment by region, and share of national unionized employment by region, 1975 and 1982*

	1975		1982	
Region	% union	% share	% union	% share
New England	24.3	5.1	18.6	5.2
Middle Atlantic	37.5	23.5	29.8	22.6
East North Central	36.0	24.6	21.0	22.6
West North Central	25.8	6.9	21.1	7.2
South Atlantic	17.2	9.3	12.8	9.6
East South Central	21.6	4.2	17.0	4.3
West South Central	17.3	5.5	12.8	6.4
Mountain	23.5	3.6	16.5	3.9
Pacific	35.7	16.7	26.7	17.7
Territories	19.4	0.6	13.1	0.5
United States	28.9	100.0	21.9	100.0

Source: Troy and Sheflin (1985, tables 7.12 and 7.14, pp. 7–13, 7–15)

American unions have had quite variable rates of success in penetrating local labor markets. Indeed, whatever the national unionization trends over the post-Second World War period, the regional patterns have been far more diverse. Table 1.3 reports unionization rates by census regions for two years, 1975 and 1982 (the latest available data). Three patterns should be immediately discernible in this table. First, national levels of American unionization were very dependent upon rates of unionization in just three regions. This was apparent for 1975, and more recently in 1982. These three regions were the Middle Atlantic, East North Central, and Pacific regions, contributing in sum 64.8 (1975) and 62.9 (1982) percent to total national unionization. Second, these same three regions had the highest rates of unionization in both years, but also had the largest declines in unionization levels between 1975 and 1982. For example the Middle Atlantic region lost nearly 8.0 percentage points during this period, while the East North Central region lost about 15.

Third, other regions had generally lower rates of unionization, especially the three southern regions of the South Atlantic and the East and West South Central. This was true for both years, although their rates of unionization did not decline as precipitously from 1975 to 1982 as was the case in the three most important regions. Their contribution to national unionization was consequently quite low, even if their relative contribution to overall unionization slightly increased over the period 1975 to 1982 (from 19.0 to 20.3 percent). Comparatively, the New England region was highly unionized, but contributed relatively little to the national level of unionization.

Rates of unionization by states for selected years 1953 to 1982 are reported in table 1.4. Similar patterns to table 1.3 are discernible in this table. That is, there were quite marked regional effects for each sample year. For instance, even in 1953, a year of strong growth for many US unions, the South Atlantic states of North and South Carolina had very low rates of unionization (8.5 and 9.4 percent respectively) compared to the New England states of Massachusetts and Rhode Island (30.4 and 28.0 percent respectively), let alone compared to a East North Central state like Michigan (44.6 percent).

This geography was relatively consistent over the whole period, even if there has been some minor convergence in rates of unionization between the states. Essentially, those states with the highest rates of unionization in 1953 lost the most over the 1953 to 1982 period. Thus the difference between the highest (54.2 percent for Washington) and lowest (8.5 percent for North Carolina) rates of state unionization in 1953 was 45.7 percentage points, compared to 30 percentage points (35.8 percent for New York and 5.8 percent for South Carolina) in 1982.

Over this period, there were some notable changes in state-level unionization. That is, from 1953 to 1960 to 1975 and to 1982, unionization declined, then increased, and then declined again for most states, including Alabama, Arkansas, and Louisiana (in the South) and Pennsylvania and New York (in the North). These years were, of course, indicative of the economic fortunes of the national economy – 1953 to 1960 average economic growth, 1960 to 1975 strong economic growth (interrupted in the early 1970s by a sharp recession), and 1975 to 1982 characterized respectively by economic growth and economic crisis.

For some other states, however, unionization declined through most of these years, including New Jersey (in the North) and California (on the west coast). In one case, Hawaii, unionization actually increased, from 14.0 percent in 1953 to 31.5 percent in 1982. There was only one other instance where an increase was recorded over the entire period, but that increase was marginal (North Carolina 8.5 to 8.9 percent). Again, it was apparent that those states with the highest rates of unionization lost the most percentage points, while those states with relatively lower, middle-order, levels of unionization lost the fewest percentage points.

To summarize, the following observations can be made about American unionization during the post-Second World War period. First, unionization appears as a process which is very geographically differentiated. Indeed, American unionization appears as a north central and west-coast phenomenon, as opposed to a national or even a multi-regional phenomenon. It also appears from table 1.4 that American unionization has been strongly geographically differentiated for many years.

Second, state unionization levels have often been affected by patterns of economic growth and decline. This is surely the lesson of table 1.4, as regards fluctuations in state unionization rates over time. Up until about 1975, unionization rates were relatively stable, albeit successively lower with each recession and recovery. Since then, perhaps because of changing economic conditions, unionization has drastically declined.

Third, given the importance of three regions to overall national levels of unionization, the decline in national unionization can be directly attributed to massive declines in state levels of unionization of those regions over the recent period 1970 to 1982. In fact, as the geographical dispersion of state unionization rates has declined, so too have the fortunes of the national union movement. It might also be contended that the failure of the union movement to penetrate other regions, especially in the South, over this period contributed to the decline of national unionization rates.

Representation election procedures

This discussion of the patterns of unionization would not be complete without a brief analysis of unions' success rates in representation elections. How successful have unions been in adding to their stock of members over this period? Since national unionization rates are ultimately derived from local representation elections, we must consider more directly the spatial and temporal patterns of these election results since 1970. Before considering the patterns of election results, it might be useful to the reader to consider first the rules of representation elections.

Typically, employees and/or unions petition the NLRB (the regional director) for certification, and supply evidence that there is sufficient interest among those relevant workers for an election. It is also possible that individuals (employees and employers) may petition for decertification of an existing union representing a relevant group of workers. The overwhelming majority of petitions are by workers for certification.

Having received the petition, the appropriate regional director of the NLRB then conducts an investigation to ascertain: (a) whether or not the employer meets the NLRB's jurisdictional standards – affecting interstate commerce and being of sufficient size; (b) whether or not there is sufficient interest on behalf of the affected workers; (c) the appropriateness of the unit of the plant for which representation is being sought; (d) whether or not an election would be consistent with the free choice of employees, and (e)

Table 1.4. *Percent of employment unionized by state, for selected years 1953–82*

State	1953	1960	1975	1982
Alabama	25.0	17.3	23.9	18.2
Alaska	52.7	46.8	41.2	30.4
Arizona	27.7	27.2	20.9	12.8
Arkansas	21.9	14.3	18.4	13.2
California	37.0	37.3	34.5	25.4
Colorado	28.2	23.6	23.6	18.0
Connecticut	27.2	23.7	27.7	18.9
Delaware	19.1	18.2	25.8	20.3
Florida	16.5	13.1	15.6	9.6
Georgia	15.1	11.8	14.4	12.7
Hawaii	14.0	20.8	34.3	31.5
Idaho	22.1	24.5	19.4	16.1
Illinois	40.7	43.2	35.1	27.5
Indiana	41.3	33.1	31.6	25.1
Iowa	26.0	25.6	23.4	20.5
Kansas	24.8	23.2	16.0	12.0
Kentucky	25.3	25.0	24.6	20.4
Louisiana	19.7	18.4	19.8	13.8
Maine	22.0	15.2	20.7	18.5
Maryland	25.8	20.1	27.5	18.6
Massachusetts	30.4	21.6	24.3	19.7
Michigan	44.6	49.1	42.2	33.7
Minnesota	38.6	32.8	29.0	24.5
Mississippi	15.0	11.9	12.6	9.3
Missouri	40.5	42.5	33.4	26.6
Montana	47.7	34.7	31.8	21.7
Nebraska	20.3	22.1	19.3	16.3
Nevada	31.2	37.4	37.4	22.1
New Hampshire	25.2	18.4	16.9	12.3
New Jersey	35.9	37.9	28.4	19.9
New Mexico	14.4	17.1	17.0	12.8
New York	35.6	31.9	43.2	35.8
North Carolina	8.5	5.3	11.0	8.9
North Dakota	15.5	12.7	19.4	14.2
Ohio	38.0	34.1	36.1	27.4
Oklahoma	16.7	13.6	19.5	12.9
Oregon	44.3	41.8	33.9	27.5
Pennsylvania	40.6	26.1	34.3	27.0
Rhode Island	28.0	21.8	26.3	19.4
South Carolina	9.4	5.8	6.8	5.8
South Dakota	14.4	8.7	13.3	10.3
Tennessee	22.6	18.8	21.7	17.3
Texas	17.4	15.1	16.0	12.5

Table 1.4 (*cont.*)

Utah	26.8	16.4	22.4	16.8
Vermont	19.5	18.1	16.3	11.9
Virginia	17.8	11.5	14.4	10.9
Washington	54.2	45.6	44.7	32.9
West Virginia	45.0	28.5	37.1	28.9
Wisconsin	39.3	35.3	31.5	24.5
Wyoming	28.4	22.3	22.6	15.6

Source: Troy and Sheflin (1985, table 7.2, p. 7–4)

whether or not an election is required given other possible options within the plant. Government employees and those employees of a company deemed to have significant supervisory authority or security responsibilities or who share confidential information with the employer are not covered under the National Labor Relations Act (NLRA).

Having certified the petition, the regional director must provide the parties with the option of a formal hearing to review matters relating to his/ her decisions before the election. In most instances, however, unions and employers either agree to a *consent election agreement* or a *stipulated election agreement*. The former type of agreement waives the formal hearing, and accepts the regional director as the final arbiter of all post-election issues. The latter agreement also waives the hearing, but assigns the arbiter role to the Board. There are other kinds of elections, including *board-directed* and *regional director-directed*, and *expedited* elections. These three types of election are administratively implemented, often to rectify problems with a previous consent or stipulated election. Since at least 1970, the vast majority of elections have been stipulated elections (see table 1.5).

Schlossberg and Scott (1983:181) suggested that the reason why consent and stipulated elections have become more common is "because employers lose little time or no time by signing them and can still object to the bargaining unit's composition by later refusing to bargain if the union wins the election." And there is no doubt that this problem has become very important in recent years.

Patterns of union representation elections

The results of NLRB-sponsored representation elections over the period 1970 to 1986, aggregated to the national level, are reported in table 1.6. Two patterns are evident in this table. First, over time, unions have become less successful in representation elections. They lost more than they won in 1986,

Table 1.5. *Summary of NLRB representation elections by type, for selected years 1970–86*

Election type	Year				
	1970	1974	1978	1982	1986
Consent					
Elections	2,159	1,315	658	172	119
Workers	84,092	37,554	16,256	4,845	2,515
Stipulated					
Elections	4,346	5,980	6,197	4,008	3,625
Workers	396,500	396,489	357,488	216,692	205,350
Board-directed					
Elections	94	45	49	50	20
Workers	10,572	5,095	3,922	5,305	3,324
Regional director-directed					
Elections	1,532	1,604	1,457	903	750
Workers	125,383	113,657	102,352	69,933	50,581
Expedited					
Elections	30	32	19	72	6
Workers	663	881	391	4,129	284

Source: National Labor Relations Board (various years)

Table 1.6. *Summary of results of NLRB representation elections for all unions, for selected years 1972–86*

Year	No. elections	% won	No. empl. won	Ave. unit size
1972	8,472	54.9	286,365	62
1974	8,368	51.0	190,038	45
1976	8,027	49.7	160,262	40
1978	7,443	48.1	157,585	44
1980	7,296	47.9	174,983	50
1982	4,320	47.7	76,659	46
1984	3,561	46.5	92,231	56
1986	4,436	41.9	105,919	57

Source: Unpublished data, National Labor Relations Board and Research Department of the AFL–CIO, Washington DC

Table 1.7. *Summary of results of NLRB representation elections for all unions by industrial division, for selected years 1970–86*

Division	Year				
	1970	1974	1978	1982	1986
Manufacturing					
No. elections	4,361	4,302	3,565	1,854	1,758
No. workers (000)	425	382	285	121	141
% won	54.2	47.9	43.2	36.7	40.7
Transportation, communication, etc.					
No. elections	861	1,039	892	659	556
No. workers (000)	87	37	33	21	16
% won	60.4	54.8	53.0	45.2	41.0
Services					
No. elections	704	1,025	1,385	1,127	991
No. workers (000)	29	49	84	65	60
% won	61.1	55.1	51.4	48.1	53.2

Source: Annual Reports (1970–82) of the National Labor Relations Board, and unpublished preliminary data (1986) made available by the NLRB, Washington DC

as opposed to 1970, when they won more than they lost. But, as important as the win/loss margin is in adding new members to unions, the actual numbers of union elections is also crucial in the process of adding new members. That is, even if the unions have tended to lose more than they win, if there were more elections they might be able to make up the difference in numbers due to the declining success rate. From table 1.6 it is obvious that as the success rate has declined, so too has the number of elections.

Indeed, over the four years 1980 to 1984, the number of representation elections practically halved. If we add in the effect of a declining average size of the election unit, then it is apparent why national unionization rates fell so precipitously in the past few years: basically unions have contested smaller elections and have lost the majority of a rapidly declining pool of elections. Only in the last couple of years has there been any improvement in the number of elections contested, though the win rate has further declined (see Dickens and Leonard 1985 for a discussion of the relative importance of these effects).

Declining numbers of elections and declining win rates were also evident for the period 1970 to 1986 for three major industrial divisions (table 1.7). In manufacturing, the win rate declined dramatically, and the number of

Table 1.8. *Summary of results of NLRB representation elections for all unions by region, for selected years 1970–86*

Region	Year				
	1970	1974	1978	1982	1986
New England					
No. elections	423	457	454	302	213
No. workers (000)	31	23	31	19	13
% won	57.0	51.6	44.1	42.4	53.9
Middle Atlantic					
No. elections	1,120	1,375	1,460	939	844
No. workers (000)	123	76	81	44	48
% won	58.1	50.6	46.1	44.4	43.8
East North Central					
No. elections	1,760	1,972	1,891	1,125	1,184
No. workers (000)	117	105	100	46	57
% won	55.8	49.9	46.2	37.7	40.6
West North Central					
No. elections	771	820	648	386	375
No. workers (000)	33	42	24	17	15
% won	40.2	47.4	52.6	41.7	43.7
South Atlantic					
No. elections	998	875	812	467	413
No. workers (000)	101	95	60	41	48
% won	49.7	45.3	40.0	37.7	47.2
East South Central					
No. elections	490	509	433	261	216
No. workers (000)	53	54	41	17	19
% won	50.0	45.6	47.6	35.2	45.0
West South Central					
No. elections	559	599	466	255	200
No. workers (000)	49	49	41	15	12
% won	57.4	48.4	47.0	39.2	44.0
Mountain					
No. elections	417	491	405	276	186
No. workers (000)	18	20	18	11	9
% won	56.1	53.0	49.1	44.2	43.5

Table 1.8 (*cont.*)

Pacific

No. elections	1,331	1,568	1,557	1,053	832
No. workers (000)	62	60	55	41	35
% won	53.3	50.5	46.3	38.3	40.6

Source: Annual Reports (1970–82) of the National Labor Relations Board, and unpublished preliminary data (1986) made available by the NLRB, Washington DC

elections more than halved. Likewise, the win rates of the other two divisions also declined, but not to the same extent. In the transportation and services divisions, the success rates were close to the national average (table 1.6), and down significantly since 1970. In this respect, the manufacturing division not only lost many more elections, but also lost its relative standing compared to the services division. Indeed, for services, even though there was a decline in elections contested from 1978 to 1986, there has been a dramatic increase in elections contested since 1970. When coupled with a relatively high success rate (53.2 percent as opposed to 40.7 percent in manufacturing), it is clear that this division is more than holding its own. It appears that the poor performance of manufacturing-oriented unions in representation elections may have been a major contributor to declining overall levels of unionization. Given that these unions have been the home of American unionism, the future of American unionism looks bleak.

This issue is taken further in table 1.8, which considers the temporal and geographical patterns of representation elections. And here, a slightly different picture emerges. In all regions there was a decline in the number of representation elections, and the regional win rate over the period 1970 to 1982. But while the number of elections contested declined by about half (1970 to 1982) in the southern regions, in the northern regions the rate of decline in elections contested was not as dramatic. On average, in 1970 the union win rate was higher in the northern regions than in the southern regions. Unfortunately for American unions, their win rates in 1982 in northern regions were not so different from their win rates in southern regions. That is, their chances of success in their traditional home regions had declined to such an extent over this period that traditionally hostile environments appeared to be just as reasonable risks. The only real exceptions to this characterization were the Middle Atlantic and New England regions, the former being far more significant than the latter in terms of overall contribution to union membership (see table 1.3). Even the Pacific region was more like the southern regions than the Middle Atlantic region with respect to win rates.

Since 1982, it is apparent that win rates in the South have increased, and now surpass those in the industrial heartland. The only exception is New England. Even so, given differences between the regions in terms of elections contested, the northern and Pacific regions remain the traditional home of American unionism. At the same time, convergence in regional win rates parallels the convergence of regional unionization levels noted previously (table 1.6). In this sense, the geography of American unionism became more universally hostile over the 1970 to 1986 period. What has often been described as the southern phenomenon (Rees 1973) – a culture of authoritarian employer–employee relations and strong community anti-union sentiment – appears to have been spread north. Given these geographical patterns, one might suppose that the reason why unions have been reluctant to embark on aggressive southern campaigns has to do with their struggle to maintain representation in their heartland regions.

Conclusion

In the United States, the unionization process is distinctly, and inherently, a geographical one. Workers choose to be represented by a union at the local (plant and sub-plant) level. Each representation election is fought at the local level, whatever the general level of unionization in the industry or region. By federal statute, workers first petition the National Labor Relations Board for a representation election, and then, if the petition is successful, vote (for and against) to have a certain union to represent them in contracts, grievances, and other work-related disputes. Overall national membership of any union is then the sum of workers who have voted separately at the local level to be represented by that union. My assumption is that the local context in which union elections are won and lost is a crucial lens for understanding the current predicament of American unions.

It is often suggested that union growth and decline are driven by the relative prosperity of the US economy.[9] However, in recent years it has become increasingly difficult to predict how and why certain macroeconomic variables affect national rates of unionization. However important structural changes in employment composition have been in reordering sectors of prosperity and decline, and however important macroeconomic fluctuations have been in affecting workers' relative wellbeing, these patterns do not explain the poor performance of unions in representation elections over the past decade. Dickens and Leonard (1985) found that after the level of aggregate economic activity had been accounted for, a significant portion of the decline of union membership was due to unions' poor performance in representation elections. They also argued that "the depressing organizing and success rates of the 1970s ... cannot be expected to disappear if the economy improves" (333).

When President Roosevelt signed the Wagner Act into law in July 1935, he noted that the Act "defines ... the right of self-organization of employees in industry for the purposes of collective bargaining."[10] Through the years, and through revisions and amendments, the goals and aspirations of the Act have changed (see Mills and Brown 1950 and Morris 1983). However, one thing has remained constant. The National Labor Relations Act (NLRA) does not guarantee unions a permanent role in industry, nor does it guarantee unions membership. Only through attracting members do unions have the right to represent workers. And only through attracting new members can unions be sure that their power is reproduced from one time period to the next. Not only are representation elections the means of maintaining membership: they are the means of legitimating union power.

Notice, though, that in this discussion I do not mean to suggest that geography is the only factor affecting union elections. In fact, local elections are set within a variety of contexts: local, national, and international as in the ebb and flow of economic activity; regional, as in state-level labor legislation; and national, as in the structure and performance of various industries and national labor legislation. A comprehensive understanding of the crisis of American unions must apprehend the intersection of these themes.

2

Understanding union growth and decline

How might patterns noted in the previous chapter be explained?[1] What theoretical perspectives are available for interpreting the decline of American unions? There is a massive literature on American unions, and the unionization process. The focus of this chapter is reserved for economic-oriented and geographical models of American unions. Two related issues are addressed: one concerns how we ought to understand the growth and decline of unions over time and place. The other concerns how we ought to conceptualize unions as organizations. In conclusion, comments are made about the methodological bases of analyses presented in subsequent parts of the book.

The literature on unions extends over a long period of time and has seen many different frameworks come and go.[2] Not surprisingly, there have been numerous attempts to review and systematize this literature, providing a steady stream of innovative modes of understanding the unionization process. Yet, for all this research, there is a great deal of pessimism about the utility of recent research. Fiorito and Greer (1982:19) observed that "[a]t present, there is no satisfactory model of union growth [or decline]." This sentiment is echoed by Hirsch and Addison (1986:72), who commented about a popular technique of analysis that "time series studies available to date tell us very little [about the current crisis of American unions]."

It appears that many researchers are uncomfortable with the heterogeneity of union experience, and would prefer an integrative framework which would eschew diversity for a standard model applicable to an average situation. Models which homogenize local experience, like cross-sectional empirical models, aggregate unions, places, times, etc. essentially deny the local heterogeneity of labor relations implicit in the very legislation that formalized American unionization. Even those studies that do appreciate the geography of union elections (to take one important issue) seem compromised. These studies are often incomplete in that certain variables are ignored; or their results are confounded by unfortunate estimation procedures which pool data across the very dimensions that should be considered in their own right – aggregating across time, locations, unions, industries, and institutional contexts. An adequate empirical strategy must be able to deal with different unions, their own electoral experience by time, place, industry, and institutional context (compare with Dickens, Wholey, and Robinson 1985).

A methodological impasse is apparent in the study of union growth and decline. I argue in this chapter that this impasse is due, in part, to an over-emphasis on aggregate national studies of unionization, and too little attention to the union representation election process. National union levels are the product, in part, of a myriad of local union elections. To ignore this issue is to ignore one of the fundamental distinguishing features of American labor law.

Structure versus history

A popular treatment of American unionization some years ago asserted that there were two schools of thought as regards the determinants of union growth. Bernstein (1954, 1961) identified these schools of thought as the saturationist or structural school, and the historical school. Adherents of the former school (including Bell 1953) argued that there was a limited set of workers available to unions as potential members: specifically, "male, blue-collar workers employed mainly by large firms in the manufacturing, mining, transportation, and construction industries in the larger urban centers of the North and West" (Bernstein 1961:131). Once these workers were organized, it was contended that the union movement would find it very difficult to make further gains amongst "the virtually impenetrable sectors – women, white-collar workers, employees in wholesale and retail trade, the service industries, the professions, government, and in agriculture, little firms, small towns, and the South" (Bernstein 1961:131). To the extent that these sectors and places became more important, as the economy expanded and diversified, the union movement would lose its relative standing amongst American workers; essentially, the market for unionization would become saturated.

The competing school of thought argued that "the labor movement is seen as increasing its size in two ways – at a modest pace over long spans of time and in sharp spurts at infrequent intervals" (Bernstein 1961:131). The modest pace of unionization was thought to derive from increasing social acceptance of unionism, while the sharp spurts were thought to derive from the growth of the economy. Bernstein (1961:157) asserted that "the growth of the union movement is inextricably linked to the growth of the economy." Growth in American unionization was argued by Bernstein to depend upon variables like output and unemployment, not the changing distribution of employment between sectors and places.

Empirically, this historical school has commanded the most attention in the literature. Ashenfelter and Pencavel's (1969) model of American union growth over the period 1900 to 1960 sought to demonstrate that "a single behavioral relationship can explain the progress of the American labor movement in the twentieth century" (434). They assumed that whether an individual belonged to a union depended upon his or her subjective assessment of benefits and costs. In contrast to Bernstein, Ashenfelter and Pencavel claimed that their single behavioral relationship obviated the need for other more social factors. Briefly, their model regressed annual percentage change in union membership against changes in consumer prices, changes in employment of the unionized sectors of the economy, unemployment, the proportion of unionized to nonunionized employment, and percentage of congressmen of the Democratic Party in the House of Representatives.

All variables were national in scale, and no attempt was made to differentiate between sectors, places, or occupations. The model was estimated in the time domain, utilizing different sub-periods, and was thus an adjustment-oriented approach to union growth. The first two independent variables were used to capture the relative costs and benefits of union membership, the unemployment variable was used to capture grievance issues, the proportion of unionized to nonunionized employment was used to capture the relative ease of membership recruiting (the higher the proportion, the harder it is to attract new members – a saturation issue?), and the relative strength of the Democratic Party was used to represent the political climate for organized labor. This model has been extended by others using different variables, and has been used recently by Neumann and Rissman (1984) and Dickens and Leonard (1985) to explain declining unionization.[3]

This approach is vulnerable to some fundamental criticisms. First, while it is (in Ashenfelter and Pencavel's words) a relatively "*compact* description of the historical growth of trade union membership" (447), it is so aggregate that it fails to do justice to the decentralized nature of American labor relations and institutions. Basically, it treats American unionization as one might treat European unionization – as a nationally integrated political system. This is despite the fact that in designing the American labor relations system, a conscious effort was made to decentralize both the rules of unionization and the process whereby unions were formed (see Stone 1981).

Second, and related to this, it is so aggregate that the processes whereby union members are added and subtracted in different places, different industries, and over different times are essentially ignored. That is, it fails to deal directly with the local electoral process, and uses national stock variables to approximate the local flow of employees in and out of union membership. Similarly, it homogenizes the experiences of different places, sectors, and times, going against the accumulated evidence marked spatial, sectoral, and temporal differentiation.[4]

There have been some attempts to establish the saturationist argument as a counterweight to the popularity of the Ashenfelter and Pencavel approach. Early work by Kornhauser (1961) on demographic, occupational, and spatial–institutional factors demonstrated that the disaggregated approach could offer useful insights into union membership characteristics. More recently, there have been some attempts to use demographic, educational, and sex-related variables to predict union membership.[5] In fact, the recent statistical work by Kokkelenberg and Sockell (1985) using the Current Population Survey to describe that characteristic of union members is well situated within this tradition.

Even so, the saturationist approach has not been as popular, perhaps because of data problems, and the inherent complexity of the perspective. Moore and Newman (1975) used a variety of so-called saturationist variables, like regional factors, local differences in institutional structure, and industry/occupational structure to argue the case for the approach, but recognized that even their attempt was hampered by data problems (444). Most recently, this literature has been given a rather different theoretical context by Hirsch and Addison (1986), who emphasize a choice-theoretic approach, rather than the earlier structural-cum-institutional focus.

I have some sympathy with the saturationist perspective. But it is difficult to agree with certain embedded assumptions. It is hard to accept that there is a structural limit to union membership. Those categories used by Bernstein and others to distinguish between potential union members and nonunion members now seem quite arbitrary. In recent years the home of American unionism, northern and western manufacturing towns and cities, has become a relatively hostile environment, even compared to the South. In addition, those groups thought impervious to unionization, professional, white-collar, and service workers (many of whom are women), are now represented in some of the nation's largest unions. In fact, these workers appear more likely candidates for unionization (going on the win rates of unions in service sectors) than traditional male blue-collar workers. Of course, it remains true that the latter are more unionized than the former. And it is the case that as a proportion of all workers, blue-collar workers are of declining national importance.

Even the saturationists hardly ever move beyond union membership as the dependent variable to the local electoral process. Despite their appreciation of the importance of local explanatory variables like institutional structure, the presumption is that structural factors dominate over any local or temporal effects. And, finally, whatever the problems with using aggregate macroeconomic variables as in Ashenfelter and Pencavel, there seems to be no reason why these types of variables should be unimportant at the local level, provided they are suitably spatially disaggregated.

Economy and community

Dunlop (1948) provided a related but more subtle explanation of union growth. He attempted to marry economic factors with social institutions, especially the community. The object of his analysis was union membership, not the electoral process. But even so, his perspective allows for a deeper appreciation of the interrelationships between different kinds of factors affecting unionization.

Dunlop made a very important observation about unions in relation to existing work practices: "no working community is ever completely unorganized. Any group of human beings associated together for any length of time develop a community in which there are recognized standards of conduct and admitted leaders" (177). For Dunlop, the process of unionization (formal organization) was intimately local, being set within the exigencies faced by a specific community of workers. As he noted, the reasons workers join unions "generally involve various aspects of the relation of the individual workman to his immediate work community and, at times, his relation to the larger locality and national life" (178). In this sense, unionization is not the result of some arbitrary association of otherwise unrelated workers. He argued that "any analysis of the development of labor organizations must proceed from the recognition that work communities, prior to formal organization, are not simply random aggregates of individual workmen" (178). Unionization is interpreted by Dunlop as workers' response to some threat to their informal rights, or a threat to the existing organization of work.

In describing the factors affecting the rate of unionization, Dunlop distinguished between long-run and short-run factors, the former likened to evolutionary factors, the latter to deviations around those trends. With respect to long-run factors, he identified four specific factors. The first was the technological position of firms and their workers: "labor organization emerges among employees who have strategic market or technological positions. They can make it hurt" (180). He defined strategic position in the following terms: "the term strategic, however, is not identical with skill. It means sheer bargaining power by virtue of location and position in the production process" (179).

Second, he argued that labor organization is only successful if workers believe that they are committed to the work community for the foreseeable future. That is, in areas of rapid turnover, migration, and job advancement, labor organization is difficult because individual interests dominate the collective interest. Third, "certain types of community institutions stimulate, and others retard, the emergence and growth of labor organizations" (184). Here, Dunlop meant to include the legal environment, national and local, as well as community institutions like schools and local governments which might affect the balance of political power between capital and labor. And fourth, Dunlop argued that community values and beliefs (the culture of work, individuals' responsibility to themselves and others, and the ethos of community) were of vital significance.

While these factors were important to differing degrees, according to circumstances, Dunlop described them as the factors driving the trend of unionization. In the short run, though, other economic factors intrude. Specifically, he associated different periods of union growth from 1827 to 1945 with the performance of the national economy. The variables mentioned included prices, wages, the demand and supply of labor, and waves of investment and innovation (perhaps a Kondratieff-like cycle). He suggested "that after prolonged periods of high unemployment for a substantial number in the work force and after years of downward pressure on wages exerted by price declines, labor organizations emerge which are apt to be critical of the fundamental tenets of the society and the economy" (192). According to Dunlop, economic forces do not necessarily dominate the long-run factors. Rather, there is a subtle interaction between community and economy. This may mean that whatever the economic patterns of a particular community, workers' reactions in terms of unionization will be highly structured by *community* culture, institutions, and technological advantage.

Dunlop's emphasis upon the community and the local labor market prompted other writers of the time to consider similar issues. So, for example, Wilcock and Sobel (1955) studied four non-metropolitan labor markets, focusing upon mobility aspects of the dual labor market. And in a paper concerned with local wage patterns and job security, Rottenberg (1956) reflected upon the meaning of choice in different local labor market settings. Shister (1953) added a further set of factors to Dunlop's framework. Specifically, he believed that Dunlop failed to deal adequately with the role of trade union leadership in the unionization process. He suggested that there "are distinct and noticeable differences" (429) between American unions. While he did not provide much in the way of examples to make his case, he did suggest that union leadership could be differentiated by four factors: first, union organizing techniques; second, the administrative structure of the union; third, the internal operation of the union; and fourth, the collective bargaining relationships between the union and the various business and government employers. This idea was then followed up by Lahne and Kovner (1955) in a brief analysis of the local organization of the UAW.

Institutions and unionization

In reviewing various perspectives on American unionization, it should be apparent that I, like Dunlop, have emphasized the importance of the local institutional context in understanding geographical patterns of American unionism. But as noted, there are many different forms that local institutions may take, ranging from schools to the courts. In the legal context, a dominant theme of American labor law has been the decentralized nature of labor relations. Fostering decentralization has been an integral goal of federal labor law, and a wide variety of government regulations and statutes. Bok (1971) identified this particular attribute, among others, of American labor law as distinguishing American labor law firmly from that of other countries. While it is not appropriate to embark upon an extensive review of the relevant legal doctrine, a number of observations can be made that relate to my critical review of the literature.

There can be no doubt that the Wagner Act (1935) and the Taft–Hartley (1947) amendments made it relatively more difficult to organize labor in the United States than in other advanced countries.[6] Unions have had to organize firms on a plant-by-plant basis, seeking representation rights for workers in different communities across the country. While they may be successful in some plants, they are required to organize all plants of a firm if they are to have a coordinated national agreement with a particular firm. Even in this case, if they are successful in organizing all plants of a firm, contract ratification often takes place at the local level. For reasons of local democracy, maintaining the power of the local union in relation to the national union organization, the union movement has had to cope with a federal legal structure deliberately designed to fragment its national power (see Cox 1954; cf. Stone 1981).

Reinforcing these statutory imperatives, the federal government has played a leading role in maintaining the integrity of local contract standards and local conditions of work. This is especially evident in laws such as the Davis–Bacon Act (Gould 1982). Passed in the early years of the Great

Table 2.1. *States with*
right-to-work legislation,
1975–82

Alabama
Arizona
Arkansas
Florida
Georgia
Iowa
Kansas (repealed in 1982)
Louisiana (enacted in 1977)
Mississippi
Nebraska
Nevada
North Carolina
North Dakota
South Carolina
South Dakota
Tennessee
Texas
Utah
Virginia
Wyoming

Sources: Troy and Sheflin
(1985, table 7.7, pp. 7–9)
and Farber (1984a, table 2,
p. 321)

Depression as a means of protecting local wage standards, over time it has
come to be a significant constraint on the ability of construction unions to
achieve effective national organization. Construction unions still support the
wage aspects of the Act, but do so at a cost: further organizing of the
industry. To the extent that government agencies have followed a similar
logic in their procurement policies, even hiring practices of blue-collar
workers, in practice the federal government has maintained the local
character of the labor market. Even in the case of the NLRB, local context
has remained a crucial test of the reasonableness of adjudication. This is
despite other trends towards uniformity through the application of national
standards of adjudication (Cox and Dunlop 1950).

In the name of federalism, the Taft–Hartley amendments encouraged
states to develop their own local labor legislation. Specifically, since 1947
right-to-work (RTW) legislation has been passed in some twenty states (see

table 2.1), and there is an ongoing campaign to pass similar legislation in
other states like Missouri and New Hampshire. This legislation has
effectively limited unions' abilities to negotiate closed union-shop agreements with firms. Indeed, the effect of these laws has been to fragment the
constituency for cross-plant collective agreements further. Basically, as there
may be local contract provisions in any general agreement between a firm
and a union, in some states the union and the firm may not be able to follow
through on accepted contract provisions, whatever the desires of local
unionists. RTW legislation is perhaps the most obvious manifestation of my
overall argument: the local institutional context has an impact on the
geographical pattern of American unionization.[7]

Precisely how important RTW legislation has been in affecting state levels
of unionization remains a problematical issue. In an early study, Palomba
and Palomba (1971) suggested that RTW states had lower levels of
unionization *prior* to the passage of these laws. They suggested too that
states with high rates of unionization lacked the political power to pass such
laws. They then concluded that the determining variable affecting whether
or not a state passed RTW legislation was the level of local economic
development. More recently, Tollefson and Pichler (1975) reworked their
data to argue that, in fact, the Palombas had under-emphasized the
significance of the level of unionization in determining the passage of RTW
legislation. Similarly, Moore, Newman, and Thomas (1975) suggested that
the proper interpretation of the relationship between unionization and
RTW legislation should stress factors originally associated with the saturationist school: the proportion of blue-collar labor, urbanization, and
southern culture.

In all this debate, the argument was over the determining significance of
unionization in the passage of RTW legislation. There has been little
empirical work on the impact of RTW legislation on unionization. Ellwood
and Fine (1983) noted that passage of RTW legislation had an immediate
negative effect on the *number* of representation elections held in those states
that passed such legislation. But they also noted that this effect was
temporary, a finding consistent with Smith's (1984) study of the effect of
RTW laws on unionization. Farber (1984a), however, found it more difficult
to come to a conclusive determination. He, like others including Dunlop
(1948), emphasized the importance of the local culture. Specifically, he
concluded that despite a strong correlation between (low) levels of unionization and the existence of RTW legislation, this "is largely a reflection of
tastes against union representation rather than a real effect of the RTW
laws" (351). While that is an interesting conclusion, one that reinforces the
importance of the local context in determining the level of unionization, it

nevertheless raises an unasked and unanswered question: in the absence of an RTW variable, how would we represent the local institutional effect?

Representation elections

As noted in the previous chapter, the representation process is the formal means whereby employees decide to have a union represent them before an employer. But, of course, to get to that point requires a good deal of informal organizing, both to generate support within the plant and, perhaps, even interest a union in taking on the case. Note that an election is not necessary if an employer voluntarily recognizes that a union commands the support of a majority of its workers. However, this is a rare instance indeed, and has become rarer in recent years (Schlossberg and Scott 1983:161–66). In the vast majority of representation cases, the employer contests the election, and often appeals the result through to the NLRB. The election process is inherently antagonistic and combative; it is little wonder that there are many instances of gaming during the election process – even fraud – on both sides of the employment relationship.

Schlossberg and Scott might also have noted that these types of elections allow significant latitude for stalling the implementation of the election results through the appeal process. Indeed, it has been asserted that the increasing importance of stipulated elections reflects employers' desires to stall the review process as long as possible by clogging the Board, as opposed to the regional directors of the NLRB (Prosten 1979). Employers can use all kinds of delaying tactics. Even by waiving the hearing, employers may effectively delay the regional director in reaching a certification determination (Roomkin and Block 1981). These tactics were readily apparent before the appointment of the Reagan NLRB. However, in recent years the scale of these tactics seems to have expanded, leading some legal scholars to suggest that declining rates of unionization can be directly attributed to the failure of the current Board to deal with the coercive resistance of employers (Weiler 1983).[8]

The regional director has the responsibility of certifying the election petition, setting the election day, tallying the votes, and dealing with any infringements of the National Labor Relations Act as it relates to the conduct of elections. But, only in few cases does the regional director have the final authority in adjudicating disputes. In many instances, employers and employees seek Board reviews, and even federal court judgments on the propriety of Board decisions. In this respect, the election process and the administration of the NLRA by the NLRB have become enmeshed in legal proceduralism. This pattern has led Dunlop (1987) to suggest that current labor law is overwhelmed with legalism, and has failed to fulfil the promise of the Wagner Act: an ordered system of industrial relations designed to promote national economic growth.

Modeling representation elections

Compared to the massive empirical literature on unionization, the empirical literature on representation elections is quite small. If the number of published papers on unionization were compared to representation elections over the past twenty years, the former would far outweigh the latter, perhaps by as much as ten to one (see Hirsch and Addison 1986 for the most recent comprehensive review of the related literature). Given that it is the election process which is the heart of American unionism, this imbalance of emphasis requires explanation.

One reason for the relative imbalance has to do with the dominant empirical methodology of economics. Aggregate econometric models have been the norm. This is of course changing, but in retrospect, the past twenty years of research in labor relations, and unionization in particular, have seen the earlier more contextual approach championed by Dunlop and others give way to a macro modeling approach. The best example of this mode of inquiry is, of course, the single equation model of unionization developed by Ashenfelter and Pencavel (1969). Modeling representation elections is more difficult to subsume under one aggregate empirical umbrella, let alone a single equation. A second reason for the dominance of aggregate union studies over election studies has much to do with the very nature of representation elections. While researchers might legitimately argue the virtues of aggregate union studies, it is more difficult to justify studies of representation elections which do not tackle the spatial specificity of each election. As Dunlop and many others have emphasized time and time again, representation elections are a local phenomenon; to apply an aggregate empirical methodology across elections is to violate a crucial aspect of the election process.

Given the importance that has been attached to Dunlop's work, it is not so surprising then that labor researchers have tended to avoid the topic of representation elections in recent years. Simply, the spatial specificity of each election does not fit easily with developments in macroeconometric theory and practice.

One result of the spatial specificity of representation elections is the lack of any thorough integrated macro model(s) which would organize the literature. This has led some researchers to lament the apparent ad hoc nature of much of the research in this area. For instance, in an extensive review of the literature, Heneman and Sandver (1983) noted that "too much of the research on union elections has not been founded on explicit theoretical frameworks. Rather, the research process has been inductive, with researchers providing post hoc theoretical explanations for the empirical relationships they uncover" (552). This observation has been echoed in a number of quarters, including Hirsch and Addison (1986). Notice that if this is in fact a fair characterization of the literature, it is difficult to use a classification scheme to describe the literature. This task is more complicated than was the case when reviewing the unionization literature.

One way to begin is to note the wide range of topics covered in this literature. There are studies on voter participation in union elections, studies on voters' preferences, studies on the role of management consultants in union representation campaigns, studies on the macro determinates of union election outcomes, and studies of different types of union elections (certification and decertification). Characteristically, these studies mix different spatial levels of data (local, state, and national), with different types of variables (individual demographic variables and economic variables), and with different times, places, unions, and institutional contexts.

So, for example, Block and Roomkin's (1982) study of voter participation in union elections began with a standard individual-oriented voter model (Downs 1957), and then used aggregate data, especially the margin of victory/defeat, to explain variations between elections in voter participation. In two studies of participation in union activities, Anderson (1979) and Kolchin and Hyclak (1984) mixed together attitudinal and demographic characteristic variables to explain levels of involvement. This kind of empirical framework has been used in studies of voters' attitudes and perceptions. For instance, Le Louarn (1980) studied the attitudes of some 95 nurses, comparing their actual votes with their intentions and a range of job and union satisfaction issues. Youngblood, Mobley, and DeNisi (1982) suggested a more general conception of the connection between these issues: "if a worker is dissatisfied with some aspect of the job, he or she will not vote (or intend to vote) for a union unless a union is perceived as being instrumental in improving the area of dissatisfaction" (246).

More macroeconomic-oriented models of union elections have focused upon industry, location, and election process variables. Becker and Miller (1981) in a study of union elections in hospitals used variables including unit size, the type of hospital, the RTW status of the state, and the metropolitan/non-metropolitan status of the hospital (mostly dummy variables), but found very little in the way of explanatory power. Hyclak (1982) used interval variables like manufacturing wages, unemployment rates, and employment growth with more success, although his sample was small, was distributed over a number of years, and included many different unions. Prosten (1979), as we noted above, considered the effect that time delays between the petition and the actual election have on the outcome of the election (a slight decline in unions' chances of winning), as Lawler (1984) has attempted to quantify the effect of management consultants on unions' chances of winning (again a slight decline).

Seeber and Cooke's (1983) study of NLRB elections over the 1970–78 period is one of the few macro-oriented studies to develop Dunlop's original framework explicitly. They included state-level data on wages, employment, legal environment, and unit size in an attempt to model the percent of votes for union representation. But, as they noted, the spatial, temporal, and union pooling of their data made it difficult to interpret their results. Recent studies by Freiberg and Dickens (1985) and Freeman (1985) have, respectively, attempted to link the impact of runaway offices on union election results and the role that the union/nonunion wage differential plays in management's opposition to union organizing.

Studies of the determinants of decertification elections have similar characteristics. These studies use very different empirical methodologies, and reflect the broad range of approaches so typical of this literature. Chafetz and Fraser (1979) conducted interviews with employers, government officials, and union leaders (even, in a couple of instances, employees) to determine the possible links between decertification and worker dissatisfaction. Anderson, Busman, and O'Reilly (1982) combined union leadership with management attitudes factors in case studies of decertification elections in California. Lynch and Sandver (1984) reported a more general cross-correlation analysis of industry characteristics. There are of course other studies that could be acknowledged. However, the point is surely obvious: to the extent that researchers have recognized the local character of union elections, their empirical methodology is more inductive than deductive, more exploratory than hypothesis-testing oriented, and more cautious of the generality of their findings. If Dunlop is taken at all seriously, it is difficult to fault these studies for their attention to the local context.

Understanding organized labor

Seventy years ago, the most developed intellectual framework for understanding the American labor movement was Hoxie's (1917) *Trade unionism in the United States.*[9] By way of introduction, Hoxie cautioned students of American unionism against possible errors which "might vitiate the whole study" of the phenomenon (27). The first error Hoxie identified would be to assume that unionism is "everywhere the same and always the same." Other possible errors included treating unions as just economic phenomena and assuming the existence of common social standards of behavior and a common social will.

Hoxie believed the union movement was best characterized as an economic and political movement, involving "a vast and heterogeneous complex of working class groups, molded by diverse environments" (35) and sustained by diverse aspirations and ideals. According to Hoxie, the patterns and processes of American unionism were very complex, being only loosely integrated through pairs of opposite tendencies like centralization versus decentralization. He also observed that "at present the *local labor union* (his italics) is the only existing unit of importance in the United States" (41), despite recurrent attempts to create a national federation of unions.[10]

Just over forty years later, Richard Lester (1958) fundamentally revised Hoxie's framework, describing American unions as mature national organizations.[11] Suggested by Lester's arguments was a spatial hierarchy of power and responsibility: power had become centralized with the national executive of unions, and tasks were assigned to different spatial levels of the union in accordance with functional bureaucratic requirements. It was now possible to talk of national unions representing whole industries across America. According to Lester the American labor movement was now a national movement like many firms and industries. At one level, he expressed a view which had been introduced by Dunlop (1944); unions could be treated as undifferentiated agents whose economic interests could be summarily treated through simple objective functions like maximizing members' real wages. In this sense they were no different than firms, consumers, and workers. All economic agents were analyzed using a standard decision framework. Empirically, this framework was the rationale for Ashenfelter and Pencavel's (1969) single equation model of union growth and decline.

At another level, Lester readily recognized that unions were evolving political institutions. He commented: "in many respects, a union resembles a political party. It has an ideology and traditions, a national organization and local branches" (17). Lester described American unions as *national labor unions* wherein members' economic interests were spatially integrated by an overall economic objective of maximizing real wages, but whose members' political interests were highly spatially differentiated and represented by local branch officials. He believed that the problems facing the union movement in 1958 were the problems he thought faced all mature organizations: the maintenance and consolidation of past success, and the management and administration of internal affairs.

Lester's model was partially successful. It became the basis of all standard treatments of American unionism, even if it is now ignored as the beginning of more recent versions (Hirsch and Addison 1986). At the same time, most analyses of American unions draw upon only one level of Lester's framework, namely the economic model. At this level, his treatment of unions as economic agents has been mimicked by many theorists, especially macroeconomic theorists. Still, while popular in the literature, it has come under increasing attack from a number of theorists.

Some microeconomic theorists have suggested that the union as economic agent fails to do justice to the union as an institution. Here, it is argued that union members (principals) ought to be distinguished from union executives (agents).[12] These two groups are thought to have different interests and powers. Other theorists argue that the standard model predicts too much and too little. On one hand, it supposes that unions have too much power – using the standard model, theorists predict that the wages of members are equal across all firms, whereas in fact wages are not so equal. On the other hand, the standard model supposes that unions have too little power – it fails to recognize the diversity of claims that unions can negotiate with firms and the effects of these claims on the economy (see the volume edited by Reid 1983 for an overview of this literature).

Obviously, I have no wish to ally myself with the new literature on the microeconomics of unions. The theoretical tools at the heart of this literature are premised upon quite radical assumptions regarding the priority of self-interest, individual choice, and economic rationality in conditions of certainty. It is as if the economic sociology of Gary Becker (1964) has been married with the rational expectations of Robert Lucas (1981) (see for example Faith and Reid 1983). Nevertheless, the points of criticism introduced by this literature recognize legitimate problems of the standard model, and mirrors my own arguments as expressed in empirical analyses of the electoral performance of the IBEW and UAW (Clark and Johnston 1987b,c,d). On the basis of these empirical analyses and the theoretical literature noted above, I would make three specific criticisms of the standard model of union behavior.

First, the standard model of union behavior is not a model of unions, nor is it a model of their behavior. The standard model is a model of a generic economic agent. The great advantage of Dunlop's (1944) model was that unions could be understood as economic actors with specific economic interests. Coming after an era when unions were primarily understood as political instruments of the Democratic Party, Dunlop's model emphasized an aspect too often ignored. However, the great disadvantage of the model was that it intellectually rationalized all union activities around a single nonpolitical economic objective function. Subsequent attempts by Dunlop (1948), and Shister (1953) and then by Lester (1958) to broaden the intellectual framework met with limited success. The internal structure of labor unions was forgotten in the rush to rationalize union behavior in terms of the dominant intellectual model of the firm.

The notion of a single objective function buries the complexities of the structural organization of union power. For instance, it was noted elsewhere (Clark and Johnston 1987c) that unions face two dialectical imperatives. One is the need to centralize power so as to be effective with firms and governments. The other is to decentralize power so as to be effective with members' economic and political interests. These imperatives interact with one another, and are not easily rationalized under one dominant interest. Indeed, to attempt such a rationalization would be to deny an embedded structural feature of modern unions. It would also make any empirical analysis premised upon such a rationalization prone to unanticipated shifts in forecast efficiency. Essentially, the single objective function model ignores the institutional character of unions as *unions*. In this criticism, my argument parallels previous points made by the new microeconomic theorists, though for different reasons.

Second, the standard model ignores a crucial aspect of union life: electoral politics. Forgotten by theorists who use the standard economic model are the principal assumptions of the legislation that gave American unions their legitimacy. While the preamble of the Wagner Act emphasized the economic benefits of more equal collective bargaining and worker self-organization, the mechanism by which workers were to organize reflected another deeply held belief – the virtues of industrial democracy. Workers were given the right to join unions, and unions were given the right to represent those workers who joined the unions. Electoral politics were taken from the political sphere of life and transposed to the work place. Unions do more than just represent the economic interests of workers (as implied by the standard economic model). Their very life is premised upon maintaining existing members, and drawing in new members. If they fail at either political function, their future prospects will be bleak. In this context, unions' political functions are prerequisites for their economic functions. Any model of union behavior must be sensitive to the electoral process. This much was recognized by Lester, but was ignored by those theorists who followed in his footsteps.

To understand why this is an important criticism, one need only consider the argument made in Clark and Johnston (1987b). There it was suggested that the electoral performance of the IBEW and UAW was partly the result of larger (national) political forces, and smaller (local) economic interests.

At the national level, unions have been understood as other national institutions. The failure of these institutions through the 1960s and 1970s to sustain the trust and confidence of the electorate is well documented (Chubb and Peterson 1985). To the extent that unions' appeal to their electorate is based on political representation functions, their electoral support has been fragmented by the general decline in the trust and confidence of all Americans in their political institutions. To the extent that unions' appeal is based on their ability to be effective in local situations, the political constituency of the American labor movement has been spatially fragmented. To suppose that the political domain of union life is either irrelevant or unimportant to union power or union behavior fundamentally mistakes the essential roots of the American union movement.

Third, the standard model fails to integrate the institutional context of national labor relations adequately with the local context in which the representation process takes place. Here, the standard model and Lester's expanded version share a similar problem. Both idealize unions as *national organizations*, ignoring the fact that the national aspect is one facet of an otherwise decentralized representation process. Of course, in relation to the world described by Hoxie (1917), there can be no doubt that the modern union is a national organization. That is, it has national officers, a national reach in terms of its representation of workers, and even national master contracts in some instances. However, both the standard model and Lester's framework fail (for different reasons) to reflect the complexity of the national–local dichotomy adequately.

With respect to the standard model, it should be readily apparent that as they have mimicked the model of the firm, they have also implicitly assumed that the operational scope of the union is spatially equivalent. But this is not a reasonable assumption. In fact, the power of firms to restructure production systems and employment relationships through relocation depends upon the fact that unions are unable to reproduce local bargains across the country. Unions cannot follow firms and automatically expect, even demand, similar working conditions to those in the firm left behind; relocation involves new social relations of production.

Those who still support Lester's approach might nevertheless claim that his model appreciated the political significance of local employment relations. But even here there remains a problem. Inherently, Lester's model of national unionism is a top–down model. That is, having established national unions it assumes that the political process acts to rationalize competing local interests in terms of the common economic interests of the union. In assuming such a rationale for union management, it supposes there are common labor relations around the country. Indeed, it assumes the existence of one technology of production, and hence one dominant mode of the organization of labor. The only differences between places are then assumed political, even personal (as indicated by local candidates for office and local grievance committees).

This assumption is quite implausible. There is an incredible variety of production technologies within specific industries, and these technologies are located according to local labor relations (Clark, Gertler, and Whiteman 1986). The mere fact that the American labor movement became a national movement did not nationalize local labor relations, nor did it nationalize local customs. The implication is that local interests are as much economic as they are political.[13]

Conclusion

Conceptually, I have argued for a richer and more complex theory of American unionism. This theoretical perspective will be worked through in subsequent chapters of the book. From this perspective, it is worth recognizing that my approach is informed by a set of essential suppositions. First, the union representation process ought to have a central place in any explanation of American trends in unionization. It is, after all, the process whereby unions claim representation of workers. In this sense, the supposition reflects a number of deeply embedded values about the virtues of industrial democracy evident in the epigraph to the book.

Just consider the ferocious response that greeted Weiler (1983) when he recommended replacing the electoral process with a less formal method of establishing majority representation (signed cards). It might be suggested that arguments against Weiler's position reflect established institutional interests, particularly those of the National Labor Relations Board. While that is no doubt true, it is just as plausible that criticism of Weiler's suggestions reflects a deeper ethical premise: the necessary virtues of representation elections *qua* elections. More empirically, though, these same elections are the mechanism by which unions garner members, and thereby represent workers in negotiation with employers. In this sense, representation elections are the heart of the American labor movement.

With the case argued for representation elections as a crucial analytical lens for understanding the fortunes of American elections, another supposition automatically follows. Because the representation election process is decentralized, there are inevitably significant local effects that generate a wide variety of election outcomes by place, time, union, and industry (to name just four possible dimensions). As we have seen these local effects may be systematic in that common variables are statistically important across different places and times (like wage variables), and these local effects may be nonsystematic in that different variables are significant in different places and/or common variables are interpreted differently in different places and times. The point is that there is a significant sphere of spatial heterogeneity in the representation process, reflecting a combination of structural imperatives and local effects. This kind of complexity is inherent in the representation process. To treat the process as not complex or as spatially homogeneous would deny a crucial attribute of the system and an important clue in how we understand the performance of different unions over time.

A third supposition is that unions ought to be treated as institutions, not simply as shallow reflections of members' interests. That is, unions are organizations and as such have a capacity to adjust and respond to the national legislative and local electoral environments. This supposition suggests another implication. Unions have many interests, and many constituencies. To imagine that unions have a single objective function is to imagine that they are so internally rationalized in terms of members' interests that all they can do is respond to members' demands. In fact, union officials have wide spheres of discretion, not exactly an institutional role with respect to other institutions that neatly maps on to a corporatist image of society. This means that in understanding the electoral fortunes of unions we must consider unions' strategies as well as workers' interests. In this sense, I do not favor the newer literature on principals and agents which retains an ideological (if not practical) commitment to the principal as the central player.

Throughout this chapter, I have dealt with the literature spawned by Lester and Dunlop. Nevertheless, these theoretical suppositions have close affinity with some of the basic assumptions of Hoxie's framework. This does not mean that I am about to turn the clock back seventy years. The American union movement is now fundamentally different than it was before the Taft–Hartley Act and the Wagner Act. Emphasizing the spatial and temporal diversity of unions' electoral performance (for example) does not mean that I wish to return to treating unions as simply local organizations. And, emphasizing the complexity and interdependencies of the processes determining union growth and decline does not mean avoiding the identification of causal relationships. Rather, the diversity of patterns and complexity of processes should be integral to any framework designed to comprehend the future of the American labor movement as a whole. In fact, the complexity of processes and diversity of patterns ought to be the object of analysis.

Inherent in this theoretical commitment is another kind of commitment: to a certain kind of theoretical aesthetic. In arguing for complexity of process and diversity of patterns, I have argued against conventional wisdom, which has it that the best theory is the simplest theory. Most concretely, the conventional wisdom as epitomized by Ashenfelter and Pencavel's (1969) model of American unionization is seriously flawed. It is flawed because it fails to recognize complexity of process, and because it fails to identify the diversity of patterns. But more than that its dependent variable, the national level of unionization, actually misrepresents the underlying process of unionization. It rationalizes an otherwise complex system through very simple and aggregate explanatory variables. It is little wonder that it has proved to be so problematic as an analytical tool in understanding the current crisis of the American labor movement.

In making the case for understanding the complexity and diversity of American unionism, I follow the lead of Hirschman (1985), who has criticized social science theories that are too parsimonious. He argued that some theories were so denuded of the texture of events and processes that theorists were led to quite unreasonable interpretations of motives, actions, and policies. Hirschman's perspective is, of course, controversial. But, it is also an important reference point for understanding my conception of this book. From case studies of union structure and behavior to empirical analyses of union performance in representation elections through to textual studies of cases and judicial decisions, I emphasize that understanding the decline of organized labor is premised upon understanding the intersection of community life and the diversity of the union movement.

PART II

Drama of economic restructuring

3

Communities and corporate location strategies

The 1980s brought considerable hardship to many people and their communities.[1] Podgursky's (1987) study of post-1980 worker displacement for the National Academy of Sciences' panel on technology and employment (see Cyert and Mowery 1987) indicated that of the many millions of industrial workers who lost jobs in recent years few were lucky enough to find similar jobs.[2] Displaced workers have suffered under-employment and unemployment with incomes (wages and benefits) much below previous levels. Employment in other expanding sectors (predominately service sectors), relocation, and higher levels of household labor market participation (typical blue-collar adjustment strategies) have rarely made up the difference.[3] Indeed, some commentators argue that economic restructuring has substantially reduced the number of well-paid manual jobs and has further polarized the distribution of wages and salaries (Bluestone and Harrison 1987; Harrison and Bluestone 1987).[4]

If economic restructuring were randomly distributed across the United States, it is doubtful its effects would have much political significance. However, economic restructuring is inherently geographically differentiated, most recently concentrated in American factory towns and cities whose histories are intimately linked to the evolution of whole industries, firms, and plants.[5] In these communities, plant closings and worker displacement are economic *and* political disasters. Plant closings often mean economic desolation, massive unemployment, and the collapse of other related businesses.

Economic restructuring can also be an intense political drama, involving state and local governments, community organizations, corporations, and unions. Local government rescue plans, union wage and benefit concessions, and public investment to encourage *in situ* corporate restructuring are one kind of political response to plant closures. The latest congressional legislative initiatives for advance notification of plant closings, limitations on the switching of work between plants, and protection of workers' pension plans are another kind of political response.[6]

The local drama of economic restructuring is the topic of this chapter (and this part of the book). Although the chapter includes a brief assessment

45

of the consequences of economic restructuring for individual and community welfare, the focus is on the roles and status of a corporation (Mack Trucks), a local union (Local 677 of the United Auto Workers), and the International executive of the United Auto Workers union (UAW), in a dispute over the planned closure of Mack Trucks' Allentown, Pennsylvania plant and the opening of a new plant in Winnsboro, South Carolina. At issue is how we should understand the interests and actions of the institutions involved in the dispute. By concentrating on the details of the dispute I hope to provide a critical perspective on the themes and issues introduced in part I. Thus the chapter has two objectives. It develops the theoretical perspective introduced in the previous chapter, and provides a critical analysis of competing theories of unionization and community economic restructuring.

Case study method

Before I discuss details of the case study, it is important to pause for the moment and consider the significance of this case (and other cases in the book), as well as the methodology I follow in presenting the case. Case studies have a problematic status in social science. By many accounts, they are not as useful or as plausible as comprehensive statistical analyses. Yin (1984) noted three common prejudices against case studies. They are supposed to lack rigor, allow little opportunity for generalization, and are written typically in such a fashion as to be too long or too complex for ready appreciation. More often than not social scientists, though not all social science theorists (see Taylor 1985) believe generalization to be an essential ingredient of scientific respectability (McMullin 1984). In contrast, case studies are thought idiosyncratic: either too specific or too vague to make general observations about theory and other circumstances.

In this study, no argument is explicitly mounted against conventional social scientific reasoning. I have made attempts elsewhere to indicate the limits of this mode of social analysis in public policy evaluation (Clark 1983) and judicial decision making (Clark 1985b). This does not imply rejection of statistical methods in all situations. There are instances where statistical methods are useful in constructing arguments about social and geographical processes. For example, Kris Johnston and I (Clark and Johnston 1987b) have argued – using probit and regression models – that the outcomes of union representation elections can be understood in terms of the intersection between the structure of US labor law and the local context of such elections. Like McCloskey (1985), I tend to think of statistical methods and similar analytical techniques of the social sciences as rhetorical devices used in the construction of interpretation and argument. Thus, use of these methods does not mean acceptance of standard scientific reasoning, despite their apparent intimate association in the literature.

I also believe that case studies can have other purposes than building prototypes. The case study analyzed here, and in other instances where case studies are presented in the book, is used in a special way. Rather than make an argument that the case study represents an average or typical situation, the case is used to throw light on our theories and categories of analysis (compare with Lauria 1986). That is, the case is used as an *exemplar* in Unger's (1986:75) meaning of the term: it provides an opportunity to reflect upon the coherence of conventional categories and explanations, and brings to the fore competing, alternative interpretations of events. Alternatively, the case might be imagined to be one of Dworkin's (1978) *hard cases*: an instance where established theories of behavior are not completely adequate, where there may be a number of plausible but conflicting interpretations of behavior, and where there may be no settled theoretical perspective for the issue at hand. These writers have their critics (see Finnis 1987 on Unger and Hutchinson and Wakefield 1982 on Dworkin). But their perspectives on the efficacy of cases is liberating; selected case studies can be extraordinarily powerful in asking difficult theoretical questions.

Why this particular case? Given a broad interest in the roles of institutions like unions and the courts, the community and corporations in restructuring, this case provides an instance where the major actors are together in a dispute that is both complex and well articulated. It involves the UAW, a union whose problems are studied throughout the book. It also involves a number of communities, a multi-plant corporation, and the institutions of arbitration and adjudication. Like other case studies in the book, it is rich enough to provide the basis for extended analysis of the crucial theoretical issues. I would also claim that the case study is significant for another reason. It is not a philosopher's "thought game," designed to represent an impossible or bizarre situation (compare with Parfit 1984). On the contrary, the case is tragic for many of the workers involved. Their individual and collective welfare is at risk, though for different reasons. Surely only the most remote of academics would imagine that the case study was unimportant.[7]

A second methodological issue concerns presentation of the case, and all case studies. The most conventional social scientists believe that facts speak for themselves, as if they simply appear and are recorded by neutral observers (Trigg 1985). It is not my intention to represent the case study, or any other case study, as simply a set of uncontested facts. Quite the contrary. Competing representations of the facts of the dispute by the parties involved is a vital issue considered in this chapter. Indeed, the chapter was conceived so as to emphasize contending interpretations of the facts, from the perspectives of those directly involved and those who read my analysis. In this sense, it is obvious that I use the case in a quite particular way. Inevitably, there is a degree of presentation bias embedded in the description of the dispute reflecting my objectives – for the chapter and for the plausibility of my argument. This is true for all narratives, whether thought of as factual as in social science or autobiographical as in literature (Eakin 1985).

The case is first presented as a narrative of events, focusing upon the reported relationship of the corporation to the union, and the interrelationships between Mack Locals and the International executive of the union. As initially presented, this narrative is naive in that events appear in an orderly sequence (White 1980). However, it must be understood that this sequence has no necessary logic other than that which was created by the various agents and the accumulated pastiche of past actions. It was not inevitable that Mack Trucks had to close the Allentown plant and open the Winnsboro plant. And, it was not inevitable that the corporation would attempt to blackmail Allentown and other communities. A second way the narrative is presented is as part of a theoretical argument. At issue is how we ought to understand the actions and motives of the parties to the dispute. Inevitably, the narrative is transformed by the theoretical discourse; my own interpretation is revealed at the end after my analysis of others' possible interpretations.

A plant closing in Allentown, Pennsylvania

According to Dun and Bradstreet's 1980 *Metalworking directory*, Mack Trucks was once the nation's largest producer of trucks over 33,000 pounds. The corporation, headquartered in Allentown, was then owned (90 percent) and controlled by Signal Companies Inc. of Beverly Hills, California. Mack Trucks employed about 12,000 in four US plants: 5,600 in Allentown, 4,200 in Hagerstown, Maryland, 1,270 in Hayward, California, and 1,000 in Macungie, Pennsylvania. These four plants produced all the parts and components for the corporation's line of truck products. The Pennsylvania plants combined assembly and manufacturing functions, while Hagerstown provided engines, wheels, axles, and chassis. The Hayward plant (which has since closed) was more limited than the Pennsylvania plants, specializing in assembly of smaller trucks.[8]

Industry commentators believe that in 1985, US manufacturing capacity in heavy-duty trucks was about twice annual sales (respectively 220,000 units as opposed to 115,000 units). Massive over-capacity coupled with increasing competition from foreign producers inside and outside of the US combined to prompt a wave of plant closings, corporate reorganization, and reinvestment throughout the industry. On 17 October 1985, Mack Trucks (then controlled by the Renault corporation of France) announced that it would close its 60-year-old Allentown facility and open a new plant (location unannounced).[9] It also announced a third quarter loss of $65 million.[10] Within a month, the corporation had modified its closure plan. It was now announced that the plant would close *unless* the Allentown UAW Local agreed to significant cost reductions "substantially equivalent to those that can be realized at the out-of-state location." At the same time, the company also announced that if the Allentown plant were to close, it would also seek other sources for its engines and parts – an announcement interpreted by UAW officials as a threat to close down the Hagerstown plant as well. The company had recently opened a small nonunion parts plant in North Carolina.[11]

Negotiations for a mid-term revision of the existing collective bargaining agreement began soon after, and continued through December 1985 to a 17 January 1986 company-imposed deadline. These negotiations involved the UAW Local unions (Allentown and Hagerstown), the UAW International, and the corporation. While local union officials were apparently willing to make concessions including cuts of $4.00 per hour in wages and benefits as well as fewer work rules and higher production rates, the UAW International proposed an alternative scheme. Workers would contribute $1.00 per hour to a reinvestment fund and significantly increase productivity. The UAW International proposal was similar to a reinvestment program already in place in the American Motors Corporation, itself partly owned by the Renault corporation (see chapter 4). UAW International officials estimated that this program would provide Mack Trucks with about $80 million per year, without having to give up $65 million in direct concessions.[12]

The company rejected the UAW International offer, and on 19 January 1986 announced again that it would close its Allentown plant and begin outsourcing parts requirements as a step towards replacing its Hagerstown facility. In Allentown, a city dominated by Mack Trucks – the largest employer and the headquarters of the company – this announcement was greeted with consternation.[13] Eugene McCarthy, president of the UAW Allentown Local, began a public campaign to overturn the UAW International proposal, with the tacit support of Mack Trucks' vice-president for corporate affairs, who was reported as saying that Mack Trucks' decision was not final. McCarthy called for a vote of local UAW members on the company's concession package, even though the UAW International would not support the package.[14] This campaign was not successful. No vote was held as the UAW International executive remained committed to their proposal. Some time later, either the end of January or February 1986, Mack Trucks announced the site for its new plant: Winnsboro, South Carolina.

This was not, however, the end of the matter. The original contract between the UAW and Mack Trucks contained a provision allowing workers to transfer between plants on the basis of seniority. The issues of who was eligible to relocate and how many would relocate became matters of dispute between the union and the corporation. Even when the new plant opened in Winnsboro in August 1987, these issues were still in litigation. Through late 1986 and early 1987, they were arbitrated and litigated, while the corporation and union renegotiated the original collective bargaining agreement which was to end its three-year term in October 1987.

In late April 1987, the UAW International union and Mack Trucks reached agreement on a five-and-a-half-year master contract involving a small cut in wages and benefits for increased job security. This was after a period of intense negotiations mediated by an outside expert. Unresolved, though, was the relevance of separate letters of agreement that the corporation had previously negotiated with its individual UAW Local unions. These agreements had included wage concessions and productivity improvements in exchange for job security, conditions thought unacceptable by the UAW International. Not only were these letters of agreement different between Locals, but the Locals had negotiated them without coordinating concessions between themselves, or even seeking UAW International approval. In renegotiating the master contract, the UAW International excluded the locals from direct participation. Ultimately, the master contract was ratified by separate votes at each Local in May 1987 at the Mack plants. The separate concession packages were not included in the ratification votes.

With agreement reached at least temporarily on a new contract (the issue exploded again in July 1987 when a UAW International official questioned the standing of the contract), binding arbitration hearings were held to resolve the issue of workers' transfer rights between Allentown and Winnsboro. The arbitrator decided that the Allentown closure and the new plant in Winnsboro did not constitute a violation of the original collective bargaining agreement (as contended by the UAW International). He also decided, though, that UAW–Mack workers laid off in Allentown had first claim to the Winnsboro jobs, thus denying Mack Trucks' position that it could refuse those workers' transfer claims.[15] This decision left the company in an awkward situation. It was now required to canvass laid-off workers it did not want to transfer so as to ensure that those workers' rights to transfer were adequately recognized. At the same time, the corporation had to put on hold 300 workers that the State of South Carolina had trained to take jobs in the new plant, just one month away from the scheduled opening of the plant.

To complicate matters further, the UAW filed suit in a federal district court in Philadelphia in mid July, charging that the corporation had set an unnecessarily quick decision date for eligible workers to decide to exercise their transfer rights. At this time, an official of the UAW International also questioned the standing of the recently negotiated contract, prompting the company to file suit against the union. A judge upheld Mack Trucks' canvassing procedure, and allowed the company to interview applicants over the balance of July in order to have those employees report for work in Winnsboro on 3 August 1987. Subsequently, the company announced that it had accepted 288 applications for transfer to Winnsboro, with some 124 pending. The UAW then sought clarification from the judge regarding the conditions of workers' transfer to Winnsboro. The judge in turn sought clarification from the arbitrator, who held hearings in late July, but then withdrew from the case.

On 3 August 1987, the Winnsboro plant opened with about 250 nonunion local graduates of the South Carolina training program, and about 210 members of the UAW who had transferred from Pennsylvania. The company had paid about $200,000 to move the transfers, though no assistance was provided for workers to find housing.[16] After a new arbitrator was appointed, the company filed suit to hire more local nonunion Winnsboro workers. The court found in favor of the company, and a further 280 were hired.[17] Whatever the final decision of the arbitrator regarding the legitimacy of the transfer procedures, the corporation had won its battle to limit the number of transfers to less than a majority of the plant work force. The UAW could not demand to be recognized immediately as the bargaining agent; a representation election would have to be held to determine if the UAW could represent workers in the new plant.

Relocation as a corporate strategy

These events have a certain logic or structure, even if only sketched and hinted at in the narrative. Implied is a question of corporate strategy, given the corporation's plant locations and desired relationship with the union. To make this logic explicit requires a more abstract or theoretical treatment, even if this treatment transforms the particularities of the dispute into a language of theory rather than the narrative. Especially important in this context is how we understand the actions and motives of the corporation and the union, and their intersection through the community of Allentown.

As we saw in the previous chapter, the standard textbook treatment of

firm location and relocation decision making is premised upon a single
behavioral imperative – cost minimization, and hence profit maximization –
and neoclassical economic assumptions of an exogenously determined
market price, pricing by the marginal costs of production, and a given
technology of production (Lloyd and Dicken 1972). By this logic location
decisions, like all other production and related decisions, turn on relative
costs represented as prices of different sets of inputs and outputs.[18] For any
single firm, the landscape is imagined as a choice set of possible locations
with different configurations of costs of production and distribution. The
aggregate landscape of production is created, if that is the right metaphor,
by the separate location-optimizing decisions of firms. It is assumed that if
all firms act rationally (that is, in relation to market prices and the costs of
production), the resulting landscape should be pareto optimal, and economically efficient. Some theorists would even argue that the spatial economy
is actually just as theorized; in equilibrium, or at least equilibrium oriented
(see Borts and Stein 1964 for a seminal contribution).[19]

Can location theory help us understand the actions and motives of Mack
Trucks? There is no doubt that the corporation faced a quite hostile market.
Chronic over-capacity in the industry, product competition and innovation
from overseas companies with plants in the US, and steady erosion of
market prices all threatened the corporation's financial viability. Given
exogenously determined market conditions for heavy trucks, Mack Trucks
could be interpreted as acting as a neoclassical firm: locating production so
as to minimize the costs of production. Not only might location analysts
interpret the actions of the corporation in the terms of neoclassical theory,
but the corporation itself sought to represent itself as simply responding to
market imperatives for lower costs of production. Throughout its dispute
with the union, the corporation demanded wage and benefit concessions at
its Allentown plant that would at least equal the lower costs of producing in
the new plant in Winnsboro, South Carolina.[20]

In this context, the choice of location was simply a matter of economics.
But, is this enough as an interpretation of the actions of Mack Trucks? Does
it do justice to the complexity of the issues as indicated by the narrative in
the previous section? I would argue that this interpretation is too simple; it
relies on a straightforward economic motive where there may have been
other motives hidden and protected by the company's public posture. In
fact, the economic motive may have served as a legitimizing device, as
opposed to being the essential reference point in the location decision-
making process. By this argument, location theorists who would support the
company's interpretation of events may be simply naive, or may misrepresent the real logic of decision making, or worse.

There are a couple of other interpretations of the corporation's motives which are not so benign as that suggested by location theory. A bilateral advantage interpretation: the public posture of the corporation may have been protecting a hidden corporate goal of radically reducing the union's power over the pace and design of the production process. In this respect, the announced closure of Allentown and the threat of out-sourcing against the Hagerstown plant could have been designed to compromise the power of the local union leadership. For Allentown and Hagerstown, Mack Trucks was the largest employer, and the economic locus of the communities for many years. Public debate over closure plans centered around the likely devastating consequences of closure, and Allentown's dependence upon the corporation. By representing the issue as an economic problem, the corporation set the communities against the local leadership of the union. The local union faced a dilemma: if it consented to concessions, it would appear weak to its members and the International; if it did not compromise, it would be held responsible for the probable economic desolation of the community.

This bilateral advantage interpretation is made plausible by the scale of community mobilization against closure, the ineffectiveness of the local union leadership, and the close links between local business elites and the corporation. In the early stages of the dispute, it was the local union that lost by appearing confused and ready to compromise. By this interpretation, media awareness of the corporation's search for sites for a new plant in the South could be thought of as part of an orchestrated campaign to force a quick union response to the corporation's demands. Similarly, the corporation's apparent willingness to negotiate even after the entry of the UAW International into the dispute may have been a calculated attempt to give the local union an option to settle, even without the International's approval. If this was the original strategy of the corporation, it must have simply miscalculated the probable response of the UAW International.

There is another interpretation, more Machiavellian than the previous interpretation, though no less plausible.[21] Perhaps, like many other US corporations, Mack Trucks sought to rid itself of the union. Not only may it have aimed at operating a new nonunion plant, but it may have also decided to use the dispute as an excuse to run down its Hagerstown facility by out-sourcing from nonunion suppliers. In pursuing such a strategy, the corporation may have deliberately attacked the credibility of its UAW Local unions, and ultimately the UAW International executive. If successful, the strategy would limit the role of the UAW in its operations, and make the union more vulnerable when the time came to renegotiate the master contract – if, in fact, the master contract was relevant by that time. In this interpretation, Mack Trucks never intended to save its Allentown plant; closure was a crucial first step in a strategy designed to limit the power of the union in its other unionized plants, and extend the significance of its nonunion operations.

However plausible as an explanation of the final outcome of the dispute between the union and the corporation, this interpretation does not immediately explain why the corporation went through an elaborate public charade of negotiating over the fate of the Allentown plant. Why insist that the plant could be saved if the union agreed to drastic concessions when the corporation had no intention of finding any settlement reasonable? Surely, it might be objected, the economic issues were more vital than I have recognized! The Machiavellian interpretation could be too complex for an otherwise simple situation.

While it is apparent that the economic issues were important in corporate planning, these same issues served a vital and subtle role at another level. The corporation could never have admitted willingly that its relocation decision was prompted by anti-union sentiment. To avoid any ambiguity of motive, Mack Trucks had to maintain and reinforce its public claim that economic considerations were the sole rationale for relocation. Indeed, to protect its hidden strategy, the corporation had to appear as the willing negotiator, while the union would best serve the interests of the corporation if it appeared as the party unwilling to compromise on economic concessions. If the union were able to provide any evidence that anti-union sentiment was an element of the corporation's decision to relocate, it may have had reason to file an unfair labor practices charge with the National Labor Relations Board. Whether successful or not, such a charge might have held up closing of the Allentown plant, forestalling relocation to the new plant.

According to the National Labor Relations Act, it is illegal for a corporation to relocate or close a plant because of anti-union sentiment. Once workers have voted for union representation, corporations are required to bargain in good faith with their union (or unions), or risk legal proceedings by the NLRB. This does not mean that corporations and unions need agree on the proper course of action. There is often considerable dispute and antagonism in the interpretation of any collective bargaining agreement. Plant closings and relocations initiated by corporations to avoid their statutory obligations to bargain are held by the NLRB and the courts to be against the intent and objectives of the NLRA. These strategies aim to circumvent an essential purpose of the Act: maintenance of the collective bargaining system.

Still, plant closings and relocations are not mandatory bargaining issues between firms and unions. These are issues that are thought to lie outside the terms and conditions of employment, and are interpreted by the NLRB as issues that reasonably relate to the property rights of corporations (see *Steelworkers Local 2179* v. *NLRB*, 1987). However, if the relocation decision depended upon labor costs, or if the relevant collective bargaining agreement included a plant closing or relocation provision, or any other provisions that could be construed as being relevant to plant closings and relocations (like transfer rights between plants), then both parties have a legal obligation to bargain over the issue and, if necessary, seek rulings on the interpretation of those provisions from arbitrators and the courts (see *Century Air Freight Inc.*, 1987). Corporations are obliged, moreover, to bargain with their unions over the effects of plant closings and relocations, even if the relocation decision does not turn on labor costs and/or no provision exists in a labor contract regarding relocation (see the Reagan Board's decision in *Otis Elevator II*, 1984).

If it was the case, as I have suggested above, that Mack Trucks' decision to relocate turned on the corporation's antiunion sentiment, it could hardly announce its decision or even allow speculation that this was its essential motive in relocating the plant. But, to relocate on the basis of labor costs, its announced reason for closing the Allentown plant, immediately meant that the corporation was obliged to bargain with the union. First, it had to establish the relative labor costs between the old plant and the proposed new plant. Second, if, as was the case, the union could not meet the concession requirements, the corporation had to bargain over the effects of closing the Allentown plant. And, since the contract contained a provision allowing for transfers between plants, the corporation also had to bargain over the terms and conditions of transfer. In these ways, the corporation adhered to the required bargaining procedures, even as it publicly blamed the union for its relocation decision.

From the UAW's perspective, so long as the corporation adhered to its bargaining obligations and maintained its reasons for relocating were primarily economic considerations, the union could not mount a serious charge of unfair labor practice, nor could it stop relocation. The arbitrator would not support the union contention that the plant closing violated the existing contract, or go along with the union's delaying tactics regarding the adequacy of the corporation's transfer provisions. The fact that a federal district court judge then upheld the corporation's request for relief from the contract's transfer provisions further reinforced the corporation's power in negotiations with the union. Thus, having rejected the company's demands for certain concessions, and having no basis to mount a charge of unfair labor practice, the UAW International could only play a delaying role

in bargaining over the plant closure. Its attempt to reintroduce the previously settled contract negotiations did not succeed in delaying the
corporation.

Of the three interpretations offered of the corporation's actions in closing
the Allentown plant and opening a new plant in South Carolina, I prefer the
Machiavellian interpretation. By my reckoning, the simple relative costs of
production explanation of relocation (that explanation favored by neoclassical location analysts and the corporation) does not do justice to
possible hidden motives of the corporation, or to the complex relationships
between the corporation, the union, and the community. The second, less
benign, interpretation, which supposes that the corporation was really
aiming to compromise the bargaining power of the Local and International
unions (rather than avoid them altogether), is plausible. But it is not as
effective as the Machiavellian interpretation in explaining the intensity with
which the corporation fought to ensure the union-free status of the new
plant. The second interpretation only asks us to imagine that the corporation was motivated by a desire to gain more leverage in bargaining
situations. By contrast, the Machiavellian interpretation argues that the
corporation's ultimate objective was to avoid the union altogether.

It is possible that all three interpretations have merit. One integrating
scenario could assume that the corporation began with economic considerations, then realized it could use the situation to gain bargaining leverage, but
finally realized that it could achieve something it had not previously planned
on – a union-free production environment. This scenario has the virtue of
replicating the narrative order of events. However, to imagine that this
narrative order stands independently of interpretation does not seem
plausible. Reporting the series of events was premised upon an initial
assumption (albeit unstated) that relocation was not an accident, the
product of failed negotiations. Implied by the order of events is an
assumption that the corporation orchestrated the events, even if it could not
actually control the actors and agents.

My Machiavellian interpretation is, of course, problematic. It rejects the
obvious as too obvious, it imagines illegal motives on behalf of the
corporation, and it produces no evidence that would justify my interpretation of motives. In fact, I may have only convinced the naive empiricist
that economic considerations are the essential explanation of corporate
relocation, and other explanations are only fabrication. Nevertheless, I
cannot accept that interpretation must be limited to Pollyanna versions of
the world, even if legitimated by a certain brand of location theory.

Fragility of union solidarity

How should we understand the role(s) and motives of the union in this dispute? Hinted at in the narrative of events, and implied to some extent in the previous section, is an interpretation of the union as relatively powerless compared to the corporation. From the perspective of the end of the dispute, the development of plans to close the Allentown plant and its relocation as a nonunion operation, the union proved incapable of stopping the corporation. According to the sequence of events of the narrative, the union appeared in a series of losing roles: the Local was too eager to negotiate concessions and the International unwilling to accept the corporation's demands. The International was unable to persuade the arbitrator and court of its interpretation of the corporation's obligations to its members and, even more critically, unable to organize the new plant. The union was internally divided, and failed to protect its interests.

Since Dunlop's (1944) pioneering work, economic theorists of labor unions have tended to treat unions as quasi-firms. While it was recognized by Dunlop that unions are quite different than firms, the analytical metaphor has nevertheless been used extensively in the literature.[22] Dunlop began with the standard assumptions of neoclassical economic models, and introduced an objective function – maximization of members' wages as defined by a wage–membership function – constrained by the costs of servicing members and protecting members from lower wage offers of nonmembers. In recent years, this model has been extended by Lazear (1983) and others in an attempt to expand upon the microeconomic theory of unions; why workers join unions, how their negotiated wages and benefits attract members, and the implications of these rewards for union/nonunion interaction. As firms are assumed to maximize profits, workers are assumed to maximize their utility. Thus, in the latest versions of union models, unions' policies are conceived as the result of the expectations of members.[23]

Is this kind of model, a hybrid macro/micro model of unions as quasi-firms, useful in understanding the poor performance of the UAW in its dispute with Mack Trucks? I would argue that the standard Dunlop-type of model does not adequately recognize the internal organizational divisions of the union into Locals and the International, nor does it adequately recognize the different interests of the Locals and the International. It should be remembered that the International over-ruled the Allentown UAW Local's agreement to corporation-demanded concessions. In addition, the president of the Local took the issue to the community in an attempt to overturn the International's decision. This action by the Local president, counter to the internal appeals system of the union, indicates a degree of internal union dissension rarely seen in public. Abstractly, it might be suggested that this kind of internal division is merely political, that there is an economic objective function which ensures the solidarity of the union. Presumably, the integrating interests are the class-based interests of UAW members, whatever their locations.

There are at least three different objections to such an abstract appeal, each of which has enough individual merit to question the plausibility of abstract analytics. First, the possibility of an over-arching national economic objective function implies a degree of US working-class collective consciousness that few researchers believe existed historically (see the volume edited by Katznelson and Zolberg 1986, comparing working-class movements in Europe and the US), or has existed in recent years (see Davis 1986). It is a romantic vision which homogenizes diverse local experiences of working-class groups, and the fragmentation of working-class solidarity by a combination of ethnic, racial, and locational cleavages (Marston 1988). Second, this notion ignores an essential institutional difference between the US and Europe. The collective bargaining system was designed to maintain the distinctiveness and legitimacy of local interests over general interests of corporations and unions as national organizations (Bok 1971). There may be local economic interests, but these are not required to relate to the interests of other groups in other locations. And, third, this notion fails to acknowledge the legitimate democratic interests of local union members, conceived in statute by the Wagner Act of 1935.[24]

The metaphor of the firm applied to the union only treats the union as a firm – an hierarchically ordered institution. The metaphor fails to do justice to the union as a working-class democracy. In these ways, use of a single objective function to explain the diverse interests of Locals and Internationals runs the risks of what Dunlop termed economic imperialism.

A more subtle interpretation of the issue is provided by Lazear. He began his analysis of wage-setting policies of unions by postulating a single objective function for workers: they maximize their expected earnings. For unions to attract members, they must negotiate wages and benefits higher than the market price of labor discounted by the costs of organizing workers. Lazear goes on to experiment with different wage policies of Locals and what he termed nationals (Internationals).[25] Lazear demonstrated that Locals set wages over or below the national optimal wage because they ignore the spill-over consequences of their policies for all workers. Thus, Internationals must monitor and standardize Locals' wage policies in the interests of all workers' welfare. According to Lazear this may require transfers of members from one Local to another, a centralized strike fund, and other similar integrating devices.

It is apparent that this model provides more insight into the actions and motives of the UAW unions than the Dunlop type of model. By Lazear's logic Allentown's UAW Local union could be accused of myopia in that its ready agreement to corporate demands for concessions threatened the welfare of other Mack Trucks UAW members and other UAW members in the US truck industry. By this interpretation, intervention by the UAW International sought to control the spill-over effects of the Local's decision to compromise in the interests of all workers in the industry even if this meant closure of the plant. This kind of action would be consistent with Lazear's theoretical predictions. However, it is an observation which is consistent with many others' interpretations of the proper role of an International union. Although Lazear suggested that his interpretation was innovative because it incorporated the spill-over effects of Locals' actions, it is well recognized that union solidarity depends upon maintaining the integrity of the union as a whole.

From discussion of theory and interpretation, as well as the narrative of events, it is fairly obvious why the union had so much difficulty in responding in an adequate fashion to the corporation. There were different interests involved: the Local sought to protect the welfare of its members and the community, while the International sought to protect the welfare of its members in other Locals and throughout the industry. Having over-ruled the Local on concessions, but then failed in its attempt to halt relocation of the plant, it was crucial for the International to relocate as many Allentown UAW members as possible. Obviously, relocation of UAW members would help the International win recognition for a new UAW Local to represent workers in the Winnsboro plant. Recognition of the UAW in the new plant would also force the corporation to bargain with the International in circumstances that would favor the union. The UAW would have control of the new plant, and possibly the future of the corporation.

But no less important, it was crucial that the International demonstrate to its other Locals that any local sacrifice would be recognized. Relocation of members provided the International with an opportunity to protect the welfare of those Local members who chose the option. For those who chose not to relocate, however, it is doubtful that they had a strong commitment to the union. More generally, if Locals began to believe their members' livelihoods were expendable in the interests of the bargaining position of the International, union solidarity would be difficult to achieve in any circumstances. It is already suspected by many UAW members that the UAW International is too closely involved with corporations in the rationalization of auto-related industries (witness the internal dissension over the UAW International's role in the Saturn Project: see chapter 9). There are other similar cases where UAW Locals have fought against the International's involvement in local matters, even leading to court cases brought by dissident Locals against the International (chapter 4). Thus, in the interests of the internal political cohesion of the union, it was necessary for the International to do everything in its power to assuage local resentment over the resolution of the dispute.

In this interpretation of the roles and actions of the UAW unions, the Allentown Local was not simply myopic. It is reasonable to suppose that the Local had legitimate interests, not served by the International. Given the political status of the Local as a partner in the UAW, it is misleading to imagine that the International had a natural or theoretical right to over-rule the decisions of the Allentown Local. The union is not, as the firm metaphor would imply, an organization hierarchically ordered according to local and national interests. It is better to interpret the union as a confederation of Locals, whose solidarity depends upon the accommodation of different local economic interests. Consequently, involvement of the International risked more than failure with respect to derailing the corporation's plans: it risked the political legitimacy of the International.

Given the motives and actions of the International, could it have done more to stop the plans of the corporation? Could it have been more successful if it had pursued a different strategy? Here the strategies of the corporation and the limits of the union as a political organization intersect. If the real motive of the corporation was to reduce the costs of production regardless of location, was the UAW International's offer of a worker-financed investment pool coupled with productivity improvements plausible? While it is impossible to answer this question with any confidence, it is apparent that the UAW offer provided the corporation with savings of a similar magnitude to its wage and benefit concession demands. Compared to the Allentown Local, the International could point to the successful experience of a similar strategy with the American Motors Corporation (AMC) as reason to justify the offer. Presumably, the corporation was aware of the AMC package, but chose instead to use the occasion to attack the International's intervention in the dispute in an attempt to alienate the Local leadership from the union executive.

If the real motive of the corporation was to compromise the powers of the Local and the International in bargaining situations, its strategy of support for the Local against the intervention of the International could have been calculated to fragment solidarity between units of the union. Assuming a measure of political legitimacy for Locals' economic interests, the corporation could be interpreted as using the decentralized political structure of the union against the union. In this strategy, the corporation could be interpreted as recognizing that it was dealing with an institution quite unlike a firm. Local interests could not be policed just as a firm would police the behavior of local plant officials; the UAW International cannot fire its Local officials like a firm. These officials are elected. If the corporation's motive was to divide and conquer, it practically succeeded. Only the constitutional affiliation of the Local UAW to the union stopped it from deliberately circumventing the International. But, perhaps it was the possibility of such divided loyalties that prompted the corporation to set the Local against the International.

If the real motive of the corporation was more Machiavellian, if it in fact aimed to rid itself of the union altogether, then its attempts to divide the union could be interpreted as a calculated effort to paralyze the union, thereby forestalling an effective response to the planned closing of Allentown and opening of the new plant in Winnsboro. Whether designed or not, one consequence of the intervention of the International was further disenchantment of Local UAW members with the union. To imagine then that the International had any hope of relocating a sufficient number of members to Winnsboro in order to sustain its demand for representation in the new plant seems, in retrospect, to have been doomed from the start. The division of loyalties between the Local and the community on one hand, and between the Local, community, and the International on the other hand seems to suggest that any possibility that UAW members would have relocated in the interests of the International's power over the corporation would have been minimal.

My interpretation of the corporation's motives and actions in this dispute suggests that the corporation sought to avoid the union by relocating to Winnsboro. I would also suggest that it used its knowledge of the internal political structure of the union to divide the union against itself. Whether or not the corporation could predict the full ramifications of its actions is not so much at issue. In effect, the corporation's strategy meant that the union could not mount an adequate strategy against the corporation in Allentown or in the new plant. The International was able to force the corporation to follow through on its legal bargaining obligations, but in doing so it simply reinforced the legitimacy of the corporation's actions. A more concerted grass-roots action against the corporation could not be mounted because the International was simply unable to accommodate the community's interests.

Community economic development

As indicated throughout the narrative and discussion of actions and motives, this dispute was not just between the union and the corporation.

The communities of Allentown, Hagerstown, and Winnsboro were intimately involved in the dispute. On many occasions, local government officials protested the breakdown of negotiations between the union and the corporation, arguing that closure and out-sourcing would do irreparable harm to Allentown and Hagerstown. For example, a county official from the Hagerstown area noted "if Mack leaves, . . . it will be very, very serious for us. Our grocery stores, our clothing stores, they depend in large part on the Mack dollar." And, as the local Mack Trucks manager for community relations remarked, "Mack *is* Hagerstown."[26] While Allentown and Hagerstown stood to lose a great deal from relocation, Winnsboro stood to gain from the dispute. The corporation's plans caused a political crisis in south-central Pennsylvania, drawing many state and local officials into the issue. At the other end, relocation to Winnsboro provided that community with the promise of expanding employment opportunities.

This kind of story, told about a union, a corporation, and three communities, is often noted in the literature on regional economic growth and decline. It is a story commonly told about the growth of the sunbelt, and the decline of the snowbelt. Part of the story might be about labor costs. But increasingly, the story is told much like the narrative: plant closures and relocation are conceived as the product of searches by corporations for localities with local social relations of production consistent with their techniques of production. At issue are local variations in union and community solidarity, and the roles taken by institutions like local governments in fostering certain kinds of local business climates.[27]

In this context, unions like the UAW and communities like Allentown and Hagerstown, with their interlocking histories as places of production, are at risk to the comparative location decisions of mobile capital. As location theorists have attempted to move beyond the simplest comparisons of relative wages and the like, this kind of case study has become the basis (albeit often unstated) of theoretical analyses of the spatial division of labor by function, product, and stage of the product cycle. Clark (1981) and Storper and Walker (1984) have provided theoretical statements that systematically structure the issues involved in this kind of location decision making. More generally, Bluestone and Harrison's (1982) book is replete with examples of plant closures and relocations that were initiated in response to local business climates – measured by union solidarity, wages, taxes.[28]

illustrate how business climates are conceived, and relate to the between the UAW and Mack Trucks, table 3.1 summarizes important climate factor rankings for Pennsylvania and South Carolina. In upon a comparative study of business climates for the forty-

Table 3.1. *Business climate factor rankings for Pennsylvania and South Carolina (), 1987*

Factor	National rank	Significance of factor
Wages	23 (6)	1
Unionization	46 (2)	2
Workers' compensation levels	28 (11)	4
Change in unionization	32 (38)	9
Manhours lost	42 (1)	11
Taxes	39 (25)	13
Cost of living	18 (24)	17
State business incentives	12 (6)	18
Overall (all factors)	38 (24)	

Note: A high ranking, where for example 24 is preferable to 38, is believed indicative of a better state business climate

Source: Grant Thornton (1987)

eight contiguous states by the management consulting firm of Grant Thornton, Pennsylvania ranked 38th and South Carolina 24th, the latter being a more desirable ranking than the former. In terms of union factors, South Carolina was thought more desirable than Pennsylvania. Comparing state rankings for wages, unionization, workers' compensation levels, and manhours lost through strikes, South Carolina ranked far better than Pennsylvania.

Indeed, a couple of factors for South Carolina ranked the highest in the nation. While it appears that it ranked low in terms of changes of unionization, this actually meant that its unionization rate declined slower than in Pennsylvania and in most of the nation. But of course, the base rate of unionization in South Carolina is very low: 3.7 percent compared to 43.1 percent for Pennsylvania, and 19.9 percent for the nation. Other factors like taxes and state business incentives also favored South Carolina over Pennsylvania.[29]

Mack Trucks relocated production from a highly unionized state to an ununionized state. It moved production from a plant which was represented by the UAW to a plant that is not represented by the UAW, and given the RTW laws of the state, is unlikely to be represented by any union. Essentially, probable lack of union representation, or at most weak representation, was a crucial decision factor for the corporation. In this context, South Carolina's union-free environment is an important economic development policy, an interpretation that has been made by others of the interaction between RTW laws and state economic growth (see Palomba and Palomba 1971). Although there is some debate over the extent of causality between RTW laws and state economic growth, there is evidence that RTW laws have had marked effects on the UAW's performance in local representation elections, as well as overall rates of unionization (see chapter 5).

In response to local criticism that the corporation had failed to draw upon Pennsylvania's community economic development resources to resolve the dispute between it and the union, the corporation responded by claiming that the dispute was "strictly a labor–management issue."[30] But, if we accept that South Carolina's labor relations climate was an important factor (if not the factor) in the corporation's decision to locate in Winnsboro, this claim seems disingenuous at best. Whereas the labor relations climate in South Carolina is partly the product of state economic development policy, the implication of the corporation's statement was that the state of Pennsylvania had no right to interfere in its decision to close the Allentown plant. A more troubling interpretation would suppose that the corporation deliberately sought to narrow the issue so as to avoid having to compromise with the union, or even provide the state of Pennsylvania with a chance to fashion a deal that would keep the corporation in Allentown.

One way or another local and state agencies were intimately involved in the dispute. In Pennsylvania, these agencies represented a threat to the corporation's plans. In South Carolina, however, these agencies facilitated the corporation's plans to rid itself of the union and its Pennsylvania operations. Community economic development as an issue in the dispute could be interpreted as simply a cover for the corporation to carry out its relocation plans.

Conclusion

This chapter, and the various themes and issues considered in it, was conceived as an interpretive project. That is, given an initial narrative about events and agents, we focused upon interpreting the motives of these agents. It is important that the chapter should not be imagined as definitive. I do not claim to have provided *the only* way of interpreting the case. In fact, the variety of possible interpretations should be taken as indicative of the significance of the case: its utility in reflecting upon the coherence of inherited theories of location, unions, and local economic development. The reader should resist the temptation of attempting his/her own totalizing integration of motives and events. While perhaps satisfying at one level – making sense of all the facts – at a more subtle level it would simply ignore the point of my argument and gloss over the possible deeper motives of those involved.

Now that the narrative has been constructed around the relationship between Mack Trucks and the UAW, it is apparent that some of the events seem more significant than others. For instance, when the company rejected the UAW International proposal for a worker-sponsored local investment fund, it became clear that relocation was an intended goal of the company. And, when the company won its appeal to the federal district judge to hire more nonunion Winnsboro workers, it became apparent that the UAW would not be able to claim immediate representation of workers in the new plant, and may in fact find it impossible to organize the plant in the future. My choice of these two events to represent the dispute should indicate immediately my interpretation of the corporation's motives in announcing the closure of the Allentown plant.

Of course, it is possible that my interpretation will offend some readers, perhaps even offend the corporation and union involved in the dispute. Some readers may still object that my evidence is not strong enough, though it should be apparent that my methodological stance is not premised upon a goal of proving my case, as a social scientist's might be. The corporation and union might separately protest my interpretation of their motives, and suggest that because I have not contacted them directly I cannot possibly know the true facts. But again, it is important to emphasize that this chapter was not designed to make the case for one true interpretation. Rather, the tensions implied by suggesting motives should be indicative of the tensions involved in any interpretation of corporate location decision making. Like Sen (1987), I prefer to be vaguely right than precisely wrong.[31]

At the beginning of the chapter, though, I suggested that the narrative was structured in a naive fashion. That is, my interpretation was not directly introduced. Rather it was embedded in the particular perspective I used to present details of the dispute. Subsequently, as I discussed the corporation, the union, and the community, it should have become more obvious that my perspective on the dispute was premised on some quite specific assumptions of the actions and motives of the parties involved in the dispute. Specifically, it was argued that the corporation was primarily motivated by a desire to avoid the union. While there may have been significant differences between Allentown and Winnsboro in the standard costs of production, after all the attempts by the union and community to accommodate the corporation, it still chose Winnsboro over Allentown. I also suggested that understanding the political structure of the union is a vital step in understanding the corporation's strategy and the union's response to that strategy. I suggested further that Mack Trucks' relocation involves a subtle appreciation of the consequences of local public policies towards unionization and economic development.

My interpretation of parties' actions and motives was premised upon a theory of location (if that is what it is called) that assumes a fundamental role for the social-cum-spatial relations of production in determining the organization of the economic landscape. By this account, local labor relations environments, what management consultants sometimes call business climates, are vital elements in corporations' locational calculations. While possibly illegal, on the assumption that *First National Maintenance* (1981) and *Otis Elevator II* (1984) hold in these circumstances, such calculations typically involve the collective bargaining process as opposed to purely economic considerations. In this way, spatial differentiation of the collective bargaining process is intimately connected to the economic prospects of towns and cities across America. Consequently, the institutions of the collective bargaining process – unions, arbitrators, courts, the NLRB, and the structure of labor law itself – are all part of the location decision frameworks of corporations.

Interpretation of the case study leads, finally, to a series of propositions about understanding the intersection between American communities and the crisis of organized labor. First, I would argue that the crisis of American unions involves a more subtle interplay of interpretation and empirical analysis than heretofore evident in the literature. Second, I would argue that the future of the American labor movement is bound up in its communities, as evident in the geography of union representation elections (for example). Third, I would also argue that institutional mediation of local relationships between labor and capital is an essential component of the differentiation of places. And fourth, I would argue that economic restructuring is a process that has made the connections between institutions, unions, and communities in ways that are only now becoming apparent.

4

Rationing jobs within the union, between communities

The United States economy is undergoing a profound transformation.[1] As we saw in the previous chapter, rapid penetration of the domestic US market by overseas producers and concomitant unanticipated reconfiguration of product markets have left many domestic producers significantly under-capitalized, and many sectors, industries, and firms in decline. These factors have drastically affected the livelihood of many thousands of workers and their communities. Corporate restructuring programs have begun rationing the remaining jobs amongst existing facilities on the basis of labor costs, labor productivity, and union cooperativeness. Some corporations like Mack Trucks have unilaterally instituted restructuring plans. But there are others which have deliberately involved their unions in the process of job rationing.

This chapter considers an instance of cooperative job rationing, and advances three related arguments. First, it is suggested that cooperative restructuring programs can pose fundamental threats to the internal politi-cal coherence of unions. Second, it is also suggested that because of the democratic imperatives faced by unions, community loyalties may fragment union solidarity. And third, cooperative restructuring programs threaten the very future of unions as institutions. The chapter is based on a case study involving United Auto Workers Local unions 12 (Toledo), 72 (Kenosha), and 75 (Milwaukee), the UAW International, and the American Motors Corporation (AMC) and its Jeep Division located in Toledo, Ohio.[2] The dispute concerned the implementation of an Employee Investment Plan (EIP) and Preferential Hiring and Corporate Seniority (PHCS) program involving the three UAW Locals over the period 1978 to 1986.

Whatever the logic of corporation-wide restructuring plans, even sup-ported by the executive of International unions, constituent Local unions may legitimately claim that their local interests are not served by such plans. Local unions are very important as political entities representing local members' interests; this function is mandated by the National Labor Relations Act and is an essential element legitimating American unions (Stone 1981). However, rationalizing Local unions' claims involves adjudi-cating fundamental questions about the constituencies of International unions and their Locals, and who is the proper agent to represent local union members' interests. Proposals for reorganizing American labor–management relations in ways that facilitate corporate restructuring and flexibility have to be cognizant of the internal political structure of unions. Understanding the future of organized labor requires an appreciation of the internal fragility of union solidarity, exacerbated by geographical and economic restructuring.

Institutional context of restructuring

It is commonplace to point to a crisis of US manufacturing.[3] Whether this is a crisis of employment alone, assuming that labor-saving investment (technology) in manufacturing has been the primary reason for declining employment, or is a more profound crisis of American corporate leadership, especially the American system of integrated corporate management and production in the newly emergent global factory, remains open for debate.

In reaction to Bluestone and Harrison's (1982:6) thesis of deindustrialization, "systematic disinvestment in the nation's productive capacity," Lawrence (1984) and others argue that American manufacturing remains competitive even if individual sectors like autos have lost their relative competitive position in the world market. According to Lawrence, massive job loss in certain sectors is evidence of ongoing structural adjustment of American industry to changing levels of world competition. While it is probably misleading to label Lawrence's thesis optimistic, he nevertheless suggested that the deindustrialization thesis mistakes evidence of structural adjustment for evidence of long-term decline of American industry as a whole. Lawrence supposes that the underlying organization of American capitalism is viable, even if certain sectors are in decline.

There are writers, however, who suppose that the real problem is deeply embedded in the logic and structure of American corporate capitalism. Halberstam (1986) argued that American corporate leadership ought to be held accountable for declining competitiveness. Through a series of case studies comparing American and Japanese corporate leadership styles, Halberstam suggested that American corporate elites are relatively risk averse, bureaucratic, and unresponsive to workers' contributions to the enterprise.[4] The result, according to Halberstam, is lower productivity and irreversible declining market shares.[5] In a less personal vein, Piore and Sabel (1984) argued that corporate America is quite inflexible. They suggested that US techniques of production are too narrowly focused upon mass production, and that workers' skills have been so devalued by these techniques that firms' labor resources are now too limited. Their thesis is that the crisis of American manufacturing is a product of institutional incapacity.

Because American management styles have been linked with corporate competitiveness and labor productivity, attention has been focused upon the *social* organization of production. The issue is whether or not labor–management relations (to take one dimension of the problem) are flexible enough to respond to competitive pressures. Dunlop (1987) and others like Kochan, Katz, and McKersie (1986) claim that the American labor relations system ought to be modified in accordance with the new economic imperatives implied by foreign competition. Not surprisingly, analysis of labor–management systems has broadened to include consideration of the role of unions in modern capitalism (see Freeman and Medoff 1984 for a detailed empirical study and Williamson 1985 for a more theoretical analysis), how unions affect the structure of production and worker productivity (see Katz 1985 for a related study of the automobile industry), and how unions might respond to these pressures given an apparently hostile environment (Kochan 1985).

At one level, it has been asserted that unions are *the* impediment to flexible management. This is surely the stance taken by the National Labor Relations Board in some of its recent decisions facilitating plant relocations (see chapters 8 and 9). At another level, however, there is unprecedented interest in labor–management cooperative partnerships between unions and management, as evidenced by the Saturn Project agreement between General Motors Corporation (GM) and the United Auto Workers union (chapter 9). There are many other examples of labor–management cooperative partnerships. Some dominate the operations of whole corporations, as is the case with National Inter-Group (the holding company of National Steel); others are more experimental, like the Saturn Project.

Not often appreciated, though, are the political pressures that these partnerships engender within unions and the concomitant dilemmas which union leaders face as they attempt to balance off contending local claims. For while labor–management cooperative partnerships and restructuring programs promise to make corporations more competitive, these partnerships typically involve radical reorganization of corporate production schemes on a plant-by-plant (Local union-by-Local union) basis. Inevitably restructuring involves significant job losses, drastically affecting some communities much more than others. As Bluestone and Harrison (1982) originally noted, and as Clark (1986a) and Hill and Negrey (1987) amongst others have recently shown, restructuring is an intensely local phenomenon. It should not be surprising, therefore, to find large multi-plant (International) unions like the UAW internally divided over the organization of cooperative partnerships and restructuring programs. The jobs of local union members are at stake, as are the futures of their local unions and communities.

If this were simply a matter of union participation in, as opposed to collective responsibility with corporations for, the rationing of jobs between workers and communities, presumably the political pressures could be endured. However, many corporations depend upon their unions to help design and implement restructuring programs. This is certainly the case in the example developed in subsequent sections of this chapter.

Union-sponsored implementation of restructuring programs raise many difficult issues. Immediately, it involves competition between Local unions in multi-plant corporations. In addition, it questions the role that International union executives ought to play in rationalizing and rationing jobs between contending Locals. These political pressures may well be contributing to the declining performance of major industrial unions in representation elections noted in later chapters. The union as an institution is caught between representing and adjudicating workers' interests at the local level and simultaneously brokering deals which would protect the future of its corporate partners. It is little wonder that unions sometimes appear weak and divided and at other times appear to be impediments to change.

Essentials of the dispute

As noted above, these issues are illustrated by a case study involving the United Auto Workers union and the American Motors Corporation. The case study analyzed in this chapter is one amongst a number of similar cases being currently litigated by the UAW International and its Locals. For example, in Springfield, Ohio there is a law suit pending against the Master Recall Transfer Rights provision of the UAW–International Harvester Agreement. This issue is also being litigated in Indianapolis, Indiana. In another less related suit, a group of workers from the Lima, Ohio General Dynamics plant are suing Chrysler Corporation for reinstatement of their Chrysler seniority rights, even though the corporation sold the plant to General Dynamics in 1982.

As noted above, the dispute involved three UAW Locals of the American Motors Corporation, the UAW International, and the corporation itself. Most generally, the dispute centered on UAW Local 12's (AMC's Jeep division located in Toledo) unwillingness to accept transferees with corporation-wide seniority rights from two other AMC plants located in Wisconsin (Local 72 – Kenosha and Local 75 – Milwaukee). While Local 12 did agree at one time (1982) to accept transferees as part of a general corporation-wide restructuring package negotiated between the Locals, the International, and the corporation, it appears that Local 12 was an unwilling participant in the scheme.

The 1982 restructuring package included two crucial elements: an Employee Investment Plan and a Preferential Hiring and Corporation Seniority program for laid-off employees of the corporation, both of which were appended to all Local UAW/AMC contracts and subsequently ratified by the membership of each Local. In contract negotiations with AMC/Jeep in late 1984, Local 12 agreed to a company proposal to delete the PHCS provision from its contract. Following that action, the Locals, the International, and the corporation became involved in a series of court appeals and arbitration hearings which were only finally resolved in late 1986. Ultimately, the International and Locals 72 and 75 prevailed over Local 12. The Toledo Local was forced to accept transferees under the PHCS program.

Traditionally, Local 12 bargained directly with AMC/Jeep and separately from the International and Wisconsin UAW/AMC Locals. Unlike other major collective bargaining agreements in the auto industry, no master contract exists between the International union and the corporation. This pattern of decentralized collective bargaining on a plant-by-plant basis is attributed by all parties to the fact that AMC's Jeep subsidiary was only relatively recently (circa 1970) purchased from the Kaiser Corporation. At the time of purchase, AMC assumed the Kaiser collective bargaining contract and did not attempt to rationalize the Kaiser/Jeep/UAW local contract in terms of its other AMC/UAW contracts. Thus, when the International and the Wisconsin Locals (72 and 75) first sought to establish a Preferential Hiring and Corporation Seniority system in their 1978 collective bargaining negotiations with the company, it was clear that such a system could only be instituted with the agreement of the Toledo Local.[6]

While it is difficult to find a detailed explanation of why the Wisconsin Locals were so interested in instituting such a system, it appears that in 1978 and 1980 there were fears that retooling and modernization of the Wisconsin facilities would displace many employees.[7] According to Local 72, the PHCS system would enable "long-standing AMC employees who are permanently laid-off at one manufacturing facility [to] obtain a preferential right to be hired at any other AMC facility which is expanding its production and work force."[8] It was important to Locals 72 and 75 to involve Local 12 because the AMC/Jeep division was the most likely place where laid-off AMC Wisconsin UAW employees might obtain a job within AMC. It is also true, as stated by Local 72, that a company-wide agreement would have "protect[ed] the jobs of *all* senior AMC employees" (italics in the original). During this period, a significant number of AMC's Wisconsin UAW employees were permanently laid off and were unemployed for several years. Because Local 12 did not agree with the policy, the preferential hiring system was not instituted in either year. Only in 1982 did Local 12 sign the agreement, and only then in the context of a deal with the other Locals and the corporation involving the establishment of an employee-based corporate investment fund.

In 1982, in the midst of the deepest economic recession since the Great Depression, the corporation requested the International and the Local unions to negotiate jointly a midterm collective agreement which would, in part, extend then current local agreements to 1985. Included in these negotiations was a proposal by the corporation to establish an Employee Investment Plan. By the terms of this plan, the corporation would retain a portion of all employees' wages to invest in modernization of AMC facilities.[9]

It is commonly agreed that the Wisconsin Locals had little to gain from participation in the plan. Modernization programs for these plants had been largely completed. Even in the depths of the recession, demand was reasonably good for AMC's newer models (Encore and Alliance), produced at the Wisconsin plants. The investment pool generated by the EIP was to be based upon the contributions of the Wisconsin Locals, whose working members far outnumbered Local 12. This pool, however, was to be used in modernizing the AMC Jeep division, which had been particularly hard hit by the recession.[10] The corporation asked for an unprecedented joint agreement between the Locals and the International to implement a restructuring program financed by the EIP. Only after Locals 72 and 75 obtained agreement from Local 12 to ratify the 1978 PHCS letter was the joint agreement signed.

The corporation-wide seniority system was to function in the following manner. It was agreed that when hiring new employees at any facility covered by the agreement the corporation would give preference to permanently laid-off AMC employees whatever their home plant location. Permanently laid-off employees were to be hired according to their corporation-wide years of seniority. And once hired at a new location, such employees would be eligible for plant-level seniority as of the date of the agreement between the Locals and the corporation (if the employees had seniority at their originating plant prior to the date of the agreement) or the date of seniority if originally hired after the date the agreement was signed. Relocating employees were eligible for relocation assistance and an equivalent job in the destination plant. Once a relocating employee claimed his/her seniority at the destination plant, the employee would lose all seniority and recall rights at his/her originating plant. Implementation of this agreement was to be the responsibility of the International union. Coupling the EIP with the PHCS was the deal or, as Local 72 termed it, the *quid pro quo* that brought the Locals together.

It took another three years before Local 12's commitment to the PHCS provision was tested. In January 1985 AMC/Jeep began a hiring program under the terms of the PHCS provision (75 laid-off Kenosha workers were hired in Toledo). But by then Local 12 and AMC/Jeep had tentatively agreed to a new contract (effective 1 February 1985) in which the PHCS provision had been deleted. The company (AMC/Jeep) had proposed deletion in late 1984, and the Local had readily agreed. However, the UAW International AMC Department Director (Majerus) demanded reinstatement of the PHCS provision, arguing that the Local had no right to withdraw unilaterally from the 1982 agreement, which involved the interests of two other Locals and the International. The corporation finally agreed with Majerus (over the objections of the Local union chairman) and reinstated the provision in May of 1985. In the next four months another 465 Kenosha employees were hired at AMC/Jeep.[11]

These actions by the International and the corporation appear to have offended the Chairman of Local 12 and many of his members greatly. As a first step, Local 12 protested to AMC/Jeep and Majerus (September 1985). Having failed at this level, the Local appealed to the UAW International Executive Board. Again Local 12 lost when the Board upheld Majerus' decision (October 1985). Finally, the Local appealed to the UAW Convention Appeal Committee (CAC), which decided in favor of the Local (late November 1985). The CAC's decision meant that Local 12 could bargain with AMC/Jeep to end the PHCS provision. At the same time, it did not rationalize or redefine Locals' 72 and 75 right to send transferees to Toledo – transferees became lost between the Locals. The CAC's decision also effectively prevented the International from siding with the Wisconsin Locals in court and arbitration hearings. But again the decision did not resolve the conflict between the Locals; the Locals could still take the matter to arbitration.

In early November AMC/Jeep began lay-offs in Toledo. By virtue of the PHCS provision, 63 of 75 Kenosha employees who would have been laid off elected to use their corporation-wide seniority rights to avoid lay-off. As a consequence, Toledo AMC/Jeep employees were laid off. This prompted Local 12 to file a grievance (no. 4374 dated 7 November 1985) alleging the company had violated its 1985 collective bargaining agreement with Local 12. And just a couple of days later, the Local filed a complaint in Federal District Court seeking an injunction to stop the company from implementing the PHCS provisions. This injunction was granted, and the company then laid off those Kenosha employees who had sought protection from lay-off under the terms of the PHCS and recalled those Toledo AMC/Jeep employees it had previously laid off.

This action by the corporation then prompted Locals 72 and 75 to file their own grievances (nos. 4062 and 85–140–675) alleging that the corporation had violated its contract in the matter of PHCS. Not only did their grievances seek reinstatement of the PHCS scheme, but Locals 72 and 75 sought to recover damages on behalf of the laid-off workers. The corporation then requested the Court to raise Local 12's bond to around $250,000, a figure related to the possible damages which would be due laid-off workers. Because Local 12 could not raise this money the suit lapsed in Federal District Court (January 1986) and the company again laid off Toledo AMC/Jeep employees and recalled eligible Kenosha employees. Finally, on 5 September 1986 the arbitrator dismissed Local 12's grievance and other related grievances filed by Locals 72 and 75.

Local 12 as an autonomous agent

Throughout the hearings before UAW appeals boards, the Court, and the permanent arbitrator, Local 12 claimed that it had the power to make its own contract with AMC/Jeep, and thus had the power to delete the PHCS provision during collective bargaining with the corporation. In its appeal to the Convention Appeals Committee, Local 12 claimed that it had only signed the 1982 EIP/PHCS agreement on the express understanding that it would expire with its contract with AMC/Jeep in January 1985. As the basis of their *Decision* supporting this position, the Committee argued: (1) continued agreement of all parties was necessary for the PHCS provision to remain in force; and (2) because there was no national collective bargaining agreement between the UAW and AMC, Local unions were the proper negotiating agents of UAW unit members. The Committee asserted that in situations like this, given the local nature of collective bargaining and the lack of a national contract, "doubts must be resolved in favor of the individual Agreements" (*Decision*: 5). Essentially, the Committee agreed with Local 12 that the local bargaining unit had the right to assert the interests of its members over the interests of other AMC/UAW Local members.

Before the Federal District Court, Local 12 sought an injunction against AMC/Jeep's implementation of the PHCS plan pending hearing of its grievance against the company regarding this issue. As before, the Local claimed: (1) Local 12 and Jeep are contractually bound to arbitrate the grievance; (2) Jeep's alleged breach of the collective bargaining agreement with Local 12 is ongoing; (3) Local 12 would suffer irreparable harm if an injunction was not granted. The first two claims were readily accepted by the Court. The Court also accepted the Local's claim that the union may be irreparably harmed in terms of its credibility with unit members. According to Local 12, its credibility was threatened by the company's actions. It could hardly claim to represent local members' interests if, after the contract had been agreed to by the union and the company and then ratified by the membership, the company acts in accord with the wishes of a third party (the International) uninvolved in negotiating the collective bargaining agreement. The Local also claimed that the company's actions threatened the unity of the union, dividing "workers against themselves."

On the basis of these arguments the Court granted Local 12's application for an injunction. Judge Walinski concluded "clearly, Jeep's implementation of the policies in question have undermined Local 12's collective bargaining power" and "Jeep has 'divided its workers against themselves,' thereby weakening or at least giving the appearance of weakening Local 12" (*Memorandum and order*: 13 and 14 respectively).[12]

As was noted above, the injunction lapsed and AMC/Jeep resumed hiring AMC/Kenosha employees. This still left the grievance which was heard in July 1986. After rehearsing the events and actions taken by the parties to the dispute, Local 12 made a four-point argument in support of its claim of autonomy. First, the Local argued that reinstatement of the PHCS plan by Majerus and Calmes was counter to the history and experience of the Local. Any previous modification of the AMC/Jeep–Local 12 collective bargaining agreement was ratified by the membership. In this case, there was no ratification of reinstatement. Second, the Local argued that Majerus had no authority to negotiate with AMC on matters dealing with the welfare of its members without prior approval of the Local. More specifically, it was asserted that Majerus was not an agent of Local 12 as defined by UAW regulations.[13] Third, Jeep had no right to negotiate with a third party about the interests of unit members who are otherwise legitimately represented by Local 12. Fourth, the Local argued that AMC/Jeep had failed to notify the Local of its intention to modify the collective bargaining agreement.

Contained and implied in all these arguments are three basic assumptions regarding the status of Local 12 and its relationship to the UAW (other AMC Locals and International). All three assumptions *idealized* the Local as a wholly autonomous and independent (exclusive) agent of local members' interests in relation to other elements of the UAW. A crucial assumption made by the Local was that it is solely responsible for negotiation of collective bargaining agreements for its members. This assumption is asserted in a number of guises: an historical narrative regarding past bargaining practices, a definition of agency that depends upon the express consent of Local members, and a claim that any intrusion on to its turf would irreparably harm its legal entitlement to represent its members. Once we accept this assumption (for the moment), the next automatically follows: that is, the Local has the power to negotiate the deletion or inclusion of any item deemed worthy of consideration by its members and/or the company. Of course, this does not mean that the Local can abrogate existing contracts or previously agreed provisions of any collective bargaining agreement. But once contract negotiations are opened, then the Local as exclusive agent of its members can propose anything consistent with members' interests. This also implies a third assumption: Local 12 has no responsibility for members of other AMC/UAW Locals, except at its discretion and within the terms of existing contracts.

To appreciate the importance of these assumptions fully requires recalling a couple of arguments made by the Local in its appeal for an injunction in the Federal District Court. Recall that the union argued, and the Court agreed, that Jeep's actions weakened the power of Local 12 by dividing "workers against themselves." The workers implied by this statement were Local 12 members and former Locals 72 and 75 members. Indeed, there was persuasive evidence introduced of plant-level fighting between these groups of workers, as well as a great deal of hostility over the fact that Toledo workers were laid off as opposed to Kenosha workers.

Hidden in the arguments by Local 12 was a presumption that the Local represented local workers first, not transferees. As such, the Local seems to have imagined that its political constituency was the local membership and by extension the community at large, not AMC/UAW employees at large or even a small portion of those employees who transferred into the plant. Also recall that the Local was very concerned about maintaining its integrity in relation to other elements of the union in the collective bargaining process. Here the presumption was that the Local, and principally its leadership, stood to lose a great deal of power if Majerus and Locals 72 and 75 prevailed. In fact, the intervention of Majerus threatened to realign the historical prerogatives of Local 12.

Local unions as bilateral partners

Locals 72 and 75 also filed grievances against the corporation charging that it had failed to implement the PHCS provision as agreed to in the 1982 collective bargaining agreement between the three Locals, the International, and the corporation. A couple of events could be thought to have initiated the grievances. Obviously Local 12's grievance was part of the issue. If successful, the grievance threatened to disrupt the PHCS system which the Wisconsin Locals had spent years developing and implementing. To protect their interests, Locals 72 and 75 had to counter Local 12's grievance with their own. The interests of the AMC's Wisconsin transferees were at stake as well. It was quite apparent that Local 12 was willing to sacrifice the interests of the transferees in order to assert the interests of its local members. In a very real sense, the Wisconsin transferees now located in Toledo needed protection. Shop-floor hostility was palpable, even though it was the nominal responsibility of the Local union to serve all workers at the plant.

The briefs filed by Locals 72 and 75 (*Prehearing brief* and *Memorandum brief* respectively) before the permanent arbitrator in July 1986 were similar and different in a number of ways. Local 72 began by asserting that AMC/Jeep and Local 12 could not rescind the PHCS provision without the consent of the other parties to the 1982 collective bargaining agreement. Indeed, both Locals argued that the common law of contracts held that AMC/Jeep and Local 12 had an obligation to Locals 72 and 75 to abide by the terms of the original agreement.

At the same time, it appears that Locals 72 and 75 differed on one crucial issue. Local 72 assumed that AMC/Jeep and Local 12 were jointly responsible for the actions taken in early 1985 leading to deletion of the PHCS provision. While discussing the law suit brought by Local 12 against AMC/Jeep, Local 72 suggested that the suit was a sham (*Prehearing brief*: 19). Rather than imagining the two parties to be genuinely at odds with one another, Local 72 believed them to be "indispensable partners" engaged in an attempt to subvert the legitimate interests of the other parties to the contract. On the other hand, Local 75 argued: "make no mistake about it, the culprit in this case is the company ... although Local 12 did become an accomplice in American Motors' attempt to breach its agreements" (*Memorandum brief*: 8).

Throughout its brief to the arbitrator, Local 72 sought to portray the issue as a question of the integrity of common law contracts. Actually, Local 72 hardly ever dealt with the issue of Local 12's right to negotiate its own contract given historical precedent, proper agency, and so forth. In this manner, Local 72 used a familiar legal strategy, its own interpretation of the bases of the dispute, to attempt to control the terms of the dispute and the bases of the arbitrator's decision (Dworkin 1986). Local 72 began by stating the issue as "whether fewer than all the parties to a multi-local, company-wide collective bargaining agreement can agree to rescind that agreement in a manner that would promote their own welfare at the expense of the remaining parties to the original agreement" (*Prehearing brief*: 1). As a means of legitimating its stance, Local 72 sought to establish the importance of the terms of the 1982 agreement, emphasizing the negotiations that led to the deal between the Locals and the International. Also emphasized was the notion of *quid quo pro*: that Local 12 and Locals 72 and 75 each exchanged interests so as to reach a deal. Local 72 also attempted to question the integrity of the chairman of Local 12, describing in detail how he apparently misrepresented his intentions to abide by the opinion of Majerus.

In terms of contract theory, Local 72's argument was quite straightforward. First, two related common law principles were invoked: (1) mutual consent is necessary for the formation and abrogation of a contract; and (2) a unilateral attempt to modify or abrogate a contract has no effect in the absence of express permission to do so as provided for in the original contract. The second step in the argument was to show that the attempt by AMC/Jeep and Local 12 to rescind the PHCS provision contravened both principles. Locals 72 and 75 and the International union all objected to their attempt to rescind the provision. Similarly, the original agreement contained no options for individual parties to withdraw unilaterally from the contract. The only instance where AMC/Jeep and Local 12 were given discretion to develop their own policy in relation to the 1982 agreement concerned the repayment of wages under the EIP plan.

According to Local 72, Local 12 and AMC/Jeep wanted to "have their cake and eat it too" (17). Having benefited from the EIP plan over the 1982–85 period, they wanted to avoid their obligations under the terms of the PHCS plan at precisely the time when the plan was implemented. By this interpretation, renegotiation of the collective bargaining agreement between Local 12 and AMC/Jeep in late 1984 came at a useful time. Deletion of the PHCS provision was a strategic ruse designed to avoid the parties' obligations.

These same issues were also raised by Local 75, along with some troubling questions about the motives of the corporation. It is apparent that the leadership of Local 12 stood to gain considerable local political advantage by abrogating the PHCS provision of the overall restructuring agreement. But what did the corporation stand to gain? In the corporation's brief to the arbitrator it sought to portray Local 12 as the perpetrator of the scheme and the corporation as a willing partner with the International union in the implementation of the PHCS program. According to the corporation, it could not be held responsible for its actions once the US District Court became involved. Nor should the corporation be held responsible for the actions of Local 12 in relation to its obligations to the other Locals and the

International union. In all these matters, the corporation claimed to be acting in good faith.

Whatever the rhetorical virtues of this position, it was apparent to the arbitrator that the corporation suggested the idea to Local 12, and promoted it in the AMC/Jeep plant in concert with the Local. In addition, officials of the corporation admitted that they had thought that rescinding the PHCS provision would pressure the International to renegotiate the EIP repayment schedule. Thus, it was asserted by Local 75 that the corporation had violated its agreement not to bargain by playing one union off another (*Arbitration award*, Grievance 4373, dated 5 September 1986, 14).[14]

By these arguments, the Wisconsin Locals sought to represent themselves and Local 12 in a quite different light than Local 12 sought to represent itself. Assumed in the Wisconsin Locals' arguments are a series of propositions describing the responsibilities of each Local and their relationships with one another and the International. First, it appears that Locals 72 and 75 believed they were joint partners with the International, the corporation, and Local 12 in a mutually beneficial contract. That all parties had ratified the contract in 1982 was taken as evidence that all parties would stand by their obligations. Second, Locals 72 and 75 assumed that the duration of the deal would either be open-ended (as in the case of Local 72) or would terminate with the EIP (as was the case with Local 75). The fact there was no mechanism for a party or parties to terminate their participation is further evidence for this assumption. Third, the parties to the contract were assumed liable to the other parties regarding their performance under the terms of the contract. In this sense, the Locals, the International, and the corporation were liable just as a person is liable for obligations willingly entered into through negotiation and agreement.

Notice that neither Local claimed that Local 12 did not have the right to represent its members. Nor did either Local claim that Local 12 had to give up its historical privilege of negotiating with AMC/Jeep. Nevertheless, whatever the political implications of the PHCS program for Local 12, as a partner with the other Locals it was required to conform to the spirit of the contract. In this setting the AMC/UAW was assumed to be a confederation of Locals with distinct spheres of local autonomy but with overlapping, albeit different interests mediated by, and represented by, the International UAW.

For those readers schooled in contemporary political theory, one might suppose that Locals 72 and 75 assumed a *corporatist* form of unionization analogous to some forms of European state capitalism. Simply described, corporatism presumes that institutions accommodate contending claims of power through bilateral power-sharing agreements amongst elites. As for internal political forces, these are thought to be accommodated through democratic representation processes and direct pay-offs. In a stable corporatist society, elite agreements are hardly ever internalized; rather members of institutions are loyal to their institutions on the basis of more general sets of rewards (see Schmitter and Lehmbruch 1979 for an overview of the literature on corporatism).[15]

The International as collective agent

The arbitrator, Paul Glendon, denied the grievances brought by Local 12 (no. 4373) and Locals 72 and 75 (consolidated in no. 4062). He found Majerus to be entirely justified in demanding that the PHCS provision deleted by AMC/Jeep and Local 12 in early 1985 be reinstated. At the same time, however, Glendon claimed that it was unnecessary to establish whether or not Majerus had the authority to force AMC/Jeep and Local 12 to reinstate the provision. Essentially, the arbitrator agreed with Local 72 that the 1982 contract was a binding agreement between the parties, an agreement which could not be unilaterally abrogated by one or more partners. In this sense, Majerus was correct in convincing the corporation to stand by the terms of the 1982 contract as opposed to the newly negotiated collective bargaining agreement of early 1985.

Glendon did note, however, that if the contract had been correctly deleted, according to the terms of the original 1978 agreement between Locals 72 and 75 it could only have been reinstated by Local 12's ratification. Generally, the arbitrator gave the corporation the benefit of the doubt, arguing that Locals 12, 72, and 75 had failed to prove bad faith on the part of officers of the corporation.

In consideration of Local 12's claim of autonomy based upon historical precedent, Glendon supposed that the precedent was simply a convenient practice as opposed to a fundamental right. It could not simultaneously benefit from a bilateral agreement while claiming that it was not accountable to the terms of that contract by reason of its historical representation functions. If history was a useful rationalization describing the relationship between AMC/Jeep and Local 12, it was also just as valid a rationalization describing the relationships between Locals 12, 72, 75, the UAW International, and the corporation. Consequently, the arbitrator held with Local 75 that the PHCS was co-terminous with the EIP. By this reasoning, the 1982 deal had precedence over any previous negotiation practice and was held as binding on Local 12. The arbitrator gave considerable weight to the imperatives facing all three unions when they negotiated the EIP and PHCS.

The arbitrator disbelieved Local 12's claim that it only signed the contract with an express understanding that it would expire in 1985.

Implied by the arbitrator's reasoning were three assumptions: one concerned the nature of UAW Locals and the other two concerned the role of the International and the relationships of UAW Locals to the International. By virtue of the arbitrator's treatment of each Local as an equal partner in the 1982 corporation-wide collective agreement, the arbitrator assumed that Locals were empowered to enter into agreements as agents representing the interests of their members. While the arbitrator chose to ignore Local 12's claims of fundamental autonomy, he nevertheless gave considerable significance to the notion that each Local had much to gain from entering into the agreement, albeit true that their interests as representatives of their local members were quite different. In this sense, the arbitrator assumed the UAW Locals were legitimate agents of members' interests, just as the officers of the corporation were the corporation's agents.

But it also seems as if the arbitrator made quite strong assumptions about the legitimate role of the International and its relationship to the Locals. Through discussion of the history and events of the dispute, the arbitrator identified a series of roles played by the International. He noted at different times the International: (1) was closely involved in negotiation of the 1982 collective agreement with the corporation; (2) was responsible for negotiating with the corporation implementation of the PHCS; (3) represented the interests of Locals 72 and 75 before the corporation and Local 12; and (4) provided an internal forum for adjudication of the dispute between Majerus and Locals 12, 72, and 75.

In all these ways, the International was closely involved with designing the EIP/PHCS program and monitoring the performance of the parties to the agreement. Through Majerus, it was also a forceful advocate for the integrity of the 1982 collective agreement. Inherent in the arbitrator's decision was an assumption that these roles were legitimate and consistent with the International's interests as one of the parties to the 1982 agreement. At this level, the arbitrator gave the International equal standing with the Locals. However, he also assumed that the Locals were answerable to the International for their performance under the terms of the collective agreement. At this level, he assumed the International to be the collective agent of all members' interests.

Upon the evidence submitted by Local 12, one might argue that these assumptions were not shared by all parties to the 1982 collective agreement. If we were to accept Local 12's claim of fundamental autonomy for the moment, by this assumption the International certainly would not warrant equal status with Local 12 or even with Locals 72 and 75. Local 12's emphasis on the fact that historically there had been no AMC/UAW master contract would seem to imply that the AMC/UAW Locals had a stronger claim as agents of their members' interests than the International. However, the arbitrator did not accept Local 12's claim to fundamental autonomy and implied that the Local forfeited its historical claim of independence from the International when it joined the collective agreement in 1982. By treating the International as an equal partner in these negotiations and by recognizing the International's claim that it had the right to bargain with the company for implementing the agreement, Local 12 essentially recognized the International as an equal.

At the same time, the Local also recognized the International as a higher authority by virtue of its appeals to various committees in the International union. Granted the Local used these committees to appeal the actions of the International. Nevertheless, the status accorded the International by the Local belied its claim of fundamental independence from the International. If the Local had really wanted that level of autonomy, it had the option to become an independent union. To do so, though, would have meant giving up the advantages of belonging to the UAW, as well as withdrawing from all subsequent agreements between the UAW and AMC. It is not clear that Local 12's membership would have accepted such a radical change in their status.

Political coherence of the union

Embedded in the dispute between Locals 12, 72, and 75, the International and the corporation were contending conceptions or models of union responsibilities and discretion. Described in the simplest terms possible, these contending models might be summarized as follows. Local 12's perspective was that Local AMC/UAW unions are *autonomous agents of their members' interests*. Locals 72 and 75 presumed that Local UAW unions are *partners with one another in relation to the corporation*. The International presumed that Local UAW unions are *responsible to the union for their actions* and that the International itself is the *collective agent representing all UAW members employed by the corporation*.

The corporation's position seemed twofold. On one hand, it obviously wanted the 1982 collective agreement signed by all Locals and the International. The corporation depended upon the International for advice regarding its actions with Local 12, for implementation of the EIP/PHCS, and for support in litigation with Local 12. In this sense, the corporation acted as if the International were the ultimate representative of the UAW. On the other hand, the corporation also used Local 12's interest in isolating itself from the other Locals as a means of advancing the corporation's interests. In this sense, the corporation was opportunistic, and used different models of union responsibilities as their interests dictated.

The arbitrator hardly addressed this issue, and preferred to look for evidence of bad faith on the part of the corporation. Finding none (or at least suggesting that the Locals had not proven their case against the corporation), the arbitrator absolved the corporation of culpability in the dispute. At this point, though, the arbitrator's decision seems disingenuous, especially given the corporation's acknowledgment that it used the issue to pressure the union (International) to renegotiate the terms of the EIP.

These competing conceptions of union responsibility also imply quite different political constituencies for the various units of the union. Local 12's *agent* model asserts that its sole constituency consisted of local union members. By this logic, Kenosha transferees were not part of the Local's responsibility. Local 72 and 75's *partners* model supposed that each Local was responsible for the interests of its own members, and once the PHCS program was implemented each union would also be responsible for other Locals' members who transferred into the Local. Thus, the political constituency implied began with the Local's members and extended to new members who joined the Local under the terms of the agreement. The International's *collective agent* model supposed that its constituency was all AMC/UAW members. In essence, these models replicated the political structure of the union, and the scales of constituency implied by its organization into local bargaining and representation units. There can be no doubt that each unit faced its own political imperatives in taking sides in the dispute over seniority transfers. To imagine otherwise would be to ignore the fundamental decentralized nature of internal UAW politics.

Given these constituencies and the terms of the EIP/PHCS agreement, a couple of other observations can be made about the politics of rationing jobs between workers and between communities. From the International's perspective, its problem was to ensure that current but laid-off AMC employees had a chance of employment within the corporation. Since seniority is such an important sorting mechanism within plants, even within the leadership of the union and corporation, seniority appears to be an ideal way of sorting laid-off employees into a priority hiring list. Corporation-wide seniority is consistent with the International's political constituency and its model of its responsibilities. In an era of declining employment in the industry and AMC in particular, the International sought to protect its oldest members irrespective of the economic conditions of each Local and AMC plant. Rationing jobs by this method was by age, assuming there were laid-off union members within the corporation willing to relocate.

From Local 12's perspective, its political constituency was local union members. Inevitably, local members are concerned not only about their own but their families' and friends' employment prospects. The Local and corporation represent, then, an important source of employment in the local community. Not surprisingly, seniority-based transfers from other communities represent impossible competition for local workers who might want employment in the plant. Thus, if there was to be job rationing, Local 12 supposed that local workers ought to have had the first chance to obtain employment.

Seniority transfers provided a series of different dilemmas for the leadership and members of the Local union and even the local management of the plant. For local union members, their loyalty to the community was set at odds with their loyalty to outside unionists. For Local union leaders who are elected to represent the interests of local members, accepting seniority transfers set them at odds with those who elected them. But, if the local leadership did not accept transfers, their loyalty to the union leadership would be severely questioned. This is a problem for a number of reasons. Most obviously, the International is able to operate more effectively with the corporation than any single Local. Thus any Local leader has an incentive to side with the International. And, finally, local management have an incentive to hire local union members. Transferees are someone else's hiring decision; management may not be confident of transferees' commitment to the plant.

Rationing jobs between workers and communities engenders tremendous political tensions in multi-plant unions. It is not always possible to resolve these tensions, given the divided loyalties implied. And resolution of these tensions is likely to generate other claims which may threaten the internal coherence of the union. For example, if Local unions accept many outside transferees they may isolate themselves from the local community. This might be possible to live with if the corporation and the International could be trusted to protect the interests of local employees and union members in the long run. However, in the long run the corporation certainly cannot be trusted to remain in the community and the International union cannot possibly guarantee local jobs in the absence of the corporation.

Thus, in the long term few union members can afford to alienate the local community. To do so would imperil their own wellbeing if they were forced to depend on the community for help because the corporation closed the local plant. It is not surprising that rationing jobs engenders such tense political relations. Local unions may find it in their long-term interests to disaffiliate from International unions, as the membership may come to believe that their interests are not served by a Local that accepts seniority transfers as part of a multi-Local deal. If this becomes the case, the leadership of Locals that participate in corporate multi-plant restructuring programs may face hostile decertification campaigns.

Conclusion

It is tempting to believe that corporate restructuring programs inevitably involve massive job displacement and unemployment. It is also tempting to believe that corporate restructuring programs inevitably pit unions against corporations; unions are alternatively portrayed as powerless and too powerful. That is, it is thought either that unions are victims of restructuring programs (assuming unions are powerless to stop corporate plans after their design and implementation) or that unions stand in the way of corporate restructuring and are impediments to change (assuming that unions are so powerful that they can veto restructuring plans). But, these suppositions do not do justice to the complexity of corporate restructuring programs and the levels of involvement by unions.

For example, based upon the case study developed in this chapter, two points can be made about the nature of job displacement. First, in some settings displacement can be mediated, indeed rationalized through intra-corporation shifts of laid-off workers. Not only has this been the case in AMC, but there is evidence of similar corporation-wide internal labor market policies within all the major American auto manufacturers. Notice, of course, that these kinds of policies are only viable if the corporation takes an active role in reinvestment and reorganization of its competitive position in the market for automobiles. These policies depend upon a continuing commitment to the industry by firms like AMC and GM, something that cannot always be said of employers in other industries, such as steel. In the absence of such a level of commitment, job displacement becomes an immediate community responsibility, albeit the case that communities can do little except provide basic subsistence support.

Second, to the extent that corporations rationalize job displacement resulting from restructuring programs through job rationing amongst existing plants, they tend to do so on the basis of seniority. This is a favorite way of rationalizing job loss, principally because it protects the welfare of older workers who have more skills and personal investment in the industry. But seniority transfers as a job rationing policy involves displacement of another kind. Assuming transfers fill expanding job slots in certain plants, these workers displace local workers who would have been hired to fill these positions. Inevitably, this creates its own tensions in destination communities as those not hired have to look for work elsewhere (other companies, industries, and places), and those hired into the community have to live and work with local citizens. The workers not hired are younger and less experienced, whereas those who transfer into the local plant are older and more experienced. Rationing jobs in this manner balkanizes the corporation's work force, and creates a relatively more mobile work force that becomes progressively older and more removed from the community. The limits on this process are early retirement schemes that facilitate displacement of the oldest workers.

It should also be apparent from the case study that job rationing by seniority and plant will likely involve unions. Indeed, the design and implementation of these programs may be at the behest of unions. International unions have become very much involved in designing policies – corporate and public-sector oriented – that at least protect their interests in representing workers in the industry. Common perceptions of unions as powerless and/or too powerful in these situations ignore the history of industrial unions like the UAW and United Steelworkers of America. These unions have had major roles in structuring employment opportunities in whole industries through bilateral collective bargaining agreements with their corporate partners. Even so, one of the lessons of the case study was that union-sponsored job rationing schemes can engender significant political tensions within the union.

Understanding the genesis of these tensions involves understanding the structure of contemporary unions. Whatever the powers of International unions in relation to corporations, it would be a mistake to imagine that unions are so highly centralized that they mimic the internal structure of corporations. In fact, despite a common assumption that this is the case in the academic literature, there are a variety of forces which sustain unions as decentralized political institutions. The representation function is one vital force which sustains decentralization. Representation is based upon local constituencies just as all congressional elections are so designed. This is not an accident. Representation at the local level reflects a deliberate policy decision made by those who designed the Wagner Act in 1935. Another vital factor is corporate interests in maintaining decentralized bargaining, even in industries which have traditionally negotiated corporation-wide and industry-wide master contracts.

If unions are to survive, they must be sensitive to members' interests at the local level. Unions' need of stable coalitions of Local units indicates a fundamental point of disjuncture between corporations and unions. Whereas corporations may want to rationalize production and investment on a plant-by-plant basis, for International unions to participate they must broker a deal that effectively serves the interests of those union members who are most at risk in corporate restructuring programs. Put slightly differently, whereas corporations treat plants as mere components of larger plans, unions must treat Locals as vital parts of the union as a whole. Otherwise, Internationals will appear as willing partners with corporations in the restructuring (displacement) of whole communities.

In some instances no deal may be possible that simultaneously serves the political and economic interests of Local and International unions. It is in these instances that unions appear powerless and too powerful. They appear powerless because of institutional incapacity: their inability to rationalize competing community interests; and because in the absence of internally negotiated strategies, all they can do is stall implementation of corporation-wide restructuring. At this point, restructuring may well become a struggle to the death between unions and corporations as unions' collective interests evaporate in relation to the strength of Local interests. In these circumstances, the very future of the union movement becomes a fundamental question.

PART III

Union performance in representation elections

5

Democracy in the guise of representation elections

On 19 June 1935, the Committee on Rules debated House Resolution 263 – a resolution to report the Wagner Act to the floor of Congress for final approval.[1] In that debate House members sought to clarify and defend provisions of the Act. While doing so Representative Mead (D – New York) said, in part, that the Act "creates a democracy within industry which gives our industrial workers the same general idea of freedom which the founding fathers conferred upon citizens of the United States. It prohibits force and intimidation and leaves men to organize or remain unorganized as they shall desire."[2] At the time, Representative Mead's interpretation of the Act, electoral democracy for industry, was one amongst a number of competing and complementary interpretations. Since passage of the Taft–Hartley amendments in 1947 it is now assumed that this interpretation was central to the Act.[3] Indeed, Stone (1981) suggested that as representation elections mimic partisan political elections, the Act embodies a fundamental ideal of American liberalism: local electoral choice.

President Roosevelt noted in signing the Wagner Act into law that it "[establishes] the right of self-organization of employees in industry for the purpose of collective bargaining, and provides methods by which the government can safeguard that legal right."[4] The National Labor Relations Board was the federal agency charged with the responsibility of holding representation elections and adjudicating appeals over conduct of the electoral process. These elections are the life-blood of any union. It is through representation elections that unions add new members. And, it is through representation elections that unions claim the right to represent workers before employers. Ultimately unions depend upon the local representation election process for their power.[5]

In this chapter, two arguments are advanced. First, it is suggested that to the extent the union representation election process mimics partisan political elections, geographical patterns of support evident in these latter kinds of elections are also evident in union representation elections. This argument has a number of implications, from the geographical scale of electoral support, through to how we ought to interpret the southern problem (chronic inability of unions to win support in the South: see Marshall 1967).

The second argument is that there are significant differences between unions in terms of their electoral performance. Part of the explanation of these differences may be in how and where unions organize, and the workers they represent. These arguments are illustrated through an analysis of the electoral performance of the International Brotherhood of Electrical Workers (IBEW) and the United Auto Workers (UAW) over the period 1970–82. Some data are also presented on the recent (1986) electoral performance of these two unions.[6]

American elections, forces of fragmentation

Union representation elections have much in common with partisan political elections. The fact that the former kind of election was explicitly conceived in relation to the latter is one obvious similarity: but there are deeper ones. Specifically, it is suggested in this section that the forces that fragment the American electorate also affect the union representation electoral process. The relative significance of local as opposed to national issues and voter alienation both have implications for unions' electoral prospects.

Verba and Nie (1972) summarized in a few lines a basic characteristic of the American political system: those who participate are more affluent, better educated, and occupy high-status occupations. They also observed that "affiliation with voluntary associations increases the disparity in participation between social levels" (336). As higher-income people are more likely to participate in voluntary associations, Verba and Nie concluded that upper-status groups are over-represented in the political process, a finding consistent with observed voting patterns. Essentially, poorer citizens with relatively inferior education and lower-status occupations do not vote in elections to the same extent as higher-status citizens. The result is a conservative polity, dominated by the interests of the middle class.

Verba and Nie equated unions with recreational groups. While membership in a union increases political participation beyond the level consistent with a person's socio-economic status, the effect is small and similar to that of participation in any other voluntary group (as opposed to a political party). Verba and Nie supposed that American unions are relatively economically rather than politically oriented. They suggested that as there are few class-oriented institutions in the political process which would draw a lower-class vote, the lower classes do not vote because no one represents their political interests. The corollary argument (though not explicitly acknowledged by Verba and Nie) is that to the extent that unions are thought to represent the lower classes' economic interests, union elections will garner higher levels of participation (if not actual electoral support) than indicated by those citizens' rates of political participation. In fact, Wolfinger and Rosenstone (1980) found that the social status effect on political participation was mediated by what is "usually called a 'stake in the system.' We did find high turnout by people with a stake in another sort of system – the patronage system that affects their jobs" (103).

In recent years there has been a proliferation of studies designed to assess the dependence of electoral success in presidential and congressional elections on national macroeconomic performance. As in Ashenfelter and Pencavel's (1969) study of the macro determinants of union growth and decline, most studies of electoral success and macroeconomic performance are aggregate in nature. That is, variables like unemployment and inflation are used to explain votes cast for different candidates in national elections (see Hibbs 1977 for a seminal paper in this context). These models are also retrospectively oriented; past macroeconomic performance of the economy is hypothesized to determine incumbents' performance in subsequent elections (see Fiorina 1981).[7]

After a number of empirical studies (Kinder and Kiewiet 1979, 1981), Kiewiet (1983) concluded that presidential elections appear to be affected by macroeconomic circumstances. But, at the same time, there is "a large, nonsystematic component to voters' choices between congressional candidates which generally does not affect their voting for president" (126). Even at the presidential level the evidence is not at all clear, partly because it seems that voters are often confused about the meaning of different macroeconomic indicators and alternative explanations offered by incumbents and competitors. Further, re-estimation of Hibbs' (1977) results have raised considerable doubts as to the robustness of his original thesis (Beck 1982). *If* it is the case that presidents are held accountable for macroeconomic performance, this effect must be limited to higher-status groups. All the evidence presented by Kiewiet (1983) suggested that for the average citizen, economic issues are quite local. Kiewiet (1983) argued that it is the local level which is most readily understood by the voter. To back his claim, he quoted Schlozman and Verba (1979:194) as suggesting that the unemployed (an instance of a group with strong economic interests) "do not see themselves as victims of broad social forces or government ineptitude but of specific events connected with their particular employment circumstances."

One implication of Kiewiet's and others' work is that there is a spatial scale effect which cuts across the national political process. At the highest level there is the national political process, dominated by the political interests of conservative elites. Participation rates and a certain ideological framework effectively conspire to narrow issues to *political* slogans (Lipset

1985). At the local level, however, there are the parochial interests of average citizens. While the average citizen may be very concerned about his/her economic status, it appears that he/she does not connect his/her local conditions with national political leaders. Rightly or wrongly, average citizens' economic interests are relatively isolated spatially and functionally from the national polity.

This conclusion is consistent with other findings that have emphasized the geographical fragmentation of the American electorate. In a recent study of the nationalization of the American electorate from 1842 to 1970, Claggett, Flanagan, and Zingale (1984) failed to "find any increase over the past 100 years in the nationalization of party voting" (89). They also observed, as Kiewiet (1983) suggested, that voting for the President does not seem to spill over into local congressional elections. In fact, they suggested that despite growing professionalization of the electoral process, and a rapidly homogenizing media environment, the crucial cleavages remain geographical, mediated by local social-status effects. Their study, like others that have emphasized the geography of partisan elections, places a high premium on the geographical differentiation of attitudes and interests.[8]

The local effect is more complicated, however, than might be first imagined. Precisely what spatial scale is implied remains quite problematic. For example, there is very good evidence that there are consistent regional effects fragmenting the national polity. Perhaps the best example of this kind of effect is to be found in differences between northern and southern states in their levels of voter participation. Northern states have consistently led southern states in voter participation over some 150 years. Rusk and Stucker (1978) attributed the consistency of this effect to institutional barriers in the South against voting; poll taxes, literacy tests, and the like.[9] While these authors were concerned with a slightly different issue, there is a crucial commonality to be recognized as regards our interests in union representation elections.[10] Those twelve southern states identified by Rusk and Stucker as having had the most stringent voting laws are also states that currently enforce right-to-work laws (see chapter 2 for more details).

Essentially, RTW laws could be reasonably interpreted as extensions of previous legal practices designed to limit voter participation in partisan political elections. According to this interpretation, RTW laws may have had no immediate effect on unionization levels, as supposed by Ellwood and Fine (1983), but may have nevertheless reinforced local elites' interests in limiting workers' access to union representation. Unfortunately, most studies of the effects of RTW laws on unionization tend to ignore the electoral process which is at the heart of unionization. Consequently, they also ignore the political context in which these laws were originally passed.

The irony is that while voter participation rates have increased in the South since the passage of the Voting Rights Act of 1965, RTW laws remain in place, reflecting an earlier time when electoral participation was actively discouraged.

This is quite clearly an example of a systematic institutional local effect. There is evidence, however, of significant nonsystematic (in Kiewiet's terms) local effects operating at a variety of spatial scales. In fact, in partisan political elections there is some evidence of partisan dealignment and voter disaffection with party voting, implying further local fragmentation in partisan voting patterns. Johnston (1982) studied the geography of voting in presidential Senate, and gubernatorial elections over the period 1946–80. He found evidence that, even at this level, voting was becoming more fragmented in terms of party voting, going against the so-called normal vote thesis (compare with Converse 1966). He also found that voting patterns were becoming more fragmented geographically. And, in congressional elections, as I have previously observed, local issues seem to hold sway.[11]

The maintenance of local context as a key aspect of voting behavior is overlapped by another phenomenon: surveys of voter confidence in the established party system is at an all time low (Wattenberg 1984). Not only do voters appear disaffected with the national party system, but they also appear less likely to make successively consistent votes by party affiliation (Cavanagh and Sundquist 1985). By all accounts, respect for social institutions has precipitously declined over the past twenty years. The electorate are less willing to trust their institutions. Perhaps not surprisingly, intraparty discipline on the floor of Congress is also in tatters. According to many commentators on the American electoral system, re-election requires closer attention to local constituents' interests than ever before, and greater distance between local candidates and national parties.

Union elections, forces of continuity

In view of the argument presented in the previous section, it should not be surprising to see a wide variety of local effects in union representation elections. The implications of the previous section for the role of economic forces in union elections were twofold. First, to the extent that potential union members associate economic issues with specific unions, these economic issues will be most likely local rather than national. Second, local economic factors may be quite idiosyncratically interpreted: to the extent that the unions suffer from voter alienation, or more reasonably voter distrust, the nonsystematic component of local elections may shatter consistent local economic effects. These expectations parallel Dunlop's (1948) argument about the local character of union elections.

It would be misleading, however, to deal only with the similarities between union elections and partisan political elections. To do so would ignore Shister's (1953) observation that unions are quite different from one another with respect to their internal organization and their capacity to mobilize workers. Unions are not simply at the mercy of the forces of electoral fragmentation. They are relatively autonomous agents, with significant bureaucratic discretion. In this respect, they are more than capable of recognizing and responding to the forces of fragmentation. After all, in recent years the UAW and the IBEW have conducted southern campaigns designed to penetrate new areas, and potential pockets of union membership. There are reasons to suppose that unions have attempted to counter the forces of fragmentation. To analyze union electoral performance in this respect is to treat unions as active agents capable of adjusting to circumstances.[12]

Clark and Johnston (1987b) explored how unions have responded to the forces of fragmentation by analyzing the similarities and differences between the IBEW and UAW. At first sight, the two unions appear similar. They are certainly of similar size, and historically have been manufacturing industry oriented, as opposed to service industry oriented. However, on closer inspection there are some major differences between the unions. The UAW, as the name implies, has been the union of the auto industry. As such it has represented assembly-line workers in large plant-level bargaining units. Craft designations, while informally important in some local unions, have not been important to the national political structure of the union. On the other hand, the IBEW is more craft oriented, and represents much smaller bargaining units, often within quite large industrial enterprises.

Given the forces of electoral fragmentation, the UAW has sought to specialize in organizing large units within the auto industry. Until the late 1970s, they often had the tacit support of the auto companies. And even now, as in the Saturn Project (see chapter 9), there has been close cooperation between auto companies and the union. This process of union integration has been further enhanced by industry-wide and company-wide collective bargaining. Master contracts with the major companies covering wages and employment have served as stable reference points for local bargaining over the terms of work. This has not absolved the union or the company from adhering to the letter of the NLRA. Local unions within the UAW still have formal responsibility for contract ratification, representing workers in grievance disputes with management and, more recently, bargaining with management over the introduction of new technology (Clark

1986b). These master contracts have also served as reference points for smaller companies in the auto industry and related industries. Indeed, it may not be too much of an exaggeration to say that the union integrated the industry over much of this century.

In contrast, the IBEW has a rather different strategy. Whereas the organization of the UAW is quite centralized, organized by industry and company, the IBEW is more decentralized. Instead of attempting to counter the forces of fragmentation by organizing a national bureaucracy, the IBEW appears to have developed local niches within the existing system. Specifically, the IBEW has concentrated in the construction industry, and in particular within the organized larger firms of that industry. For many years, the wages and conditions of this industry have been set by union standards, protected by the federal government through construction contracting laws such as the Davis–Bacon Act. The IBEW has also sought representation in a couple of other industries (communications for example), representing craft workers rather than assembly workers. In these instances, as in the construction industry, larger firms have been relatively friendly environments. The local IBEW has been a source of skilled labor and apprenticeship schemes, and has provided firms with the capacity to meet federal regulations relating to job specifications, affirmative action hiring, and the like.

Notice that both the UAW and, to a lesser extent, the IBEW have been firmly entrenched in sectors of the economy which have national markets, tend to be dominated by larger firms, or are dominated by federal government regulations. The UAW sought to counter the forces of fragmentation by organizing on a firm and industry level. By the nature of the industry and the size of the production units, this implied large bargaining units. The IBEW, on the other hand, has operated within more competitive industries by organizing key craft workers. In those instances where internal referencing with regard to wages and conditions has been desirable (as in the case of the communications industry), government regulations standardizing prices and services have tended to counter the forces of fragmentation. In other instances, where local conditions have been *the* bases for bargaining (as in the construction industry), the union has situated itself within major firms and/or has so specialized with regard to its representation of skilled workers that the IBEW has protected itself against fragmentation. In both types of strategies, the IBEW has organized small units, and has maintained a quite decentralized organizational structure.

Union elections are then similar to, and different from, partisan political elections. At a most general level, the original legislation deliberately sought to mimic partisan elections. In doing so, the union representation process became intimately tied to the schisms of the American electorate. In this

Table 5.1. *Percent distribution of IBEW and UAW representation elections by type of election, for selected years 1970–86*

Election type	IBEW					UAW				
	1970	1974	1978	1982	1986	1970	1974	1978	1982	1986
Board	1.7	0.6	0.4	1.8	1.0	0.3	0.3	0.3	2.1	0.8
Consent	29.1	11.1	7.2	2.4	2.0	14.6	6.9	1.5	1.4	1.5
Expedited	0.8	0.3		4.2					0.7	
Regional dir.	20.5	18.2	16.6	15.6	17.3	17.3	14.2	12.7	11.3	15.9
Stipulated	47.9	69.7	75.7	75.8	79.6	67.8	78.6	85.5	84.5	81.8

Sources: Clark and Johnston (1987b, table 1, p. 160) and author's calculation

setting, geographical fragmentation of the electorate, especially in relation to economic issues, has had a profound effect on the nature of union elections. On the other hand, unions are highly developed institutions. The UAW and the IBEW have evolved quite different strategies to deal with the forces of electoral fragmentation. For the former union this has led to a highly centralized organization. In the latter case, decentralization has been the typical response. Notice though, in both instances these unions have become highly specialized – with respect both to industry and to the types of workers represented by each union. So as to mediate the local effects embedded in the representation process, unions have sought to sustain continuity by relying upon certain niches in the economy.

Electoral performance of the IBEW and UAW

It was noted in chapter 1 that most representation elections are either regional-director directed or stipulated elections. This was also true for the IBEW and UAW (table 5.1).[13] In 1970 a significant proportion (nearly 30 percent) of IBEW elections were consent elections; that is, elections agreed upon by management and labor without a formal hearing, nominating the regional director as arbiter of any disputes. By 1986, however, consent elections accounted for about 2.0 percent of all their elections. Thus, the IBEW and UAW were more similar on this issue at the end of the period than at the beginning. There seems to have been little evidence of year-to-year shifts in the types of elections favored by management and labor. Rather, there was a quite clear trend towards stipulated elections as *the* desired election type. Perhaps this trend reflects increasing use by management of full Board hearings as a means of delaying the representation process.

Table 5.2. *Summary of IBEW and UAW representation election results, for selected years 1970–86*

	IBEW		UAW	
Year	Elections	% wins	Elections	% wins
1970	234	55.6	336	56.2
1974	324	50.3	346	47.9
1978	235	42.1	268	45.9
1982	165	36.9	142	41.5
1986	138	43.9	192	42.4

Sources: Clark and Johnston (1987b, table 2, p. 160) and author's calculations

As for election wins and losses, table 5.2 summarizes each union's performance for the years 1970, 1974, 1978, 1982, and 1986.[14] Two patterns are immediately evident in this table. First, both unions suffered drastic changes of fortune in terms of election wins over this period. In 1970, on average they won more elections than they lost. But, even in 1974, long before the precipitous decline in union fortunes identified at the national level in chapter 1, the IBEW tended to win as many as it lost, and the UAW tended to lose more than it won. By 1982, on average the unions lost significantly more than they won. Four years later (1986), this trend was still very much apparent. A second pattern was evident. Not only were there drastic declines in unions' electoral performance, but actual numbers of elections contested also declined. This was apparent in the latter years of the 1970s, and most marked in 1982 and 1986 (although in 1986 the UAW did improve its number of elections contested compared to 1982). In contrast, in 1974 the number of elections contested increased for both unions over the 1970 total. Patterns observed at the national level – declining win rates and declining numbers of elections contested – were also evident in the electoral performance of the IBEW and the UAW. It is not difficult to see how both unions lost nearly 350,000 members each over the period 1974–86.

Clark and Johnston (1987b) summarize the distribution of representation elections by unit, and industry, for each union. Over the period 1970–82, it was apparent that the UAW became less focused upon industrial production units in representation campaigns, and more diverse in terms of the types of units in which they sought representation. Even so, in 1982 traditional production units still dominated their representation campaigns (table 5.3), a pattern which returned to greater significance in 1986. There were slight increases in 1974 and 1978 in the proportionate share by other types of electoral units. In contrast, IBEW representation campaigns became more

Table 5.3. *Percent distribution of IBEW and UAW representation elections by election units with 2.0 or more percent share of all elections, for selected years 1970–86*

Election unit	IBEW					UAW				
	1970	1974	1978	1982	1986	1970	1974	1978	1982	1986
Industrial/production	39.3	41.1	43.4	47.9	46.9	73.5	70.2	72.0	64.1	83.3
Craft	8.1	9.6	7.7	6.1	13.3					
Departmental	9.4	3.4	4.7	12.7	9.2	2.1	3.8	5.6	6.3	3.0
Professional/technical	14.5	14.2	13.6	11.5	5.1	4.4	5.8		7.7	
Clerical/office workers	7.3	11.7	11.9	11.5	14.3	10.4	6.4	7.5	10.6	6.1
Other	20.1	19.7	17.9	8.5	11.2	7.4	13.0	12.3	9.2	5.3

Sources: Clark and Johnston (1987b, table 3, p. 160) and author's calculations

concentrated on production units over the period. The IBEW also sought greater representation in departmental and clerical units. It remained more diverse in terms of its representation election strategies than the UAW. This was despite a rather dramatic decline in 1982 of the proportion of production unit elections contested by the UAW. Compared to the IBEW, the UAW was more functionally specialized, both with respect to workers' tasks (production) and with respect to product types (related to the automobile and motor transportation generally).

In terms of their representation elections by industry, in 1970 the IBEW contested 75 percent of all their representation in just four industries. Not surprisingly, these industries included special trade construction (SIC 17), electrical and electronic equipment (SIC 36), and the communications (SIC 48) and electrical services (SIC 49) industries. In 1974 and 1978, these four industries accounted for 80 and 78 percent respectively of all elections. By 1986, however, these four industries had slipped in terms of their share of all elections. Over the period 1970–86, those four core industries became progressively less hospitable as sources of union membership. In 1970, the IBEW won 66 percent of construction representation elections, but in 1982, it won only 22 percent. Similar changes in electoral fortune were apparent for SICs 48 and 49; in the case of the electrical and electronic equipment industry, the union never was able to win more than it lost over the entire period. In those few industries it was able to win more than lose, the number of elections contested in these industries was so small that overall decline in the rate of union success was hardly affected.

Likewise the UAW contested representation elections in just a handful of

Table 5.4. *Summary of IBEW and UAW representation election results (numbers of elections and percent wins) by region, for selected years 1970–86*

Region	1970 Elect/ % win		1974 Elect/ % win		1978 Elect/ % win		1982 Elect/ % win		1986 Elect/ % win	
IBEW										
North	109	52.3	150	44.0	119	37.8	100	43.0	54	42.6
South/RTW	41	61.0	68	55.9	47	44.7	17	11.7	16	25.0
South and West	67	53.7	77	55.8	53	43.4	38	39.5	18	61.1
West/RTW	5	80.0	11	54.5	10	60.0	6	16.7	3	0.0
Central/RTW	12	66.7	18	55.6	6	66.7	4	00.0	3	66.7
UAW										
North	239	56.5	279	46.6	219	46.1	118	42.4	62	40.3
South/RTW	42	64.3	25	60.0	26	38.5	13	46.1	14	35.7
South and West	44	45.4	34	47.1	14	50.0	9	22.2	1	100.0
West/RTW	1	100.0			1	100.0				
Central/RTW	10	60.0	8	62.5	8	50.0	2	50.0	3	66.7

Sources: Clark and Johnston (1987b, table 6, p. 162) and author's calculations

industries. It should also be apparent that this union was less concentrated than the IBEW; over the period 1970–82, the top four industries accounted for 62 percent (1970), 55 percent (1974), 73 percent (1978), and 48 percent (1982) of all UAW representation elections. Although there was a slight increase in the share of these industries of total UAW elections in 1986, the pattern remained much the same relative to the IBEW. The union fought most of its elections in about six industries, all of which were related to the auto industry. As was the case for the IBEW, the UAW lost much of its support in its core industries. Where the union was able to maintain its support, in the durable wholesale industry (SIC 50), for example, actual numbers of contested elections were very small. Notice, though, that even in 1978 both unions experienced significant (negative) shifts in their electoral fortunes in their core industries, and appeared unable to develop alternative options which would have stemmed the tide.

Regionally, the IBEW appeared to lose more than the UAW. That is, from table 5.4, it seems that as the former union was more spatially diverse than the latter union in terms of its representation election strategy, in 1982 (but not in 1986) that diversity appeared to inflict heavy losses on the overall win rate of the union. Compared to the UAW, the IBEW fought proportionately many more elections in the South/RTW, the South and West, and the West/ RTW regions over the period 1970–86. Whereas win rates in these regions were above win rates in the North for 1970, 1974, 1978, and 1986, in 1982 win rates in these regions were very low compared to the North. On the other hand, the UAW has remained very much in the northern region of the country. It may be the case that the declining fortunes of the IBEW, compared to the UAW, in 1978 and 1982 can be attributed in part to the spatial diversity of the IBEW, and the radical decline in win rates in southern and western regions.

It was suggested in the previous section that the unions have sought to avoid the forces of electoral fragmentation through general policies of regional and industrial specialization, and work task and functional specialization. But, according to our evidence, this strategy proved to be less and less effective over the 1970–86 period. While the strategy maintained electoral support through the early years of the period, since 1978 electoral fortunes have consistently gone against the unions. The balance between fragmentation and continuity slipped from continuity to fragmentation over the period under study.

Local factors in union performance

We also analyzed union performance in terms of local factors. This involved three kinds of variables. There were structural variables, like those utilized in the previous section. These variables, including region, industry, and unit, represented the overall organization of the unions and the NLRB election process. There were local economic variables, collected from the US Department of Commerce at the county level, and reflecting the local economic conditions of firms, industries, and counties. There were a set of institutional variables, reflecting legislation like RTW laws, and local levels of unionization (see appendix 1).

In terms of the local economic variables, two kinds of dimension were included. First, an attempt was made to place the representation election in context: that is, in relation to local conditions. This meant collecting data on other firms in the area and industry. Second, an attempt was also made to deal with changes in the local economic environment. Thus, not only were there cross-sectional data, like the number of business establishments in an SIC in the county in 1970, but there were also time-dependent data, like percentage change in the number of business establishments in an SIC in the county over the period 1968–70. Not all elections could be linked directly to county-level data on local economic performance. There were coverage problems with some of the county-level data, affecting about 15 percent of the elections.

No attempt was made to establish causal links between election results and local economic performance. The results of this subsequent project are reported in the next chapter. The aim of the analysis reported here was to establish significant statistical associations, describing patterns of union representation elections in relation to a set of likely related variables over the period 1970–82 (the only county-level data currently available). It is important to re-emphasize at this point that there was no attempt in this stage of the analysis to determine the relative size of a local effect (as opposed to its statistical significance), nor did we determine whether or not a particular variable negatively or positively affected a union's win–loss record. A more sophisticated testing procedure was needed to make this kind of determination.[15]

A series of conclusions were made of the MANOVA results, simultaneously considering the significance of specific variables. First, the win–loss records of both unions were found to be significantly associated with cross-sectional local economic variables. So for example, in 1970 the IBEW's win–loss record was associated with the number of establishments in the local industry. The win–loss record of the UAW in 1970 was associated with employment and wages. Second, it was also apparent that for all the variety of local economic performance variables, only a relatively small set of variables were significantly associated with the unions' win–loss records. Especially important were the employment and pay variables. These variables are basic to any contractual relationship (Williamson 1975). They reflect the immediate material interests of workers and management. On one side of the contractual relation, employment and wages are the determinants of workers' nominal wages. On the other side, these two variables are the determinants of firms' variable labor costs. To the extent that firms operate in a competitive product environment, these variables intimately affect short-run profits and long-run investment (Clark, Gertler, and Whiteman 1986). It is little wonder that firms and workers would directly associate these variables with union representation elections.

The win–loss records of both unions were significantly associated with local economic factors in two of the four years; specifically in 1970 and 1978, years of relative (national) economic growth. In those two years of relative (national) economic decline (1974) and deep recession (1982), local economic factors were practically irrelevant. This was a very important finding. It suggests that there is a pronounced temporal effect in union representation elections, an effect that reflects national (as opposed to local) economic conditions. This finding was hinted at in the preceding section, when we discussed temporal patterns of unions' wins and losses. Here, we added another spatial dimension to the issue: national economic conditions affect the relevance of local economic factors.

It should be apparent, however, that there is some overlap between these patterns and those noted in the previous section. Unions' 1982 election results were difficult to rationalize by any appeal to general structural or local variables. It appears that there were important, but nonsystematic, local factors during recession that affected union representation elections. In this context, Kiewiet's findings regarding partisan political elections offer some useful insights. He argued that partisan political elections are increasingly dominated by what he termed local nonsystematic effects. As a result, he doubted whether or not party loyalty or even presidential voting patterns were general enough to order local elections. It may also be the case that he identified an issue that is temporally specific; that is, linked to the phase of the national economic cycle.

Our results implied two kinds of local effects in union representation elections. Traditional local wage and employment variables may be important during relatively prosperous times. Here, the issue might be characterized in terms of distribution: the share of income and employment between the parties to a contractual relationship. Dunlop's (1944) model of union behavior is in fact premised upon this supposition. It assumes, as representation election voters may in times of economic growth, that unions (as opposed to staff associations and other nonunion labor organizations) are able to lever greater shares of incomes given stable or expanding levels of employment. But during recession and economic decline, the traditional contract variables do not appear statistically associated with unions' win–loss records. Instead of issues of distribution being dealt with, other issues intrude, including the likelihood of the firm or plant surviving. In these circumstances, local factors are nonsystematic. Employment is not guaranteed, wages and profits are squeezed, and contractual relations are severely strained. In times of economic decline local representation elections are likely fought on the basis of very parochial factors; loyalty, leadership, etc. There may be no local variables, like the contract variables, which would be general across localities.

In 1982 the one significant variable associated with the UAW's win–loss record was the level of participation in representation elections. Our analysis indicated that the number of eligible voters in each election also was significantly associated with the unions' win–loss records. This was particularly the case for the UAW (1970, 1974, and 1978); less so for the IBEW (just 1970).

Participation, size, and electoral performance

No study of elections, union or partisan political, would be complete without some analysis of the patterns of participation. From the previous discussion of American electoral and participation patterns, we should expect that participation rates for representation elections are higher than participation rates for partisan political elections. As Wolfinger and Rosenstone (1980) observed, participation rates are highest when people believe they have a stake in the outcome. There can be no doubt that this is the case in union representation elections. By their very nature, union representation elections are fundamentally about the material interests of workers and employers.

Apart from these general observations, there are a couple of reasons for expecting participation rates to be *very* high in representation elections. Time and again it has been observed that the representation process typically begins at the local level amongst disaffected employees. In many cases, relationships between workers and management are highly polarized *before* union organizers become involved. While this is difficult to document, it is generally held by unions and management alike that a poor local labor relations climate practically invites a union to organize a plant. Dunlop (1948) observed many years ago that the absence of a union in a plant does not mean that workers are unorganized. In point of fact, the NLRB union representation election certification process requires a high degree of worker mobilization prior to the election itself. Otherwise, the NLRB would have no evidence to suppose that an election is justified. If by chance some workers may be initially indifferent about the election process, both unions and management have a vested interest in securing their vote. Indeed, given the amounts of money spent by companies on management consultants whose sole purpose it is to defeat unions in the representation election, it would be a rare worker who would be unaffected or unsolicited during a campaign.

For the 16-year period 1970–86, practically two-thirds of all union representation elections had participation rates of 91 percent or greater (table 5.5). This was especially true of IBEW elections, and was also the case in UAW elections (excepting 1982 and 1986). Furthermore, for each union and year analyzed, over 85 percent of all union representation elections had participation rates of 81 percent or more. When compared to partisan political election participation rates (see Verba and Nie 1972), these are remarkably high levels of electoral participation. It can be observed that there was some variation in the proportion of representation elections with 80 percent or less participation rates. It also appears that the proportion of

Table 5.5. *Percentage distribution of union representation elections (IBEW and UAW) by participation rates, for selected years 1970–86*

Union	Year	Participation rates		
		0.0–0.8	0.81–0.9	0.91–100.0
IBEW				
	1970	8.5	22.6	68.9
	1974	12.9	17.9	69.2
	1978	11.1	23.0	65.9
	1982	13.3	18.2	68.5
	1986	10.2	20.4	69.4
UAW				
	1970	8.6	25.6	65.8
	1974	13.3	21.4	65.3
	1978	8.2	25.7	66.1
	1982	14.1	24.0	61.9
	1986	10.6	32.6	56.8

Sources: Clark and Johnston (1987b, table 8, p. 166) and author's calculations

elections with participation rates of more than 91 percent remained relatively stable throughout this period. For both the UAW and the IBEW, 1974 and 1982 were the years when the proportion of elections with less than 81 percent was highest. Even here, though, the vast majority of elections in this category had participation rates of 70 percent or more.

In Clark and Johnston (1987b) we used a MANOVA analysis to determine if there was any systematic pattern in these variations, focusing upon structural, local, and institutional variables. For the IBEW, there were slight significant variations in participation rates for industries and regions in 1974 and 1978, and 1982 (industries only). It appears that in industries where the IBEW had little involvement (that is, conducted few elections) participation rates were lower than average (around 87 percent), and in regions where the IBEW had little involvement participation rates were higher than average (around 95 percent). For the UAW, in 1978 and 1982 it appears that participation rates were slightly lower in elections it lost as opposed to elections it won. But the differences were slight – only about two or three percentage points around the 91 percent participation level. It was more difficult to make clear distinctions between types of units as regards variations in their participation rates.

Quite startling patterns of unit sizes were observed (table 5.6). Generally, the IBEW and UAW were very different in terms of the average size of their

Table 5.6. *Summary of IBEW and UAW representation election results (number of elections and percent wins) by unit size (number of eligible voters), for selected years 1970–86*

	1970		1974		1978		1982		1986	
Size	Elect/	% win	Elect/	% win	Elect/	% win	Elect/	% win	Elect/	% win
IBEW										
0–9	79	68.4	112	64.3	56	48.2	45	42.2	37	62.2
10–19	58	65.5	79	44.3	61	49.2	50	34.0	27	25.9
20–29	25	40.0	44	50.0	34	38.2	20	50.0	7	57.1
30–49	26	38.5	31	41.9	30	33.3	32	21.9	12	25.0
50–99	46	39.1	24	33.3	25	28.0			8	37.5
>100			34	38.2	29	41.4	18	44.4	7	42.9
UAW										
0–9	34	82.4	23	65.2	28	64.3	17	64.7	16	68.8
10–19	59	52.5	58	69.0	36	64.0	26	50.0	18	50.0
20–29	39	71.8	34	41.2	31	51.6	20	50.0	18	55.6
30–49	49	71.4	62	50.0	31	35.5	25	32.0	22	54.5
50–99	63	54.0	53	39.6	51	47.0	23	34.8	23	26.1
100–199	48	39.6	62	48.4	50	40.0	31	29.0	22	31.8
>200	44	31.8	54	27.8	41	26.8			13	7.7

Sources: Clark and Johnston (1987b, table 10, p. 167) and author's calculations

electoral unit. Over the whole period, the average size of an IBEW electoral unit was between 10 and 19 workers. In contrast, the average size of the UAW unit was between 50 and 99 workers. The difference in size was a reflection of the basic difference between the unions: the IBEW was craft oriented, and the UAW, production oriented.

In 1970, the IBEW won the majority of elections in units with 19 or fewer workers. In 1974, it won the majority of units with 9 or fewer workers. After that time, there was no winning size until 1986. The union did win 50 percent of elections held in units of 20 to 29, but this was not a systematic pattern. The UAW had a similar experience in that its winning unit size shrank drastically over the 1970–86 period. In 1970, the UAW won the majority of elections it contested with 50 to 99 workers. The winning size shrank in 1974 to between 30 to 49 workers, and in 1978 and 1982 to 20 to 29 workers. Only in 1986 was there any reason to imagine that the UAW's performance had improved in this matter.

Nevertheless, given the size of most auto plants, the traditional focus of the UAW on organizing whole plants as opposed to units within plants, and the tremendous costs involved in organizing and maintaining small units, these patterns have been viewed with great alarm by the UAW and the labor movement in general. It is a pattern which other unions have experienced, and one which few observers are able to explain.

Anecdotal evidence suggests that the smaller the election, the more personal the campaign. That is, instead of voting for the union per se, people vote according to the appeal (or otherwise) of the local leadership. If this is true, and we have no direct evidence which would decide one way or the other, it would be consistent with trends in partisan political elections. It has been observed that as congressional elections have become more local in focus, stressing local leadership as opposed to party affiliation, personal contact with candidates has become a crucial factor in deciding election outcomes. In partisan elections this often turns on mobilizing people to vote (participation). In union elections, participation is not so problematic. Nevertheless, in an era of voter alienation from political institutions, it may well be the case that the appeal of unionism is secondary to the slate of local union officials who are personally known to the voters.

We conducted a MANOVA test for systematic and statistically significant associations between unit size and other dependent variables. We were unable to ascertain any associations between the winning size of a representation election and other variables. But we were able to find some significant associations between size in general and other variables. Even so, the actual contribution of these variables to variations in size was very small. In 1970, the average size of representation elections was slightly smaller in RTW states, as opposed to non-RTW states. Likewise, in 1978 the average size of UAW representation elections in the northern region was larger than in the southern region. Not surprisingly, winning and losing were associated with size, as was industry (see the results in the section above).

Conclusion

All the evidence presented in this chapter suggests that the IBEW and the UAW have fared poorly in union representation elections over the past few years. In 1970 these two unions won more elections than they lost. By 1986, they lost many more elections than they won, and contested markedly fewer representation elections. It is no wonder that they have experienced dramatic losses of membership in the past five to seven years. These patterns are not particularly recent. That is, the balance between winning and losing turned in the mid 1970s. While the recent 1982 recession magnified the dimensions of the problem, both unions were under pressure in the late 1970s to improve their win rates. These patterns are particularly significant given that both unions have been historically two of the largest and most successful unions. The relative decline of the American union movement has as much to do with the declining electoral fortunes of unions such as the IBEW and UAW as with industrial and geographical shifts in employment.

Two arguments were advanced in this chapter. One was that the two unions were quite different in terms of their patterns of success and failure. For example, the relative geographical diversity of the IBEW appeared to hurt it more in terms of electoral success in 1982, compared to the UAW, which was more concentrated in the northern regions of the country. While both unions were relatively industrially concentrated, they tended to cover different industries. The unions were quite different too in terms of the types of workers they represented: the IBEW tended to represent skilled craft workers, and the UAW, production workers. One result of this specialization was the very small size of the average IBEW election unit. Size appears to have been an important variable in union representation success and failure. Both unions saw the average size of their winning unit shrink dramatically.

The other argument concerned the union representation election process. As it is modeled on the partisan political election process, it shares many of its problems. Specifically, the fragmentation of the American electorate, so evident in partisan elections, also affects union representation elections. Politically, this has meant that fewer and fewer electors trust established institutions like parties, and tend to favor local candidates on the basis of what Kiewiet termed nonsystematic factors. We have argued that similar processes are at work in union representation elections, although the significance of these effects appears to be associated with the phase of the national business cycle. Indeed, evidence presented on associations between unions' win–loss records and local economic factors suggests that fragmentation has accelerated in the past few years. Traditional variables, like industry affiliation, regional association, and wages and employment do not seem to provide the continuity of electoral support they once might have.

One implication of this argument is that traditional ideas of organizing new union members may no longer be appropriate. It is not enough to proclaim that northern auto workers *will* belong to the UAW. And it is not plausible to claim, as a matter of custom, that workers will want to join unions to protect their wages and employment. Economic conditions are obviously important, but so too are less tangible nonsystematic effects. Union elections have become more personal, more antagonistic. In this regard, unions, like political parties, face an uphill battle to convince the American public that they are to be trusted. Unfortunately for the union movement, the factors fragmenting trust in national political institutions have also fundamentally affected union representation election success.

6

Organizing strategies in the heartland and the South

From all the data so far presented, it is apparent that the American labor movement is in the grips of a profound crisis.[1] Unions are winning proportionally fewer representation elections, contesting fewer elections, and winning in smaller units. These patterns are especially evident in the electoral performance of industrial production-oriented unions in the northern industrial states over the past ten years. Since the early 1950s, it has often been asserted that the union movement would inevitably decline because of its lack of appeal to the growing service-sector occupations and to the southern region of the US. And yet, some thirty years later, it seems that the union movement is most vulnerable in those sectors and areas once thought to be the heartland of American unionism.

In the previous chapter it was noted that there are distinct differences between unions in their organizing strategies. For example, the IBEW has concentrated on skilled tradesmen in a variety of electrical-oriented sectors located across the US. In contrast, the UAW has concentrated on a group of auto-related industries located in just a few regions. One goal of this chapter is to provide a rationale for this organized strategy. Most of the literature fails to integrate the macro-structural determinants of unionization with the local context of representation elections. The geographical diversity of representation elections, so obvious in election outcomes, seems too often lost in the rush to prove single equation (parsimonious) models of unionization. A second goal of this chapter is to provide an understanding of unions' electoral performance which integrates structural determinants with local context, thereby retaining the complexity of the latter, so important in current problems of the American labor movement.[2]

The model of union organization at the heart of this chapter assumes unions operate within a set of ordered structures or rules of the game. These structures are primarily national, reflecting legal, economic, and institutional forces: the requirements of the National Labor Relations Act and its regulatory agency, the National Labor Relations Board; state-level right-to-work legislation; and national legislation regarding property rights. These are macro-structural imperatives. Yet, they are not complete in the sense that there is a one-to-one correspondence between these structures and local outcomes. Not only are the rules of the labor relations system interpreted by the NLRB with reference to local conditions, but the system itself was designed to ensure a wide measure of discretion at the local level.

It is at the local level, where context and structure are integrated through union representation elections, that American unions ultimately grow and decline. This means that knowing the regulatory environment is not enough to predict the outcome of a local election.[3] Farber (1984b) was pessimistic regarding the possibility of *general* conclusions given this kind of framework. He noted in part that "the structural, institutional, and political characteristics that govern collective bargaining are sufficiently variable that the union objective function will differ considerably across contexts" (43). I contend that this is inevitable, and that it is best to understand union representation elections *in* context as opposed to *outside of* context.

A model of union organization

At the outset, it is assumed that unions can be described in terms of their objective functions. At one level, a union is an institution like other institutions: an organization fundamentally concerned with the growth, maintenance, and reproduction of its power. This assumption is consistent with at least two streams of literature. As in Dunlop (1944), it is assumed that unions can be described by a well-defined objective function. The union maximizes something, even if it is vaguely specified as power. Nevertheless, I also tend to side with Shister's (1953) more expansive version of the union as a bureaucratic entity. Consistent with the new institutional movement unions are assumed to be agents in that they deal as unitary organizations with other organizations. In this sense, power is a relational concept; it has to do with the ability of organizations to assert their interests in bilateral negotiations with other organizations.[4]

Unions are also political organizations. In fact they are legally constituted as representatives of members' interests, and are internally organized according to political constituencies. As noted previously, the Wagner Act and the Taft–Hartley Act sought to introduce democracy to industry. The Wagner Act designated unions as workers' representatives in collective bargaining, and the Taft–Hartley Act designated members as equal partners with leaders in the political organization of union affairs. In this sense, the proposed model retains aspects of Ross' (1948) model of union behavior, with its recognition of worker heterogeneity and the differing interests of members and leaders. However, unlike Ross (and more like Farber 1984b), the proposed model retains Dunlop's notion of an objective function. This simply implies that unions act with respect to certain goals and objectives. But it does not imply that unions are consistent in specifying a particular goal as their primary objective, or that unions are rational in the sense that they choose *the* optimal strategy which would achieve their goals. Unions have little unilateral power; they must respond pragmatically to perceived circumstances, internal and external.[5]

Relative to unions' objective functions, I would assert that unions' representation and political functions should be understood as constraints. Assuming unions are concerned to reproduce their power, their representation and political functions are necessary conditions for attaining their goals. This is a reasonable interpretation as long as the reference point is union behavior at a given time and place. However, over time, the continuity of a union is dependent upon these two functions. Without the representation function employers could easily ignore unions, and without the political function unions could easily be dismissed as nonrepresentative or self-interested corporations (witness the attacks by dissidents and government officials upon the leadership of the Teamsters union).

Given the legal imperatives faced by the union movement, exercise of union power is conditional upon the integrity of its representation and political functions. This means that unions require members so as to make claims for power. And, it means that members must sanction union activities in order for unions to legitimize their power. But it does not mean that unions' only power is their membership rolls. While there are clearly advantages in having a large union, both in terms of assets and income, a large union could be paralyzed by overwhelming requirements for representation and the need to sustain internal political cohesion. A union could be very powerful in its dealings with other institutions (as defined above), even if it is relatively small and specialized. What each union requires is an effective organizing strategy which can reproduce union power, but which is also sensitive to the costs of representation and political functions.

So far unions and corporations have been treated as single unitary entities. In fact, unions are hierarchical organizations, with many different levels of activity, ranging from locals through to national and international offices. Union locals are, in the first instance, the legal location of union members. They represent bargaining units in plants and companies in many different communities around the country. At this level, unions contest representation elections, thereby gaining or losing members and representing members in bargaining and grievance disputes.

The spatial organization of American unions reflects another structural imperative: provisions of the NLRA, which have placed a premium upon local democracy. Not only is this evident in the organization of representation elections, but provisions of the Act allow for and facilitate state-level labor legislation like RTW laws and local labor practices not formally codified in state legislation. As Stone (1981) and others have noted, retention of local labor practices has been thought a key attribute of the American labor relations system as compared to European and Australian systems, which are far more centralized. It is this facet of American labor relations which Farber (1984b) referred to in discussing the prospects for a general model of union behavior applicable to many different contexts.

In a sense, national labor legislation is structurally incomplete. That is, we cannot read off local reflections of union imperatives for power because local discretion is built in to the union movement. The representation and political functions of unions are hierarchically and spatially decentralized. Any organizing strategy must be not only sensitive to the costs of representation and internal political coherence, but must also be sensitive to the map (context) of local labor practices.

Local labor practices reflect and describe dominant employment relationships (Clark 1981a). However, while there may be many different local employment relationships, they are themselves bound by common rules regarding property rights and (capitalist) roles of management and labor. Conventionally, American employment relationships, whether bound by contract or not, involve at least the following variables: conditions of employment and lay-off, wage levels (nominal and real – often including cost of living adjustments), benefits, the organization of production (including productivity, the pace of production, etc.), and the role and introduction of technology. In an idealized capitalist economy, employment and wages are intimately related to the marginal product of labor – the productivity value of labor.

However, in an economy characterized by significant adjustment costs, operating in disequilibrium (not equilibrium), employment (workers and the hours they work) and wages are used as separate variables to regulate the cost of production. These same variables regulate the nominal wage of labor and, hence, the real wage, once aggregate price movements are accounted for by labor. Thus, even local labor practices are set within a structural imperative. This means that some variables will be more important than others in different contexts, and that some variables may be interpreted quite differently in different contexts. It also means there are a set of structurally determined variables which *generally* describe local labor relations.

And yet, whatever the importance of the local context, it is just as clear that many American unions are national organizations. They operate at higher spatial scales than the local level, especially in their dealings with corporations and governments. This is the arena of institutional power, as distinct from the relations of one union Local to another, and to the national office. Corporations are organized nationally and internationally. Whole industries reach across different communities, as corporations respond to and restructure the map of labor practices (Clark, Gertler, and Whiteman, 1986). Ownership rights, constitutional statutes like the Commerce Clause, and federal legislation like the Commercial Code which pre-empt state-level legislation have effectively nationalized American industry over the past two hundred years (Clark 1981b; Johnston 1986). And, it is clear that the National Labor Relations Board has protected firms' rights to locate (and relocate) industry where appropriate, even in circumstances where labor has had existing contracts. The national organization of industry is yet another structural imperative outside the control of unions. Like national labor legislation, the organization of industry structures the organizing environment of the American union movement.

Thus unions face two counter-imperatives. To be effective in dealing with corporations and governments, they must mimic those organizations. Power must be centralized, and interests negotiable between these institutions. At the same time, because of their representation and political functions, unions are effectively decentralized and dispersed. Unions and firms operate in two quite different institutional worlds. As unions are the representatives of labor, they must inevitably reflect local labor practices. In contrast, firms are often controlled at much higher tiers of the spatial hierarchy and have no statutory responsibility for sustaining the integrity of local representation. Differences in local labor practices appear as opportunities for corporate planners (compare with chapter 3), while these same differences appear to unions as impediments in their attempts to negotiate with corporations (compare with chapter 4). These tensions are reflected in the organizing strategies of American unions.

Organizing strategies and electoral performance

How might unions respond to these structural imperatives? A number of propositions can be made regarding unions' organizing strategies, and ultimately their electoral performance. To give this discussion greater specificity, and incidentally deal with the first goal of the chapter – a rationale for unions' organizing strategies – these suppositions are applied to the IBEW and the UAW.

First, in order to contain the costs of representation and internal political coherence, and to negotiate at a level most consistent with the organization of corporations and governments, *unions will tend to specialize by repre-*

senting particular segments of the work force. In this context, union organizing strategies would include the following:

1. Specialization by particular work functions, skills and/or occupations.
2. Specialization by particular industries.
3. Specialization by particular areas or regions. The IBEW appears to have specialized in certain craft occupations, especially related to electrical and electronic equipment. In contrast, the UAW has tended to specialize in industries closely related to the auto industry. Occupational or skill differentiation has been less important since most union members are production workers.

Second, so as to contain the diversity of labor practices, especially institutional forms of labor relations, *unions will tend to localize.* Organizational strategies would include the following:

1. Operating in particular institutional settings; for example RTW as opposed to non-RTW settings.
2. Operating in particular geographical settings; representing particular informal labor practices. The UAW has certainly maintained a regional strategy, coupled with the locational practices of the auto industry, but informed perhaps by basic differences between northern and southern regions in local labor relations practices. The UAW has tended to operate in non-RTW settings as opposed to RTW settings.

Third, given union practices of specialization and localization, in negotiating with corporations and governments *unions will either centralize or decentralize their negotiation strategy.* The choice of strategy will be dictated by the following:

1. Whether or not the union represents particular skill or work functions as opposed to industries. If a union like the IBEW represents craft workers, then the optimal negotiation policy will be decentralization, given the very different product and industry affiliations of members. If a union tends to represent production workers of particular industries, like the UAW, the optimal policy will be to centralize negotiation.
2. Whether or not the union is localized or spread throughout the nation. This will also depend upon whether the union represents particular work functions or industries. In the former case, decentralization will be the rule and the union will tend to be located in many different regions of the country. In the latter case, centralization will be the rule and the union will tend to locate only where the particular industry is located.

Fourth, given certain levels of localization and specialization, a relatively constant institutional (policy) environment, and the costs of representation and internal coherence, *unions will tend to reinforce their chosen strategy by virtue of their experience.* This may mean, though, that in the long run unions become dependent upon their specialized niches for a continual flow of new members. The corollary implication is that with such dependence, unions may become very vulnerable to overall patterns of economic growth and decline in their chosen niches. Thus, the UAW will continue to depend on the auto industry even as the industry is fundamentally restructured and employment levels drastically reduced. Likewise, the IBEW will continue to depend upon its niches in larger industries and firms even as those industries and firms de-skill the craft functions that the union represents.

These propositions provide a series of crucial institutional variables that should be considered in analyzing the determinants of union electoral performance. Industry affiliation, location, and the legal environment are all important, as are other variables like state levels of unionization which could be thought to be good proxies for local labor relations cultures. These suppositions also provide an expectation that there will be differences between unions, given different organizational strategies, in how well they perform in different contexts. And, finally, these propositions imply significant differences between the unions in terms of their units' sizes and the number of eligible voters. As a decentralized union representing craft workers, the IBEW inevitably contests representation elections in very small units. For this union to represent larger units would require a fundamental shift in its organizing strategy. Likewise, the much larger electoral units contested by the UAW illustrate the UAW's strategy of industry representation, as opposed to craft representation.

There are two obvious implications from the previous discussion. First, as unions become dependent upon certain niches (craft, industry, location) for their membership, their electoral fortunes will reflect the fortunes of their niches. Thus, for example, as the auto industry grew, UAW membership greatly expanded, given a relatively specialized and localized niche. On the other hand, as restructuring of the auto industry has advanced, the union has lost significant numbers of members.

Clearly this is to be expected: fewer employees translates into fewer potential union members. But, it appears that the union has lost working members as well: those workers who have become disillusioned with the auto union's policy of centralized negotiation.[6] In fact, there is some evidence that the UAW has tended to cooperate in the rationalization of the industry, thereby providing little support to union locals who have fought the restructuring policies of the motor corporations (chapter 4). In this case, the union has lost more representation elections because of radically changing local circumstances. In addition, disillusionment with the centralized policies of the union links with more general public distrust of established institutions. The result is general distrust of the union, and local votes against the union as circumstances dictate.

A second implication is that as circumstances change, especially decline, in these niches, union membership becomes a contentious issue for management and workers alike. This is particularly apparent in industries and regions dominated by unions. In these instances, declining local levels of wages, benefits, and employment may precipitate a vote against union representation simply because local workers wish to differentiate themselves from perceived competing locals. The union itself becomes the issue as workers in different plants strive to restructure local production relations in the face of threats or hints from management regarding their relative standing amongst other similar plants operated by the company.

This scenario is relevant to the IBEW, even though it typically represents very small numbers of union members in larger enterprises. The local representation election becomes the battleground for union and management, where the union representation issue is directly and immediately linked to the economic performance of the local plant. The scenario is also entirely consistent with evidence that voters in congressional elections relate their economic prospects to local circumstances, not the national policy context or the international industry-competitive situation.

By the very nature of the legal arrangement of the American labor relations system, there is a significant sphere of local discretion in any union representation election. The union organizing strategies considered here exist precisely because of the incompleteness of the structural arrangement of unions' powers in relation to the local context. There can be no doubt that those designing the rules of union power and those interpreting these rules have seen local discretion as one way of controlling national union power. While there are many more plausible scenarios linking union strategies with possible electoral outcomes, surely the message is clear: there can be no complete integration of macro-structural imperatives with local outcomes.

Empirical framework and model specification

In Clark and Johnston (1987c) we utilized this framework to interpret the electoral performance of the IBEW and the UAW over the period 1970–82 (the latest available data). Essentially, the argument was that union electoral performance can be understood as the result of the interaction between structure and context. More simply, two sets of independent variables and a dependent variable are implied by this model. There are those independent variables that describe the institutional and political structure of union organizing strategies, and those that describe the local context of union elections. The dependent variable was the outcome of union representation elections.

That is:

OUTCOME = f(STRUCTURE, CONTEXT)   (6.1)

In the literature on union representation elections, the dependent variable is specified either as a continuous variable or as a dichotomous variable (Heneman and Sandver 1983). Continuous variables are either the percentage of pro-union votes or the percentage of union victories. The latter variable is typically used in aggregate national studies of unionization where the object is to link union victories to a series of national economic determinants (Mitchell 1980). This approach is very similar to Ashenfelter and Pencavel's (1969), and shares the problems of that approach. It is very difficult to integrate structure and context and deal with the geographical diversity of representation election outcomes.

More relevant in this context is the former variable, the percentage of pro-union votes, which can retain the specificity of structure and context. However, there were two basic problems with this variable. First, it does not measure the outcome of union representation elections in the sense that after tallying the votes, the NLRB either certifies union representation or denies certification. There is no intermediate role for a union depending upon the percentage of votes cast for it in a representation election. Unions can only win or lose a representation election. Second, the percentage of pro-union votes does not adequately capture the voting process embedded in union representation elections. Eligible voters face a dichotomous choice: yes to union representation or no to union representation. In this respect, the voting process is like other dichotomous choices faced by individuals and firms in many situations. In the union representation elections, it is difficult to imagine individuals voting according to some desired percentage pro-union vote without first deciding whether or not to vote for or against union representation.[7]

Conceptually, the better dependent variable was a dichotomous variable (1 = union victory, 0 = union loss). It measures the outcome of a union representation election directly, and is more consistent with voters' choice behavior. Of course, this does not necessarily mean that we had direct knowledge of voters' choices. No attempt was made to model individual voter behavior.[8]

As for the independent variables, structure and context were described by a series of dichotomous and continuous variables. The institutional and political structure of union representation elections was represented by three types of variables. These included a state-level variable indicating the presence (= 1) or absence (= 0) of RTW legislation, a variable indicating whether the election is stipulated (STIP) (= 1) or not (= 0), and a variable indicating whether the election is in a CORE industry (= 1) or not (= 0).[9] The first and second variables represent the legal structure of union representation elections (state-level and national), while the third represents the inherited industrial structure and organization of the union. It is often assumed that the presence of state-level RTW legislation adversely affects the chances that a union will win a representation election. There is some evidence that this is the case for the IBEW and the UAW. We expected that the RTW parameter coefficient would have a negative sign, although the significance of the coefficient could vary with the union since the IBEW has been more geographically dispersed, and organizationally decentralized, than the UAW. For these reasons, we also expected the CORE variable to have variable parameter signs and significance levels.

In the past few years, the number of STIP elections has dramatically increased as a proportion of all elections. Some writers have suggested that this form of election has been used by employers to harass unions and delay the representation process (Weiler 1983). By itself, it was expected that the STIP parameter coefficient would have a negative sign. Initially, it was planned to use other related variables, such as whether or not there had been an election in the plant in the previous couple of years. However, there were very few instances of this in the years studied, and certainly too few to include in statistical analysis. More generally, though, there are very few data available which would allow direct analyses of employers' tactics. A related variable, the size of the electoral unit measured by the number of eligible voters (ELIG), straddles the line between structure and context. There is no doubt that the average size of the winning electoral unit has declined for virtually all unions over the past fifteen years. Perhaps one reason for this has been overly narrow interpretations of the appropriate electoral unit by the NLRB and regional directors. Like the STIP variable, ELIG could be reasonably interpreted as a proxy for the institutional context.

The local context of the election was described by a series of county-level economic variables. These included local industry-specific employment (EMPLOY) and nominal wages (PAY), the number of firms in the local area (ESTAR), the number of firms in the relevant SIC in the area (ESTSIC), and the number of firms with fewer than 19 employees in the area and SIC (LESS). More complex versions of these variables were derived, including time-dependent transformations, and dichotomous representations of whether there was positive (= 1) or negative (= 0) change in the variable over the previous couple of years. This data set was described in more detail in appendix 1 and Clark and Johnston (1987b).

Given these local economic variables, it was assumed that voters evaluate union representation on the basis of the past and current economic performance of the unit in relation to local standards. In this sense, the model assumes an adaptive expectations framework, as opposed to a more radical framework (perhaps rational expectations: see Lucas 1981). As in other macroeconomic voter models (Fiorina 1981), it is assumed that voters use past experience to evaluate the respective claims of the company and union regarding the likely impact of union representation on their economic wellbeing. Notice, though, that it was also assumed that voters evaluate these claims in a larger community setting than simply the electoral unit. And like Hoxie (1917) and Dunlop (1948), we assumed that the community context provides an interpretive lens through which these claims are assessed. Different variables may be significant in different contexts, and common variables interpreted differently in different contexts.[10]

Generally, the model estimated was specified as:

$$\text{OUTCOME}_{it} = f(\text{CORE, RTW, STIP, ELIG, EMPLOY,...LESS})_{jt,t+n} \qquad (6.2)$$

where OUTCOME was specified for a given union (i) and year (t), and the independent variables were structural, area (j), and time (t, t + n) specific. The model was estimated for the IBEW and the UAW over the years 1970, 1974, 1978, and 1982. These years were selected so as to broadly represent changes over the national business cycle. The first year could be described as a year of relative economic decline (relative to the previous couple of years). The last year was the worst recession since the Great Depression of the 1930s. In between was a year of economic growth and sharp decline (1974) and an economic boom (1978).

There are a couple of problems with using an ordinary least squares (OLS) regression routine in these situations. First, because the dependent variable was dichotomous, use of an OLS routine would violate a crucial assumption: constant error variance. Second, in working in the probability domain, as we would be if an OLS regression routine was used, predicted values of the dependent variable may be outside a meaningful range of probability.[11] The better option for all these problems was to use either a Logit or Probit model. In the dichotomous case, both models produce essentially the same results, the choice being dictated by the availability of software. Here, Probit models are estimated by using a maximum likelihood technique through HotzTran (Avery and Hotz 1985).

Results of Probit analysis

This section summarizes the Probit results through a brief discussion of the derived parameter coefficients' signs and significance levels. In the next section, the implications of these results are discussed with reference to possible organizing strategies that the unions might have used over the period 1970–82. In order to select the relevant independent variables, given the range of possible variables introduced above and in the appendix of Clark and Johnston (1987b), an analysis was undertaken to select variables so as to minimize variables' cross-correlations.

As a consequence, the following model was estimated for both unions over the four sample times:

$$\text{OUTCOME}_{it} = f(\text{CORE, RTW, STIP, ELIG, PESTAR, PEMPLOY, PAVPAY,} \\ \text{AVPAY})_t \tag{6.3}$$

where PESTAR, PEMPLOY, and PAVPAY represented percentage change in the number of area/industry establishments, employment, and wages respectively over the previous two years. Only the AVPAY variable was a level variable.

Consistent with our earlier findings, as time progressed (1970 to 1982) fewer and fewer independent variables could be significantly and consistently related to the outcomes of IBEW representation elections. In 1970, a year of relatively slow national economic growth, the union won just over 55 percent of all its representation elections. Two parameter coefficients (RTW and ELIG) were found highly significant, and one (STIP) was found significant at a lower level. All three could be interpreted as standing for the institutional structure of representation elections. There were no significant local parameter coefficients. The RTW parameter was found to have a positive coefficient, STIP, a negative parameter coefficient, and ELIG, a negative parameter coefficient. That is, the IBEW tended to win more in RTW states, tended to lose elections in large units, and tended to lose STIP elections. In 1974 the union won 50 percent of its elections. Only the ELIG variable was found to have a highly significant parameter coefficient, again negative. Two parameter coefficients were found significant at a much lower level: CORE and STIP. The union tended to win in CORE industries and in STIP elections.

In 1978, a year of relatively strong economic growth, no parameter coefficient was found to be highly or even slightly significant. The union lost the majority of elections it contested, but appeared to contest elections in many different sectors, occupations, regions, and institutional contexts. By this time the vast majority of elections were STIP as compared to 1970, when fewer than 50 percent were STIP. In 1982, the worst post-Depression year for national economic performance, the union was winning just under 40 percent of the elections it contested. In this year, though, it tended to lose elections in RTW states, a switch from 1970. It also tended to lose in areas characterized by relative economic growth in the number of establishments (PESTAR) and high average wages (AVPAY). Still, the parameters on these two variables were significant at a relatively lower level than was the case for the RTW parameter. The union contested relatively few elections during 1982, and failed to win in sectors traditionally associated with it.

There were some similarities between the unions in terms of the parameter coefficients found to be significant, and in terms of the years in which there were more significant parameter coefficients. For example, the RTW parameter coefficient was important in 1970 for both unions. In both cases, the sign on the coefficient was positive. This was also the case for the UAW in 1974. Over all the years, the ELIG parameter coefficient was found significant for the UAW. Basically, the union won in progressively smaller and smaller units. In contrast, there was no winning size for the IBEW in 1982. Whereas the IBEW was found to have significant local parameter coefficients in 1982, the UAW was found to have a significant local parameter coefficient in 1970. The UAW tended to lose in areas where wages were rapidly increasing. In 1970, the union was also winning in RTW states. The implication is surely obvious: the union's southern strategy was working. In 1974, just the RTW and ELIG parameter coefficients were significant. And in 1978 only the ELIG parameter coefficient was highly significant, although the AVPAY parameter was slightly significant. In 1982, one of the worst years for auto sales on record, the other significant parameter coefficient (recognizing ELIG) was CORE. Given the sign on this coefficient, the union was only winning representation elections in non-auto-related sectors.[12]

Different variables may be important in different contexts, and the same variables interpreted differently in different contexts. And, of course, some crucial variables like local leadership and loyalty to the union were not considered. We were not surprised to find few instances of a variable being consistent between contexts: this is a product of local discretion built in to the structure of American labor relations. Put slightly differently, Kiewiet's (1983) nonsystematic component seems to have been crucial in local union elections. The next part of Clark and Johnston (1987c) evaluated these results in terms of possible union organizing strategies. It must be recognized that these strategies are considered at a highly abstract level, as if local factors were in fact systematic between contexts. Thus our analysis should be considered as a series of experiments, not definitive statements of the proper course of action.

Implications for union organizing

Based on the evidence presented above, the highly concentrated industry strategy of the UAW had significant costs and benefits over the 1970–82 period. To the extent that the union was able to organize in the South, following the location decisions of the industry, the union clearly benefited. But, such concentration brought large costs in 1982, when the whole industry practically collapsed during the recession. No auto centers were spared in the recession; the union could not escape to other local havens because the industry is spatially integrated in terms of its production systems. On the other hand, the IBEW strategy of decentralization seems to have protected the union marginally in 1982. That is, by localizing organizing drives, by focusing upon the northern non-RTW states, and by targeting relative growth areas, the IBEW was able to win in an otherwise very hostile national economic climate.

The IBEW's and the UAW's options were, and remain, relatively narrow. Given an inherited industrial base, a geographical orientation (centralized and decentralized), and the costs of representation and internal political coherence, unions can hardly change their organizing focus overnight. To consider the implications of the previously reported Probit results, we must be sensitive to the *possible* options of the unions. Given the estimated relationships between election outcomes and the structure and context of union representation elections, what is the probability that the IBEW and UAW would have won an election if they had followed a particular organizing strategy? The probability of winning is considered for each union and each strategy over the four years 1970, 1974, 1978, and 1982. The basis of these calculations was the estimated parameter coefficients, regardless of their levels of significance.[13]

Five strategies were identified as arguably relevant for the period 1970–82. The first three were structurally oriented, being based on a combination of industrial and geographical factors, with the North–South distinction serving as a proxy for different labor relations practices including RTW legislation. The second group of strategies were more contextual, being based on local variables. Specifically, the strategies evaluated were:

(1) a heartland strategy focusing upon northern core/noncore industries;
(2) a southern strategy focusing upon southern core/noncore industries;
(3) an industry strategy focusing upon core and noncore industries;

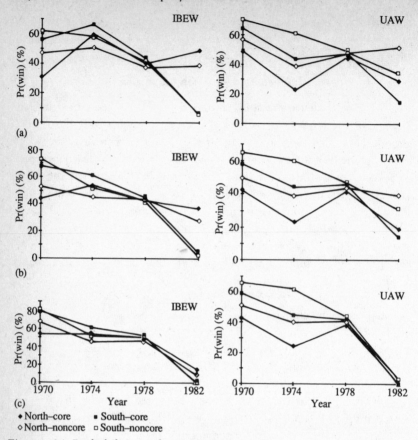

Figure 6.1 Probabilities of IBEW and UAW winning representation elections under various strategies: (a) heartland strategy; (b) strategy targeting employment growth; (c) strategy targeting enterprise growth

(4) an area growth strategy focusing upon localities characterized by high rates of employment growth relative to enterprise growth;
(5) an area growth strategy focusing upon localities characterized by high growth rates in the number of local enterprises relative to employment growth.

The estimated probabilities of winning of the five strategies are summarized in figure 6.1. Beginning with the heartland strategy, there were clear differences between the unions over time in terms of their likely probability of winning. In 1970, the IBEW had a much lower probability of winning in their North–core than the UAW. But by 1982 the IBEW had the higher probability of winning. When we considered North–noncore sectors, a less polarized picture emerged: both the IBEW's and the UAW's probabilities of winning declined over the period 1970 to 1982. And by 1982, both unions had very similar probabilities of winning in the northern noncore sectors. We have noted that the UAW contested relatively few North–noncore representation elections in 1982, although clearly more than in 1970. Thus, a heartland strategy in 1982 would obviously have benefited the IBEW, but hardly have helped the UAW (figure 6.1). Indeed, the poor performance of the UAW during 1982 could easily be linked to the union's concentration on this strategy in the face of overwhelming odds. On the other hand, however useful a heartland strategy might have been to the IBEW, it is just as clear that this union remained relatively decentralized.

This last point is crucial to understanding the performance of the IBEW during this period. Whereas both unions began in 1970 with relatively similar probabilities of winning in southern core sectors, by 1982 disaster had struck the IBEW. In fact, a remarkable spatial shift occurred in the electoral fortunes of the IBEW over this period. In 1970, a heartland strategy for the IBEW would have been judged irrelevant given its probability for winning representation elections in the South. But in 1982, its southern strategy had collapsed; its only options for success were in the North, especially in its core industries. Being decentralized, spread throughout the US, saved the union from imminent collapse. Over the 1970–82 period, the experience of the UAW was rather different: its southern strategy did reasonably well. The union would have prospered using this strategy since the probability of winning in the North in 1974 had declined so that it had a greater probability of winning in the South. In 1978, there were significant differences between the North and the South in terms of the union's probability of winning. Even in 1982, its southern strategy would have been a very reasonable alternative to its conventional heartland strategy.

Discussion of geographical union organizing strategies has woven together another strategy: an industrial one. It has been noted many times that both unions have tended to concentrate their organizing on relatively small (but different) groups of core industries. There are many good reasons for such concentration, ranging from minimizing the costs of representation through to maintaining internal political coherence. Embedded in the tables are a couple of implications regarding the likely future utility of this strategy. For the UAW, the election results of 1982 imply a difficult future. Its highest probabilities of winning are in noncore industries and the South more generally. If this pattern were to continue through the 1980s, the union would be divided within itself. That is, with more noncore members, the union executive has to respond to the challenge of representing these new members in sectors in which they have little expertise while ensuring the loyalty of these new members, and at the same time dealing with increasingly vocal dissident groups within the traditional heartland core sectors of the union. Notice that these patterns were evident as early as 1970, and have been important since 1974.

In contrast, the IBEW's industry strategy seems less problematical. Even though its southern strategy collapsed in 1982, and even though it remains relatively decentralized in areas where it could not win in 1982, the results suggest that its northern core-industry strategy was the only strategy which saved the union from complete disaster. This is obviously a viable strategy in the short run. The danger is, though, that its centralization strategy could fail in a couple of years. If that were to happen, the union could be faced with the UAW's dilemma: expansion into noncore sectors could threaten its internal coherence. Moreover, if the IBEW continues to concentrate in northern core sectors, then its hard-won gains in the South could be in danger of being lost. After all, over much of the 1970–82 period, the union had much higher probabilities of winning in the South than in the North.

What would be the implications of a more locally oriented strategy, one focused upon areas of economic growth? Instead of planning on the basis of large geographical and industrial units, what would be the implications of planning union organizing strategy around variations in local economic prosperity?[14] The consequences of targeting high employment growth areas for organizing drives on the probability of the IBEW winning representation elections could have been twofold (see figure 6.1).

First, focusing upon such areas would have only marginally increased the union's overall win rate in the North for 1970 and 1978. In the South, such a strategy could have had a more marked positive effect in 1970, given the magnitude of differences between the estimated win probabilities. Second, such a strategy would have seriously eroded the union's overall win rate in 1974 and 1982, in both the North and the South. In fact, such a strategy would have taken the union to the brink of disaster in 1982. An employment growth strategy would have benefited the UAW in 1978, and would have seriously compromised its membership in 1982. In 1970 and in 1974 such a strategy would not have affected the chances of winning in the North and the South. Only in 1978, in the North, would an area-based employment growth organizing strategy have significantly increased the union's chances of winning.

What of the relative merits of targeting areas of high enterprise growth as opposed to areas of high employment growth? An enterprise growth strategy would have benefited the IBEW in 1970 and 1978 even more than an employment growth strategy. An enterprise growth strategy would have been preferable to a standard region/industry strategy in 1978. But in 1974 and most obviously in 1982, an employment strategy would have been preferable to an enterprise growth strategy, while a more conventional heartland strategy would have been preferable to the previous two area-based strategies. As for the UAW, an enterprise growth strategy would have been marginally preferable to an employment growth strategy in 1970, and would have made no difference in 1974. An enterprise growth strategy in 1982 would have spelled disaster for the union.

Intuitively, there are a couple of reasons why an enterprise growth strategy would more likely benefit the IBEW rather than the UAW. Most new enterprises are small. If they have any construction requirements they will employ electrical workers of one kind or another. In contrast, few new enterprises would hire UAW workers, and would be unlikely to be of any significant size. The IBEW is a union with a great deal of experience with small firms, and small bargaining units. The UAW is a union whose experience has been predominately in large production enterprises. There is such a special relationship between the UAW and auto companies that a general enterprise strategy would be irrelevant.

Conclusion

Unions' organizing strategies are bound by general structural imperatives which do not necessarily reach through to the local level in any systematic way. This argument parallels a previous argument that voters in representation elections often vote according to local issues which have no immediate outside relevance for other union representation elections. In this respect, like Kiewiet's (1983) argument regarding congressional elections, there is a significant nonsystematic local effect in union representation elections.

From the unions' perspective, there are similar issues to be considered in analyzing the chances of a union winning a particular representation election. While election procedures are set within well-regulated institutional, political, and industrial environments, these macro-structures are incomplete in the sense that knowing these environments is not enough for us to be able to predict the outcome of an election in any given place or time. The context of representation elections is a crucial part of the story; indeed, without knowing the context of an election, anyone predicting the outcome of a local election could be very mistaken. It is in the interaction between structure and context that union electoral prospects are created.

The model of union organizing strategies developed in this chapter has retained aspects of Dunlop's (1944) theory of the union as an active decision maker, and Ross' (1948) theory of it as a political institution. Unions' organizing strategies were discussed with reference to two dimensions. First, it was suggested that unions organize so as to reproduce themselves. There are two basic constraints to this process: the costs of representation and the costs of internal coherence. The second dimension of this discussion concerned how these general imperatives were played out in particular circumstances, and how the two unions developed organizing strategies to cope with these imperatives. The result was a series of propositions regarding likely organizing strategies, and a series of identified structural variables which would be important in understanding the electoral performance of the unions over the past decade or so.

Empirically, outcomes of union representation elections were related to a series of structural and contextual variables. The former included the type of the election, the existence of RTW legislation, and so forth. The latter included local economic variables, especially employment, income, and enterprise variables. It was found that there was no one model of union representation outcomes that could work for all times and places. It was also found that in some years there were no significant and consistent local effects, or even structural effects. There appear too many situations where local nonsystematic effects determine the outcome of elections.

Organizing strategies were considered for their likely impacts on unions' probabilities of winning elections. Strategies which are based on the structure of representation elections – industry, region, and their interaction – could be quite clearly differentiated in terms of their impacts on the unions' probabilities of winning. Similarly, locally oriented strategies could be shown to have quite distinctive and differential effects on unions' winning chances. Not only was there a mix of structural and local effects, but over time there were also some significant differences regarding the effectiveness of these strategies. This means that there is no simple recipe for union organizing, whether structural, contextual, or some combination. As macroeconomic circumstances have changed since 1970, so too have viable union organizing strategies. For example, in the 1970s the IBEW was quite successful in the South, as compared to the North. But in 1982, its northern heartland strategy was the only one that saved the union from disaster. In contrast, the UAW's chances of winning representation elections were very good in southern/noncore regions over the entire period 1970 to 1982. The variety of different effects by time, structure, and context makes general conclusions about the effectiveness of any one strategy very problematic. Given our theoretical perspective, where structure is incomplete and context crucial, these results were entirely appropriate.

However, it would be misleading to concentrate on strategies according to their probabilities of winning. There is more to attracting new members than concentrating on strategies with high probabilities of success. For example, in 1982 the UAW could have chosen to concentrate on southern/

noncore sectors and northern/noncore sectors, even areas characterized by high rates of employment growth. There were really very few such opportunities. Such a southern strategy would have targeted sectors and areas of the country where the union had very little prior representation. And, in any event, would such a strategy have returned as many new members as a more general strategy wherein no attention was paid to potential winning versus non-winning situations? That is, there may be more new members to be gained using strategies which have relatively low chances of success. The much greater number of elections in situations where the chances of winning are lower may itself make up the difference between low-chance strategies and high-chance strategies. The cost of organizing has to be balanced between the chances of success and the potential flow of new members.

This issue is very complicated. At one level, the union as an organization has nothing to gain by spending its resources on so-called lost causes. Perhaps this is the reason why both the UAW and the IBEW have contested far fewer elections in recent years. In this context, a strategy which targeted areas of high employment growth would have been consistent with their financial resources. But at another level, unions have to deal with more than simply the optimal use of their resources. Ultimately, their legitimacy resides in their representation functions. To the extent that these unions represent large numbers of workers in particular industries, their power relative to employers and governments must be enhanced.

Thus, it may pay the union to go after lost causes even if such a strategy bankrupts the union. By concentrating on particular sectors, unions minimize the costs of representation, and maintain internal political coherence. A sectorally and geographically diffused membership, concentrated in areas of rapid economic growth, may make impossible demands on the executive of a union. Imagine the problems that the UAW would face if it had to represent unemployed auto workers in northern cities, and service workers in southern cities. The interests of these two groups are so different that it is very doubtful if the leadership of the union could survive politically. Given the structural imperatives facing unions, it is very difficult for them to alter their organizing strategies radically.

7

At the margin of the rules of the game

In a recent decision, a panel of the National Labor Relations Board set aside a narrow union victory in a representation election involving the Retail, Wholesale and Department Store Union Local 1034 and the Bristol Textile Company.[1] During an acrimonious election campaign two employees were overheard saying that they would slash the tires of employees who opposed the union. The union won the election by a 15–12 vote, with two ballots challenged. The company filed an objection with the NLRB claiming that the threat to slash tires so affected the atmosphere of the election that a second election was warranted. On appeal, the NLRB panel held that the threat was "plainly coercive." Because of the closeness of the margin of victory, and the fact that at least seven voters were aware of the threat before the election, the panel ordered a new election.

In another case, this time involving the United Food and Commercial Workers and a supermarket chain, the Board ordered a new election because a management consultant "unlawfully interrogated" employees about their prior union experience just before the election.[2] In this instance, the union lost by a vote of 27–51 and appealed to the Board claiming (in part) that the management consultant's questions had a coercive affect on employees. Chairman Dotson dissented from the majority opinion, arguing that the interrogation was an isolated event, which would have had no effect on the outcome of the election. There are many more examples of similar appeals to the NLRB to overturn election results. These appeals come from unions and management alike, and typically involve the NLRB in adjudicating the significance of alleged election misconduct with respect to the margins of victory or loss.

If the Board is convinced that a group of voters were coerced, and if these voters could have altered the outcome of the election, then the Board appears quite willing to set aside the election result. In essence, this is the Board's definition of a close election result. So, for example, in *Bristol* the close margin of victory precipitated a new election; in *Michael's Markets* the fact the election result was not close led Dotson (but not the Board) to reject the union's claim for a new election. It should be apparent that the Board does not always evaluate the significance of election misconduct with respect to the margins of victory and loss. Nevertheless, the closeness of an election figures prominently in many appeals to the Board, and appeals to the courts.[3] For unions and management involved in representation elections, the closeness of an election magnifies the differences between the parties' interests and competing claims.

Despite the significance of close elections as a distinct class of elections for the NLRB and unions and management alike, there has been little systematic study of the phenomenon. It is not immediately obvious how important close elections are in terms of the overall distribution of election outcomes. *If* close elections are quantitatively important, little is known about how they might differ from non-close elections. Based on Clark and Johnston (1987d), this chapter analyzes the patterns of close elections for the IBEW and UAW over the period 1970–86.

Close elections and campaign strategy

In their review of the academic literature on representation elections, Heneman and Sandver (1983) did not consider close elections, and only identified one article (Block and Roomkin 1982) which could be construed as being relevant. Block and Roomkin were concerned with the relationship between voter participation in representation elections and the margin of victory.

It might be reasonably expected that studies of the impact of management consultants on election outcomes would consider the closeness of an election as an important datum point in evaluating the effectiveness of these consultants. Lawler (1984) observed that management consultants depress the probability of union victory, a finding which runs counter to Getman, Goldberg, and Herman's (1976) conclusion that managements' election campaigns have no effect on voting preferences. Dickens (1983), writing on the same topic, sided with Lawler, noting "the practical importance of even small changes in the probability of workers voting union in determining the outcome of union representation elections" (574). In this context, one might imagine that close elections are the preferred terrain of management consultants.

It has been contended by Weiler (1983:1769–70) that "a major factor in the decline of unions' success rates in representation campaigns has been the skyrocketing use of coercive and illegal tactics . . . by employers determined to prevent the unionization of their employees."[4] Weiler's (1984a) proposals for redesigning the union representation election process have met with considerable debate, argument, and some support (see Frankel 1985). Most of Weiler's critics have focused upon his arguments concerning the impact of employer-initiated delays in the NLRB's election process on election out-comes.[5] It has been argued that there is no necessary relationship between delays in the election process and election outcomes. For that matter, it has been suggested that employers' dirty tricks are essentially irrelevant. Here critics have returned to Getman, Goldberg, and Herman (1976) for evidence to counter Weiler's claims. Not often appreciated is the fact that Weiler was not concerned with all elections. Like Lawler and Dickens he suggested that employers' dirty tricks would be most effective in close elections.

Weiler attempted to explain the comparative effectiveness of management in close elections by a sketch theory of management behavior. His argument went as follows: employers' efforts to frustrate union organizing campaigns "will probably be concentrated on swing voters in close elections"; in close elections workers believe that "their votes will really make a difference"; and thus "they pay more attention to the employer's threats about the dire consequences of a union victory." He also suggested that in units where there is only mixed interest in union representation, "intimidation is more likely to be effective." Using Getman et al's data he then sought to demonstrate that "even a slight impact from employer unfair labor practices may seriously reduce union success" (1787). This claim was illustrated by reference to Dickens' (1983) reworking of the same data. Having introduced this argument, Weiler spent the balance of his article considering legislative alternatives, especially the Canadian option.[6]

Despite the vociferous criticism of Weiler's approach there are reasons to believe that his sketch theory of employer strategies in relation to the closeness of elections has merit. Before beginning a campaign, management and unions have significant information about the preferences of voters. The names of those who signed cards authorizing the union to petition the NLRB regional director for a representation election provide clues as to the depth and range of sentiment in favor of representation. Moreover, exper-ienced managers are able to identify those involved in the internal campaign for certification even before a union representation election is set by the NLRB. The personal nature of this information is most reliable and available in small units, where each person is known to union organizers and management. In larger units, it may be more difficult to use this information to judge the level of support for union representation. In these units, individual workers are relatively isolated from management, even from union organizers. It should be readily apparent that small represen-tation elections (the home domain of the IBEW) are likely to be more personal, more focused upon individual workers' opinions and attitudes than larger representation elections (the home domain of the UAW).

Signed authorization cards indicate some basic support for union representation. However, in most situations there is likely to be worker opposition to union representation – few petitions are signed by all eligible employees; many petitions are signed by a minority of employees. In most circumstances there is a cadre of union supporters and a relatively large proportion of uncommitted voters. Since unions must convince a bare majority to vote for representation, unions and management do not have to convince all eligible voters of their claims for and against representation. Given initial levels of support and opposition, unions and management compete for uncommitted (swing) voters. In these situations, management and unions face similar decisions regarding expenditure levels and tactics: how much to spend, and whom to target.

On the union side, the expenditure level is set by reference to estimated returns from winning (union dues) discounted over a finite and limited time horizon (the likely length of the first set of contracts), and the costs of representation: establishing and maintaining a contract with management. It is assumed that unions will spend up until the point where the costs of organizing equal expected returns, given a fixed time horizon.[7] It is also assumed there are increasing returns to scale in servicing contracts so that a union may be willing to spend proportionally more per voter in larger units than in small ones. Assuming firms are profit-maximizers and operate in competitive environments, management have an incentive to minimize their campaign expenditures (compare with Freeman 1985). The limit to their campaign budget would be defined by the estimated costs of unionization discounted over the future life of the existing capital stock. This may mean that the higher the union/nonunion wage differential and the higher the costs of maintaining collective bargaining, the more a firm may be willing to pay to avoid unionization.

This implies that management are unlikely to commit significant resources to lost causes. In these instances, perhaps the best option for management is to divert resources and investment to other plants located in union-free environments. There is evidence which suggests that corporate relocations in the United States are tied to such decision criteria (see chapter 1). And there have been instances where firms have unilaterally abrogated existing union contracts by relocating production from union to nonunion plants (see Johnston 1986). Even so, these kinds of tactics have been subject to intense litigation, and have been found to be illegal in a number of instances.[8]

Institutional context of close elections

One of the themes running through Weiler's analysis of employers' election tactics is an assumption that the legal framework of American labor relations is in some way responsible for the number and patterns of close elections. Specifically, Weiler argued that the NLRB has been too permissive in allowing certain employer campaign tactics, and too cautious about enforcing the rules of the game. The presumption is that the NLRB has rewarded those employers who have been most aggressive in anti-union campaigns by failing to police these campaigns adequately. Another presumption embedded in Weiler's argument is that increasing levels of employer resistance have led to proportionally more close elections and a lower union success rate.

Since the passage of the Taft–Hartley Act in 1947, scholars have identified five, perhaps six, different regulatory regimes of representation election conduct (Williams 1985, ch. 2). In accordance with section 8(c) of the Taft–Hartley Act, the Board has responsibility for ensuring that unions and management act in a way consistent with the best interests of voters: providing an atmosphere which facilitates free and reasoned choice. This policy was enunciated in *General Shoe* (1948), wherein the Board declared its intention to provide "a laboratory in which an experiment may be conducted, under conditions as nearly ideal as possible, to determine the uninhibited desires of employees" (1341). This policy dominated the NLRB's early adjudication of appeals regarding parties' election conduct.

In practice, interpretation of laboratory conditions has evolved from a very narrow and regulated notion to a relatively expansive and permissive conception of proper behavior. From 1948 to 1962, the *General Shoe* model dominated, beginning with the NLRB's own narrow reading of laboratory conditions, and then the courts' narrow reading of them. According to Williams (1985) the courts were more willing to enforce a narrow interpretation in the later years of this period than was the NLRB. It was quickly recognized that representation elections take place in highly charged situations, and that idealization of the democratic process may in practice deny effective implementation of the law. In 1962, the NLRB revised its policy, holding in *Hollywood Ceramics Co.* (1962) that "an election should be set aside only where there has been a misrepresentation or similar campaign trickery" (1601). The Board also suggested that if the injured party had no chance to respond to such trickery, and if there was a reasonable basis for believing trickery had a significant impact on the election outcome, then the Board had a responsibility to rerun the election. From that point the Board became enmeshed in disputes over the veracity of all kinds of propaganda, and the likely impact of misrepresentations on the election process.

Williams (1985) believed that *Hollywood Ceramics* "practically guaranteed the absence of consistent, predictable guidelines" (41). It appears that in the intervening years to 1977, the Board was faced with more and more cases of misrepresentation, and greater confusion about its own position in each subsequent case; the Board had either to return to a narrower reading of laboratory conditions or abandon the misrepresentation criteria. It chose the latter course of action. In 1977, the Board drew a temporary halt to *Hollywood Ceramics* and decided that it would "no longer set aside elections on the basis of misleading campaign statements" (Williams 1985:47).

Rather, in *Shopping Kart* (1977) it assumed that employees could recognize propaganda "for what it is." The Board was very influenced by Getman, Goldberg, and Herman's (1976) study, which purported to show that employer campaigning did not change employees' attitudes. But this did not last: *Hollywood Ceramics* was reintroduced in 1978 through *General Knit* (1978). From 1978 to 1982 *Hollywood Ceramics* held sway, even though it was severely attacked in the courts and by individual members of the Board. In 1982 it was again replaced by *Shopping Kart* through *Midland National Life* (1982), and has since been clarified in *Clark Equipment* (1986).

The essential point here is that since 1948 the NLRB's policies regulating the conduct of representation elections have become progressively permissive, complex, and confused. While this is not the place for a full-fledged analysis of the evolution of election campaign policy, it can be reasonably argued that the period subsequent to *Hollywood Ceramics* fundamentally compromised the NLRB's policy. Indeed a number of commentators have argued that by 1978 the policy was in a shambles. The period 1978 to 1982 did little to resolve the issue, and made revision of *Hollywood Ceramics* a virtual necessity. Since the Reagan NLRB was constituted in 1981, it appears that its policies have become more relaxed, and less concerned with each campaign event than with how an event may have effected the outcome of the election. This has meant that the Board has been willing to tolerate campaign tactics like misrepresentations of parties' opinions, actions that would have been grounds for ordering a new election in the early 1960s.[9] Both unions and management have complained about the *Midland* policy, although it appears to favor management.

Patterns of close elections

Four suppositions, two general and two particular, about union and management campaign strategies in close elections follow from this brief discussion. First, a general supposition: management will campaign most actively in close elections. Because relatively few voters are crucial to the outcome of such elections, and because management have an incentive to minimize the costs of campaigning, the target efficiency of expended funds will be highest in close elections. The corollary is that where union support far outweighs any internal opposition management will respond through relocation strategies. A second general supposition is that the increasingly complex and confused regulatory environment has increased managements' returns for contesting close elections. In fact, according to Weiler, over time the confused regulatory environment has generated proportionally more close elections.

A third supposition, which follows directly from these two suppositions, is that management have tended to win more and more close elections over the past couple of decades. The fourth supposition, which also follows from the above, is that the target efficiency of campaign expenditures will be highest in small units. In such personalized and tense situations, individual workers are more likely to be held directly accountable for their views. This implies two further sub-suppositions: (a) management and organized labor are more able to monitor voting preferences in close elections in small units than in larger ones; and (b) participation rates will be higher in close elections in small electoral units than in close elections in much larger ones.

However plausible these suppositions, there are few data available on the significance of close elections. There have been no studies of the patterns of close elections for different unions over time. Nationally, there was a striking coincidence between the evolution of the NLRB's election campaign policy and the explosion of unfair labor practices by employers in the early 1970s. From 1960 to 1970, labor's charges of unfair labor practices by management doubled. From 1970 to 1975, the number of charges practically doubled again, and from 1975 to 1980 it increased by 50 per cent (see Weiler 1983:1780). With respect to the IBEW and UAW, we were not able to collect any evidence directly linking employers' unfair labor practices with the closeness of union representation elections (Clark and Johnston 1987d). There is no evidence available to support or contradict the first supposition. But we were able to comment on the plausibility of the others.

From data collected and described in an earlier chapter, close elections were defined by the difference between votes for and against union representation standardized by the overall vote and multiplied by 100. To accommodate scale effects, a high percentage difference (20 percent) was used in very small units (0–10 voters), declining in a linear fashion through to a low percentage difference (5 percent) for very large units (100 or more voters). These percentage rules were used after considering the distribution of votes for and against unionization by size of electoral unit for both unions. Since we were especially concerned to identify those elections where changing just a few workers' votes might have changed the outcome of the election, a sliding scale of percentage difference by size of unit was

Table 7.1. *Percentage distribution of all representation elections by win/loss and close/nonclose for the IBEW and UAW, for selected years 1970–86**

Union/Year	Close elections			Nonclose elections		
	Win	Loss	Total	Win	Loss	Total
IBEW						
1970	9.0	6.0	15.0	50.0	35.0	85.0
1974	6.0	13.0	19.0	44.0	37.0	81.0
1978	8.0	13.0	21.0	34.0	45.0	79.0
1982	3.0	12.0	15.0	34.0	52.0	86.0
1986	9.2	18.4	27.6	34.7	37.8	72.5
UAW						
1970	8.0	9.0	17.0	48.0	35.0	83.0
1974	7.0	12.0	19.0	41.0	40.0	81.0
1978	6.0	15.0	21.0	39.0	39.0	78.0
1982	8.0	10.0	18.0	33.0	49.0	82.0
1986	15.9	30.3	46.2	26.5	27.3	53.8

Note: * Rows may not sum to 100.0 because of rounding errors

Source: Clark and Johnston (1987d, p. 454, and author's calculations)

necessary. For instance, a 20 percent difference between votes for and against union representation in a unit of twenty workers is still very small, whereas the same rule applied to a unit of one hundred workers would give drastically different qualitative results.[10]

For the first three sample years (1970, 1974, and 1978), the percentage of close elections increased from around 15 percent to around 20 percent for both unions, and then decreased to around 15 percent in 1982 (table 7.1). In 1986, the significance of close elections dramatically increased for both unions. Generally, the UAW had proportionally more close elections than the IBEW, especially in 1986. With respect to electoral performance, it is clear that the IBEW and UAW lost the majority of close representation elections for all years. In fact, compared to nonclose elections, these two unions performed quite badly in close elections, with win rates in close elections consistently well below the win rates of nonclose elections (table 7.1). Notice, though, that the temporal patterns of win rates in close elections were quite different between the two unions. From 1970 to 1982, the IBEW's win rate in both kinds of elections declined, and most precipitously in close elections. Comparatively, the UAW's win rate in close elections remained relatively stable while its win rate in nonclose elections declined quite dramatically.

Given that these two unions are very different in many ways – they represent quite different types of workers stratified by geography, industry, and occupation, amongst many other dimensions – the consistency of the identified patterns through to and including 1986 is quite striking. It was noted above that the number of close elections has significantly increased as management's chances of winning such elections also increased or at least remained constant. Of course, it must be readily acknowledged that the proportion of close elections was generally small compared to that of nonclose elections. The numbers involved were about 50 elections for each union in 1978, about 29 for the IBEW and 21 for the UAW in 1982, and even fewer in 1986. Still, it is close elections which seem to generate so much dissent and legal manoeuvering. We must not be overly sanguine about the relatively low percentage of close elections.

Was there any evidence supporting the claim that close elections in small units are more precisely monitored by labor and management? And that close elections have higher participation rates than nonclose elections? As one indication of the precision of close election campaigns implied by supposition four, it was found that between 25 percent (1974 and 1978) and 33.3 percent (1970 and 1982) of all IBEW close elections had a split 50–50 percent vote for and against union representation. The average size of an IBEW electoral unit is very small (10 workers) compared to the average size of a UAW electoral unit (near 100). Thus, the above supposition regarding the importance of the size of electoral units in monitoring efficiency seemed warranted.

It is not surprising that the proportion of UAW close elections with a split 50–50 percent vote was low over this period. It is less clear why the number of split votes declined from around 18 percent in 1970 to about 4 percent in 1982. The relatively large proportion of split votes for the IBEW implies a great deal of precise planning and monitoring of voters' attitudes by management. We are not aware of any other similar findings for all unions or other particular unions. These findings support Weiler's (1983) contention of the crucial importance of limited but targeted management anti-union activities, even if we were unable to identify directly specific management actions in particular union representation elections.

·Elsewhere we observed that there appears to be little significant variation in union representation election participation rates by union, year, or location (Clark and Johnston 1987b). However, for close elections there are reasons to suppose that voter participation will be generally higher than in nonclose ones, and highest in close elections in small units. To assess this supposition an analysis of variance was undertaken, comparing close and nonclose elections according to their participation rates for each union and each year. For the IBEW (the union with very small electoral units) it was found that in 1970 and 1978 there were statistically significant (at least at the 90 percent level) differences between close and nonclose elections according to their levels of participation. In contrast, for the UAW it was found that only in 1978 could a case be made that close and nonclose elections were statistically different in terms of their participation rates. Given the general lack of variance in overall participation rates, perhaps these results were not so surprising.

Modeling the margins of victory and loss

In analyzing the patterns of close elections, the focus was upon aggregate national patterns. While this was useful in setting the issue in a general policy context, previous chapters emphasized the importance of the local context in understanding unions' performance in representation elections. In chapter 2, it was observed that aggregate models of union growth and decline have failed to explain the current crisis of the American labor movement because these models do not take into account the decentralized character of American labor relations. The spatial diversity of unions' electoral performance was illustrated in chapter 5, along with an argument for a significant nonsystematic local component in union representation elections. And, in the previous chapter, the outcomes of union representation elections were modeled using a series of structural and local variables.

The question analyzed in Clark and Johnston (1987d) was simply: what are the local determinants of the margin of victory and loss? There were two basic reasons for this emphasis. First, in the context of the NLRB's review of the conduct of union representation elections a crucial adjudicatory variable is the margin of victory or loss. As we have seen, the Board often uses the margin as a means of deciding the relative significance of electoral campaign behavior. Likewise, labor and management frame appeals to the NLRB regarding the conduct of one another in representation elections according to the margins of victory and loss. The margin is then a behavioral variable. Second, the margins of victory and loss are a continuous variable. Some elections are very close, others not close at all. Using the margin of victory or loss allowed us to discriminate between close elections and nonclose elections while dealing directly with the reference point of the NLRB. All elections were treated as observations in this approach. The margins of union victory and loss were analyzed using common local and structural independent variables.

We were not concerned with modeling the outcomes of close representation elections.[11] Even so, a similar empirical framework was used where the margin of victory or loss was a function of a set of institutional or structural variables and a set of local or contextual variables:

MARGIN = f(STRUCTURE, CONTEXT)   (7.1)

Since MARGIN is a continuous variable, we were able to estimate the formal model using a standard ordinary least squares regression routine.[12]

As in previous chapters, the structure of labor relations relevant to the IBEW and the UAW were represented by three independent variables: a state-level variable indicating the presence (= 1) or absence (= 0) of right-to-work (RTW) legislation; a variable indicating whether or not the election was stipulated (STIP) (= 1) or not (= 0); and a variable (CORE) representing the inherited industrial structure of the union (industries where the unions have had a long relationship were identified by 1; 0 otherwise).[13] The size of the electoral unit (ELIG) was included as an independent variable, as was the participation rate (PARTIC). A set of local economic variables were included, specifically employment in the relevant county and industry (EMPLOY), the payroll of firms in the relevant county and industry (PAY), and the number of establishments in the relevant county (ESTAR) and industry (ESTSIC). These economic variables generally describe the employment relationship (EMPLOY and PAY), and the level of industrial concentration and competition for labor in the county (ESTAR and ESTSIC).[14]

The model estimated could be generally specified as:

$$\text{MARGIN}_{it} = f(\text{CORE, RTW, STIP, ELIG, PARTIC, EMPLOY, ESTAR/ESTSIC, PAY ...})_t \qquad (7.2)$$

where MARGIN_{it} stood for either VMARGIN (the margin of victory) or LMARGIN (the margin of loss) for a given union (i) and year (t). VMARGIN and LMARGIN were measured as percentages with respect to the overall vote in each election. The independent variables were those specified above. Also included as independent variables were variations on those basic local economic variables, including change in employment etc., as well as average pay (AVPAY) and change in average pay over the past two years (PAVPAY). The model was estimated for the IBEW and UAW over the period 1970–82, specifically the years 1970, 1974, 1978, and 1982 (the latest data available).

Before considering the results of estimating this class of models, it is important to pause for a moment to *hypothesize* the likely causal effects of these independent variables on the dependent variable. Theoretically, because CORE industries have long been the home domains of the unions, in instances of a union victory the historic dominance of the union should amplify the margin of success and narrow the margin of failure in union losses. However, it has been observed that unions' success rates in CORE industries declined over the 1970–82 period. Thus readers should not be surprised to see different effects by different years. Generally, it is expected that the existence of state-level RTW legislation would narrow the margin of victory and amplify the margin of loss. RTW legislation can be thought of as embodying a fundamental anti-union culture, sustained through law and reflected in other variables like the local level of unionization (see Ellwood and Fine 1983 and Farber 1984a).

Stipulated elections (STIP) have rapidly increased as the preferred management type of election. They provide the option of delaying implementation of a union victory through appeals to the NLRB and do not allow for local adjudication of management tactics. This may mean that the local election environment is tense and antagonistic. At the same time, though, it is unclear if such an environment would narrow or widen the margins of victory and loss. There are reasons for both expectations. Of course, these institutional variables need not be significant. And, in fact, it was doubtful whether STIP would be particularly important in this regard.

As has already been noted, the size of an electoral unit (ELIG) may have an important negative effect on union success. Generally, one might imagine that a small ELIG would narrow the margin of victory and amplify the margin of loss, *if* the likelihood of victory was relatively low. On the other hand in more open circumstances a small electoral unit may witness considerable polarization of opinion, leading perhaps to large margins of victory and loss. With respect to the level of participation (PARTIC), it is expected that a high PARTIC will narrow the margin of victory and amplify the margin of loss. In small units management are more able to monitor individuals' opinions, and in units characterized by high rates of participation those otherwise uninterested workers are more likely to be influenced by management than labor (Weiler 1983). Simply the greater resources of management would likely sustain this effect.

In areas of high levels of employment, high levels of wages, and a large number of establishments, employers' competition for labor is likely to be quite pronounced. Organized labor will have a bilateral advantage in these areas. Consequently, support for unionization should be high as individual workers attempt to ratchet up their income. In these cases the issue is quite simply the relative shares of income. We expected that high levels of employment and pay and a large number of local establishments would have similar effects on the margins of victory and loss. They should amplify the margins of victory and narrow the margins of loss.

There are also a couple of reasons for expecting distinct temporal effects that will swamp these general expectations. Local economic effects appear strongest in times of national economic growth. In particular, it was observed for the UAW that the years 1970 and 1978 elicited statistically significant local wage and employment effects. Of course, the auto industry is a national industry dominated by large multinational corporations. In contrast, many of the IBEW's firms are local. In recession, though, there appear to be no local effects, whether for the UAW or the IBEW. In these times the issue is one of rationalizing employment, not redistributing income. Thus there may be a union–industry effect related to the macro-economic circumstances.

Determinants of the margins of victory and loss

The appendix to Clark and Johnston (1987d) reports the full results of the regression analyses including measures of model performance and levels of significance of the estimated parameter coefficients. Generally speaking model (2) performed best in explaining the margin of victory as opposed to the margin of loss. Coefficients of determination (R^2) were consistently higher for VMARGIN than LMARGIN for both unions over all years. One point of distinction in this regard between the two unions involved the relative performance of the model over the four years. With respect to the IBEW, it was found that the model performed best for both VMARGIN and LMARGIN in the early years 1970 and 1974, whereas in the UAW case the model performed best for both VMARGIN and LMARGIN in the last year, 1982. There tended to be more significant parameter coefficients for VMARGIN than LMARGIN over the four years and two unions.[15]

In the case of the IBEW, most of the significant parameter coefficients were on the local economic variables. The only structural exception to this generalization was the RTW parameter, which was found to be significant for VMARGIN in 1970 and 1974. In 1970 the positive sign on the parameter coefficient implied that there were higher margins of victory in RTW states than in nonRTW states. This was reversed, however, in 1974. While RTW states were for a time quite hospitable areas for union organizing, this changed quickly for the IBEW. For the UAW two different structural variables' parameters were significant – CORE in 1978 and 1982 and STIP in 1978. The negative parameter sign on the CORE coefficient implied that the margin of victory (1978) and loss (1982) was lowest in CORE industries. The positive sign on the STIP coefficient (1978) implied that the margin of victory was highest in stipulated elections, the type of election most preferred by management. Perhaps management prefer STIP elections because they know of significant anti-management sentiment amongst eligible voters.

As expected, theoretically and empirically, the size of the electoral unit (ELIG) was systematically important for both unions. For the IBEW this was the case for VMARGIN in all years, and LMARGIN in 1974 and 1978. The sign on this parameter coefficient was invariably negative, implying that as the size of an electoral unit increases, the VMARGIN and LMARGIN decreases. We had expected that a small ELIG would narrow the margin of victory and amplify the margin of loss. Actually we found that the smaller the size of the electoral unit, the larger the VMARGIN and the LMARGIN (holding participation rates constant). Participation rates were found to be significant for the UAW but not the IBEW. The sign on the PARTIC parameter coefficient was invariably negative, implying that as participation rates increase the VMARGIN and LMARGIN decrease. This was expected. Since the average size of an IBEW electoral unit is so small and participation rates in such units often very high (for reasons advanced by Weiler and others), it should not come as a surprise that PARTIC was insignificant for the IBEW. The amount of variance in the IBEW's participation rate is very small compared to the UAW.

So as to understand the effects of the various local economic variables on VMARGIN and LMARGIN, a series of scenarios were constructed which are temporally specific. Beginning with the IBEW, in 1970 two variables' parameter coefficients were found statistically significant (PEMPLOY and PAVPAY – the percentage change in local industry employment and the percentage change in local industry average pay). From 1968 through to 1970, the national economy grew rather slowly and even declined in some industries compared to previous years. The signs on the coefficients imply that in areas of large rates of decline in employment and average pay, the margins of loss were largest. Conversely, in areas of low rates of decline, the margins of loss were smallest. Similar scenarios can be constructed for the UAW. In areas of high average pay (AVPAY), the margin of victory was highest. In areas of high employment *growth*, the margin of victory was also high. Essentially, in those areas comparatively well off with vibrant auto industries the UAW was able to garner overwhelming victories in representation campaigns.

From 1972 through to the final quarter of 1974, the national economy expanded and then suddenly contracted. Rates of inflation were quite high as Nixon's wage and price controls came to an end in late 1972 (Clark 1985a). The negative signs on the IBEW's PAVPAY and AVPAY parameter coefficients implied respectively that in areas of low relative pay growth the margin of victory was highest, and in areas of low average pay the margin of loss was highest. Perhaps in areas of rapid wage growth potential IBEW workers voted overwhelmingly in favor of union representation so as to ensure their share of high future wage gains. Areas of low average pay are invariably located in the South. Thus, the margin of loss may simply reflect a deeply embedded anti-union bias. For the UAW another explanation was warranted. The positive sign on the PAVPAY parameter implied that in areas of high growth in average pay, the margin of victory was also high, whereas in areas of low employment growth the margin of loss was largest. Perhaps in the former case workers recognized the role of the union in sustaining high rates of income growth and voted accordingly, while in areas of low employment growth the union was blamed for this trend and so perhaps workers also voted accordingly.

Over the two-year period 1976 to 1978 the national economy grew quite rapidly, albeit at lower rates than in the golden era of the mid 1960s (Gordon 1980). Notice in these conditions there were few if any significant parameter coefficients for either union. For the IBEW, in areas characterized by a high number of establishments the margin of victory was highest. Following on from the previous discussion, this pattern was the result of competition between large numbers of employers in an era of rapid economic growth which allowed the IBEW more latitude in organizing potential members. The result of minimal employer resistance was evidenced through expanded margins of victory in union representation elections.

The year 1982 was the worst national recession since the 1930s. From 1980 through to 1982, the economy stagnated and shrank. This was especially the case in auto production and in construction; unemployment in some mid-western auto towns hovered around 30 percent (Clark 1986a). Both unions suffered tremendously in terms of win/loss rates and the very low number of representation elections that were held in 1982. Notice that significant parameter coefficients were concentrated in just one union (the IBEW) and just the margin of victory.

Given that the IBEW won relatively few elections during 1982, the results of estimating model (2) for VMARGIN had some surprises. In areas of few establishments (ESTAR) and low rates of decline in those establishments (PESTAR), the margin of victory was highest. But in areas and industries characterized by high rates of decline in employment (PEMPLOY) and average pay (PAVPAY), the margins of victory were also very high. Perhaps the union succeeded in isolated, protected niches: areas of low relative decline, and segments within areas and industries of high relative decline. In these two contexts the trades skills of average IBEW workers may have sustained a high demand for labor even as employment declined in the local economy. With respect to the UAW, which was also found to have its highest win margins in areas characterized by rapid decline in the number of local establishments, perhaps the strong pro-union vote was a protest against management.

Conclusion

This chapter was concerned with the patterns of close elections and the determinants of the margins of victory and loss. It has been suggested by Weiler (1983) and others that the poor performance of American unions can be traced to the explosion of management unfair labor practices, and the failure of the NLRB to act consistently and conscientiously to enforce the rules of the game regarding fair representation election conduct. At least two patterns are said to follow from these factors. First it is suggested that there are many more close elections than before; and second that unions have tended to lose more and more of these elections. With respect to the electoral performance of the IBEW and the UAW over the period 1970–86, it is apparent that both suppositions can be generally sustained.

One qualification to this general claim has to do with the electoral performance of these two unions in 1982. The proportion of close elections declined in this year, and the IBEW won more close elections than nonclose elections in that year. Of course, 1982 was a very bad year for American unions and the IBEW in particular. Both unions contested relatively few representation elections and won very few of those elections they contested. Compared to 1986, 1982 was an exception to a general trend towards more and more close elections.

Given a set of close wins and losses, we attempted to model the margins of victory and loss for each union and year. The margin issue is important to all parties in representation elections. The NLRB often uses the margin of victory or loss as a reference point in evaluating the importance or otherwise of appeals regarding election conduct. The closer the margin the more likely the NLRB is to seriously consider overturning the election result. Management are also very interested in the margins of victory and loss. At one level their interest is economic: the target efficiency of anti-union campaigning is reflected in the votes cast against representation, and the closeness of an election result. It is claimed in some quarters that management consultants have become very skilled in identifying the needed margin of victory, and targeting their propaganda accordingly. Indeed, for the IBEW at least we found evidence which would support this supposition. Up to a third of all IBEW close elections finished with a split 50–50 percent vote for and against union representation (by law a union loss). But in larger electoral units, typical of the UAW, it appears to be very hard for management to achieve such target efficiency.

In modeling the margins of victory and loss, we concentrated on two types of determinants: structural and contextual. The first type included the existence of RTW legislation, the type of election (STIP), and so forth. The second group were local economic variables. Notice that we do not claim to have considered all possible sources of determination of the margins of victory and loss. Some variables like union loyalty are difficult to quantify, and others are so local that they are not systematic across all places. As noted elsewhere, there are significant nonsystematic local effects which are not adequately captured by models which use common cross-spatial variables. However, it was apparent that we were often successful in modeling the margin of victory. The crucial variables tended to be local economic ones rather than structural ones, as well as variables reflecting the size of the electoral unit and the participation rate (especially for the UAW) of the representation election.

Management consultants and union officials cannot change the characteristics of the local economy just to win representation elections. Nevertheless, they can target some places rather than others in terms of their organizing and anti-organizing campaigns. The strength of the local economic effects for both unions indicates that a place-sensitive strategy would pay dividends. However, the variability of these effects year to year indicates that there is no easy recipe for predicting the margin of victory by location. The significance and direction of effect of local economic variables vary by macroeconomic trends in the national economy.

Management consultants and union officials can affect the size of the electoral unit and the level of participation in union representation elections. Paradoxically, whatever the target efficiency of small units, larger units have smaller margins of victory than smaller ones. Perhaps this is because larger units are more heterogeneous in terms of workers' interests and goals. Thus, they may have a built-in anti-union bias simply because it is difficult to convince a wide range of workers that all their interests would be served by being represented by one union.

For management, this possibility represents a dilemma. If they narrow the coverage of the electoral unit by appeal to the regional director or the Board they isolate the union influence if the union wins the representation election. On the other hand if they broaden the electoral unit, they have more of a chance of convincing a few uncommitted voters to vote against union representation, and thus defeat the union. Given the small size of IBEW units, participation rates are very high in most, if not all, IBEW elections. For the UAW, however, if management can increase participation, they have a good chance of narrowing the margin of union victory, even defeating the union. In this context, management have options not shared by unions.

They can lobby workers on the shop floor, they can use subtle and not so subtle inducements to turnover uncommitted workers, and they can divide the union vote by treating different segments differently.

Close union representation elections are particularly troubling to the NLRB. These kinds of elections are the source of many appeals from labor and management regarding election conduct. The closer the margin of union victory or loss the more likely the losing party will appeal to the Board to set aside the election result. The grounds for appeal may be irrelevant, even frivolous. However, if the Board can be convinced that the claimed infraction could have altered the election result, then such appeals may have a good deal of merit for the injured party. From the cases and examples cited, it is clear that the Board often evaluates the importance of supposed infractions by reference to the margin of victory or loss. Thus, the credibility of the Board's adjudicatory apparatus is most tested in close elections.

As noted above, Weiler (1983) suggested that the increasing numbers of close elections and the poor win/loss records of unions contesting these elections can be explained by the failure of the NLRB to enforce the rules of the game regarding proper election conduct. There can be no doubt that there are many instances of illegal election conduct, and instances where even if such conduct is legal, it ought to be illegal. While the evidence presented here and elsewhere seems to support Weiler's suppositions, there are a couple of reasons for remaining cautious about the scope of our results. First, an autonomous increase in close elections would inevitably generate more appeals to the Board, and more claims of unfair management practice. Second, with more and more claims and greater scrutiny of the Board's decision criteria it is inevitable that its rules would come under increasing attack. The Board is charged with responding to each case on the merits of each case. General rules will often fail to provide adequate guidance in particular instances. Thus, the failure of general rules might be construed as a failure of will, or worse, the product of political interests.

It is not my intention to defend the Board against its critics, or support particular interpretive practices of the Board. Quite the contrary. In subsequent chapters I am very critical of the Board and its decisions. It is more than possible that the NLRB has become enmeshed in controversy because of its own internal failure to respond to the issues relating to close elections. And it is just as possible that the increasing numbers of close elections have more to do with declining electoral fortunes of the union movement in general. An autonomous rise in the number of close elections would provide significant advantages to management attempting to avoid unionization, and would threaten the integrity of the NLRB's decision criteria. In these circumstances, it is readily apparent why unions would tend to lose close elections.

Is it likely that there has been an autonomous increase in close elections? For the IBEW and the UAW, I would suggest the answer is yes. In previous chapters I argued that the declining fortunes of the American labor movement can be linked to two factors. First, as the representation electoral process mimics the partisan political process, so it also shares in its problems. Specifically, declining levels of partisanship for political parties and trust in the institutions of politics (see Wattenberg 1984) may have spilled over to unions. This does not mean that individual workers need trust management more than unions. It simply means that levels of alienation have increased and with it has come a greater skepticism of established unions. There may be more close elections because individual workers are less committed to the union movement.

Second, the American union movement is not a monolithic centralized structure. In fact it is highly decentralized, according to legislative imperatives. One consequence is the overwhelming significance of local issues; not just wages but employment, leadership, trust, and commitment are all very important. The highly personalized nature of such local issues when coupled with a general distrust of formal institutions may reinforce existing divisions between workers. Unlike most national and state-level partisan electoral units, larger union representation electoral units are characterized by significant cleavages by class, sex, and race. As a result of such segmentation, union organizers may find it very difficult to build overwhelming coalitions of interests. Close elections would result because of the deeply embedded divisions of society.

Thus, however important close elections are to unions, management, and the NLRB, there seem to be few simple rules for understanding observed patterns. It is clear, though, that close elections represent opportunities for management to manipulate and coerce individual workers. But, it is not clear that close elections are the product of such coercion.

PART IV

Regulating local labor–management relations

8

Integrity of the National Labor Relations Board

Any understanding of the interrelationships between organized labor and American communities must inevitably consider the role and status of the administrative arm of federal labor law, the National Labor Relations Board. It is the NLRB which is responsible for the administration and interpretation of the National Labor Relations Act. In addition, it is decisions of the Board which have had profound impacts on the economic health of American communities, the success and failure of organized labor in local representation elections, and the extent of managements' prerogatives in terms of the relocation of work, to cite just three of many related dimensions.

The current NLRB was a product of the Wagner Act, signed into law by President Franklin D. Roosevelt on 5 July 1935. Drawing upon the experience of immediate predecessors (the National Labor Board of 1933 and the National Labor Relations Board of 1934),[1] sponsors of the new Board hoped that it would be a unifying but independent force for the administration of federal labor law (see *First annual report* of the NLRB 1935: ch. 3). In retrospect, achievements of the Act and the Board went well beyond supporters' goals and President Roosevelt's modest ambitions: "an important step toward the achievement of just and peaceful labor relations in industry."[2] Fifty years or so later, the NLRB is thought by many to have been a vital institutional innovation in building the United States' decentralized system of labor relations and collective bargaining (see Morris's 1987b introduction to his edited volume), and is often favorably compared to European experience of more bureaucratic and centralized control of the collective bargaining process (Bok 1971).[3]

Despite its importance in the evolution of collective bargaining, the NLRB is often surrounded by political controversy. While it is currently popular with management organizations, spokespersons for organized labor argue that unions ought to avoid the Reagan Board as much as possible. Some commentators would say that the Reagan administration tainted the Board with its appointment of conservative management-oriented lawyers. But others observe that the NLRB's popularity with unions and management has always varied with the political affiliation of the incumbent president

They suggest that recent debates about possible management bias of the Reagan NLRB are not so different from previous debates over the supposed management bias of the (for example) Eisenhower NLRB.[4]

The question of bias is quite complex, made so by deep political tensions between the different parties involved. In this chapter, bias is considered in relation to a specific issue: the NLRB's integrity as an adjudicatory authority. At issue are the internal coherence of the NLRB as a decision-making body, how it makes decisions, and how its decisions may ultimately bring into question the overall political power of the institution. Also considered is the significance of institutions like the NLRB in the creation and reproduction of the economic landscape. These issues are explored with respect to recent decisions of the NLRB in *Otis Elevator* (1981, 1984, 1987). This dispute involved Local 989 of the United Auto Workers (UAW) and Otis Elevator Company and centered upon whether the employer was required to bargain over the relocation of work from one facility to another.

Institutions and the economic landscape

The location of production is a popular research topic in economics, geography, and regional science. There is a massive set of literature devoted to many different dimensions of the topic (see Lloyd and Dicken 1972 for an original text treatment). But, for all the research on the location of production, it remains dominated by a quite simple theory of location decision making. Drawing upon the work of Weber (1929), the dominant paradigm is economic and neoclassical in theoretical orientation. That is, the map of production is thought to be the result of many separate optimizing decisions by firms to locate their plants on the basis of the lowest relative input prices given a set of marketplaces (see chapters 1 and 3).

There have been many critiques of the literature spawned by this theory. Most critiques focus upon the questionable plausibility of neoclassical assumptions of certainty and flexible price adjustment, as well as the whole notion of spatial price equilibrium.[5] These critiques have obvious merit. Yet, perhaps unwittingly, there remains a tendency to accept the neoclassical image of labor and capital as just factor inputs, thereby ignoring their separate and collective political interests. One consequence of this inchoate economic anthropology is a reluctance to treat labor and capital (management) as human agents, capable of forming contracts covering issues like what to produce and where to produce. Not only does conventional location theory strip agents of their capacity to act outside of the structural imperatives of prices and profits, but it treats the political organization of production as irrelevant or inconsequential to the creation of value.

Based on an assumption of the importance of agency and political interests, a new kind of location theory is evolving. In previous chapters it was noted that this new type of location theory is one more sensitive to the social relations of production – the relationship between labor and management, and the political structure of different agents' rights and obligations. At present, this theory does not have the analytical simplicity of neoclassical location theory. One reason for its complexity has to do with its attention to case studies and fine-grained analyses of different locales. It is also apparent that a crucial element of the project is explanation of spatial economic differentiation. To understand spatial economic differentiation requires a greater appreciation of labor and capital in the political environment. But, unfortunately, neoclassical stripped-down versions of location decision making have significant costs, not least of which is an inability to deal with the political structure of labor–management relations.

Focus upon the relationships between labor and capital inevitably leads to consideration of how labor contracts and collective bargaining agreements between unions and companies affect the location of production. And, once these institutional representations of the social relations of production are acknowledged, we must also consider how regulation of these relationships by state agencies like the NLRB affects both the form and substance of the economic landscape. Ultimately, the location of production is affected by a range of institutions and agents. Compared to neoclassical location theory, there is no longer a simple determining reference (market prices for factor inputs and commodities) for location decisions. One implication is that there are a set of agents and institutions competing for political dominance in the location decision-making process (as in many other facets of production).

Understanding the role of political institutions like the NLRB in adjudicating disputes over the location of work should be considered a necessary step for understanding the production and reproduction of the economic landscape. At the minimum, this involves consideration of the decision-making methods of such political agents. In this context, the integrity of the NLRB is a problem of economic and political geography; its ability to rationalize and justify its decisions regarding the location of work has direct and substantial consequences for the map of production.

Discussion of the integrity of the NLRB could have been framed as a discussion of its political legitimacy. In a Weberian sense, the legitimacy of a political institution refers to the degree to which the polity accepts (explicitly or implicitly) its rules as a plausible framework for social action (Hyde

1983). This is a society-centered definition of legitimacy, wherein the democratic caucus is the essential reference point. It is also a positive theory of legitimacy – the legitimacy of an institution is evidenced by the actions (and non-actions) of the democratic caucus – and is related to H. L. A. Hart's (1961) theory of law, which holds that law is defined by observed customary action. There are many problems with positive theories of legitimacy and law, not least of which is their dependence upon society as the reference point in determining the virtue or otherwise of political institutions (see Clark 1988c). With regard to the topic of this chapter, a critical problem with positive theories is their ignorance of the power of institutions to foster, even create, legitimacy as a means of reproducing power.

Elsewhere, I have analyzed the legitimacy of the capitalist state, concentrating upon the autonomy and status of state apparatuses (Clark and Dear 1984). This approach was state-centered rather than society-centered, and analyzed the state as an institution rather than a derivative symbol of democratic politics. It was noted that law has a very special place in the American state, and a degree of autonomy that has given the practice of adjudication a quite distinct location outside of democratic politics. Nevertheless, the status of law and legal agencies like the NLRB is problematic. As an institution, as opposed to an ideal, law operates in a political arena. In this chapter I am most concerned with the actions of the NLRB as a political institution and how its actions affect its political integrity.

While the concept of legitimacy might be useful in this context, its meaning in this instance would be confused by the standard Weberian interpretation. Thus, I prefer Dworkin's (1986) concept of integrity. By Dworkin's definition, integrity is directly related to the political performance of institutions, and in particular their adjudicative authority. Dworkin (1986:176) distinguished between two types of integrity: "a legislative principle, which asks lawmakers to try to make the total set of laws morally coherent, and an adjudicative principle which instructs that the law be seen as coherent in that way as far as possible." In this chapter, I concentrate on the latter principle; in the next chapter, aspects of the former principle are considered in relation to the NLRB, the Saturn Project, and economic justice.

Collective bargaining and the location of work

To illustrate the concrete effects of NLRB decision making for the economic landscape, the case considered here is *Otis Elevator*, an instance of the

Board's adjudication of a dispute concerning the relocation of work. This case is important for a number of reasons. Coupled with other NLRB cases like *Milwaukee Spring* (1982, 1984) and the decision of the US Supreme Court in *First National Maintenance* (1981), *Otis Elevator* is often cited as evidence of anti-union sentiment on behalf of the Reagan NLRB.

Connerton (1987) used *Milwaukee Spring* and *Otis Elevator* to argue that the Board has mounted a full-scale attack against "the very foundations of collective bargaining." From that position, Connerton questioned the integrity of the Board by asking "whether it continues to serve the purposes for which it was originally chartered." At another level, *Otis Elevator* has been invoked as evidence by those critical of delays and confusion in the NLRB's adjudicative process. It remains to be seen how the final decision in *Otis Elevator* will affect other cases. Case law is a "moving target." Nevertheless, it is clear that the case raised serious questions about the NLRB's adjudicative integrity (for an assessment see St. Antoine 1987).

Relocation of work appears to be an especially troublesome issue for organized labor. There is evidence that the threat of relocation and relocation itself are a powerful weapon used by management in their attempts to dissuade workers from union activities. Getman (1986) cited the *Weather Tamer* (1980) case as a particularly obvious instance, while others have noted the negative effect that such threats can have on union performance in representation elections (Freiberg and Dickens 1985). Such threats are thought to be very powerful management election propaganda, particularly in communities and regions already adversely affected by plant closings.[6] Given that many industrial unions have fared very poorly in representation elections in these types of regions in recent years, union officials have come to believe that relocation of production is as much an anti-union strategy as it is a legitimate business decision based upon "purely" economic considerations.

Bluestone and Harrison (1982) suggested evidence consistent with this assessment, and demonstrated that plant closings and the relocation of work are closely related to corporate investment policy. Instead of treating investment as simply a capital asset, it is thought that management now couple investment with labor relations strategies that deliberately seek to avoid unions (as for example in Westinghouse Corporation) or basically compromise the power of unions in existing work places (a strategy pursued by manufacturers such as Mack Trucks). Bluestone and Harrison's argument was given a more theoretical and statistical treatment in Clark, Gertler, and Whiteman (1986:ch. 3), wherein it was shown that the location of investment and relocation of capital can be directly associated with geographical patterns of union strength. Essentially, *Otis Elevator* was an instance in which these issues were explicitly played out in litigation.

In *Otis Elevator*, a charge of unfair labor practice was brought by Local 989 of the UAW against Otis Elevator company under Section 8(a)(1) and (5) of the NLRA ("to refuse to bargain collectively with the representatives of his employees") on 7 June 1978.[7] The company had previously notified the union that some members of the bargaining unit were to be transferred from the plant located in Mahwah (New Jersey) to another facility located near the United Technologies' (the parent company of Otis Elevator) research center in East Hartford, Connecticut.[8]

The union had represented employees in the Mahwah plant since about 1950, and had negotiated the contract then in force through to March 1980.[9] Instead of dealing with the union on this matter, the company went directly to the individual employees who would be affected. By doing so, the union charged the company failed to recognize the union as "the sole and exclusive bargaining agent" of members' interests.[10] At issue were three specific charges: (1) the company had refused to bargain with the union over the decision to relocate work; (2) the company had refused to provide information concerning the reasons for its decision; and (3) the company had refused to bargain over the effects of its decision to relocate work.[11]

On 29 November 1979 Irwin Kaplan, an administrative law judge, concluded that the company had in fact violated Section 8(a)(1) and (5), and ordered it to bargain with the union. Over a year later (25 March 1981), the Board upheld the judge's conclusion (*Otis Elevator I*) and filed a motion in the US Court of Appeals (Washington DC) to have its decision and order enforced. This decision was also appealed to the US District Court by the union and the company. However, in August of that year the Court granted an NLRB motion to reconsider the case in the light of the decision of the US Supreme Court in *First National Maintenance*. After considerable delay, on 6 April 1984 the Board issued another decision (*Otis Elevator II*), reversing *Otis Elevator I*. The Board remanded allegations that the company had refused to bargain over the effects of the relocation of work back to the administrative law judge. At that point, the judge re-examined the entire case, and reasserted his original findings. Nearly nine years after the filing of the original charge, the Board issued a second and final supplemental decision (*Otis Elevator III*) on 13 March 1987. In that decision, a majority of the Board agreed that the company had failed to bargain over the effects of the relocation issue, but was otherwise not liable for its failure to bargain over the relocation decision.

Through to mid 1982, Local 989 continued to press for action on its charge and filed other charges alleging further violations of Section 8(a)(5).

Without action on its charges, even at the time of the Board's *Otis Elevator I* ruling, membership of the bargaining unit had practically halved. By 2 June 1982, when the president of the union wrote to the Board protesting delays in the proceedings, the bargaining unit was much smaller again; fewer than 37 members down from about 270 in early 1978. As the president of the Local noted, "since the employer [appealed] the Board's decision they felt no obligation to cease [relocation]." The president of the Local believed his bargaining unit was "being destroyed, presented by a *fait accompli* by an employer who refuses to bargain over decisions to remove work and who surfaces bargains on impact [italics in the original]."[12] The president believed also that the planned relocation of work was originally conceived as a negotiating ploy, but had become a reality because of delays in the NLRB's adjudicative process. All subsequent rulings by the Board became irrelevant to the survival of the bargaining unit.

Critics of the NLRB

How should we evaluate the controversy surrounding the NLRB's decisions in *Otis Elevator*? How much credibility ought to be accorded Connerton's contention that the Board was attacking the very foundations of collective bargaining? To understand these issues, we must first consider some standard treatments of the integrity issue.

Board members are appointed by the President for overlapping fixed terms. Thus, it is inevitable that the NLRB would be subject to periodic criticism. The election of a new President makes the composition of the Board an important political topic for labor and employer representatives. Even with an incumbent President, the expiration of Board members' terms and the appointment of new members provide congressional critics with recurrent opportunities to voice their approval or disapproval of the Board and its decisions.[13] Since Board decisions are sometimes reviewed by federal courts, there is always the possibility of judicial criticism of Board decisions. The NLRB does not exist in a political vacuum; it is an "adaptive" agency subject to a variety of external pressures (if not control) (Moe 1985).

In this sense, controversy over the Board (its composition and decisions) does not mean necessarily that the Board has failed in its mission. Controversy is inevitable, and part of the political process which, by design, envelops the NLRB. Thus, we need not support critics of the current Board who would dismiss it as fundamentally compromised just because it is controversial, as if the existence of controversy is sufficient evidence to justify their claims.

Partisan politics aside, there are other criticisms of the Board, its adjudicative practices and its substantive assumptions, which are not so easily deflected. In this respect, there appear to be three different types of criticism. Some critics accuse the Board of neglecting the "higher purpose" (President Roosevelt's phrase) of the NLRA, especially the economic policy goals that were an essential rationale for passage of the Wagner Act (see Dunlop 1987 and Marshall 1987). Other critics accuse the Board of failing in its duty to provide effective and timely adjudication of disputes (St. Antoine 1987 and Weiler 1983, 1984a). And a third set of critics accuse the Board of conservatism: of failing to support legitimate class interests of organized labor (Goldfield 1987). In its search for defensible solutions to disputes, critics of the NLRB as a decision-making organization claim that the integrity of the NLRB is fundamentally at risk. By this logic, the issue is the internal coherence of the Board, rather than its popularity with different political constituencies.

Dunlop (1987) argued that the Board is swamped by lawyers. His frustration with the Board's procedures mirrors other economists' concerns that it has become too focused upon issues of legal etiquette as opposed to the substantive consequences of its decisions for the economy. As emphasis, economist critics of the Board typically recall the preamble (Section 1, "Findings and policy") of the Wagner Act, which noted as fact the utility of collective bargaining rights in facilitating the "channels of commerce." In much the same vein, Marshall (1987:16) recently suggested "there are close relationships between an industrial relations system and the economic performance of an enterprise or economy." Many critics contend that the Board has failed to sustain the substantive economic goals of the NLRA, preferring to treat adjudication as simply an exercise of law within the terms of the NLRA (case law and precedent) not economic policy.

If the economic consequences of NLRB decisions have not been accorded as much significance as these critics believe is warranted, other critics believe that the NLRB's adjudicatory process has failed to live up to promises made to organized labor during congressional hearings on the Wagner and Taft–Hartley Acts. Weiler (1983, 1984a) has been a particularly harsh critic of the effectiveness of NLRB decision making. He argued that the Board has failed to contain and police unfair labor practices associated with management behavior in representation elections and collective bargaining. He also claimed that this failure is not simply a function of the Reagan administration's appointment of management-oriented lawyers (though such appointments may have exacerbated the problem). Rather, like St. Antoine (1987), he believes that failure to police employer behavior adequately is related to a reluctance by the NLRB to support an essential substantive goal of the Wagner Act: "restor[ation of] equality of bargaining power between employers and employees."[14]

There can be little doubt that the massive wave of unfair labor practices and the consequent litigation explosion have substantially affected the NLRB's capacity to make timely and consistent decisions over a wide range of issues (see Flanagan 1987 for details). Though Weiler's position has been attacked by many management lawyers (but compare with the position taken by union lawyers such as Frankel 1985), his argument received some support in Flanagan's study of the litigation explosion. Nevertheless, questions remain. How should these patterns be interpreted? Do criticisms indicate adjudicatory ineptitude or a mistaken emphasis on the adjudicative process at the expense of substance? Or, are these criticisms symptomatic of a deeper flaw in the NLRB and the NLRA in general?

According to Klare (1978, 1981) and Goldfield (1987), the integrity of the NLRB was compromised long ago. They have argued that the Wagner Act itself was flawed, the result of too many strategic concessions done in the interests of coalition building during congressional debate over passage of the Act. Subsequent revisions to the NLRA (for example, the Taft–Hartley Act of 1947) limited the legitimate exercise of organized labor's power while decisions of the NLRB have favored a narrow "rights" interpretation of workers' and managers' interests. Although both writers would acknowledge that the NLRB was of great significance in protecting and facilitating organizing activities of the emerging union movement, they also argue that federal labor law has become progressively more conservative. Klare called this process "the deradicalization of the Wagner Act." In a similar context, Goldfield referred to a "growing conservatism of national labor law" which has reduced the NLRB's effectiveness in combating anti-union animus.

Three dilemmas of adjudicative integrity

What is so important about the critics noted above, and the perspectives they represent, is their questioning of the integrity of the NLRB as a decision-making institution. For writers such as Dunlop, the problem with the NLRB is not political controversy. Rather, by Dworkin's (1986) conception of integrity the NLRB as an institution is vulnerable at two distinct levels. At the legislative level, Klare, Goldfield, and others question the moral coherence of the NLRA and hence the possible scope and power of the Board. At the adjudicative level, Weiler, St. Antoine, and others question the coherence of the NLRB's adjudicative practices, focusing upon the substantive bases of adjudication and the efficacy of decision making.

Here, I concentrate upon the latter level. This is not the occasion to launch a full-fledged critique of the NLRA. It is easy enough to imagine that the Act is less than adequate given the exigencies faced by unions in recent years (witness attempts to reform labor law). But to reduce the NLRB to a mere shadow of the NLRA would ignore other important issues that relate to the integrity of the NLRB as a decision-making institution.

When signing the Wagner Act, President Franklin D. Roosevelt sketched the statutory responsibilities and limits of the NLRB. He observed that the Act provided for the NLRB "to hear and determine cases in which it is charged that this legal right [of workers' self-organization for the purposes of collective bargaining] is abridged, and to hold fair elections to ascertain who are the chosen representatives of employees."[15] Reflecting congressional debates over the proper functions of the NLRB, the President noted that the NLRB was not to act as a "mediator or conciliator in labor disputes." The Board was designed to be an "independent quasi-judicial body," responsible only for the "interpretation and enforcement of the law."[16] These brief phrases, summarizing crucial elements of the Wagner Act, invested the NLRB with two essential functions: enforcement and interpretation of provisions of the Act, and adjudication of disputes relating to the collective bargaining process.

Both functions have proved problematic for the Board, unions, and management. If these functions were obvious and clear cut fifty years ago (though this was by no means necessarily the case), they are no longer so obvious. The adjudicative integrity of the Board is at risk because of the opaqueness of these functions. As a consequence, over the years the Board has faced three dilemmas: (1) *A dilemma of substantive choice*: how should the NLRB choose between substantive goals that are embedded in provisions of the Act? (2) *A dilemma of interpretive practice*: how should the Board judge the behavior of parties in a dispute? (3) *A dilemma of legal practice*: how should the Board rationalize its decisions with regard to previous decisions – that is, with regard to inherited case law and decisions of federal district courts? These three dilemmas combined render adjudication incredibly complex and involved. They also make it fragile and contentious.

In a sense, though, the significance of the Board has grown because of the problematic status of its adjudicative practice. In the absence of clear-cut rules regarding substantive goals, interpretation, and legal practice, each new dispute has to be addressed on its merits. A single-issue dispute can generate many charges of unfair labor practices as parties attempt to represent themselves in the most favorable light or confuse the legitimacy of the claims of other parties. If a party to a dispute is dissatisfied with the Board's ruling, the problematic status of the Board provides an easy rationale for appeal to a federal court. Thus, the history of the Board could be easily read as a succession of attempts to resolve these dilemmas while simultaneously adding in to case law new rulings and new precedents that are used against it in federal court. This is one way of explaining the litigation explosion.

Some abstract examples can illustrate the significance of these dilemmas. Beginning with the substantive goals dilemma, as noted above many economists believe that the essential rationale for the NLRA was its role in facilitating the "current of commerce" (maximum economic growth). Dunlop among others (the Reagan administration included) would judge the adjudicative integrity of the Board by simply referencing the extent to which it achieved this goal. While it is readily apparent that this goal is important, few scholars of the NLRA would accept that this was the *only* or even the *most important* goal provided for by the Wagner Act (see Atleson 1983 and Gould 1982). In fact, there are other substantive goals that have legitimate claims, a point made recently by Morris (1987a).

For some legal scholars, there is no question that the goal of maximum economic growth should dominate all other substantive goals. Posner (1979, 1980) suggested that wealth maximization (a close proxy to maximum economic growth) is uniquely desirable, since it is a more coherent basis for adjudication and less contentious than other competing claims. Even so, it is also apparent that these suggestions have been met with a great deal of skepticism (see Dworkin 1985). Not only have the bases of Posner's model been challenged on logical grounds, but it is also argued in Clark (1985b) that this suggestion does immense damage to a crucial democratic value: respect for others' interpretations and goals. Surely, the Wagner Act was passed because it embodied a range of goals, representing the interests of many different constituents.

To claim that one goal should transcend all others would be to impose a solution to the dilemma of substantive choice. While such a solution may have the virtue of tractability, allowing the NLRB to order substantive goals in terms of their relationship to maximum economic growth, such a strategy may simply escalate the issue into further dispute. In this context, those who value other substantive goals may reasonably challenge the integrity of the NLRB's whole decision-making logic.

The dilemma of interpretive practice is similarly problematic, though for different reasons. Weiler claims that the NLRB has failed to police and contain unfair labor practices (originating mainly with management), as well as infringements of employees' rights to representation and collective bargaining. His position on this issue is unambiguous. He and other critics believe that the NLRB has not dealt with an essential ingredient of the original Wagner Act represented by President Roosevelt's statement that enforcement of employees' rights is "both an act of common justice and economic advance." Weiler also believes that lack of enforcement is one of the chief causes of declining union success rates in representation elections. By this logic the union movement is threatened with extinction because of the NLRB's adjudicative practices.

Although Weiler is probably correct that the NLRB is one cause of declining union success rates in representation elections, he has not recognized a deeper problem. The dilemma faced by the NLRB in this context goes as follows. If it uses notions like fairness, equality, and justice as the bases of evaluating the behavior of parties to a dispute, its adjudication of such disputes runs the risk of being labeled as biased. These terms demand a judgment about persons' behavior, and are normative standards implying some kind of moral worth. Inevitably, moral judgments are political, whether by implication (an unstated theory of right or wrong) or by explicit referencing of a theory of justice (see Kennedy 1976 on the differences between standards and procedures). On the other hand, if the NLRB eschews such judgments for safer terrain, such as the rights of employers and employees, it runs the risk of being labeled as narrow and overly legalistic. At issue is the extent to which the NLRB is sensitive to the motives and actions of individuals in specific disputes.

The dilemma of interpretive practice is not easily resolved, if at all. Moral standards provide the NLRB with a means of being sensitive to specific motives. But, these standards may prompt political retribution, evidenced by campaigns against the Board in Congress and the media. A retreat to a "rights" approach may avoid normative evaluations of agents' actions, but may also prompt further moves against decisions of the Board in courts of appeal. Neither option is a safe haven for the Board: it is caught between moral imperatives and legal imperatives.

This brings us to the third dilemma, that of legal practice. An often-made criticism of the Board's procedures is that they are both time-consuming and overly legal (Dunlop 1987). What was once a "quasi-legal" adjudicative agency has become dominated by the legal process. Congressional critics of the NLRB's procedures have observed that delays in case processing, decision making, and the appeal process are endemic to the agency.[17] In a very real sense, delays in case processing and the overwhelmingly legal nature of NLRB proceedings seriously affect the effectiveness of the Board in responding to specific events. As justice is delayed and transformed into legal doctrine from the specific issues it is doubtful if the Board is ever able to deliver on Roosevelt's original promise of "a better relationship between labor and management."[18]

Rationalizing legal practice is difficult for other reasons. The NLRB is required to consider disputes in terms of its own case law and that of the federal courts. Theoretically, every unfair labor practice could involve the NLRB in choosing between substantive goals of the NLRA, choosing between moral standards and "rights" theories of individual entitlement, and setting their adjudication within a similarly complex set of previous decisions. Any decision could be challenged on substantive grounds (by groups whose interests are represented in the decisions of the NLRB), on political grounds (reflecting supposed bias against different parties), and legal grounds (the logic of separate decisions with respect to all of the above).

For these reasons, it should be also apparent why the integrity of the NLRB is so fragile. Adjudicative practice implies a series of unresolved dilemmas, situated within an already charged political environment. This does not mean that the NLRB is paralyzed by these dilemmas. It must act on charges of unfair labor practices even if its actions generate further disputes over the integrity of its adjudicative practices. The NLRB is beset by a never-ending spiral of decisions, appeals, and questions regarding its adjudicative integrity.

Integrity of the NLRB

Before considering details of the case in relation to adjudicative practices of the NLRB, the political significance of the case should be re-examined. *Otis Elevator I* and *Milwaukee Spring I* were decided in 1981 and 1982 (respectively) around the time of President Reagan's firing of 11,000 striking PATCO air traffic controllers. At a time when organized labor felt particularly vulnerable, these decisions were hailed by labor as a constructive defense against the political power of management organizations. However, both cases were decided by an NLRB majority originally appointed by President Carter. These members were described by Irving (1983:550) as "liberals," responsible for "excesses" in their "meddlesome efforts to bar relocations." Irving hoped these decisions would be overturned when Reagan appointees to the NLRB gained a majority on the Board. He was not disappointed. Both cases were returned to the Board by federal courts for reconsideration, and were subsequently reversed in 1984 by the Reagan-appointed majority.

In response, labor's spokespersons characterized the Reagan NLRB as a rogue elephant let loose by right-wing business interests. They sought to damage the political integrity of the NLRB and force some moderation of its views regarding management powers. But, of course, this tactic was unlikely to succeed. By virtue of the appointment process, the NLRB reflects dominant political interests. Its decisions (for and against organized labor) whatever the affiliation of the incumbent President have a measure of political integrity simply because of the appointment process. Another tactic had to be used.

Organized labor was more successful in Congress. A campaign was mounted against the NLRB by attacking its adjudicative integrity. In the Democratic controlled House, hearings were held on the timeliness of decisions, the statutory criteria used to evaluate labor and management behavior, and the internal organization of the Board's reviews. In addition, legislation was initiated directly related to these cases on issues such as plant closings and relocations (see Harrison 1984). While Republicans controlled the Senate, actions by the House Democrats could be contained and treated as harassment, even if the chairman of the Board were forced to account publicly for his decisions. However, with capture of the Senate by a majority of Democrats in 1986, political pressure on the Board came from another side. Not only were legislative initiatives of more consequence, but the President himself was vulnerable to charges of delaying reform. In this setting, the NLRB was less powerful politically, even if relatively insulated from direct control. It could no longer depend upon supporters in Congress to stymie attacks upon its adjudicative integrity.

Three dilemmas were identified above as sources of the NLRB's vulnerability. They were all related to NLRB adjudicative practices. While they may not have an immediate origin in the political location of the Board with respect to Congress and the President, it is apparent that these dilemmas can have significant political consequences. Enemies of the Reagan NLRB (inside and outside of Congress) used these dilemmas of adjudicative practice against the Board, in ways that were more effective than direct questioning of the Board's political agenda.

The first dilemma identified was that of substantive choice. The issue facing the Board in this respect has to do with choosing the substantive basis of its decisions amongst a set of plausible goals of the NLRA. In upholding the union's charge against Otis Elevator, the Carter Board argued that the collective bargaining process had to be respected. Indeed, the Board took as its "threshold question ... whether [the] Respondent was required to bargain with the Union concerning its decision to transfer certain unit employees to a new facility in Connecticut" (*Otis Elevator* I:235). The company argued that any negotiation with the union over its decision to relocate would have abridged its "freedom to invest capital and manage its business" (236). The company claimed that its property rights were fundamental, and gave it a unilateral arena of unrestricted discretion unlimited by any bilateral collective bargaining agreement.

The Carter Board disagreed with the company. Although the Board accepted the principle that firms have a right to manage their business, it argued in this instance that bargaining with the union would not have been "a significant abridgement" of the company's property rights. The Board cited *International Harvester* (1977) and *First National Maintenance* to justify its reasoning. The Board found in favor of the union on all three charges and ordered the company to bargain with the union.

However, just after this decision and before the Board obtained an order enforcing its decision, the US Supreme Court decided against the Board in an unrelated review of *First National Maintenance*. The Supreme Court held that the company in that instance was only required to bargain about the effects of its decision to close its facility, as opposed to bargaining over the decision to close. And in contrast to a prior decision in *Fibreboard Paper Products* (1964), the Court also held that a decision to shut a facility for purely economic reasons was not part of the legislative mandate for collective bargaining as set out in Section 8(a) of the NLRA. Two further points were made by the Court. First, the Court supported the idea that collective bargaining was a fundamental aim of the NLRA, but argued that Congress had not meant that union officials would become equal partners in running a business. Second, they also asserted that in this instance, infringement of the employers' need for unencumbered decision making outweighed any benefit "for labor–management relations and the collective bargaining process" (666–67).

Implicitly, the Court questioned the logic of the NLRB in *Otis Elevator I*. However, this did not mean that the NLRB was necessarily incorrect in its decision. Rather there were simply grounds for reconsideration of the circumstances of *Otis Elevator I*, if not its reversal.

The Reagan Board's decision in *Otis Elevator II* reversing *Otis Elevator I* began with an unequivocal statement: "[i]n the light of the Supreme Court's opinion in *First National Maintenance*, [w]e conclude that the Respondent [the company] was free to decide to ... [relocate] ... unrestrained by Sections 8(a)(5) and 8(d) of the Act" (891). The Board was well aware of the importance of the company's decision for the survival of the bargaining unit but believed that the relocation decision "was not subject to mandatory bargaining" (892). Two of the three charges of unfair labor practices brought by the union against the company were dismissed: failure to bargain over the decision, and failure to provide information relevant to the decision to relocate. The third charge, that the company had failed to bargain over the effects, was upheld and returned to the administrative judge for rehearing. In justifying these decisions, the Board cited the same reasons cited in *First National Maintenance*: "management's need for predictability, flexibility, speed, secrecy, and to operate profitably," these being legitimate business decisions excluded from mandatory bargaining (893).

The implications of *Otis Elevator II* are fourfold. First, it is apparent that unions' collective bargaining rights are only enforceable if an essential condition can be met: that management have settled on a strategy of what to produce, where to produce, and how to produce. Second, it appears that it is management's prerogative to decide if this condition is met or if, for whatever reason, management can exercise their unilateral power. Third, it appears as if bargaining between management and labor is limited to wages and conditions of work, not relocation of work or any other issue that might ordinarily be construed to impinge upon management's discretion to organize production in ways they deem most appropriate to their mission. Fourth, where a contract does exist, management are still required to bargain over the effects of their decision. However, labor have no right to expect any concession by the company on its management prerogatives. For all these reasons, the Board essentially compromised the status of collective bargaining while promoting the economic power of management.

The Board's choice of priorities amongst the substantive goals of the NLRA was widely attacked by organized labor. Some critics questioned the integrity of the Board by suggesting that in effect the Board no longer supported "basic" goals of the NLRA: the promotion of collective bargaining and in particular "equality of bargaining power between employers and employees," "an act of common justice," or "a better relationship between labor and management." This was Connerton's position. On the other hand, Board supporters were able to justify the decision by asserting the importance of arranging the collective bargaining process with respect to the economic goals of the Act: "to eliminate the causes of certain substantial obstructions to the free flow of commerce." In this sense, the Board's decisions in *Otis Elevator* were neither wrong nor right. Rather they reflected different political interests served by choosing to support certain substantive goals of the Act.

Even so, reversal of *Otis Elevator I* brought into public focus deep dilemmas of adjudication, and the question of the NLRB's integrity. While we have spent most time discussing the dilemma of substantive choice, the other dilemmas added to the sense of crisis of integrity engendered by this dispute. Throughout the hearings and adjudication of the charges of unfair labor practices, the administrative judge portrayed the company and in particular Dr. William Foley, Otis Elevator's vice-president, as "unreliable." In fact, Judge Kaplan was quite "unimpressed with Dr. Foley as a witness.

The record disclosed that at times he was evasive and equivocal and less than responsive or forthright" (*Otis Elevator III*:D-5).[19] In all issues of fact, the judge believed the union, not the company. At issue here was the dilemma of interpretive practice: assessing the motives of the company in by-passing the union and refusing to cooperate with it with information and/or recognition of its negotiating rights vis-à-vis the decision to relocate production.

The judge also argued that the company and vice-president Foley exhibited bad faith in their relationship with the union. Like the NLRB in *Otis Elevator I*, the judge believed that the company was not originally committed to relocation but became so after the union made what Foley thought to be an unreasonable response to the company's plans to reorganize the plant. By this interpretation, the company subverted the collective bargaining process after it realized that it would not achieve its goals. In contrast, the Reagan NLRB refused to speculate upon the motives of the company, and retreated to an abstract interpretation of management's rights. To make this interpretation plausible, it had to make an absolute distinction between "purely" economic interests and collective bargaining rights as if they are completely separate decisions. For the judge, relocation was just a bargaining tactic used by the company to exploit the union's weakness. For the Reagan NLRB, relocation was a separate business decision unrelated to the collective bargaining process and classed as an essential entrepreneurial function of management.

The failure of the Reagan Board to rationalize its abstract interpretation of motives in relation to the administrative judge's more personal interpretation of motives provided another opportunity for enemies of the Board to attack its integrity. In this instance, one enemy was from within (the judge) and another was from the past (the findings of the previous Board). Yet another enemy was the union, especially the union's leaders, whose credibility was judged to be far superior to that of the company. In this setting, the integrity issue was not just a question of possible bias; it was also a question of "common justice" – many commentators believe that the Reagan Board failed to take into account the circumstances of this particular dispute in its rush to rationalize its decision of support for management's economic interests.

And, finally, what of the dilemma of legal practice? All adjudication involves fitting the details of specific disputes into a wider (case law) context. The challenge facing the Board and all similar agencies is to make the fit in a way that satisfies the exigencies of the dispute at hand and higher tiers of the legal process. In this instance, the decisions of the Board were challenged at both levels, and its integrity compromised by both levels. Obviously, the decision of the US Supreme Court in *First National Maintenance* was a direct challenge to the integrity of the Board. At the same time, the time taken by the Board to reach its decisions, the failure of the Reagan Board to deal with the motives of the company, and the consequences of the company's actions for the survival of the bargaining unit also questioned the integrity of the Board.

In this context, it is not surprising that critics of the Board accuse it of "legalese." All the evidence collected in this chapter concerning the decisions of the Board point to a decision-making process overwhelmed by a need to set its decisions within a plausible legal framework even as the actions of the company destroyed the bargaining unit. Even if the original decision of the Board had been enforced (despite *First National Maintenance*), it is difficult to see how an appropriate remedy could have been instituted. By virtue of the company's actions through the period leading up to the administrative law judge's initial decision, it would have been impossible to restore the circumstances existing at the time the collective bargaining process collapsed.

In effect, the company relocated production and then developed a legal rationale to justify its decision. There is little doubt that the company undertook a risky strategy once it was committed to relocation. Up until the decision of the US Supreme Court in *First National Maintenance*, there was every reason to expect that the terms of the collective bargaining process would have been broadly interpreted. And, there is reason to believe that even this decision might have been accommodated by the NLRB if it had been interested in establishing a way of balancing the significance of the collective bargaining process with management's economic rights. After all the Supreme Court, like the NLRB, is also liable for its actions in the sense that it too has to be able to accommodate competing interpretations of society's goals.[20]

But the company was lucky. What was previously a questionable bargaining tactic and possibly an illegal *fait accompli* became a legitimate business decision justified by a revised legal doctrine and an institution committed to expanding management power, limiting the exercise of unions' collective bargaining rights, and facilitating economic growth. Alternatively, what we might interpret as luck could also be interpreted as an instance where the questionable integrity of the NLRB worked in favor of the company. This need not be true in all cases.

Conclusion

There is not much doubt that political debate over decisions by the NLRB will be important in the future. The nature of the institution, the appointment of members to the Board, and the vital character of the issues adjudicated all indicate that the integrity of the Board will remain an open question. Inevitably, there is no way that the NLRB can avoid dispute: the contingent nature of political support for the Board is embedded in its structure.

If unions and corporations were to avoid the Board (which has been threatened by union officials), then perhaps the NLRB would be less vital in the design of the economic landscape. However, this seems unlikely given the pace of corporate economic and geographical restructuring in recent years. For unions, there are few other institutions that can provide protection from the unilateral decisions of corporations. In this context, labor contracts are more than just bilateral agreements: they are legal representations of relative power. The NLRB is not only caught within the fabric of power relations, but actually makes power in the reading it gives of the nature and character of collective bargaining agreements. This is what was promised by the Wagner Act. It is also possible that a different President could significantly alter the composition of the Board and the substantive goals that it would pursue. By this logic, the spatial structure of employment and production is a political issue.

In contrast, it is often supposed that the location of work is simply the result of separate decisions taken with respect to the landscape of input (factor prices) and output (sales and market) opportunities. In this chapter, it was argued that the location of work is a more complex political process than represented by this ideal image of atomistic capitalism. Actually, the location of work is the result of conflicts and agreements between agents and political institutions, all of which claim certain legal powers in relation to their interests and others' actions. Given these claims, adjudicatory institutions such as the NLRB and the courts are crucial location decision makers, affecting the welfare of separate agents and the form of the economic landscape in general.

The case study explored in this chapter sought to demonstrate some of the essential processes creating the economic landscape. Specifically, analysis of *Otis Elevator* allowed us to understand how and why the powers of control of the spatial structure of production have changed for labor and capital. Some commentators argue that these changes were simply the result of changes in the composition of the NLRB, of changes of bias within the NLRB for and against the interests of organized labor. However, I hope that discussion of the dilemmas of adjudicatory practice indicate the limits of this approach. The NLRB is not only an adjudicator of law, but is also a political agent, and an institution whose long-term interests depend upon maintaining a modicum of integrity separate from its immediate political constituency.

Three implications immediately follow from this expanded conception of location decision making. First, ideal images of capital and labor as separate forces of production fail to do justice to the complexity of their relationships in production. Collective bargaining agreements are just one formal image of these relationships. But contracts between labor and capital need not be explicit, nor should we imagine that collective bargaining is a discrete event which once completed (as in the form of a contract) is not challenged until the next contract is due. In fact, the relationship between labor and capital in production and exchange is always problematic, and bargaining an ongoing process. In some instances, of course, collective bargaining agreements may provide a form of security regarding customary conditions of work. But, as this case study demonstrated, tensions between labor and capital may spill over into the political domain and implicate those institutions charged with the responsibility of stabilizing collective bargaining.

Second, the regulatory environment ought to be regarded as just as problematic as the relationships between labor and capital. It would be a mistake to imagine that regulatory institutions simply adjudicate between agents as if the adjudicatory function is simply a matter of determining which agent wins and which loses. Here, it was shown that the NLRB is subject to many political pressures and internal dilemmas regarding its adjudicative practices. For a variety of reasons, the location of work has been a particularly explosive issue for the NLRB, not least because reversal of its decisions on the basis of political interest has opened up the agency to intense scrutiny. In *Otis Elevator* the NLRB's integrity was challenged on many different grounds: from the implied and explicit substantive bases of its decisions to the consequences of delays in the adjudicative process. What an agency decides and how it decides can have substantial implications for the powers of different agents and the ultimate form of the economic landscape.

Third, we must also be cautious of ascribing too much power to agents and institutions. That is, having identified the bases of one set of decisions we should not be induced to imagine that these decisions will hold in all subsequent cases. Again, the evidence presented in this chapter should be enough to persuade those who imagine adjudication to be final to realize that this is rarely true. There may be instances where a case is exhausted. But the landscape is littered with the results of previous decisions, some consistent with the past, others quite contrary to the latest incarnation. The map of adjudication must be rationalized, if only to convince others of the integrity of the NLRB.

9

Options for restructuring the US economy

In the first half of this decade, the United States economy went through a remarkable cycle of fortune.[1] From the severest recession since the Great Depression, the national economy has prospered to the point where some believe that its success threatens the integrity of the whole economy. While the economy is not quite at full employment, domestic macroeconomic indicators appear robust when compared to European conditions. Even so, the economic recovery has been very uneven, sectorally and spatially. Restructuring and deindustrialization have accompanied the recovery so that even as the economy has added new jobs, other union jobs have been lost. The new jobs created are quite different, by skill, sector, union representation, and location, to the jobs lost. There appears to be a new economic geography, markedly different than the post-war era.[2]

In terms of labor policy, there remain important issues to be considered in how restructuring should be designed and accommodated. One fundamental issue has to do with how local labor relations might be modified so that American industries, particularly heavy manufacturing industries, remain economically competitive in the face of foreign competition. This is not simply a question of economic efficiency, or of policy inventiveness. While many citizens, whether labor or management, Democratic or Republican, secular or nonsecular, desire economic success, there are just and unjust ways of ensuring future prosperity. Current policy options for redesigning local labor relations have significant equity dimensions which may be as important as their economic consequences. These options also have vital implications for the future of the American labor movement, and the role of organized labor in facilitating economic restructuring.

It is contended in this chapter that the labor relations policies of the Reagan administration, and especially of the National Labor Relations Board, are essentially unjust. If these policies work in the short run, they may achieve an economic prosperity that none of us value as just. If, in a restructured national economy, many workers are employed at $5.00 an hour, the economy will surely be worse off than before. This concern for justice should not be dismissed as merely utopianism or tilting at windmills. The Wagner Act of 1935 and the Taft–Hartley Act of 1947 explicitly linked stable wage levels and employment with harmonious and equitable local labor relations in maintaining the prosperity of the nation. In this sense, how economic success (like full employment) is valued depends on what it means, and how it is achieved (see Walzer 1983).

This chapter deals with a fundamental question of public policy: how the institutional framework of American labor relations ought to be designed so that local labor practices are consistent with the imperatives of macroeconomic efficiency and social justice. As such it considers the NLRB in terms of Dworkin's (1986) second dimension of integrity – the moral coherence of the NLRB's decisions regarding the location of work.

Economic restructuring and labor policy

Economic restructuring is an ongoing aspect of modern economies. In recent years, though, the pace of restructuring seems to have quickened, and its reach broadened to encompass the whole US economy. These changes have been partly in response to the impact of international trade on the US economy. It is clear that the nation's competitive position in many basic industries, including steel, has been eroded.[3] But, at the same time, there has been growing dissatisfaction with the role and stature of the NLRB. As we noted in the previous chapter, there has always been debate and argument over Board decisions; recent controversial decisions have re-emphasized the Board's vulnerability to public scrutiny. One consequence of this debate over the integrity of the Board has been reconsideration of how current labor relations practices ought to be designed in order to respond to economic and geographical restructuring.

The US has become very vulnerable to overseas firms exporting to the US domestic market, and to the international marketplace. Just ten years ago, imported products were of negligible significance compared with the US domestic-oriented manufacturing production. But now imports are of vital significance to the US economy and growing dramatically in importance (Lawrence 1984). Suddenly, it appears that the US economy is part of what Grunwald and Flamm (1985) have termed the global factory. Not only is there competition from imported finished commodities, but in some sectors a large proportion of the components for domestically assembled products are also imported (see, for example, Sanderson, Williams, et al 1987).

Extraordinarily high federal budget deficits have exacerbated these problems. Until recently high real interest rates prompted massive capital inflows, and an historically high value for the US dollar prompted a balance of trade crisis. Unfortunately, the high value of the US dollar against other currencies (notably the Japanese yen) drastically affected the competitiveness of much of the US's traditional manufacturing base. While real interest rates have declined, the damage has been considerable. Imports remain very high, and exports lag. The US has turned from being a net creditor to a net debtor nation. Though the value of the dollar has fallen dramatically, the whole Midwest region has undergone a dramatic restructuring, affecting workers, communities, and whole industries.[4]

The consequences of this situation for local communities and the nation's industrial structure have hardly been addressed, except in the most trivial fashion. The popular press has been inundated with recipes for curing the crisis of American manufacturing. Most fall short of even a rudimentary theoretical perspective, preferring instead to blame or extol the virtues of management (Reich 1983). Still, there has been some interest, albeit academic (see Hamermesh 1984), shown in the costs and benefits of individuals' adjustment to the changing fortunes of different regions and industries.

The current legislative and budgetary impasse in Congress does not bode well for developing plausible policy responses. But if it were solely an economic crisis, we might be more sanguine about possible remedies. However, there is another crisis overlaying the economic crisis: one of labor relations. In a period where there ought to be a concerted policy response from the federal government, involving management and labor, all the evidence presented here and in previous chapters suggests that labor relations are in turmoil.

As noted in chapter 8, the current Board was recently described as being the most conservative in the fifty years of its existence (Murphy 1987). Unions loudly protest Board decisions, while management congratulate the Board on returning to the true meaning of US labor law.[5] The irony is that while business leaders were very hostile to federal labor legislation (like the NLRA) in the past, the interpretation of these same statutes has been so changed by the current Board that business now supports federal labor legislation whereas labor does not. Labor leaders now call for a completely new labor Act, one which would be more consistent with their interests. Whatever the truth or otherwise of these contending claims, it is clear that the Board does not command respect from a broad cross-section of society.

Of the many criticisms made of the Board, one particular set deserve re-emphasis given the object of this chapter. John Dunlop (1987) and Ray Marshall (1987), both noted labor economists and previous US Secretaries of Labor, argue that the current labor relations system is not adequate in the face of the international competitive threat. They contend that the Board is too slow to make decisions, is too legalistic in terms of its procedures, and is not sensitive to the changing economic conditions facing both firms and unions. As a consequence, they argue that the US is severely hampered economically in terms of its capacity to adjust to the changing economic environment. Economic efficiency seems to come a very poor third to other apparently more important quasi-legal objectives: due process and adjudication. Many lawyers and labor specialists would agree with Dunlop and Marshall, especially as regards the procedural morass that faces all participants when seeking a decision from the Board.[6]

The economic costs of this system are difficult to quantify. Nevertheless, it is reasonably easy to indicate the types of costs engendered by the current labor relations system. For instance, by delaying resolution of labor–management disputes, all parties pay either in direct costs or opportunity costs. Similarly, by emphasizing due process as opposed to timely adjustment to changing circumstances, the whole economy is stymied in its attempts to meet new competitive threats. It is also clear that the current Board may not be willing to experiment with new labor relations innovations which are primarily economic oriented as opposed to legalistic. According to Dunlop, the labor relations system, which began as a response to the Great Depression, has become overwhelmed by legal issues. In an era of economic crisis, Dunlop suggests that the NLRB fundamentally compromises the economic system.

As we have seen, lawyers are very critical of the Board because of supposed flip-flops in the interpretation of the National Labor Relations Act and in the adjudication of particular disputes. While the Board's decisions have always been sensitive to members' political opinions, the current Reagan Board is held by critics to be much less reliable than previous Boards. The fact that it has held to quite conservative interpretations of the meaning and intent of the Act has further focused criticisms of the Board. One consequence of this tangled web of issues is that labor and management are increasingly attempting to avoid the Board, favoring other forms of arbitration where possible as well as more primitive unilateral decisions based on the respective powers of actors in local disputes. Another consequence is a growing perception among labor's representatives that the Board is arbitrary and unjust.[7]

If economists, lawyers, unions, and management are so critical of the Board, what is its future? John Dunlop has contended that current problems of the Board are symptomatic of deeper structural issues. Whatever the peculiarities of current Board members' views, Dunlop believes the Act itself is inadequate for current circumstances. That is, even if a more labor-oriented Board were appointed, it is entirely probable that the Board would be unable to help resolve the larger issues regarding international competitiveness. While the Act was a fundamental building block for the economy in the working out of the Great Depression, it is now seen as dated, even an historical anachronism hindering further economic adjustment and development. Some unions and management believe (for different reasons) the Board and the Act stand in the way of their achieving just and equitable solutions to their problems. As a result there is mounting pressure for a new Act and a new mode of conflict resolution, one that is simultaneously adaptive, just, and responsive to current circumstances.

Unfortunately for the current Board, it is being asked by a variety of constituents to respond to issues which may be beyond its historical purview. Rarely has the Board had to act outside its traditional adjudicatory domain; public policy concerns have been relatively neglected as opposed to substantive legal issues (Morris 1982). Yet for all these criticisms, the Board has acted in recent times to address the national economic efficiency issue. Indeed, in its *Milwaukee Spring II* (1984) decision, it laid the foundation for a radical reorganization of American industry – across regions and across industries, and between unions and management. This alternative model of American labor relations is set within the terms of the current Act, but interprets its intent quite differently than before. Recent innovations, like joint determination, expanded terms of bargaining, and employee participation are less relevant than a narrow interpretation of employers' and employees' rights. This model of labor relations does retain one assumption of the original Act: the inevitability of economic warfare between management and labor.[8]

In contrast, the recent agreement between the UAW and GM to develop the Saturn Project in Spring Hill, Tennessee has been invoked as a quite different model for future legislation. In contrast to the current Act, the Saturn Project promises a collaborative co-determination agreement which eschews conflict for collective interest bargaining. While this agreement is still in the planning stages (construction has just begun), supporters of the agreement argue that it is the first step in restructuring the underlying logic and tenor of American labor relations.

The second option, the Saturn Project model, may involve a major reform of the National Labor Relations Act. As Dunlop has noted, though, this need not be thought of as an impossible task. All major labor legislation in the US has been born in periods of economic crisis. In fact, when attempts have been made to reform labor relations in periods of relative prosperity, such attempts have foundered upon indifference and special interests (witness the failure of the reform legislation introduced by the Carter administration). The NLRB option has as its logic a radical conservative interpretation of the current Act. Both options aim at accommodating the forces of economic restructuring. If both have similar ends – presumably economic prosperity and full employment – which option is more desirable in terms of economic justice?

These two opposed options for the future of American labor relations enable us to evaluate the integrity of the NLRB in a broad and comprehensive way. Of course, these options do not exhaust all possible options, and current labor–management practices may be somewhere between these two. Even so, there is considerable value in setting the two as polar opposites, if only for the exposure of the embedded political interests. In what follows, their claims to integrity are considered in the light of the theory of justice.

Modes of economic justice

To understand what is meant by economic justice in this analysis, it is necessary to make some preliminary observations regarding the theory of justice. Because the issue here is the underlying logic of the American labor relations system, implied are issues of substantive justice. That is, we are concerned with the design of a labor relations system that embodies principles of justice within the structure of the legislation. In contrast, when public policy makers deal with justice, if they do so at all, more often than not they deal with justice as a problem of redistribution or compensation. After the creation through economic policy of a certain set of outcomes (like employment, wages, and unemployment in different regions of the country), the issues become either redistributing wealth (if there are unacceptable inequalities between people and places) or compensating those who somehow lost in the process of creating others' wealth.[9]

Substantive justice is concerned with the ex ante design of a just economic system; redistribution and compensation are typically ex post modifications to planned economic outcomes. The former should entail an intimate link between ends and means – how full employment is to be achieved is as important as the goal – while the latter presumes no necessary link between what was anticipated and how outcomes are then modified. Put another way, substantive justice is internal to the system of rules or regulations that define the relationships between employers, employees, and government. In contrast, redistribution depends upon a set of external judgments made of the virtues or otherwise of outcomes previously designed, or previously intended. Substantive justice is the concern of this chapter.[10]

Of the many different conceptions of distributive justice, two dominate current debates in philosophy and public policy. Indeed, one might easily argue that these two conceptions are the fundamental datum points in contemporary arguments over what society ought to be in a most general sense. Without regard to order, these two are best summarized as equality of opportunity (EOO) and equality of resources (EOR).

The former is characterized by Dworkin (1981) as a starting gate theory. That is, assuming all people begin as equals, a just society would ensure that all people have the opportunity to attain their individual goals. The emphasis is on ensuring all people start on an equal footing. A good metaphor for understanding this theory is a horse race. No judgment is made of the justice or otherwise of the final result as long as the race was begun as if all people are equal. Equality of resources as a theory of justice goes beyond ensuring a fair race. The issue here is the fairness of the outcomes as much as the procedures by which the race is run.[11] In Dworkin's theory of equality of resources it is not enough to begin the race on an equal footing; the race must be continually monitored to ensure the justness of the procedures, as well as the justness of the outcomes.

EOO is probably the most recognizable theory of justice. It is embedded in the dominant ideology (Posner 1981), and finds ready acceptance in more conservative quarters of government. On the one hand it appears just, as it treats people as equals. On the other hand, as long as the starting gate is relatively well defined, there is no necessary role for government in adjudicating the virtues or otherwise of outcomes of this process. So, for example, if it is assumed that employers and employees are equal in the sense of their individual rights to due process and access to the courts, then whatever results from labor negotiation depends upon the interests of the parties to negotiation, and is not a legitimate issue of adjudication for the NLRB. Of course, there is a good deal of debate over how the starting gate ought to be designed. Recent arguments over affirmative action, individual unions' status in disputes with employers, and even the behavior of employers in union certification elections are issues all related to the question of how equal people are when they begin the race.

Theoretically, EOO is a utilitarian theory of justice, wherein the desires and goals of individuals are thought to be personal and subjective. Thus, no regulated outcome would be fair to the separate desires of particular individuals. Action is assumed voluntary; if not, coercion would violate assumed inalienable rights of individuals to being treated as equals. Notice that there is little regard shown for the material status of individuals. As long as their material status does not interfere with their status as free individuals, then the fact that some individuals are employers and others employees is less relevant than the fact that they are assumed to be individuals who are free to choose whom they wish to associate with in labor contracts. Likewise, little regard is shown for the integrity of groups of workers and employers, given that individuals have a fundamental right to exercise their choice at any time.

It could be suggested that it is this conception of justice which is an important theme behind the logic of the Reagan NLRB.[12] It might also be suggested that state courts' increasing intervention in labor relations through their scrutiny of the employment-at-will doctrine is based on this rights theory of justice.

Equality of resources is a more materialist theory of justice. Instead of beginning with the free status of individuals as the rationale for justice, EOR begins with their material circumstances. Clearly, individuals are assumed to have desires and interests, and they are accorded a prominent role in society at large. Yet, their equality is judged as being circumstantial. This means employees and employers are judged with respect to one another in terms of their material advantages and disadvantages. Not only does the theory suppose that people ought to begin with roughly equal economic power, but it is presumed the state should make a determination of the fairness of the original distribution of resources. Thus, unlike the EOO model of justice, the state has a fundamental role in defining the public standards of equality, even if some individuals may value their resources differently.

But the EOR model of justice is more than a starting gate model. It also claims that the state must continuously review the progress of people, through the course of the race, and to the final outcome. The key principle justifying state intervention is what Dworkin and others have referred to as the envy test. Essentially, it is asserted that people should not be at the mercy of initial decisions regarding race tactics throughout the course of the race. There must be an avenue for changing horses in mid race. This appears to be a very strong principle, and may at first sight appear to reward those who make bad decisions, or even capricious decisions. However, the intent of the principle is to encourage people to take risks, in conditions of uncertainty and accidental advantage and disadvantage. For instance, if we were serious about justice, we would surely not penalize those who fall into a ditch beside the race track because they didn't know it existed or, worse, if they were pushed into the ditch by other horses. Likewise, we would not want to reward a person who had the good fortune to find a short cut to the finish line, while others simply followed the regular race track.

Thus there is a continual interplay between people's material circumstances, the circumstances in which they make strategic choices, and the end result. Economic justice in this model integrates the means and ends of economic outcomes while retaining an ethical public standard about what is desirable and not desirable. In contrast to EOO, EOR aims to ensure justice throughout the horse race. Paradoxically, EOO may in fact legitimize inequality of results in the name of equality of opportunity. Because no ethical standards are applied to people's positions throughout the race, and because material circumstances are largely irrelevant compared to the rights of individuals, full employment may be unjust, but be justified by an appeal to justice.

Economic justice is not an unambiguous concept. As a policy goal, it is a very difficult concept to apply to current circumstances. One reason is that it has a variety of meanings, and these meanings are derived from a diverse set of theoretical rationales. But, more critically, which standard of justice is chosen will depend on the significance we attach to issues like individual rights as opposed to material circumstances. In this sense, economic justice is foremost an ideological conception of the proper design of society. The choice we make between these two visions is a choice between two fundamental values; they are and remain essentially incommensurate.

It should be clear, though, that one need not be agnostic about which theory of justice is desirable. As will become apparent when *Milwaukee Spring II* and the Saturn Project are discussed, we can come to quite distinct views regarding the justice of these two different approaches to local labor relations. Before moving to these options, the elements of the subsequent argument can be briefly stated. First, it is contended that EOO is conceptually flawed, because it legitimizes injustice in the name of justice. To the extent that *Milwaukee Spring II* is based on logic derived from EOO, there are good reasons for supposing the NLRB is acting unjustly. Second, it is contended that as EOO makes no allowances for economic circumstances it is inevitably compromised as a policy model relevant for future labor relations. Its legal image ignores the real significance of contemporary circumstances because it idealizes the relationships between employers and employees. Third, the NLRB approach will likely exacerbate tensions between employers and unions, at a time when collective collaboration is at a premium. The fundamental problem with the NLRB approach is that it is unjust.

On the other hand, the Saturn Project model appears *relatively* more just. To the extent that it follows the logic of EOR, it can claim to offer a just solution to current international problems. That is, the Saturn Project appears sensitive to the relative material conditions facing unions and management. In addition, because it is premised upon co-determination, where everything is negotiable, then whatever the rewards for the parties involved, the means by which these outcomes are achieved should be relatively just. This does not mean that there need be total equality between the parties to the contract. Rather, the implication is that the end result will be just, even if nominally unequal. In this way, the Saturn Project may be a more desirable model for achieving full employment.

Milwaukee Spring II

In *Milwaukee Spring*, the NLRB was involved in adjudicating whether or not an employer could relocate production from one unionized plant to another, nonunionized, plant during the term of a collective bargaining contract (Johnston 1986). The firm had shifted production from its Milwaukee plant to another in Illinois after failing to win wage concessions from the union. The UAW brought suit against the company before the NLRB in 1982, claiming that the firm could not escape the terms of the current contract. The Carter Board decided in favor of the union, arguing that the firm was bound by its obligations as implied and expressly stated in the contract. The employer appealed to a federal district court and, on a technical point, the case was returned to the NLRB for rehearing. In 1984, the Reagan NLRB decided in favor of the firm. The Board argued that the firm was allowed to shift production unilaterally because there were no clauses in the contract explicitly prohibiting such relocations.

As was noted in the previous chapter, the Reagan Board also reversed another related decision of the Carter Board in *Otis Elevator II* (1984). The Board held that the firm in question was not required to bargain with the union over plant closings and production consolidation in another plant despite the fact that the contract was still in force. Their decisions in *Milwaukee Spring II* and *Otis Elevator II* were based upon a decision of the US Supreme Court in *First National Maintenance* (1981). There the Court argued that management had a prerogative in matters relating to their operations so long as local labor costs were not *the* determinate factor in deciding to relocate production. The crucial issue for the Board has become the right of management to conduct their business without undue interference from labor over decisions to restructure operations, close and open plants, introduce labor-saving technology, and the like. Put slightly differently, the Board has narrowed the scope of collective bargaining by narrowing the legitimate interests of labor to issues of compensation.

According to some commentators these cases, and other related ones, constitute a concerted attack by the Board on meaningful collective bargaining (St. Antoine 1987). All issues other than compensation (narrowly interpreted) become non-mandatory bargaining issues, and as a consequence organized labor are drastically limited in their attempts to bargain over the changing economic environment.

It is tempting to interpret the actions of the Reagan Board as yet another instance of the Reagan administration's hostility to organized labor. While such an interpretation may have merit, the issues are deeper than simple vindictiveness. In a way, the Board is developing an economic policy by broadening managements' prerogatives when responding to changing economic circumstances. As was mentioned earlier, one aim of the Board, and the Reagan administration, is to foster economic competitiveness. Maximum national economic growth is the objective, economic efficiency is the rule. And if, as a result of current interpretations of local labor–management rights, the strength of unions is whittled away, one cannot imagine that the Board would find this an unfortunate consequence.

Is this policy just? Clearly there is evidence to conclude that it is not. But it is not enough to disagree with the policy's outcomes. That would leave its rationale intact and would focus attention on compensation or redistribution, rather than its underlying logic. To repeat, substantive justice is more about the design of the rules of an economic system than about adjudicating outcomes. In this context, the underlying logic of the Board appears to be fundamentally flawed in terms of substantive justice. To the extent that the Board uses EOO as a reference point (albeit implicitly) to justify its interpretations of management rights, it shares in the logical faults of this model of justice. In particular, its assumption that management and labor are substantially equal in terms of their legal rights allows the Board to justify injustice. How is this sleight of hand accomplished?

Embedded in the *Milwaukee Spring II* decision are a series of related moves and assumptions. The Board begins by invoking a rights theory of justice, wherein labor and management are treated equally in terms of their legal standing as free individuals. Without regard to their respective material circumstances, the Board then assigns to labor and management certain functional roles. Management manages, labor labors. These functional roles take precedence over collective bargaining and have an almost natural status; it appears that the Board assumes these roles to be natural. Then, the Board supposes that since these are their normal roles, their respective rights allow them a wide range of discretion within their proper domains. Since it is also assumed that labor and management freely chose their roles, there can be no coercion, or indeed any reason to suspect that the respective parties are unequal.

Of course, the Board is not interested in material equality so much as legal equality. Any interference with the exercise of the parties' free will (given their prescribed functional responsibilities) would then be interpreted as unjust. Given this rationale, it is little wonder that collective bargaining comes a very poor third to due process and adjudication. The Board could easily argue that collective bargaining is an unwarranted invasion of managements' legal rights. Indeed, this is precisely their rationale.

A related move the Board makes in reaching its decisions is to idealize the roles of management and labor. This is accomplished by its functional definition of management and labor. But, of course, the Board is very selective in its functional definition of these roles. It does not use customary management–labor practices. Rather, it seems to use an idealized conception that owes more to Adam Smith and the eighteenth century than to contemporary circumstances. Essentially labor and management are type-cast by reference to an ideal image of competitive capitalism. This idealization has some less obvious implications for management. It implies that managers are the immediate agents of stock holders, that management are only the instruments of others' interests. But this seems no more plausible than the type-casting of workers' interests. After all, management in the modern corporation are more than agents. Their interests (job security, benefits, autonomy, etc.) may be more closely identified with workers' interests than with shareholders' interests (returns on investment, the market value of shares, etc.).

The parallels with neoclassical economic theory are readily apparent. A very common theoretical device is to idealize economic relations by the use of an island metaphor. Imagine there are two people isolated on an island, Robinson Crusoe and Man Friday. What would be the most efficient division of labor, given their respective skills? Notice there is no institutional system of collective bargaining, or for that matter any firms. Material circumstances are unimportant except in the resources available. Each individual is treated as a legal equal. Indeed, these two gentlemen are in a state of nature, unencumbered by the supposed unwarranted interference from the state. This metaphor is used in teaching to demonstrate how free exchange can maximize total wealth, as long as each person does what he does best. Perhaps the Board has been reading introductory economics texts, or perhaps it has been influenced by the Chicago School of law and economics (championed by a couple of federal Appeals judges: see Posner 1985).

One does not have to be a professional philosopher to see the problems of this model of justice. There is circularity built into its logic: people are assigned universal rights, functions are invoked to define people's legitimate terrain, and then rights are used to justify this terrain. The fact that we do not inhabit the ideal world of neoclassical economics appears irrelevant. The fact that no attention is paid to the historical *relationships* between labor and management is also irrelevant. It is no wonder that labor see this kind of decision as unjust. It ignores material circumstances when assigning rights, but then idealizes functional roles to provide a terrain for management discretion. Their selectivity in defining functional roles is clearly biased, and their emphasis on ideal rights appears unrelated to material circumstances. Injustice is thus justified by an appeal to a particular theory of justice.

Of course, the Board may well be justified in using an EOO model of justice in that there are different theories of justice that command respect in our society. The choice of any theory of justice is a political act, as the Board itself is a political body. Members of the Board are, of course, appointed by the President. Similarly, any appeal to material circumstances as the basis for judging justice implies a quite different conception of justice (perhaps EOR). So, we have to be cautious in arguing that the Board is unjust in terms which are outside the logic of its own model of justice. But, the suspicion amongst organized labor (and even some management) is that its reasoning is a callous attempt to justify a radical restructuring of local labor relations. The fact that current Board members come from corporate backgrounds and were known to be anti-labor does not help the Board in justifying its interpretations of statute and precedent, or in justifying its underlying conception of justice.[13]

Assuming that this model of local labor relations will nevertheless be followed by the NLRB, what are its implications for labor, and labor–management relations? It is clear that the integrity of the Board will come under increasing scrutiny. To the extent that critiques of the Board, such as the one in this chapter, make a difference in the respect accorded to the Board, we should expect a further loss of confidence in the established institutions of American labor law. This may mean that unions will avoid the Board as much as possible, and even management may find that appeal to the Board will only jeopardize already fragile labor relations. At a time when there is already tremendous stress between management and labor over issues such as plant closing, restructuring, and technological innovation in the work place firms can hardly afford outright confrontations with labor. Yet, there is an attitude amongst management that the Board's bias represents an opportunity to settle old scores. The danger is that the Board's position on so many issues will lead to further labor strife.

A widespread perception that the Board is unjust will also likely damage its effectiveness. Ultimately, the Board depends upon management and unions for its continuity. If the unions do not trust the Board, its capacity to bring order and purpose to the labor relations system will be very limited. Not only will the nation suffer, but there is good reason for doubting the future of the Board itself. The irony is that the Board's goal of a competitive economy may well be compromised by its policies. The Board would have us return to the pre-Wagner Act era; economic warfare is just around the corner.

The Saturn Project

In the last few years, the American auto industry has accomplished a remarkable turnaround. From disaster during the 1981–82 recession, when sales of domestically produced autos fell to record lows and foreign auto companies (notably Japanese) appeared poised to take over the domestic market, to relative prosperity in recent years, the fortunes of firms and workers have swung 180 degrees. This is not to say that foreign competition has receded or that all laid-off workers have been rehired. In point of fact, General Motors, to cite just one company, has shed thousands of workers in the past five years, affecting the economies of many towns and cities of the Midwest. The cost of economic rationalization has been very high, and even now it is not clear that the auto firms have recovered from their past failures (Clark 1986a). Nevertheless, American auto firms are about to embark on a series of major investments in domestic small car manufacturing, something that was thought impossible just a few years ago.

In undertaking this investment program, Ford and Chrysler have signed joint venture agreements with Japanese auto firms. Ford has signed with Mazda Motor Company, and Chrysler has signed with Mitsubishi to form a new company – the Diamond–Star Motor Company. GM has chosen to go it alone in its Saturn Project, and join with Toyota in their joint company called NUMMI. The aim for all companies is to produce a competitive domestic small car for the US market. We should recognize, of course, that all companies continue to import and assemble foreign autos produced by their European and Japanese affiliates.

What is most important about these ventures is the emphasis of all firms on a new form of labor relations. Given the Japanese involvement in these plans it should not come as a surprise that there should be a different form of labor relations; after all, it is often suggested that it is their labor relations system which makes the Japanese so competitive (Gould 1984). But, for GM's Saturn Project at least, the new model of labor relations *depends* on a joint partnership agreement with the UAW. In this Project, the partner is not another foreign auto company, but the union. The Saturn Corporation is the result of a series of intensive GM–UAW committees, including personnel from all levels of the parent Corporation. It is a wholly owned subsidiary of GM, linked to the UAW in a joint venture.

Other companies' attempts at restructuring their production systems have retained some form of affiliation with the UAW. But unlike the Saturn

Project, they have not made any partnership agreements with the union, nor have they made so well-defined agreements with the union regarding preferential hiring of UAW members. And there remain some sensitive issues to be resolved between the UAW and these new ventures. For example, the UAW sought to bargain with Diamond–Star over out-sourcing and the use of foreign components. As well, the UAW sought to make Diamond–Star a bargaining item with Chrysler when it went through renegotiation of its contracts with Chrysler's core facilities. While the Japanese are involved as partners with domestic firms, and as managers of these new plants, it is not obvious that labor relations will be very different from before.

Details of the Saturn Project are sketchy (see Ephlin 1986 and Warren 1986).[14] It is located in Spring Hill, Tennessee, just twenty-two miles from the new Nissan plant in Smyrna.[15] The plant will employ about 6,000 workers, drawn from UAW members employed at other GM facilities (active and inactive). It will pay workers close to current rates in other GM plants, and will have the customary COLA adjustments and related benefits. But, there will be few job classifications (only one production and three to five skilled classifications), compared to over 400 job classifications in other auto plants, and most workers will be covered by permanent job security. More importantly, there will be a conscious effort to eliminate distinctions between management and labor – from cafeteria and parking areas to job assignments and production responsibilities. Indeed, whatever the benefits of the new plant for its workers, the crucial difference between the Saturn Project and other GM facilities will be in the labor–management environment. In these ways, the goal is to create a new labor relations system, organized around principles of co-determination and collective interest.

According to GM and UAW spokesmen, the Saturn Project represents a new form of labor relations in the sense that cooperative interest bargaining is to be the basic mode of labor–management relations. Instead of economic warfare over management rights, the goal is to facilitate the cooperation of labor and management in the creation, design, and production of their new automobile. Instead of economic warfare over wages and working conditions, the goal is to make these issues conditional upon the success of the joint partnership. And, instead of depending upon the NLRB as the forum for adjudicating irreconcilable differences between the parties to the partnership, the goal is to make all matters subject to internal collective bargaining procedures. Essentially, collective bargaining as it is known in the NLRA is to be replaced with local co-determination premised upon the mutual interests of the partnership. The Saturn Project will attempt to duplicate the Nissan experiment, while maintaining a union environment.

Not everyone is enamored of the Saturn Project. There have been some internal tensions within the UAW over the compromises implied by the Saturn Agreement. It is apparent that traditional adversary roles do not fit within the rubric of the new labor relations. It is also apparent that few people know where this kind of model will lead the labor movement. More serious, though, have been the suits brought against the UAW and GM by conservative interests, including the National Right-To-Work Legal Defense Foundation. Tennessee is a right-to-work state, dominated by conservative labor legislation.

Actually there have been a couple of challenges to the Saturn Project. In a complaint filed by the Associated Builders and Contractors (ABC) with the NLRB regional director in Memphis, the ABC alleged that the project contractor had entered into an illegal prehire agreement with construction unions. While the regional director rejected the claim, arguing that the prehire agreement was in fact legal, the ABC sought a ruling from the Board.[16] More serious was the complaint filed with the NLRB's Detroit office: the Foundation charged the UAW and GM with violating the free choice of individuals, and discriminating against nonunion workers.[17] The issue went before the General Council of the NLRB, who rejected this suit as well. The legal challenge was based upon a rights-oriented conception of economic justice.

Is the Saturn Project a more just approach to economic efficiency? Perhaps. To answer this question adequately we must pause for a moment to consider the implied bases of the Saturn Agreement. Trust between labor and management has always been a most fragile aspect of local labor relations. The reasons for this situation are not hard to find. Essentially, American labor law was built upon an assumption of economic warfare. Reconciliation of labor's and management's interests was thought possible only through third-party arbitration or the NLRB. Class antagonisms, based on property ownership rights and labor's dependence upon a ruling elite, are the implied fundamental impediments against mutual trust.

Likewise, reciprocity (mutual sharing and sacrifice) has always foundered upon the historical legacy of American labor relations. It is then obvious why co-determination eschews rights for mutual interests as the basis of negotiation. In such an open-ended partnership, trust and reciprocity can only be developed if both parties are willing to sacrifice their historical rights. Everything must be negotiable. If either party appeals to an outside authority to resolve their differences, the appeal process must be sensitive to maintaining trust and reciprocity. Without trust and reciprocity, both parties will quickly retreat to protecting their own interests, not the interests of the partnership. Thus it is crucial that there be consistency between the underlying logic of the partnership and the basis of adjudication.

However, the conception of economic justice implied by the Saturn Project is very different than that implied in the decisions of the Reagan NLRB. The Saturn agreement begins with an explicit recognition of the parties' material interests. To accommodate these interests, both labor and management sacrifice their legal rights. That is, collective bargaining depends in the first instance upon material circumstances. Universal rights are not important. More critically, though, the first bargain is not supposed to be anything but a notice of intent. Co-determination requires continual negotiation and renegotiation as circumstances change. Consequently, no party is held hostage to past commitments if the material circumstances change so as to alter their evaluation of the bargain.

Economic justice in the Saturn Agreement appears similar to the EOR model of justice reviewed previously. Instead of an ahistorical ordering of universal rights, and an arbitrary definition of functional roles, the agreement attempts to account for material circumstances. Instead of the justifying of outcomes by reference to initial entitlements, outcomes are continuously monitored for their fairness in relation to the goals of the partnership. And, instead of ignoring the chances of fate, the continuous bargaining clause allows for revision in the agreement without having to appeal to a universal set of laws which define in general ideal interests, as opposed to material interests. Notice that economic justice is conceived as a necessary condition for the success of the Saturn Project. Due regard for the parties' interests is part of the procedures for achieving economic success. In this sense, there is a quite specific model of substantive justice built into the partnership agreement between the UAW and GM.

Conclusion

Is the Saturn Project co-determination agreement the way forward for the American labor movement, and local labor relations? On the basis of the argument presented in this chapter, it might be claimed that it is preferable to the current policy of the NLRB. On purely economic justice grounds it seems far superior, and may even deliver more economic success than the NLRB policy. But, we should pause for a moment to consider some of its implications before rushing to canonize the agreement as *the* alternative.

We need to be cautious because the agreement is an experiment. For all the publicity associated with it, there is no tangible evidence regarding its real consequences. Given the time frame for the whole Project, it will be many years before we will be able to evaluate its successes and failures. Since it is in its beginning stages, neither the union nor management are able to provide much more than superficial sketches of the provisions and how it will work. On the other hand, the Project does represent the basis of a quite different philosophy towards labor relations, a philosophy which has adherents in other auto companies and other sectors of American industry.

If it is successful, what might be some of its more important implications? At the outset, it is clear that the agreement is quite exclusionary. To sustain the kind of collaborative enterprise envisioned by the agreement, it is very important to have loyal and committed workers (labor and management). Practically, this means workers with previous experience in the auto industry who are committed to a different form of labor–management relations. The Saturn Project will be a kind of graduate school for workers who are adept at auto production and human relations. Necessarily this means that only a few workers will have the chance to work in the Project. This is bound to have political ramifications.

Just consider the State of Tennessee. In the last few years, the legislature and the Governor have essentially bought an industry with the locational inducement packages they have offered GM and Nissan. Yet Tennessee residents will not automatically have access to the GM jobs, nor will nonunion workers be able to take jobs in the company. Now, this need not imply fundamental criticisms of the Project. Rather, the point is that whatever the benefits of the plant, these benefits will be narrowly distributed. The logic of the agreement requires highly integrated social relations. For the NLRB to force the company to hire nonunion workers and workers who have little experience in the industry would seriously compromise the internal coherence of the new labor–management system. The Saturn Project would no longer be the graduate school for labor relations.

Similarly, there may be internal political problems in the union because of the distinctiveness of the agreement vis-à-vis existing auto contracts. At a time when the UAW is negotiating with other automakers for new contracts aimed at increasing workers' wages and benefits, the union is also sanctioning the Saturn Agreement, which will be quite unlike the industry norm. The union is under pressure from all quarters, firms, governments, the press, and their own members to compromise on all manner of contract issues. Rightly or wrongly there is a public perception that the unions are to blame for America's lack of competitive muscle. At the same time, Japanese companies which are beginning production in the US are also demanding different treatment from the union. In these circumstances, the union must simultaneously support the Saturn Project (thereby supporting an important innovation in labor relations designed to create a competitive domestic small car) and limit the spillover effects of the agreement into other contracts (thereby supporting the interests of the rank and file of the union). The union leadership are facing a difficult time. They have to rationalize their decisions, and win support from the rank and file.

The Saturn Project has very important implications for the future of organized labor. As the agreement is between the UAW and GM, it is between two institutions as opposed to between individuals. The parties' interests are not, in the first instance at least, individual members' (whether labor or management) separate interests; rather they are the interests of the union and GM. In this respect, the union is more than a body representing members' interests: the union made the agreement prior to any of its members being hired. Indeed, one might argue that the agreement was only possible because the union was willing to go beyond its conventional role as just a representative of members' interests.

Of course, many American unions have been entrepreneurial in the past. Union officers have often had as one of their roles the responsibility of developing new employment opportunities for their members. But the Saturn Project goes beyond business unionism. The agreement has close parallels with European corporatism – a system of public agreements between leaders of major organizations to facilitate the cooperation of their respective members in furthering national objectives (see Przeworski 1985; Schmitter and Lehmbruch 1979). While we have some way to go before corporatism is the dominant political model of the US (the skeptics amongst us might reasonably argue that corporatism is impossible in the US), corporatism does offer unions an important role in society at a time when they are fighting for survival.

The Saturn Project not only bolsters union strength, but actually requires a well-developed worker organization to be successful. That is, the underlying logic of co-determination is premised upon the existence of institutions who are able to bargain on behalf of workers and management. Furthermore, it is not enough that these institutions simply exist; they must have a measure of authority over their individual members. Thus, the Saturn Project is only possible if there are unions, a point that has not been lost on RTW opponents of the agreement. For unions to play such a vital role in co-determination, they must be protected from those in government and business who would want to destroy them. If the NLRB is successful in narrowing the powers of unions, and further limiting the effectiveness of their organizing drives, it is debatable whether the current policies of the NLRB are consistent with the philosophy underlying the Saturn Project.

So, the nation faces a fundamental choice in the next few years. At one level, the choice is between two different models of economic justice, two different ways of achieving economic prosperity, two different ways of accommodating economic restructuring. At another level, though, the choice is between alternative forms of society. The Saturn Project implies a form of corporatism. Indeed, it implies quite different political values: group interests as opposed to individual interests, co-determination as opposed to economic warfare, and a culture of collective action as opposed to American individualism.

PART V

Prospects for organized labor

IO

Republicans, Democrats, and the southern veto

Given evidence of the decline of organized labor, it is not surprising that there should be pressure to reform the rules governing the representation process, the National Labor Relations Board, and American labor law in general.[1] In recent years, there have been a series of hearings in Congress reviewing the integrity and efficacy of federal labor law. In 1984 there were hearings on the question: Has labor law failed? Evidence collected during hearings on this question concerned management practices in representation elections, the NLRB's adjudication of disputes arising out of representation elections, and the design and enforcement of current statutes relating to the representation election process. The majority report of the House Subcommittee on Labor–Management Relations concluded that labor law had failed and had been "deteriorating throughout the 1970s [and] has currently reached crisis proportions" (1).[2]

Implied, even sometimes explicitly identified in these hearings, were a couple of assumptions. First, it was assumed that reforming the regulatory environment (rules of representation elections, treatment of unfair labor practices, etc.) would substantially improve labor unions' electoral performance. Second, it was further assumed that only labor law reform could ensure the future of organized labor as an American institution.[3] It is obvious that labor law reform was not a priority of the Reagan administration; if there had been labor law reform during this era, it would have been very hostile to the interests of organized labor. It is argued in this chapter that significant labor law reform is unlikely even if Congress and the presidency were controlled by the Democratic Party. Previous attempts to reform labor law in better circumstances failed because labor's congressional supporters were not able to marshal support from southern Democrats. Sectional or local interests have dominated partisanship in previous crucial votes for labor law reform.

These arguments are explored through an analysis of post-1960 labor-initiated labor law reform movements. Included are the 1965/66 campaign to repeal Section 14(b) of the National Labor Relations Act (the right-to-work provision),[4] campaigns to rescind application of Section 8(b) 4(A) concerning secondary boycotts in the construction industry, and the labor law reform bill of 1977. Also considered are recent attempts to soften the stance and decisions of the NLRB. Despite Democrat Presidents and large Democrat majorities in Congress during the first and 1977 secondary boycott campaigns, organized labor's best chances for revision and strengthening of the Act were stymied by opposition from Senate Republicans and southern Democrats. More recently, with the blessing of the Reagan administration leading Republicans introduced a series of bills designed to return organized labor to its nineteenth-century status as just another form of restraint of trade, or worse, a criminal conspiracy.[5]

A brief historical perspective

Labor law reform has a long and varied history. As in so many other areas of social and economic policy, President Franklin D. Roosevelt's New Deal was the watershed of national labor–management relations policy.[6] In his message to Congress on 24 May 1937 regarding the importance of the Fair Labor Standards Act Roosevelt expressed a sentiment which informed so much of the labor law reform legislation of the New Deal era. He observed in part that "goods produced under conditions which do not meet rudimentary standards of decency should be regarded as contraband and ought not be allowed to pollute the channels of interstate trade." Having noted industry and regional variations in employment standards, Roosevelt suggested that "there are a few rudimentary standards of which we may properly ask general and widespread observance. Failure to observe them must be regarded as socially and economically unwarranted under almost any circumstance" (quoted in Whittaker and Ciccone 1978:11).

In the early years of this century, labor law reform movements were concerned with instituting and strengthening state legislation mandating minimum standards of factory employment, and ensuring adequate regulation of child employment. Fewer than half the states of the Union had passed statutes proscribing a minimum age for work in 1900. Most of those states with minimum age laws restricted coverage to factory work; agricultural work was exempted, as was work in more dangerous sectors such as mining. By 1913, the year the federal government established the Department of Labor, many states had legislated fourteen as the minimum age for factory work, although there were still numerous forms of exemption. In an historical survey of labor laws, the Bureau of Labor Statistics (1962:14) remarked that as of 1913, "the elementary principles of modern state child labor laws were already established" even though these laws "left much to be desired." Only after the passage of the Fair Labor Standards Act in 1938,[7] and its constitutional test before the US Supreme Court in 1941,[8] were there reasonable cross-state minimum standards of employment.[9]

Prior to the passage of the National Labor Relations Act in 1935, federal regulation of organized labor was based upon anti-trust commercial trade laws and *laissez-faire* conceptions of free contract, neither of which were explicitly designed to apply to collective bargaining. The Sherman Act served as the statutory basis for the US Supreme Court in the *Danbury Hatters* case treating union contracts as a form of "restraint of trade or commerce."[10] Section 1 of the Act began: "every contract, combination in the form of a trust or otherwise, or conspiracy, in restraint of trade or commerce ... is hereby declared to be illegal." The Clayton Act of 1914, which amended the Sherman Act, is thought to have been designed to distinguish a sphere of action for organized labor: a sphere unencumbered by doctrinaire applications of the Sherman Act to labor unions. Despite the opening phrase of Section 6 of the Clayton Act, which asserted "that the labor of a human being is not a commodity or article of commerce," successively narrow interpretations of the Act by the US Supreme Court based upon earlier case law effectively emasculated the power of organized labor.[11]

Through a series of acts and amendments, including the Norris–LaGuardia Act of 1932, amendments to the Railway Labor Act in 1934 and 1936, and the NLRA, the federal government established a national code for the conduct of local labor relations which has been the basis of American labor law through to the present day.[12] New Deal labor legislation sought to establish an affirmative policy for collective bargaining, union organizing, and labor–management relations. There can be no doubt that the labor code was conceived at the time as a radical shift in the federal government's sentiment towards unions as legitimate institutions. The last paragraph of Section 1 of the Wagner Act effectively summarized the sense of legitimacy bestowed on unions: "It is hereby declared to be the policy of the United States ... [to] encourage the practice and procedure of collective bargaining ... the exercise by workers of full freedom of association, self-organization, and designation of representatives of their own choosing for the purpose of negotiating the terms and conditions of their employment."[13]

In many respects, however, the package of labor laws passed in the early 1930s are not the labor laws of the 1980s. From the moment the Wagner Act was passed, campaigns were begun to repeal, amend, and revise the Act. Both management and labor have sponsored such legislative initiatives, though arguably only management have been particularly successful. By amendment, judicial interpretation, and passage of new labor laws, organized labor's legal environment has become progressively more conservative over the past fifty years. Karl Klare (1978) argued that the judiciary systematically deradicalized the Wagner Act by limiting the applicability of the Act and failing to enforce decisions vigorously by the NLRB. By many accounts (see Morris 1983), the Taft–Hartley amendments of 1947 also dramatically limited the powers of unions with respect to their members, and with respect to states' right-to-work laws. Whether because of a genuine concern for the democratic rights of unionists, or for more likely conservative interests in limiting the exercise of union power, the result was much the same. And others have suggested that the Landrum–Griffin Act of 1959 unfairly discriminated against labor by requiring certain reporting to the federal government by unions but not management.

The campaign to repeal Section 14(b)

Passed as part of the 1947 Taft–Hartley amendments to the NLRA, Section 14(b) holds that:

[N]othing in this Act shall be construed as authorizing the execution or application of agreements requiring membership in a labor organization as a condition of employment in any State or Territory in which such execution or application is prohibited by State or Territorial law.

In conjunction with Section 8(a)(3), which outlaws discrimination in hiring and employment tenure with respect to membership or nonmembership in labor organizations, Section 14(b) enabled states to pass their own laws regulating union shop agreements. These laws are, by definition, more restrictive than the provisions of the Taft–Hartley amendments; Section 8(a)(3) effectively restricts states from passing laws which would provide for greater union security. Commonly described, Section 14(b) is the provision which enables state RTW legislation. By the end of 1947 11 southern and western states and one midwestern state (Iowa) had passed RTW legislation; by 1953/54 five other southern and western states (Nevada) had passed RTW laws, and by 1965 (the year of the repeal campaign analyzed here) there were 19 states with RTW laws (see table 10.1).

Since passage of the amendments there have been a number of attempts to revise and repeal Section 14(b).[14] Not all attempts at revision have been initiated by labor. During the 83rd Congress (1953/54), the Eisenhower administration sponsored and supported Senate bills which would have strengthened states' regulation of organized labor. There were a number of proposals to repeal Section 14(b) so as to encourage states to broaden their application of anti-labor legislation to cover compulsory arbitration, strikes, and local matters (see Cox 1954 for a wide-ranging review). Senator Smith

Table 10.1. *States by right-to-work (*) status and region, 1965*

North/Midwest	South/Southwest	West/Mountain
Connecticut	Alabama (*)	Alaska
Illinois	Arizona (*)	California
Indiana	Arkansas (*)	Colorado
Iowa (*)	Delaware	Hawaii
Kansas (*)	Florida (*)	Idaho
Maine	Georgia (*)	Montana
Massachusetts	Kentucky	Nebraska (*)
Michigan	Louisiana	North Dakota (*)
Minnesota	Maryland	Oklahoma
Missouri	Mississippi (*)	Oregon
New Hampshire	Nevada (*)	South Dakota (*)
New Jersey	New Mexico	Utah (*)
New York	North Carolina (*)	Washington
Ohio	South Carolina (*)	Wyoming (*)
Pennsylvania	Tennessee (*)	
Rhode Island	Texas (*)	
Vermont	Virginia (*)	
West Virginia		
Wisconsin		

(R – Florida) introduced a bill which would have allowed the NLRB to decline jurisdiction in cases where effects of labor disputes on interstate commerce were small. Another bill introduced by Senator Goldwater (R – Arizona) would have given states the power to regulate strikes and picketing in firms and industries covered by the NLRB.

At the time, the argument for repeal and revision of Section 14(b) was promoted by Republicans in terms of states' rights. But as a labor-oriented pamphlet noted, the "proposals would give the States only the power to add their own anti-union restrictions to those of the federal law – while keeping the federal law also in effect" (Congress of Industrial Organizations, 1955:31). These attempts to strengthen states' powers over organized labor were not successful.

The 1965/66 campaign to repeal Section 14(b) was a labor-initiated campaign. It was led by House Democrats and had the support of President Lyndon Johnson. In his State of the Union message to Congress on 4 January 1965, the President announced at the end of his speech that he would "propose to Congress changes in the Taft–Hartley Act, including Section 14(b). I will do so hoping to reduce conflicts that for several years have divided Americans in various states of our union."[15] On the same day, Representative Frank Thompson (D – New Jersey), chairman of the Special

Labor Subcommittee of the House Education and Labor Committee, introduced a bill (HR 77) to delete Section 14(b), thus obviating state RTW provisions.

Opponents of repeal included the New Citizens Committee to Preserve Taft–Hartley (formed through an alliance of the National Association of Manufacturers, the US Chamber of Commerce, and the National Right To Work Committee), and Adam Clayton Powell (D – New York), chairman of the House Education and Labor Committee. Given the previous campaigns by business groups to amend the NLRA, culminating in the Taft–Hartley Act of 1947 and their unsuccessful campaign in 1953/54 to extend the powers of states over organized labor, the opposition of business groups to the repeal of Section 14(b) was expected. Not expected was Powell's opposition. He argued that repeal would place "the factories and industries in the south in the hands of unions that will not allow Negroes to join them."[16] Powell announced that he would not support repeal unless anti-discrimination provisions were written into the Taft–Hartley Act. Ultimately, Powell withdrew his opposition to repeal, making a deal with House leaders for support of a bill he introduced (HR 9222) extending Title VII of the Civil Rights Act of 1964 to all industries employing eight or more people. Business groups remained fundamentally opposed.

Hearings were held on the bill to repeal Section 14(b) in May and June of 1965. It was voted and reported to the House by Powell on 17 June, and finally passed by the House on 28 July with a close 221–203 vote in favor of the measure. During hearings and passage of the bill, it became evident that few Republicans supported repeal and few southern Representatives, whether Republican or Democrat, supported repeal.

A simple but profound pattern was apparent in the voting record for and against repeal. Northern Democrats voted overwhelmingly in favor of repeal; southern Democrats from RTW states voted overwhelmingly against repeal (compared to a 2–1 vote margin in favor of repeal in southern non-RTW states); and western Democrats also voted overwhelmingly in favor of repeal, whatever their state RTW status. Without support from northern Republicans, the measure would not have been passed. In fact, the eighteen vote margin in favor of repeal was all Republican, and all but one of the Republican votes in favor of repeal came from northern states. Fourteen of those positive Republican votes came from just three states: Massachusetts (2 votes), New York (6 votes), and Pennsylvania (6 votes). Essentially, a combination of regional sentiment and RTW status amongst southern Democrats nearly defeated the measure. Without support from Republicans from northern industrial states, the repeal measure would have had little chance of passage.

Table 10.2. *Senate voting patterns by political party, right-to-work status, and geographical region for and against cloture of debate on repeal of Section 14(b), 11 October 1965*

Region/ RTW status	Democrats		Republicans		Total
	For	Against	For	Against	
North*	22	2	3	9	36
South					
RTW	1	14		2	17
n-RTW	3	3	1	3	10
West					
RTW	4	1		7	12
n-RTW	10	1	1	5	17
Total	40	21	5	26	92

Note: * Includes Iowa and Kansas, both RTW states

Having been passed by the House, the campaign shifted to the Senate. Hearings had begun on the Senate version (S 256) in late June. By August, the Senate Committee on Labor and Education had approved consideration of the measure, and in September the measure was reported to the floor of the Senate. In early October, a filibuster was initiated by Dirksen (R – Illinois), forcing a cloture vote on 11 October. With 92 senators voting, cloture was lost by a 45–47 vote margin, far short of the necessary 62 votes required for cloture. As in the House vote, the Senate cloture vote reflected regional sentiment and RTW status. Northern and western Democrats voted overwhelmingly in favor of cloture; southern Democrats voted overwhelmingly against cloture (the Democrat vote in southern non-RTW states was split 3–3 for and against cloture). Only 3 of 12 northern Republicans voted for cloture, including Smith of Maine, Case of New Jersey, and Javits of New York. Combined with a Republican 5–26 vote against cloture, southern Democrats effectively vetoed any chance of taking a vote to repeal Section 14(b) (see table 10.2).

Two further cloture votes were taken. In his State of the Union address to Congress on 24 January 1966, President Johnson once again affirmed his support of the repeal of Section 14(b). Under the heading of union security agreements, the President argued that "strong and responsible collective bargaining is an important instrument of a free and healthy economy. To improve its functioning and to make the national labor policy uniform throughout the country, I again urge the Congress to repeal Section 14(b)."[17] This was the strongest public appeal by the President for passage of repeal over the whole campaign. The basic claim made by Johnson was for a *national* labor policy, as opposed to a geographically fragmented system of regulation. In making this claim, Johnson reflected the reality of the coalitions for and against repeal; sectional interests dominated party affiliations.

On the same day as Johnson's State of the Union address, the Democrat Majority Leader (Mansfield) reintroduced a motion to bring the repeal bill to a vote. Dirksen again initiated a filibuster. Cloture was called for but lost on 8 and 10 February. On both occasions, there was a slim majority in favor of cloture (51–48 on 8 February and 50–49 on 10 February), but in both instances the vote in favor of cloture fell far short of the necessary 66 votes required. The difference between the first cloture vote and the latter two votes was only that seven senators who did not vote in the first cloture call voted in the second and third cloture votes. These senators voted according to their announced (but unvoted) positions in the first vote. Only one senator changed his vote regarding cloture over the three calls for cloture. McGovern (D – South Dakota) voted no to cloture on the first vote, yes on the second, and no on the third. South Dakota is, and was at that time, a RTW state. With the failure of the third cloture vote, the campaign to repeal Section 14(b) was abandoned.

In retrospect, the campaign to repeal Section 14(b) appears to have been ambitious in scope, bound for failure, and yet another beginning in a much longer campaign to reform American labor law. It was ambitious because of its central premise: repeal of Section 14(b) was a necessary step to nationalize American labor policy. In this sense, the campaign sought to return to basic suppositions of the New Deal era. The federal government was to have *the* crucial role in regulating and facilitating organized labor. A national labor policy was to be an important means of sustaining national economic prosperity. And local (state) issues were to be adjudicated with reference to one common law. In terms of the rhetoric of the New Deal, the repeal campaign asserted that only the national government could fairly administer labor law. It was also ambitious in the sense of its timing. Coming just eighteen years after passage of the Taft–Hartley Act of 1947 and a decade of domestic turmoil about supposed communist infiltration of government and organized labor, the campaign to repeal Section 14(b) sought to reverse congressional sentiment of the 1950s. Instead of allowing states further avenues for controlling the power of organized labor, a common aim of 1950s reform legislation, the aim of the campaign to repeal Section 14(b), was to strip states of any power to regulate unions.

The campaign was bound to fail for a variety of reasons. Most obviously, repeal of Section 14(b) threatened southern economic interests. A dominant view amongst business interests at the time was that RTW legislation had made a positive contribution to southern economic development. While the evidence for this view is debatable (see Congress of Industrial Organizations 1955), during debate and hearings on repeal this argument was advanced by southern interests time and time again. It was claimed that RTW legislation was necessary to industrialize the South. This claim when coupled with claims for state rights and the distinctive heritage of southern labor relations combined to make support of repeal a sectional issue as opposed to a partisan issue for southern Democrats. Even so, the repeal measure passed the House.

In the Senate, the arguments were the same. But at this level, it appears unlikely that the measure would have been voted upon even if all Democrats had supported cloture. With 99 senators voting, 66 votes were required for cloture. However, there were just 61 Democrats. To gain cloture would have required the cooperation of the 5 Republicans who voted in favor of cloture in a losing cause plus the complete loyalty of all 61 Democrats. It is very doubtful if all 5 would have voted against their party's leadership in a strictly partisan contest. And, even if cloture had been achieved by extraordinary partisan solidarity, it is even more doubtful if a majority would have been mustered to pass the repeal bill.

One of the most articulate and forceful Republican supporters of repeal was Senator Javits of New York. A month before the first cloture vote, Javits argued for a more extensive repeal measure that would include expedited representation elections and enforcement of unfair labor practice decisions. Javits suggested that the repeal legislation was too narrow: "I view 14(b) as only part of a much larger problem – the need for a general review and revision of the Labor–Management Relations Act in a number of important respects" (31).[18] While a comprehensive labor law reform package was to take another twelve years before it was introduced in Congress, Javits' sentiments were apparently shared by many House Democrats. It was also apparent from the record of debates and speeches that the perspective taken by President Lyndon Johnson and House leaders was broader and more encompassing. Perhaps the whole campaign was misconceived in the first place. Perhaps the best strategy would have been to tackle labor law reform directly without focusing so much attention on Section 14(b).

Common-site picketing and labor law reform

With the election of Jimmy Carter as President of the United States in late 1976, and a Congress dominated by the Democrat Party, it appeared that organized labor would finally be able to achieve its legislative agenda.[19] By common consent, it was assumed that President Carter would return the legislative agenda set in the early years of Johnson's administration. Very early in 1977, Representative Frank Thompson (D – New Jersey) introduced two labor law reform bills. The first bill (HR 77), introduced on 4 January 1977, was described by Thompson as a labor law reform package designed to reform the administration and implementation of the NLRA. The second measure (HR 3500), introduced on 16 February 1977, was designed to allow common-site picketing in the construction industry. Both measures sought revision of federal labor law, and both had the support of organized labor. In a sense, both pieces of legislation were to be the culmination of years of lobbying by labor to revise federal labor statutes.

Labor's optimism and the legislative paths of labor law reform during the period 1976–78 were based, in part, upon a previous attempt by congressional leaders and the US Secretary of Labor (John Dunlop) during the Ford administration to overrule the 1951 decision of the US Supreme Court in *NLRB* v. *Denver Building and Construction Trades Council* (1951). In that case, the Court upheld a decision by the NLRB that it was an unfair labor practice for unions to picket the general contractor on a common-situs construction project in order to force him to cease doing business with a nonunion sub-contractor. The NLRB based its decision on the Taft–Hartley amendments to the NLRA, specifically Section 8(b)(4)(A), which outlaws secondary boycotts.

Despite close relationships between general contractors and sub-contractors in the construction industry, the NLRB argued in *Denver* that the sub-contractor was in fact the primary target of the union and that the general contractor was a third party in the dispute between the sub-contractor and the union. By this line of reasoning, the sub-contractor was treated as a separate business, unrelated to the general contractor. This assumption was necessary to sustain the argument that picketing the general contractor was a secondary boycott. This opinion was then supported by two further decisions of the Court in *International Brotherhood of Electrical Workers, Local 501* v. *NLRB* (1951) and *NLRB* v. *International Rice Milling Co* (1951).[20]

Since the 1951 decision, there have been many attempts to legalize secondary boycotts in the construction industry. As early as 1954, the Senate recommitted an omnibus labor bill which would have reversed the ruling. In 1959, 1960, and 1965 attempts were made to bring the issue to a vote in both the House and the Senate. In April 1975, Frank Thompson brought the issue to the House in the form of a bill Protecting the Economic Rights of Labor (HR 5900). With the support of the US Secretary of Labor (John Dunlop), hearings were held on the bill in June 1975, and the bill was reported to the

Table 10.3. *Senate voting patterns by political party, right-to-work status, and geographical region for and against common-site picketing, 19 November 1975 (HR 5900)*

Region/ RTW status	Democrats		Republicans		Total
	For	Against	For	Against	
North*	21	3	8	4	36
South					
RTW		15		9	24
n-RTW	4	2	1	2	9
West					
RTW	5			7	12
n-RTW	11		2	3	16
Total	41	20	11	25	97

Note: * Includes Iowa and Kansas, both RTW states

House on 18 July 1975. Thompson met with President Ford during this period and reported that the President supported the bill so long as a clause was added instituting a new form of collective bargaining in the construction industry. After debate and amendment, the House passed the bill on 25 July 1975 by a 230–178 margin. The margin of victory was the result of two strategies. House leaders were able to attract some southern (Democrat) votes in favor of the bill, and convince others (Democrats and Republicans) not in favor not to cast their votes. So as to garner support from southern Representatives, an amendment was accepted allowing states to pass their own common-site laws.

The measure was debated in the Senate, passed by a 52–45 margin (19 November 1975), and forwarded to a conference committee. In terms of voting patterns, the measure was passed by the Senate through a coalition of northern Democrats and Republicans and western Democrats (table 10.3). As in previous attempts to pass labor law reform through the Senate, southern Democrats and Republicans were strongly opposed to passage. With further amendments, the conference committee report was then accepted by both Houses of Congress and presented to the President for signature. On 2 January 1976, to the surprise of many in both parties, Gerald Ford vetoed the bill.[21] In his message to Congress Ford indicated that his previous support of the bill was unfounded and that the bill itself did not include necessary provisions which would ensure stability in the construction industry. John Dunlop resigned in protest. Since there was insufficient support in Congress to override the veto, the leadership of the House dropped further consideration of the measure.

One year later, with a new Democrat President just inaugurated, Frank Thompson introduced a series of bills designed to reform federal labor law systematically. With respect to common-situs picketing, Thompson introduced (16 February 1977) HR 3500, a bill allowing for Equal Treatment of Craft and Industrial Workers. Like HR 5900, the bill was designed to allow secondary boycotts in the construction industry. The bill proposed to amend Section 8(b) to make the construction industry an exception to the general provisions of the Taft–Hartley Act. Also included were provisions of HR 5900 related to collective bargaining in the construction industry. Thompson's modified bill (HR 4250) was reported to the House in March 1977, and was voted upon on 23 March 1977. Another surprise was in store for labor's supporters. The modified common-situs bill, previously supported by the House in 1975, was defeated by a 205–217 margin. Compared to passage of HR 5900 in 1975, HR 4250 was lost in the House because of defections by northern Republicans, and many more votes cast against the bill by southern Democrats. In retrospect, it appears that the leadership of the House assumed passage of the bill to be guaranteed. Their lobbying attention was focused upon the Senate, which they believed was the real impediment to legislative reform. They failed to appreciate the effectiveness of employer organizations' lobbying efforts.

On 19 July 1977, Thompson reintroduced his labor law reform bill, the Labor Law Reform Act of 1977 (HR 8410), in conjunction with Javits (R – New York) in the Senate. On the previous day, President Carter had sent a message to Congress in support of the bill, emphasizing that reforms were necessary to "guarantee employees the right to choose freely their representatives." According to Carter the bill was designed "to make NLRB procedures fairer, prompter, and more predictable," and "protect the rights of labor and management by strengthening NLRB sanctions against those who break the law."[22] Provisions of the bill included expanding the NLRB to seven members, instituting a summary review procedure for ALJ decisions, expediting elections so that they were held within fifteen days, providing equal access to unions and management alike in election campaigns, and resolving disputes over unit determination by rule. There were also provisions to penalize employers found guilty of consistent violations of the law by withholding federal contracts.

Essentially, the labor law reform package aimed to improve the electoral procedures of representation campaigns. Deliberately not included were provisions like repeal of Section 14(b) and modification of Section 8(b) 4(A) for the construction industry. In this sense, Thompson's bill was quite conservative. It dealt primarily with the rules of the union representation election process, not the overall conception of the rules of American labor–management relations. The goal was to improve the procedures of the electoral process. In opposition to Thompson's bill, John Erlenborn (R – Illinois) introduced a more radical reform bill for labor law just five days before Thompson introduced the labor law reform bill. Erlenborn's bill, HR 8310, An Employee's Bill of Rights, was designed to strengthen members' rights against unions. It was not acted upon in committee or on the floor of the House.

Hearings on the bill were conducted in Washington DC and Roanoke Rapids, North Carolina. Evidence in support of the bill came from previous Secretaries of Labor, unions, and the NLRB. Evidence against the bill came from employer organizations and public-interest groups like the National Right to Work Committee. Conscious of the failure to pass revision of Section 8(b) in the House just a few months previously, organized labor undertook a massive lobbying exercise. At the same time employer groups took the offensive. It was probably the most intensive and protracted lobbying campaign on any single piece of legislation during the Carter presidency. Unfortunately for labor, the bill failed to pass both Houses of Congress.

The bill was passed in the House of Representatives by an overwhelming margin of 257–163 on 6 October 1977. Compared to the votes cast for and against the common-situs bill in March, support for the bill came from northern Democrats and Republicans, and a significant number (though not a majority) of southern Democrats. In fact, organized labor was able to collect 88 southern and western Democrat votes and 28 northern Republican votes in favor of labor law reform, whereas previously they had only been able to marshal 62 and 12 votes respectively.

When the campaign to reform labor law moved to the Senate, it became quickly apparent that it would be difficult to bring the measure to a vote. The Republican leadership announced a filibuster to stall the legislation. Debate on the measure began in May 1978. From 7 June 1978 to 22 June 1978 six cloture votes were conducted. All failed. The first cloture vote failed even to record a majority in favor, and was lost by a 42–47 vote margin (60 votes were necessary for cloture) (table 10.4). The closest cloture vote came on 14 June 1978, where the motion was won by a 58–41 margin but failed to find the necessary 60 votes to force cloture. Not only did all cloture votes fail, but the Democrat leadership were forced to amend the bill drastically to garner support from northern Republicans.

On 8 June 1978 Senator Byrd introduced a series of amendments to limit the equal access provision for unions to employers' plants to after-hours,

Table 10.4. *Senate voting patterns by political party, right-to-work status, and geographical region for and against cloture of debate on labor law reform, 7 June [14 June] 1978 (HR 8140)*

Region/ RTW status	Democrats		Republicans		Total
	For	Against	For	Against	
North*	21 [24]	1	5 [10]	7 [4]	34 [38]
South					
RTW	1 [2]	15 [14]		7 [7]	23 [23]
n-RTW	2 [4]	2 [2]	1 [1]	3 [3]	8 [10]
West					
RTW	2 [3]	1 [1]		8 [8]	11 [12]
n-RTW	8 [11]		2 [3]	3 [2]	13 [16]
Total	34 [44]	19 [17]	8 [14]	28 [24]	89 [99]

Note: * Includes Iowa and Kansas, both RTW states

extend the deadline for union representation elections to 35 days, widen the reference point for determination of make whole remedies, and allow employers to receive government contracts once they had shown that they had remedied unfair labor practices. In these ways the labor law reform bill was stripped of any real reform. The contest to achieve cloture became a symbolic struggle between lobbyists employed by organized labor and employer groups rather than a struggle over substance.

Comparison of the first and closest cloture votes (table 10.4) provides a lesson in the continuity of geography and the fragility of partisanship. For all the lobbying efforts of organized labor, they were unable to alter the overwhelming vote against cloture by southern Democrats. It does appear that organized labor was able to shift a significant number of northern Republican votes in favor of cloture, and mobilize a small group of western and northern Democrats to participate in the vote for cloture. When it might have made a significant difference to the outcome of the penultimate cloture vote, the President was unable to convince even one of the two Democrat senators from Georgia to support cloture.[23] These two senators voted against cloture in every vote. In fact, over the course of the labor law reform movement, 1976–78, Georgia's all-Democrat congressional delegation fundamentally opposed reform, voting against it in most instances and for weakening the reform measures at every opportunity (see table 10.5).

The campaign to reform labor law nearly succeeded. And yet, if we take an historical perspective, it seems to have been destined to fail. Since passage of the Taft–Hartley Act in 1947, there has been a solid congressional bloc

Table 10.5. *Voting patterns (Y = for; N = against) of Georgia's House of Representatives (Democratic) delegation, common-site picketing (HR 4250) and labor law reform (HR 8410), March and October 1977*

House bill	Vote	House action	Vote margin	Date
Common-site picketing				
1. Consideration	7Y 2N	Adopted	297–112	23 March 1977
2. Amendment	7Y 2N	Adopted	212–209	
3. Amendment	4Y 5N	Rejected	181–241	
4. Amendment	9Y	Adopted	252–167	
5. Amendment	2Y 7N	Rejected	115–304	
6. Amendment	9N	Adopted	246–177	
7. Passage	9N	Rejected	205–217	
Labor law reform				
1. Consideration	6Y 4N	Adopted	267–152	4 October 1977
2. Consideration	7Y 3N	Adopted	291–128	
3. Consideration	9Y	Adopted	384–5	5 October 1977
4. Amendment	9Y 1N	Rejected	168–247	
5. Amendment	10Y	Adopted	408–8	
6. Amendment	8Y 2N	Adopted	246–174	
7. Amendment	5Y 5N	Rejected	185–229	
8. Amendment	10Y	Adopted	418–0	
9. Amendment	3Y 7N	Rejected	111–301	
10. Amendment	10Y	Adopted	394–8	
11. Amendment	2Y 6N	Rejected	162–250	6 October 1977
12. Amendment	4Y 6N	Rejected	139–279	
13. Passage	10N	Adopted	257–163	

opposed to labor law reform, especially any labor law reform which would bolster the electoral fortunes of organized labor. To illustrate, one has only to compare Senate woting patterns over three separate reform movements. The campaigns to repeal Section 14(b) and pass Labor Law Reform both failed in the Senate because cloture could not be achieved. While cloture was achieved on the common-site picketing bill, the vote in favor of the bill was very close.

Voting on all three measures shared common patterns. For example, in comparing voting patterns in all three tables it should be apparent that there were a core group of Republican senators against all three measures: 26 against repeal of Section 14(b), 25 against the common-site picketing bill, and 28 [24] against labor law reform. Similarly, there were a core group of Democrat senators who voted against all three measures. These senators were from the South: 17 against repeal of Section 14(b), 17 against the common-site picketing bill, and 17 [16] against labor law reform. Passage of the common-site picketing bill, and indeed any other labor law reform measure, required the defection of a small group of northern liberal Republicans and the complete loyalty of northern Democrats.

Leaders of the 1977 movement to pass the common-site picketing bill were essentially correct. They rightly assumed that passage through the Senate would be difficult, even impossible. However, by focusing their lobbying efforts on the Senate, and consequently neglecting the House, they failed even to gain passage through the House. This failure brought to light another issue. Despite Democrat majorities in the House and Senate and a Democrat President, the constituency for labor law reform is weak and fragile.

As in the Senate there are whole blocks of Representatives opposed to pro-labor law reform. The majority of southern Democrats voted against all labor law reform measures reviewed above. Of course, some votes were closer than others: repeal of Section 14(b) saw 26 southern Democrats vote in favor compared to 71 against, whereas labor law reform saw 40 southern Democrats vote in favor compared to 53 against. Southern Republicans gained in strength over the period 1960 to 1978, but only twice did *one* southern Republican support labor law reform. The voting patterns of northern Republicans tended to mimic the voting patterns of southern Democrats: there was a consistent majority of northern Republican Representatives against labor reform measures. In the House, passage of labor law reform measures was only possible because of a coalition of northern Democrats and western Democrats. Conversely, defeat of labor law reform measures, like the 1977 common-site picketing bill, could be engineered by a coalition of southern Democrats and Republicans with strong support from northern Republicans.

Given these congressional voting patterns, it is clear that labor law reform would be very difficult to achieve even in the most benign of circumstances. If the Democrat Party were to sweep northern congressional districts and win most, if not all, northern Senate seats, then labor law reform might succeed. This assumes, of course, a northern Democrat President. It is unlikely that such a Democrat-controlled Congress could override a presidential veto. Alternatively, a Republican President and a coalition of northern Democrats and Republicans may be able to form an effective coalition in favor of labor reform. This was nearly the result in the 1975 common-site picketing campaign. But the chances of this occurring seem remote given the current success of the Reagan administration. Moreover, population trends seem to be conspiring against such a possibility in the future. As the population in the South and Southwest grows faster than in the North, the balance of the House is shifting more towards the South. Even if new Representatives are Democratic as opposed to Republican, historical voting patterns on labor law reform imply that there will be few, if any, new supporters of organized labor.

Labor law reform in the Reagan era

In recent years, the federal legislative agenda has been dominated by the Reagan administration and the budget crisis. Landslide victories by Ronald Reagan in 1980 and 1984 drastically altered the power relations between Congress and the presidency. Even though the Democrats retained control of the House in 1980, and expanded their numbers in 1984, there is evidence that the political alignment of members of Congress became more conservative with each congressional election (Cavanagh and Sundquist 1985). The relationship between Congress and the President was set very early in Reagan's first term; he forced a restructuring of budget priorities in accordance with his ambitions to build military superiority over the Soviet Union. New domestic policy initiatives were rare as Congress was forced to rationalize and cut back social programs in relation to defense expenditures. Of the few initiatives introduced and passed through both Houses of Congress, the Tax Reform Act of 1986 was a rare instance of congressional party politics. Even this Act, though, was premised upon conservative (Democrat and Republican) support in Congress. Because Republicans controlled the Senate neither party was able to mount a coherent legislative program.

In its 1984 end-of-year survey of organized labor and its legislative agenda, the *Congressional Quarterly Weekly Report* summarized labor's prospects under the heading "Organized Labor Braces for 'Four more years'" (29 December 1984:3166). Representative William Clay (D – Missouri), chairman of the House Education and Labor subcommittee on Labor–Management Relations (a position previously held by Frank Thompson, author of many previous labor law reform measures) was quoted as saying "I see the same forces in power that are basically anti-union," and "unfortunately, I don't see any real prospects of legislating to deal with the situation under current circumstances" (3166).

At the same time, however, Orrin Hatch (R – Utah) claimed that organized labor was still the most powerful lobby in Washington. In a sense, Hatch was partially correct. His own attempt at (conservative) labor law reform (S 1774), ao amendment to the Hobbs Act to apply the Act to union violence, failed to reach cloture in the Senate on 16 April 1986. Cloture was lost by a 44–54 margin, 16 votes short of the 60 needed to bring the measure to a vote. While there was no chance for labor law reform, House Democrat leaders were effective at another level. In the Senate they were able to block anti-union legislation like Hatch's amendment to the Hobbs Act. In the House of Representatives their critical oversight hearings on the Reagan administration's labor policies and practices, and decisions of the NLRB have challenged the fairness of the labor–management relations system.

Many of the issues raised in oversight hearings on labor law conducted by various House sub-committees were related to previous campaigns to reform labor law. For example, in the House sub-committee on Labor–Management Relations hearings on labor law and the construction industry held in March 1983, problems of collective bargaining, common-site picketing, and the special circumstances of the industry were emphasized. Arguments were elicited in favor of labor law reform, but especially against the adjudication practices of the Reagan-appointed NLRB. In July 1985, a bill to strengthen collective bargaining rights in the construction industry and limit the use of double-breasting by employers in the industry was approved by the House Committee on Education and Labor. It was subsequently passed by the House by a 229–173 vote on 17 April 1986, but then languished in the Senate.

During much of 1984, the Democrat leadership of the House campaigned against the NLRB and the Department of Labor's administration of the NLRA. Oversight hearings on the administration of the Landrum–Griffin Act were begun on 7 February 1984 by Representative Clay and the sub-committee on Labor–Management Relations. Clay suggested the hearings were necessary in order to review the effectiveness of the Department of Labor's regulation of employers' management consultants. In their report to Congress in late 1984, a majority of the sub-committee argued that the Department of Labor had failed to enforce the law adequately: that the law had been forgotten. The majority report began by stating its overall conclusion that "there is widespread noncompliance by employers and labor relations consultants with the disclosure provisions of Title 11 [of the Landrum–Griffin Act]" (1). While the Republican minority report noted problems with monitoring compliance and enforcing the Act, it was suggested that these problems were the "result of resource limitations" (19), not any underlying anti-union animus on the part of the Department of Labor.

Beginning on 21 March 1984, oversight hearings were conducted by a sub-committee of the House Committee on Government Operations on the subject of the NLRB's use of Section 10(j) injunctions against unfair labor practices. The issue addressed concerned how injunctions might be used to expedite the NLRB's review of the exploding number of management-initiated unfair labor practices in representation elections. At issue were the administration, activities, and views of the Reagan-appointed NLRB. In a similar vein, joint oversight hearings were held by the sub-committee on Labor–Management Relations and the sub-committee on Health and Safety in June 1984 on the performance of the Occupational Safety and Health Administration. These hearings concentrated on labor–management relations and health and safety at the General Dynamics Corporation. In both sets of hearings evidence was taken from unions, management, the administrative agencies, and individual workers. The crucial issue raised time and time again in these hearings concerned the commitment of the Reagan administration and its agencies to enforce current labor laws. Essentially, the various agencies responsible for labor law were placed on trial. Labor law reform was not the issue in these hearings; rather the focus was on the enforcement practices of line agencies.

In conjunction with congressional campaigns to ensure enforcement of existing labor law, hearings were also held in June 1984 on the question: Has labor law failed? The focus of these hearings was on the substantive structure of American labor law including the origins of the Wagner Act, the role of the NLRB, and the causes (as related to labor law and its enforcement) of the precipitous decline of unions' success rates in representation elections. Many groups and individuals were asked to testify before the House sub-committee on Labor–Management Relations.

Richard Freeman (1984) began his prepared statement by asserting that "if the purpose of federal labor law is to enable workers to organize without undue management pressures ... developments in the past two decades suggest that federal labor law has failed" (115). To support his contention, Freeman cited the exploding number of management violations of the NLRA (specifically dismissal of employees engaged in union organizing activities), the consequent virtual collapse of union organizing through the NLRB, and the breakdown of NLRB representation election procedures. He claimed that there was a direct causal link between the massive increase in employer violations of the NLRA and the precipitous decline in union organizing success rates. Paul Weiler (1984b) was then introduced and expanded on the themes introduced by Freeman. According to Weiler, the "real problem is that the legal system has not, in practice, been able to mount sufficient counterincentives as the law was supposed to do" (120). He suggested that labor law had failed not simply because there were incentives to break the law, but because the law itself was not adequately enforced. The penalties for violating the law are low relative to the advantages of doing so, and the enforcement system is cumbersome and slow.

While the sub-committee had no real opportunities to develop a legislative agenda that would address the many problems of the union representation process identified by witnesses at the hearings, the report of the sub-committee established a basic reference point for those involved in the political battle to discipline the Reagan NLRB. The report of the sub-committee began by simply noting that labor law had indeed failed. The title of the report symbolized the sub-committee's majority opinion (and incidentally mimicked the title of Weiler's 1983 article): *The failure of labor law: a betrayal of American workers.* In reaction the minority report of the sub-committee accused the majority of engaging in pure rhetoric. It said, in part, "the history of the continuing debate on national labor law policy has been characterized by overstatement, overdramatization, and other forms of hyperbolic rhetoric. This report is no exception" (26). At the same time, even commentators much more removed from the immediate issues have concluded that federal labor law has failed to sustain the vision embodied in the preamble to the Wagner Act (Murphy 1987).

Is labor law reform possible?

The reform movements to repeal Section 14(b), rescind Section 8(b) 4(A), and reform the representation process (Labor Law Reform Act of 1977), sought to bring about a radical change in the rules by which labor and management acted in relation to one another and the federal government. Put slightly differently, these movements aimed to modify the rules of the game, thereby improving workers' power in relation to individual employers and the power of organized labor in relation to the national political establishment. Each reform would have made a substantial difference to the organizing potential of unions covered by the rules of representation. For example, repeal of Section 14(b) would have spatially integrated labor law, establishing the dominance of national labor standards regarding the relationships of labor and management. Section 14(b) sustains and legitimizes local state standards of behavior, and further fractures the cross-locality organizing power of industrial unions. Combined, Sections 14(b) and 8(b) 4(A) promote the idea that workers' interests are distinctive and necessarily different between and within employers, places, and issues.

The Labor Law Reform Act of 1977 as initially conceived was not so radical and, by the time of the last cloture vote in the Senate, was largely symbolic in importance. Nevertheless, its original provisions promised to revise the representation process dramatically by expediting elections, and ensuring the adjudicatory integrity of NLRB-sponsored review procedures. The Board was to be expanded, severe penalties for noncompliance were introduced, and legalistic delaying tactics were to be avoided by a summary review process. By and large, these were the same kinds of provisions promoted by Weiler and others in the 1984 hearings on labor law reform. Weiler had recommended an expedited injunction process as another means of ensuring speedy resolution of representation disputes. However, comparing 1977 to 1984, there were some basic differences between the years which would lead one to give greater credibility to the utility of such reform measures in 1977 as opposed to 1984.

In retrospect, the scale of opposition that greeted Weiler when he published his findings on the role of unfair dismissals in prompting declining union success rates in representation elections seems even more problematic than at the time. The very basis of the proposed 1977 reforms was observations of similar patterns a decade previously. Clearly the scale of management unfair practices in representation elections had significantly increased since 1977. But, overall, the procedural reforms promoted during the reform campaign were responses to previously well-recognized patterns: patterns that could only escalate with the failure of labor law reform. Indeed, by the time Weiler published his article, the possibility that a procedural revision of the representation process could resolve the deeper structural problems of federal labor law seemed past. One can only conclude that opposition to Weiler's findings was politically motivated, coming at a time when the Reagan administration was on the defensive regarding the management of the Department of Labor and the NLRB.

By this logic, labor law reform appears to be either impossible or, if passed in the near future, largely irrelevant. That is, given the consistent and concerted opposition of southern Democrats to reforming the underlying rules of federal labor law, it appears highly unlikely that a reform package which included repeal of Section 14(b) and rescinding Section 8(b) 4(A) would have any chance of success. A reform package which focused just on the representation process might have a greater chance of success. However, given the scale of unfair labor practices, and the extent to which management have institutionalized the role that these practices play in their responses to representation campaigns, any procedural reform is likely to reap few benefits. While it is readily apparent that procedural reform would be in the interests of fairness, it is not so clear that procedural reform would enable unions to recover the ground lost in the past decade.

Conclusion

Labor law reform during the Reagan administration had a rather different complexion than related movements in earlier administrations. The leadership of the House sought to limit and contain the powers of the regulatory agencies responsible for the implementation of federal labor law. Thus, the various hearings on labor law reform held by House committees in 1984 and 1985, and especially the hearings on Has labor law failed? should be interpreted as a holding strategy: a means of asserting the political interests of organized labor in an environment fundamentally opposed to labor's interests. This strategy has been very successful in a number of ways. First, the publicity generated by these hearings forced the Reagan administration to justify its administration of labor arbitration and adjudication (the NLRB), and thus the existing labor law system itself.

And yet, in the abstract, the conservative ideology of the Reagan administration was such that it would not have been otherwise interested in supporting current federal labor laws. In the beginning of the Reagan administration, labor law reform was an important priority. Orrin Hatch's attempts at reforming labor law through the application of nineteenth-century anti-trust laws to labor unions was one example of the underlying legislative agenda of the administration. Ironically, the political fire engendered by House hearings on labor law reform and the NLRB forced the administration to support existing labor law. Whether by design or by response, the Reagan administration became more involved in facilitating a narrow legalistic interpretation of federal labor law than campaigning in favor of Senate Republican versions of labor law reform.

Second, these hearings and the forum provided organized labor by virtue of the publicity surrounding the administration of the NLRB, have focused public attention on management's behavior in representation elections. The extent of violations of the law, the numbers of workers unlawfully dismissed for exercising their rights of self-organization, and the unscrupulous activities of management's labor relations consultants have all served to focus attention on employers' activities in representation elections. Management organizations have been on the defensive, and have been forced to support existing procedures which they previously decried as being anti-management. As a consequence, greater enforcement of election procedures has become an important means for the NLRB, and the Department of Labor more generally, to sustain their claims of legitimacy. In this sense, organized labor have been able to use the labor law reform movement to maintain themselves politically.

Ironically, though, through the focusing of so much attention on the enforcement of election procedures, the broader agenda of labor law reform, so important in previous reform movements, has been ignored. It is very doubtful if the recent political success of organized labor could be translated into greater success rates in representation elections. In fact, there are few supporters of organized labor who would claim that procedural solutions to enforcement problems of current labor law are the means for sustaining the long-run growth of the American labor movement. To imagine so would be to mistake the political agenda of labor for its organizing strategy. What remains unclear, though, is whether or not organized labor has an effective representation election strategy which goes beyond political action.

Of recent strategy proposals, the most acclaimed in the press and within the AFL–CIO has been the manifesto sketched in *The changing situation of workers and their unions* (AFL–CIO 1985). This manifesto begins with an assumption that labor law reform is not possible in the near future. Its goal is to use the existing rules of the game to fashion a new organizing strategy, one which is sensitive to the changing work place. The manifesto recommended experimenting with different forms of collective bargaining, instituting new categories of union membership not immediately tied to specific employer bargaining units, introducing commercial services designed to attract new and existing union members, and better use of communications for corporate campaigns and reaching out to the public in general.

In a sense, the labor law reform movement during the Reagan era failed to advance any general conception of the future of federal labor policy. Both the Reagan administration and the House leadership have been stymied in their attempts to advance the legislative interests of management and organized labor. While it was recognized that some kind of reform is needed, the debate over labor law reform did not generate an obvious bipartisan legislative agenda. The AFL–CIO's new manifesto recognizes that there will be no meaningful reform by the Reagan administration, but also appears to have lost contact with the terms and agenda of previous reform movements.

As currently conceived, labor law reform as procedural reform would hardly address the crucial dimensions of labor–management relations. But a more substantively oriented reform of the rules of American labor–management relations seems very unlikely given past congressional voting patterns and sectional interests. If there is to be reform, it must come from outside the federal legislative and administrative environment. If this is to be the case the question becomes: what is the future of American labor–management relations?

11

Employment contracts without unions

There is a certain irony in the decline of organized labor and the problematic status of federal labor policy.[1] Although union contracts protect fewer workers from employers' arbitrary decisions, and the National Labor Relations Board appears less reliable in protecting workers' rights as defined by collective bargaining agreements, employers' discretion regarding the treatment of their employees actually seems to have narrowed over the past decade. At the local level, experiments with new forms of labor–management collaboration in nonunion settings have sometimes involved considerable commitment of employers to the welfare of their workers; quasi-union conditions are typical in these settings.[2] In union situations, there have been attempts to broaden workers' discretion in the production process in the hope of increasing labor productivity (witness the partnerships between the United Auto Workers Union and General Motors Corporation in the Saturn Project and the NUMMI plant).[3]

At a broader level, there have been important state-level public policy innovations in nonunion labor–management relations, especially involving limits upon employers' rights of dismissal. Many states have modified the applicability of employment-at-will, the common law doctrine controlling employment relations in nonunion, noncollective bargaining situations.[4] As proscribed in the leading case *Payne* v. *The Western & Atlantic Railroad* (1884), employment-at-will provides employers with the right to hire and fire for any reason or no reason, at whatever time they desire. Originally, employment-at-will was simply a practice, legitimated by case law as opposed to statute. But in recent years many state legislatures have modified employment-at-will through statutory exemptions pertaining to the public interest, as their courts have also limited the scope of the doctrine. According to scholars and observers of employment relations policy, the doctrine of employment-at-will has been significantly eroded in a majority of states.[5]

The irony is that as unions have declined in importance, and the NLRB has been forced to retreat because of employer resistance, state courts now play a vital role in regulating nonunion employment relations. In doing so, state courts may now "afford unorganized employees an opportunity to prove ... a claim for arbitrary and retaliatory discharge."[6] In many jurisdictions, courts hold that at-will employees may be protected by implicit contracts. As a consequence, there is an emerging new American model of (nonunion) employment relations, albeit a patchwork quilt of state-level actions. This chapter analyzes the implications of this new policy innovation for unions and communities: what unions may become, and how communities may be reconceptualized. The logic and theoretical bases of state-level exemptions to the doctrine are discussed. These exemptions are described in a number of ways, including with reference to their spatial patterns with regard to other state-level labor relations policies like right-to-work legislation.

To illustrate the changing status of employment-at-will, a federal district court case is analyzed, specifically *Ohanian* v. *Avis Rent a Car System, Inc.* (1985). This case involved the integrity of a promise of lifetime employment as opposed to a claim by the company (Avis) that it had the right to fire Ohanian at will. The logic of this case is more complex than simply being about employment-at-will. At issue were considerations of the proper grounds by which a person could be fired, the relevance of written as opposed to oral contracts, and the extent of parties' obligations to one another under the terms of inherited statute and common law. While it is tempting to imagine that employment-at-will is an historical anachronism, the significance and likely generality of exemptions to employment-at-will remain open for debate.

Origins of employment-at-will

The textual origins of employment-at-will are more ambiguous than one might first imagine (compare Feinman 1976 and Jacoby 1982). While practically every discussion of the meaning of employment-at-will begins with an 1884 decision of the Tennessee Supreme Court in *Payne* (see for example Roberts 1986:183), the case itself did not originate in a dispute over employees' rights of employment and just procedures of termination. Employment-at-will was a tangential issue, raised by the defendant (the railroad) to justify their threat of immediate dismissal against any employee who would trade with a third party (Payne). One looks in vain in the original decision for references and sources which would provide background and justification for the judges' decision. It appears that the Court used the defendant's arguments as opposed to other possible "readings" of the case law and the issue at hand.

The Court accepted and advanced the doctrine as if it were obviously well regarded. At a couple of crucial junctures in the majority's opinion, the Court defined employment-at-will in the following terms (507, 519, 519–20):

men must be left, without interference to buy and sell where they please, and to discharge or retain employees at will for good cause, or even bad cause without thereby being guilty of an unlawful act per se ... [a]ll [employers] may dismiss their employees at will, be they many or few, for good cause, for no cause or even for cause morally wrong, without thereby being guilty of legal wrong.

By the Court's reasoning, employment relations were to be treated just like any other trading relationship: a free exchange between consenting partners (520). But, rather than goods being exchanged, the commodity involved in the transaction was labor. As in other trading relationships, employment-at-will could be only constrained by contracts which *a priori* defined the terms of employment and termination (517). Only if an employment contract was breached could "the law" interfere in the relationship between the parties (520). Since it appears that the employees concerned were not covered by an employment contract, the Court agreed with the defendant that employment-at-will held in this instance. Consequently, the Court asserted that it had no power to intercede on behalf of the plaintiff with regard to the particular issue litigated in *Payne*.

With respect to American employment case law, these few sentences used by the Tennessee court to define employment-at-will have had a remarkably resilient life. They serve as the beginning point of all histories of the idea, and as the rationale of defenses of the notion (see Epstein 1985a). For a century, the doctrine as expressed in *Payne* was the primary rationale justifying the actions of employers accused of arbitrarily terminating employees without notice and without cause.[7] In addition, the doctrine served as the basis of intellectual claims for the virtues of the free market as opposed to "interventionist" public policy. Even now, employment-at-will has strong advocates. Most recently the doctrine was invoked by McKenzie (1984) as an argument against proposed plant closing legislation, a response to rigidities of local labor market adjustment to capital mobility. It has also been used as the basis of a critique of federal labor law, especially the Wagner Act of 1935 (see Epstein 1983).

Yet the virtues of the doctrine were not that obvious to everyone involved in *Payne*. In a trenchant critique of the majority opinion, Judge Freeman focused more on the issue at hand and the implications of their opinion than employment-at-will. He made a couple of crucial points in rebuttal. First he suggested that "we have no precedent precisely covering the facts to guide us" (530). While he recognized that "the exigencies of our advancing civilization" (530) may demand new principles and that "cases are seldom alike" (531), he suggested that the majority had failed to consider more relevant principles, especially those relating to fraud and conspiracies. More critically, he argued against the idea that employees could be forced (by threat of dismissal) to withdraw their trade from a person their employer deemed inappropriate.

At one level, it might be assumed that Justice Freeman conceded the plausibility of the notion of employment-at-will, but constrained the applicability of the doctrine for a variety of reasons, including the interests of public policy. At the same time, while noting that his critique did not "in any way interfere with the legal right to discharge an employee for good cause, or without any reason assigned if the contract justifies it" (542), Freeman also argued that the doctrine did not justify an employer "hold[ing] the threat over the employee *in terrorem* to fetter the freedom of the employee, and for the purposes of injuring an obnoxious third party" (542). He then suggested that such conduct was not morally justified and "ought not be in law" (542). He suggested that if such power were granted to employers, it could ultimately cripple the economy.[8]

In developing his argument, Freeman made two crucial points. First, he observed that as capital was being rapidly concentrated the "masters of aggregated capital" may crush free trade if allowed to use their employees as weapons against merchants they wish to control. Second, he claimed that employment was so important to the average worker that the "perfect freedom of capital" ought to be regulated in the interests of public policy and "all the best interests of society" (544). According to Justice Freeman, capital may become so powerful that it "may control the employment of others to an extent that in time may sap the foundations of our free institutions" (544). In essence, Freeman argued that employment-at-will was not an absolute right: it was set within the context of what society at large deemed to be morally right and appropriate given broader public policy interests. He concluded for these reasons that the majority opinion was fundamentally misguided.

Vestiges of the counter-arguments introduced by Judge Freeman's dissent have survived into the modern era both as public policy exemptions to the doctrine (see Murg and Scharman 1982 for a detailed exposition) and as theoretical arguments against the logic of the doctrine (see Blades 1967). Compared to the Court's decision in *Payne*, however, it is not as often acknowledged that the minority opinion in *Payne* contained the critique now invoked to narrow the applicability of employment-at-will. Perhaps one reason for neglect of Freeman's dissent was the nature of his critique. Whereas the majority asserted a simple principle, the minority opinion was less abstract, more complex, and driven by the circumstances of the case.

In retrospect, the *Payne* case was important for a number of reasons. It explicitly and summarily defined a "new" common law doctrine of American employment and contract which was to hold sway in many states for another century. Even though employment-at-will is perceived by many contemporary theorists to be inherited from ancient common law, there appear to be no previous definitions of the doctrine as contained in *Payne*. It also marked a crucial point of divergence of American case law from the English tradition. Though obviously important in many American states, the intellectual logic embodied in *Payne* (as opposed to the decision itself, which would have been ignored in England if it had been known) failed to advance in England and was ultimately supplanted by a more pragmatic conception of government regulation of the terms of employment.

Atiyah (1979) demonstrated that English *laissez-faire* economic theorists like Jevons and Marshall were very wary of abstract notions like individual rights and the application of notions like freedom of contract in an absolute manner.[9] Their pragmatic sense of law and the role of public policy was summarized by Atiyah (1979:615) in three quotations taken from Stanley Jevons' *The state in relation to labour* (1882). Essentially, Atiyah's quotations from Jevons described (1) the harsh realities of work; (2) denied the relevance of absolute principles like freedom of contract given these harsh realities; and (3) argued the case for government regulation of employment conditions so long as the interests of all society were advanced.

While these propositions would probably have found favor with Justice Freeman, it is clear that the majority of the Court in *Payne* eschewed such pragmatism for an ideal image of the relationship between labor and capital. For many years the majority's opinion dominated pragmatic public policy interests. And more recently, when the abstract principle of employment-at-will has given way in some states to public policy interests, the intellectual claims for employment-at-will remain in dispute.

Exemptions from employment-at-will

In *Geary* v. *United States Steel Corp.* (1974), a majority of the Pennsylvania Supreme Court decided that the company was within its rights to terminate Geary because, as an at-will employee, he had "no right of action against his employer for wrongful discharge" (185). According to the Court, its majority opinion was consistent with other states' interpretations of the rights of employers to hire and fire at will, and the standard interpretation of torts. Although the Court recognized that the power of corporations relative to their employees had vastly increased since the late nineteenth century, and that there was some debate over the status of public policy interests in the conduct of private nonunion employment relationships, it was unwilling "to impose judicial restrictions on an employer's power of discharge" (177). It could not find a "clear mandate of public policy" (185) to overturn nearly a hundred years of precedent.

A little less than ten years later, Clyde Summers (1983) used the *Geary* decision to demonstrate just how quickly the consensus supporting employment-at-will had evaporated. *Geary* was quoted by Summers as illustrating an anachronism: a "misbegotten legal doctrine" (201). In contrast, the *Geary* dissenting minority opinion in favor of protecting unorganized employees as a matter of public policy was quoted by Summers as a watershed opinion which quickly became an avalanche. This opinion, the article by Blades (1967), and a Note (1974) in the *Stanford Law Review* are cited by many (friend and foe of employment-at-will) as the intellectual bases for the rush to limit the application of the doctrine (see for example Epstein 1985a).

Three different grounds for limiting the application of employment-at-will or exempting its application altogether are normally identified: employment-at-will may be limited for reasons of public policy; because of the existence of implied contracts of employment; and/or because of implied covenants requiring certain standards of treatment of employees. Generally, public policy exemptions are for protecting the public interest in maintaining employees' statutory rights. For example, in states like Pennsylvania employers are not allowed to unilaterally terminate employees who perform public obligations like jury duty (*Reuther* v. *Fowler and Williams Inc.* (1978)), who refuse to submit to an unlawful act like a lie detector test (*Perks* v. *Firestone Tire and Rubber Co.* (1979)), who exercise their legal rights like filing a workman's compensation claim (*Butler* v. *Negley House* (1981)), or who protest a company action to a state authority (see for example *Kilpatrick* v. *Delaware County SPCA* (1986)).[10] By this logic Geary may have been protected from discharge because his actions advanced the public good.[11]

With respect to implied contracts and covenants, employers may be held to performance criteria and dismissal procedures stated in employment manuals or verbally communicated at the time of employment. So, for example, in Pennsylvania, employers are bound by provisions in employee handbooks that relate to job security and termination procedures (*Cook* v. *Heck's Inc.* (1986)), as well as implied conditions of employment or standards of treatment (*Banas* v. *Matthews International Corp.* (1985)). Employee handbooks or manuals are often interpreted by courts to be legitimate bases for employees' expectations, and as implicit contracts binding upon employers and employees alike.[12] Even if employees are not covered by a union contract or represented by a staff association and the like, these manuals are often treated by the courts as equivalent binding documents.[13] In recent years this kind of interpretation has extended to federal courts' interpretation of company manuals.[14]

Of course, in reality few termination decisions of employers are accountable to the conditions of these exemptions.[15] Few terminations contravene the public interest as defined by case law or are counter to the terms and conditions of company manuals, and in some circumstances employers are careful not to imply any limits to their arbitrary discretion. In fact, companies have become more sophisticated in recent years regarding their use of employee manuals and the authority granted managers to make commitments to potential employees regarding job security and conditions of termination. For example Sears, Roebuck & Co. require job applicants to acknowledge their status as at-will employees, and General Motors include a disclaimer in their nonunion employee handbooks to the effect that handbooks are not to be interpreted as contracts or as defining conditions of employment.[16]

Public policy reasons for limiting the application of employment-at-will are widely accepted in many states, as evidenced in tables 11.1 and 11.2. Of the 50 states, 29 allow exemptions for this kind of reason, with no obvious strong geographical patterns amongst states that allow or disallow exemptions. However, with respect to the existence of implicit contracts as grounds for allowing exemption from employment-at-will, a strong geographical pattern is evident in table 11.2. Of Southern and Southwest states dominated by RTW legislation, only 6 states out of 17 allowed an exemption compared to 12 states out of 19 states in the North and Midwest. By comparison, states in the West and Mountain regions were about split on allowing or not allowing exemptions. Very few states indeed allowed exemptions on the basis of implied covenant. On the basis of these data, it is difficult to discriminate reasonably between regions of the United States on this issue.

On the other hand, it is quite apparent that the notion of a labor contract in the South – whether explicit as in union settings or implicit as in nonunion settings – is quite problematic. Only a minority of southern states allow for exemptions to employment-at-will on the basis of implied or promised contracts. It also appears that wrongful discharge suits against employers in southern states rarely get beyond the lowest state courts. Typically, such suits are summarily dismissed. Perhaps resistance in the South to employment contracts in any form reflects customary employment practices of last century, as suggested by Roback (1985) and implied in chapter 5 of this book. Alternatively, the conservative economic development-oriented ethos espoused by many current southern judges leads to the same conclusion (a possibility consistent with Palomba and Palomba's 1971 interpretation of RTW laws). Both explanations are plausible. Close correspondence between patterns of RTW laws and state courts' treatment of implicit contracts suggests the importance of local customary labor practices as evidenced in labor law, but not solely determined by labor law.

As there is a geography of unionization evident in patterns of union growth and decline there also is an equivalent geography of nonunionization evident in the patterns and scope of exemptions to employment-at-will. Crudely described, there is a North–South split in the protection of nonunionized employees from arbitrary dismissal. Not surprisingly, patterns of exemptions to employment-at-will on the basis of implicit contracts tend to map union strength. And perhaps not surprisingly, these patterns reflect the reference point noted by the dissenting judge in *Geary*: local nonunion employees deserve to be protected by the courts as local unionized employees are protected by collective bargaining agreements. Recognition of this geography of exemptions to employment-at-will has prompted some writers to call for federal statutes to rationalize the diversity of exemptions evident in these patterns (Stieber and Murray 1983).

Now that these patterns have been noted, it is important to recognize two fundamental qualifications to the comparisons drawn immediately above. First, because many exemptions (especially relating to implicit contracts) have evolved through litigation and the exigencies of specific cases, a mode of evolution entirely consistent with the common law tradition of employment-at-will, state comparisons may not be very sensitive to the local circumstances that have been vital to the development of each exemption. Second, since exemptions have evolved in an incremental manner, it is possible that what are now plausible exemptions may not be in the future. In these ways, Kiewiet's (1983) nonsystematic component of local partisan elections and union representation elections may be vital here as in other instances. The local conditions embedded in categories of exemption may be as significant as any consistent cross-state component of the categories. Thus we should be wary of any claim which supposes that common exemptions mean the same thing between jurisdictions.

There are, of course, statutory bases for most public policy exemptions to employment-at-will. For this reason, we might expect greater consistency (type and issue) between states on this class of exemptions. But, the more difficult issue – implicit contracts – may be even more variable between states, especially in terms of interpretation, than simply recording the existence of such exemptions may suggest. This is an area of litigation that is rapidly changing.

Table 11.1. *States by employment-at-will exemption criteria, right-to-work (*) status, and region, 1986*

	Exemption criteria		
Region/state	Public policy	Implied contract	Implied covenant
North/Midwest			
Connecticut	Yes	No	No
Illinois	Yes	Yes	No
Indiana	Yes	Yes	Yes
Iowa (*)	No	No	No
Kansas	Yes	No	No
Maine	Yes	Yes	No
Massachusetts	Yes	Yes	No
Michigan	Yes	Yes	No
Minnesota	No	Yes	No
Missouri	Yes	Yes	No
New Hampshire	Yes	No	No
New Jersey	Yes	Yes	No
New York	No	Yes	No
Ohio	No	Yes	No
Pennsylvania	Yes	Yes	No
Rhode Island	No	No	No
Vermont	No	No	No
West Virginia	Yes	No	No
Wisconsin	No	Yes	No
South/Southwest			
Alabama (*)	No	No	No
Arizona (*)	Yes	Yes	No
Arkansas (*)	Yes	Yes	No
Delaware	No	No	No
Florida (*)	Yes	No	No
Georgia (*)	Yes	No	No
Kentucky	Yes	Yes	No
Louisiana (*)	No	No	No
Maryland	Yes	No	No
Mississippi (*)	No	No	No
Nevada (*)	No	Yes	No
New Mexico	Yes	Yes	No
North Carolina (*)	Yes	No	No
South Carolina (*)	No	No	No
Tennessee (*)	Yes	No	No
Texas (*)	Yes	No	No
Virginia (*)	No	Yes	No

Table 11.1 (*contd.*)

West/Mountain

Alaska	No	Yes	No
California	Yes	Yes	Yes
Colorado	No	No	No
Hawaii	Yes	No	No
Idaho (*)	Yes	Yes	No
Montana	Yes	Yes	No
Nebraska (*)	No	Yes	No
North Dakota (*)	No	No	Yes
Oklahoma (*)	No	Yes	No
Oregon	Yes	Yes	No
South Dakota (*)	Employment-at-will abrogated		
Utah (*)	No	No	No
Washington	Yes	No	No
Wyoming (*)	Yes	No	No

Sources: Bureau of National Affairs, October 1986, and the *Daily Labor Report*, 6 November 1986 (no. 215), A–9–A–10

Table 11.2. *Summary of state employment-at-will exemptions by criteria and region, 1986*

	Exemption criteria		
Region	Public policy	Implied contract	Implied covenant
North/Midwest	12 Yes	12 Yes	1 Yes
	7 No	6 No	18 No
South/Southwest	10 Yes	6 Yes	
	7 No	11 No	17 No
West/Mountain	7 Yes	7 Yes	2 Yes
	6 No	6 No	11 No
	1 N/A	1 N/A	1 N/A
State totals	29 Yes	25 Yes	3 Yes
	20 No	24 No	46 No
	1 N/A	1 N/A	1 N/A
Total	50	50	50

Source: Bureau of National Affairs, October 1986

Contract and the grounds of dismissal

In *Ohanian* (1985), the company (Avis Rent a Car System) and an employee (Robert Ohanian) brought suit against one another in a federal appeals court over the terms of a previous decision of a lower federal district court. In the lower court decision, the company was found to have breached its oral contract (promise) to Ohanian of lifetime employment. The jury in this case awarded Ohanian $304,693 for lost wages and benefits. On appeal, the company sought to have the decision overturned, arguing that the statute of frauds barred the kind of implicit contract that Ohanian claimed as his right. Ohanian appealed to have his damages increased, arguing that the jury had made a mistake in calculating damages. Neither appeal was accepted by the court; it affirmed the decision of the lower court.

This is an important decision for a number of reasons. It provides a useful illustration of the changing legal status of common law employment contracts at the federal level. The logic of the decision at the lower level illustrates the importance placed upon oral commitments, promises, as evidence of employment contracts over and above written documents like company procedures and routines. By the decision of the lower court, this case is an instance where conventional common law employment doctrine was set aside in the interests of one party (Ohanian) to the contract. Whereas the company sought to portray the relationship between the parties as simply an at-will contract and the dispute as only an instance where one party (the company) exercised its right to terminate the contract, the court rejected both the company's interpretation of the relationship between the parties and the notion (based upon the statute of frauds) that the parties should be treated equally.

Ohanian was first employed by Avis in 1967, when he worked in Boston. Over the years, Ohanian worked up through the company, reaching by 1980 the position of vice-president for sales in Avis' western regional office located in San Francisco. According to a former Avis general manager and witness in the lower court trial, Ohanian was thought to have done an outstanding job in that position, and was held to have been one of the company's best performers. On the basis of his experience and ability, in the fall of 1980 Ohanian was recruited by officials of Avis' world headquarters to become vice-president for sales in the northeast region, in which Avis had performed very poorly over the previous few years.

By all accounts Ohanian was reluctant to move. His family liked living in the San Francisco bay area; he was pleased with his success in the western region; and, more than anything else, he was wary of leaving the security of his position in the western region for the northeast region, which he believed was dominated by the internal company politics of Avis world headquarters. To make it possible, the general manager of Avis promised Ohanian lifetime employment and assured him that "unless [he] screw[e]d up badly, there is no way [he was] going to get fired ... [he would] never get hurt here in this company."[17] On the basis of this promise (in reliance), and heavy lobbying by high officials of the company, Ohanian relocated to the New York area in early 1981.

Ohanian was successful in his new position, and was promoted to national vice-president of sales in late 1981. As a consequence of this promotion, he began working in Avis world headquarters. However, he became "dissatisfied" with that job, and asked to return (an option he had been promised when promoted to the national sales job) in June 1982 to his immediately previous job as vice-president for sales for the northeast region. One month later Ohanian was fired without severance. At that time, he was earning a yearly salary of $68,400 and had not been paid a bonus of $17,100. Three months later, he had obtained a new job as vice-president for sales of American International Rent A Car, earning a yearly salary of $50,000 and a bonus of $20,000. Ohanian brought suit in federal district court against the company for damages.

The jury decided in favor of Ohanian and against the company. In doing so, the jury found that the company had agreed to employ Ohanian until retirement barring dismissal for just cause (if he "screwed up"). The jury also found there were no grounds for believing Ohanian had been dismissed for just cause. The jury awarded him the present value (1985) of Ohanian's lost pay and pension benefits, the bonus he was owed by the company, and incidental relocation costs. In sum, he was awarded $304,693. Clearly, Ohanian had won over the company. But, his damage award was far less than his argued entitlement. The company appealed against the decision and award; Ohanian appealed against the award.

The company appealed against the award by invoking a rather "anachronistic" doctrine: the statute of frauds.[18] The company argued two positions using this doctrine. First, it suggested that since its promise of lifetime employment could not be performed within a year (a requirement of the statute), the contract was barred by the statute.[19] Here, the court countered by suggesting that the company had too narrowly interpreted the intent of the statute, and suggested that common law interpretations of contract allowed for promises to endure over long periods of time without contravening the intent of the statute. Second, the company also asserted that the promise was barred by the statute because only Ohanian had the right to withdraw from the contract.[20] But, here, the court reminded the company that it too had the right to terminate for just cause.[21]

The company also argued that Ohanian had in fact agreed to be treated as an at-will employee. It based its assertion on a form Ohanian had signed in April 1981 to claim his relocation allowances, some months after joining the northeast regional office. Part of the form dealt with relocation expenses. But it also contained the following:

I also hereby confirm my understanding that nothing contained herein or in connection with the change in my position with Avis shall be deemed to constitute an obligation on the part of Avis to employ me for any period of time, and both the company and I can terminate my employment at will (6709).

In testimony, Ohanian suggested that he did not read this passage, nor did he mean to imply that he had changed the terms of the oral contract. The court argued that the purpose of the form was to claim relocation expenses and could not be held as evidence of a new contract. Moreover, the court argued that Ohanian had given his implicit agreement to the terms of the oral promise by having relocated to the east coast.[22] The court also did not accept the company's claim that the grounds of "just cause" were too ambiguous to be definitive and thus could not be enforced. The court rejected the company's claim that damages should have been computed after accounting for Ohanian's salary with his current employer. The court also rejected Ohanian's contention that the damages were "so low as to constitute a miscarriage of justice" (6722). Basically, the company was held to the terms of the promises made to Ohanian; these promises constituted the employment contract.

Throughout the trial, the company attempted to portray Ohanian in the worst possible light. They suggested he was a "dishonest" employee, an "insubordinate" employee, and accused him of "disloyal acts" (6736–37). It was asserted that he had "padded" his expense account, and had abused the trust of the company by making trips with a friend. The jury, though, did not believe there was any plausible evidence of "just cause" for dismissal. While the meaning of "just cause" appears to have been quite ambiguous, as indicated by the dissenting judge, its use as the literal translation of "screwed up" was effective in orienting the court and the jury. Not only was it given judicial integrity by the court's citation of close examples in case law, but it was also given practical meaning by referencing companies' employment manuals and dismissal procedures which use the phrases as guards against arbitrary dismissal.

The jury sided with Ohanian against the company, believing (apparently) that Ohanian was a victim of a power-play in the upper management of Avis. Ohanian's reluctance to move to the northeast region, given the reputation of Avis' world headquarters for political intrigue, seems to have been entirely warranted. In a sense, his cautiousness regarding employment security and the extensive lobbying it took to convince him to relocate all reinforced his credibility. Failure of the company to prove a substantial "just cause" case simply reinforced the appeals court's opinion that Ohanian was wise to be cautious. Unfortunately for Ohanian, the damages were quite small relative to the costs of the suit.

Promise as contract

This case is interesting for all kinds of reasons. Clearly, it provides an illustration of the complexity of employment law in nonunion noncollective bargaining situations. And, in this sense, it illustrates just how far the courts have come since the majority opinion decision in *Geary*. By this logic employment-at-will, and the inherited statutes and common law doctrines that provided it with legal integrity, are increasingly labeled as anachronistic. But, if *Ohanian* is an indication of the future of employment contract law in nonunion situations, what is implied in terms of the theory of contract? And do cases like *Ohanian* come close to realizing the ambition of the dissenting judge in *Geary*? That is, does it indicate that unorganized employees now have protection from "the arbitrary dismissal powers of employers" like their friends in organized labor (192)?

The case involving Robert Ohanian is about both employment-at-will and a distinctive theory of contract. The emphasis of the court, the language of the discourse between the parties, and the direct association made by the court between the terms of the oral contract and the notion of promise all indicate that the dominant conception of contract theory in this instance was liberal. As conceived by Fried (1981), the liberal theory of contract can be described by three essential assumptions about the nature of individuals and their roles in society, and a logical argument about commitment and moral obligations. This theory is not without its critics, both from the left (Atiyah 1986:ch. 6) and the right (Epstein 1985).

The three assumptions of liberal contract theory will be immediately recognized by anyone familiar with liberal theory in its various guises (compare with Dworkin's 1981 assessment of different theories of justice). These assumptions are (no special order is implied): (1) that individuals have fundamental integrity as self-contained emotional and calculating agents; (2) that individuals' actions and desires are the basis of personal happiness and, as such, ought to be protected as long as their pursuit does not harm others; and (3) that for individuals to achieve their greatest good, some form of cooperation may be necessary in some cases – dictated by the separate goals and circumstances of each person. As a consequence of these assumptions, it is then supposed that individuals will only enter into cooperation (exchange, transactions, and contract) with others as long as their needs are mutually served by the terms of cooperation. That is, all contracts are assumed voluntary and undertaken as long as one person is made better off without the other being made worse off.

These assumptions are common to many theories of contract, and are evident in much of the literature on law and economics (see Posner 1985). What is special about the Friedian liberal theory of contract is its claim that contracts are actually promises: more than statements of intention, they are actually commitments to abide by the terms of mutually binding obligations made prior to their anticipated and defined performance. This kind of theory makes use of the moral component of promising so as to indicate the difference between contract and other forms of less vital voluntary associations. It also ensures that breaches of contract are evaluated more critically than may otherwise be the case given that cooperation is a secondary aspect of life in a liberal world. The connection between contracts and promises is such that contracts are assumed to carry moral rights and obligations to others.

Once we recognize that this theory was the basis of adjudication in *Ohanian* it should be quite apparent why and how Ohanian was able to prevail over Avis. In the narrowest sense of the theory, having made a promise to Ohanian of lifetime employment, the company was literally responsible for fulfilling its obligations. It made no difference if the burden of obligation fell most heavily on the company (Ohanian could leave at will while the company was required to guarantee employment), nor did it matter that the terms of the contract were vague and ill defined (as in "screwed up"). Likewise, it did not matter that Ohanian unknowingly signed a form indicating his status as an at-will employee. What counted as evidence was the original oral promise; the liability of the company was judged by its subsequent behavior in breaching that promise.

In terms of damages, the Friedian theory of contract supports the notion of expectational damages – that is, the full value of the promised performance. In this case, damages would have amounted to Ohanian's wages and benefits over the course of his career at Avis to retirement at age 65 (possibly 15 years or more). But in this case the jury seems only to have considered his earnings up until the date of their decision holding the company liable. This was the basis of Ohanian's contention that the jury had made a gross error of calculation whereby the limited scale of damages was inconsistent with the (Friedian) theory of contract. In effect, the error by the jury impugned the significance of the decision itself.

The company, on the other hand, did not accept that the promise had been made, refused to accept its terms and conditions, refused to honor its contractual obligations, and then sought to change the method of calculating damages – its method would have awarded only the difference between Ohanian's current earnings and those promised up until the date of the jury's decision. While we might suppose that the company disagreed with the terms of the contract, another interpretation would be that through its actions there is enough evidence to suppose that the company disagreed with the theory of contract itself.

There are other theories of contract, and other formulations of the liberal theory of contract (for a review see Atiyah 1981). With respect to the latter issue, I wish to mention two possible options, both of which reject Fried's view though not necessarily his assumptions about the nature of individuals and the desirability of collective action, as well as a more radical approach. One option, commonly identified with Atiyah (1979), would reduce the significance of contract and fold it into more general considerations of tort liability. Another option, commonly associated with Epstein (1985b), would reassert the significance of at-will contracts in the interests of economic efficiency. Both theorists reject Fried's normative theory of contract.

Atiyah argues a modified realist position to the effect that the liberal theory of contract has collapsed. By his logic, enforcing contracts in a manner consistent with Fried is a losing proposition for two reasons. First, he argues that no one should be held accountable for the performance of a contract that no longer has utility for the parties involved. This does not mean that Avis would be allowed to treat Ohanian as an at-will employee. Rather, Atiyah's position is that the penalties for breaking a contract should not be so severe as to force the performance of a contract against the will of one or more parties. If they were, an essential assumption of liberal theory would be violated. Atiyah would prefer to assess damages with respect to the plaintiff's actual costs of reliance – either those costs incurred or opportunities foregone by relying upon the performance of the contract. Second, Atiyah doubts the virtues of the moral component of liberal theory, largely because it is actually a philosophy of life (an ideal), not a commonly accepted representation of social structure and actions.

On the other hand, Epstein has argued the case for at-will contracts as the essential building block of economic relations. Epstein notes that not all contracts should be at-will contracts. Nevertheless, he argues that at-will contracts should be both available for agents if they choose to use this form of agreement and the presumptive basis for interpreting common law agreements not otherwise formally specified by the parties to an exchange, transaction, or the like. According to Epstein, at-will contracts have two virtues. First, they are thought to promote efficiency – in their simplest version they are self-regulating and thus do not involve the social costs typically associated with regulation. Second, because these kinds of contracts are terminable at will, economic efficiency is thought to be enhanced because resources would be allocated to the highest return (discounted by the costs of compensating others for nonperformance) speedily and effectively. The result, assuming a competitive economic world, should be higher aggregate welfare.

By Epstein's logic, Fried's normative theory is not the strongest defense of contract. He would assert that the efficiency contract is not normative, but rather positive and empirical. Moreover, Fried's version of contract may involve significant social costs in terms of lower overall wealth because promises might be enforced for no other reason than the moral integrity of a promise as opposed to the costs and benefits of breaking a contract. Indeed, in terms of employment contracts, Epstein has argued that questions of redistribution as they arise in evaluating the terms of contracts are best left to social policy. The distinction Epstein has in mind is critical both of Fried's theory and the emerging new theory of common law employment law. Whereas Fried's position might be used to justify "fairness" in contract, Epstein argues that these normative conceptions of contract performance only confuse the market. It is better, according to Epstein, to allow at-will contract behavior and then institute ameliorative policies if the effects run counter to desired social norms.

Thus, Atiyah and Epstein reject Fried's theory of contract as promise for rather different reasons. Atiyah believes that contract has become subsumed under more general theories of tort liability and idealizes relationships as opposed to offering a reliable guide to judicial decision making. Epstein would also reject the notion of contract as promise because he believes that normative ideals have no place in economic arrangements, and that such ideals are possibly counter to the interests of economic efficiency. Both would reject the decision of the jury in *Ohanian*, though they might find something favorable in the jury's assessment of damages. Atiyah might interpret these damages as mimicking the costs of reliance, while Epstein might argue that although excessive, these damages are those necessary to break the contract. Neither would assess the full expectational costs desired by Ohanian.

Notice, as well, that Atiyah and Epstein would have little sympathy with the kinds of public policy exemptions to employment-at-will noted in previous sections of this chapter. In fact, Epstein has been particularly critical of these kinds of interventions into the labor market. Compared to the well-developed theories of Fried, Atiyah, and Epstein these exemptions are driven largely by recognition of the stark economic and social realities as opposed to representing even implicitly a coherent theory of contract. Judge Freeman's critique of the majority opinion in *Payne*, the dissenting opinion in *Geary*, and the accumulated social problems of an unfettered labor market are the standard reference points for those who wish to overcome the subtle attraction of theory *qua* theory.

By virtue of the methods of common law adjudication, its emphasis on case-by-case assessment of circumstances and the relevance of policies conspire to make the pattern of exemptions to employment-at-will a patchwork quilt of options and lost options. In this sense, these exemptions are wholly ad hoc in design and conception. On the other hand, it is tempting to imagine that cases like *Ohanian* are a vital sign post along the way to a new theory of contract. Clearly, it represented the application of a particular kind of contract theory – at least in the rhetoric of theory, if not application. But even here, I suggested there are reasons to doubt the theoretical plausibility of the approach embodied in the case. Like exemptions, a case like *Ohanian* represents the evolution of the theory of employment contracts coupled with a quite pragmatic conception of the costs of breaching a contract. *Ohanian* is not the ultimate case that will make sense out of the patchwork quilt of state employment laws and case law.

Unions as law firms

What implications can be drawn from the preceding discussion of nonunion employment contracts for unions? If unions continue to lose members, and collective bargaining as an institution becomes even further removed from the work life of the average worker, one possibility is that unions (especially the largest unions with the greatest legal expertise) become legal advocates for nonrepresented workers in their contract disputes with employers. Such a policy would be consistent with recent proposals by the AFL–CIO (1985) to become more service oriented. Such a policy might draw upon the loyalty and support of a large minority of workers who consistently vote for representation in losing causes. Like VISA cards, insurance, and political representation, legal representation in contract disputes could be a service provided to paying associate members of the union.

Organizing such a program would be a Herculean task. The standard methods used in representation elections would seem to be quite irrelevant for these circumstances. Perhaps it would be possible to harness the direct-mail solicitation techniques of political interest groups, or even the store-front advertising methods of some smaller independent law firms. Perhaps workers could sign up for legal representation as most people do when they buy insurance policies. There could be risk premiums, experience rating, and similar techniques to match the potential costs of representing different types of workers. However imaginative we become about possible union strategies for "organizing" the unorganized into associate programs, there is little value in speculating further on how unions might approach the organizing challenge. A more vital issue is to identify possible implications regarding the themes of this book which would follow from such a policy.

Consider the implications of such a policy for the vitality of American communities. As was noted in previous sections of this chapter, exemptions to employment-at-will are state specific, based upon local public policy goals and the adjudicative practices of the courts. Though there is evidence of an increasing involvement of federal courts in adjudicating the performance of nonunion employment contracts (witness *Ohanian*), the strength of local exemptions tends to map the patterns of union strength. This means, of course, that those states which have been the traditional heartland of American unionism (northern and northcentral states) are those states with the most developed case law on exemptions to employment-at-will, and those which have been hostile to organized labor (southern states) are the states with least innovation in nonunion employment contracts.

Given these patterns, one possible implication of an associates policy for unorganized workers is that those northern communities with strong histories of union representation would be the communities in which unorganized workers could take advantage of exemptions to employment-at-will. In southern states with limited histories of union representation, opportunities for court appeal against employment-at-will are very limited, as are the activities of unions generally. Essentially, the protection of workers from arbitrary dismissal inside and outside of unions is more a northern phenomenon than a southern one; an associates program could simply reinforce this geography of advantage and disadvantage. A related implication is also apparent – an associates program may simply reinforce the balkanization of the labor movement into northern states.

It is obvious from all the evidence introduced in the previous chapters that the labor movement is fighting for survival. Its isolation from new areas and fields of employment growth is palpable, as is its inability to reach beyond traditional areas of strength. One goal of the Wagner Act and the package of New Deal legislation envisaged by congressional leaders was to integrate the nation in terms of customary labor practices and protection of the rights of workers. Collapse of the union movement threatens to undermine this goal in manufacturing sectors. An associates program based upon the patterns of state exemptions to employment-at-will would surely further limit the reach of national standards of employment and conditions of work. Essentially, the state-by-state pattern of adjudication simply reinforces local practices over desired national standards. An associates program based on state exemptions could be interpreted as further evidence of the failure of national labor legislation.

With respect to the institutions of labor–management relations, an associates program would further fracture an already fragile institutional environment. The relevance of the National Labor Relations Board would fall further behind the practice of labor relations. This is already apparent in the NLRB's response to economic restructuring, and unions may feel little sorrow in seeing the current Board disappear into oblivion. But apart from the NLRB, also at risk here is the very mandate for regulating local labor relations that the federal government seized in the 1930s. So is the very structure of federal labor relations policies, so often premised upon a belief in a strong union system (whether in hope or by design). By this scenario, the degeneration of unions into associates programs offering legal representation in disputes over personal employment contracts would indicate more than the failure of federal labor law. It would signal the end of federal responsibility for labor–management relations.

For the unions, Lester's (1958) conception of the postwar era as the mature phase of unions as national organizations mimicking the hierarchical power of corporations and the structure of governmental authority may never be realized. Rather, the forces of decentralization will have won, fracturing the power of unions and redefining the unit of an employment contract – from groups of individuals organized into associations designed to protect their collective interests to just individuals, from collective bargaining agreements to personal services contracts (or non-contracts, depending upon local circumstances), from union–management grievance committees and boards of adjudication at the local level to state courts and even federal courts. In these ways, the decentralization of labor–management relations will have far-reaching consequences for unions as organizations and for the possibility of collective action.

The latter implication is one that deserves greatest scrutiny. Unions do much more than simply protect workers from arbitrary dismissal. Throughout the book we have seen unions in many roles. For example, they were shown to be instrumental in redesigning the nature and organization of work in the face of massive economic restructuring in US industry (see chapter 4 on the United Auto Workers investment program in AMC corporation, and chapter 9 on the UAW–GM Saturn project). In addition, unions were shown to be vital institutions for community welfare even if they are not always successful in rationalizing internal political interests (see chapter 3 on the Mack Trucks dispute). They were also shown to be important institutions for representing the interests of groups of workers (as in the *Otis Elevator* case: see chapter 8), as well as the political interests of the working class as a whole (see chapter 10 on attempts at labor law reform). While we could imagine that unions and the AFL–CIO might take over the political representation function as yet another political interest group, the prospects for collective action at the work place would disappear with unions.

In a very real sense, unions are democracies, forums for the expression of collective interests. To retreat to them as associates programs for unorganized workers would be to give up a fundamental ideal of the Wagner Act – "a democracy within industry" (Representative Mead, D – New York). Now, I do not wish to romanticize unions, or imagine that they are always preferable to courts and other modes of representation. There are, of course, many other forms of representation which are quite legitimate. In fact, unions have been quite successful in using the courts to advance their interests even if justice is often delayed. At the same time, to imagine that they could simply reorganize themselves as associates programs while remaining consistent with their heritage radically mistakes the underlying histories of unions as working-class institutions. Such a naive understanding of unions would make Verba and Nie's (1972) mistake of interpretation ("unions are just like clubs": see chapter 2 above) a practical reality.

Conclusion

There is not much doubt that the new forms of employment contract will become more important in northern states over the coming years. The ideal expressed in the dissenting opinion in *Geary* of protecting unorganized labor from the arbitrary actions of employers in the courts just as unionized workers are protected by collective bargaining agreements will likely be expanded. Instead of simply matching the conditions of organized labor, the courts and state legislatures will be asked to take the lead in employment policy; public policy exemptions to employment-at-will are just the start of a more general move in many states to rationalize workers' rights in the work place. To the extent that unions decline even further in importance, state employment policies will have to be more coherent and ambitious than imagined by previous commentators. Practically speaking, the states are being asked to replace unions and the federal government as the principal institutions for protecting workers.

It is apparent, though, that not all states are about to join this movement. Historically, southern states have been hostile to unions: that is obvious in the relative failure of unions to win representation in these states and the opposition of southern congressmen to labor law reform. Southern states also appear quite hostile to recent attempts at reforming employment-at-will for all but the most compelling public policy interests. Thus, if there is to be a new environment for labor–management relations outside of unions, the NLRB, and federal government policy, it will be an environment geographically shaped and splintered by deep divisions between the working-class histories of the North and South. To put the matter most starkly, whereas right-to-work laws were used by southern elites against the growth of unions in the interests of local economic growth, maintenance of employment-at-will could serve the same interests and elites.

Consequently, we must be wary of ascribing too much to the exemptions movement. While important to many millions of workers, its increasing significance is as much a testament to the failure of the Wagner Act and fifty years of federal regulation of labor–management relations as it is a positive move towards greater protection of individual workers' rights. In this sense, the inability of unions to achieve labor law reform has two sides. One side is well recognized, and has to do with the prospects for unions in representation elections (amongst other issues; see chapter 10). But there is another side to labor law reform. While not operating at the federal level, labor law reform has accelerated in recent years at the state level in the guise of exemptions to employment-at-will. In this instance, though, the results of reform are rather distant from the interests of unions, and fail to provide national coverage to all workers, especially southern workers.

Underlying many arguments about exemptions to employment-at-will are fundamental questions about the nature of American society. For example, I noted above that exemptions from employment-at-will have to do with workers' individual rights rather than their rights as members of unions or other organizations. This distinction is critical for a number of reasons. Most obviously, exemptions are applied on a case-by-case basis, and are not automatically relevant to any particular dispute between a worker and employer. In contrast, the great value of belonging to a union was that workers' rights were allocated on the basis of group affiliation. Individual workers were protected under an umbrella of union representation. Less obviously, exemptions treat all workers as separate individuals and do not allow for group rights. This means that the unit of dispute is always the individual; implied is actually a liberal theory of society where collective action is problematic and contingent. In contrast, the Wagner Act gave institutions primacy in labor–management disputes – indicating a rather different (if inchoate) social democratic theory of society.

On these terms, it seems apparent that the decline of unions and the increasing significance of exemptions to employment-at-will indicate a more fundamental intellectual transformation of the theory of labor–management relations. These patterns represent a retreat from concerted political action involving coalitions of classes and elites to a rights theory of society where progress is measured in terms of individuals' freedom as opposed to their social rights derived from their membership of unions.

12

Unions and communities unarmed

We have come a long way in this book. It began with a brief statement on
the importance of a community-oriented perspective for understanding the
current crisis of organized labor, and moved quickly to two case studies
which sketched some of the basic issues. This relatively simple presentation
of the book's underlying thesis was replaced chapter by chapter with more
complex interpretations of the intersection between unions and communities. In this way, other ingredients were added to my thesis and were
evaluated in terms of their significance. Included were analyses of the
impacts of geographical and economic restructuring and the tensions
involved in orchestrating international union solidarity. From empirical
models of unions' performance in representation elections through to
detailed case studies of institutions and the status of labor law, my goal was
to illustrate the many different ways of understanding the union–community
connection.[1]

At the outset I noted that no one test of the union–community connection
would be introduced to demonstrate its utility for understanding the current
crisis of organized labor. In this sense, I do not claim to have proved my
case, as a simple-minded empiricist might want me to proclaim.[2] Indeed, the
various ways shown of conceptualizing the union–community connection
should be reason enough to suppose that any one test would be inadequate.
Nevertheless, by itself each way of illustrating the union–community
connection provides an empirical perspective on the problems facing the
American labor movement. For example, a number of chapters indicated
that cross-community competition for jobs can do incredible harm to union
cohesiveness. In instances where local union members are forced to choose
between their union and their community, union solidarity is fragile at best.
These kinds of pressures feed into unions' problems at the local level,
illustrated here by studies of the electoral performance of the United Auto
Workers and the International Brotherhood of Electrical Workers.

The richness and complexity of this material mean that the reader is
probably owed a restatement of my argument(s); a step towards a conclusion to the book. As will become apparent, though, I am not sure that an all-
encompassing conclusion should be crafted out of this material.[3] Neverthe-

less, some commentators are sure that there is an essential explanation for unions' problems and, as a consequence, a clear agenda for revising public policies and/or union policies. A good example of this kind of conclusion is to be found in Freeman and Medoff (1984), who supposed that unions could be saved if the positive contribution they make to economic competitiveness is recognized. If the reader is uncomfortable with this conclusion, Goldfield (1987) provides a more radical diagnosis. He identified the failures of federal labor legislation and its haphazard enforcement by the National Labor Relations Board as essential ingredients of the decline of organized labor. While appealing as a rhetorical strategy, such essentialist conclusions do great harm to building a comprehensive understanding of the complexity of the issue and promise a solution where there may be no solutions.[4]

In contrast, this chapter argues that there is no single enemy of labor that can be held responsible for its current problems. By implication, I suggest that the geography of American unionism is not *the* explanation of union decline, nor is rationalization of this geography the necessary solution. Rather, the crisis of organized labor ought to be understood as the result of an unfortunate juxtaposition in time of three semi-autonomous factors operating at the local level: structural–legislative imperatives, economic and geographical restructuring, and the accumulated inertia, or worse, sclerosis, of the major institutions of American labor law.

Crisis of organized labor

When discussing the crisis of organized labor most commentators focus upon the collapse of union membership in the 1980s. There is no doubt that this collapse has reached crisis proportions. By Farber's (1987) reckoning, union membership in private nonagricultural sectors fell some 7 percentage points from around 20 percent in 1980 to 13 percent in 1988.[5] Considering that union membership was relatively stable through most of the 1970s (at around 25 percent), this decline has been nothing short of phenomenal. These patterns are discussed at length in chapter 1 above.

In the various chapters of this book, three sources of declining union membership were analyzed. The union movement has lost membership because of wholesale retrenchment of employment in heavily unionized sectors such as steel, autos, rubber, and chemicals. Unions have lost members through the relocation of employment from northern unionized and industrialized communities (what I termed in chapter 6 the heartland of American unionism) to nonunionized areas of the United States and overseas. And, unions have failed to win their share of representation elections in their own areas and sectors. They have failed to maintain their share of manufacturing employment as the total number of manufacturing employees has declined. The relative success of service unions over the same period of time has not made up the difference.

However important these sources of declining membership, the current crisis of organized labor is more than a crisis of membership. Throughout the book, I have emphasized that industrial unions today are facing very hostile situations in their home domain: their traditional centers of power and support. Unions are held accountable for the prosperity (or lack thereof) of communities and regions across the United States. Rightly or wrongly, plant closings and plant relocations are seen as directly attributable to unions' relationships to employers. The case studies presented in this book that deal with this issue (in chapters 3 and 4, for example) are indicative of the deep political divisions generated by these situations. While employers are probably accountable and have much to gain in these situations, the failure of unions to mount effective counter-policies has further alienated their traditional constituencies. The crisis of organized labor is more than the loss of membership; it is deeper and perhaps more fundamental: the welfare of unions is no longer consistent with the welfare of communities.

Since the history of so many unions is bound up with the evolution of particular communities, sustained by close community alliances involving local working-class elites and even merchant classes, the separation of union welfare from community welfare has had radical debilitating effects on intra-union solidarity. In a couple of case studies, I noted the cruel choices faced by union leaders. While it is difficult to fault union leaders for attempting to preserve their institutions by sacrificing some local unions (for example), deep divisions between members of the same union are one result. Another result is less willingness to join, and less willingness to abide by union policies regarding concessions and the terms of agreements with corporations. The crisis of organized labor should be understood as an internal political crisis as much as a crisis of membership.

I suggested earlier that this crisis is the result of an unfortunate juxtaposition in time of three factors: the structural–legislative imperatives of the Wagner Act and subsequent federal and state legislation; the geographical patterns and processes of economic restructuring; and the inertia of institutions like the National Labor Relations Board. Structural–legislative imperatives are simply the rules of labor–management relations: those rules that have fostered decentralized labor relations by industry and community. From representation elections to the ratification and even the negotiation of contracts, the presumption of federal labor legislation is that these labor–management relations belong at the local level.

Of course, unions and employers have made attempts to build across communities – witness the growth of master contracts – and unions themselves have attempted to match the spatial diversification of employers. But for all these institutional innovations, unions remain vulnerable to the peculiarities of local circumstances. This was predicted even at the time of passage of the Wagner Act in 1935. Representative Gildea (D – Pennsylvania) commented that the Wagner Act threatened to localize unions, and thereby rob them of their ability to operate as national organizations (see the epigraphy to this book). On the basis of the material presented in the book, who would be confident in arguing that Gildea was wrong? Unfortunately for the union movement, Gildea's insight or intuition about the possible consequences of the Wagner Act has proved right.

By themselves, the rules of labor–management relations are not totally determinate. There is no one model of local labor–management relations; in fact there are many different modes of relationships that vary by place and situation. These rules allow a great deal of discretion in the evolution of local practices and the development of local labor relations cultures. Most obviously this is apparent in the development of labor relations in right-to-work states. But, even if not so obvious in northern non-RTW states, there are many differences between communities in terms of their relationships with employers even in the same industry (see chapter 4 above on the American Motors Corporation and the UAW).

The second major factor which has contributed to the crisis of organized labor is the restructuring of the US economy. So much is written about this phenomenon that the reader might be excused for wishing to pass on quickly to other issues. As noted above, restructuring has led to massive job losses and internal political tensions within unions. It is clear that restructuring has cost many unionized workers their jobs. And many communities have been drastically affected (Bluestone and Harrison 1982). The case studies in this book illustrate this with some eloquence. But the geographical effects of restructuring are not uniform. In fact, restructuring is highly spatially differentiated. And, there is considerable evidence that the design of corporate restructuring programs is often very sensitive to local labor–management relations conditions. In this sense, restructuring not only impacts communities, but its very character is shaped by differences between communities in their histories of labor–management relations.[6]

The significance of the third factor is also immediately obvious. The National Labor Relations Board and the courts (state and federal) have inherited a complex set of doctrines, case histories and precedents, all of which are part of the discourse of adjudication and administration of labor law. Whether by design or by default, the Reagan NLRB seems less able to cope than before. It is overwhelmed by charges and counter-charges, from the most trivial issues through to fundamental issues of the future of the labor movement and the design of new forms of labor relations (see chapters 7 and 9). Moreover, as I indicated in chapter 8, there are good reasons to suppose that the Board faces basic internal problems in rationalizing its decisions – its integrity is questionable because of internal dilemmas of adjudicative practice, let alone because of possible management bias in its decisions. On these grounds, I tend to think that the NLRB is a major impediment to the labor movement.

Still, I do not doubt that the labor unions have faced each of these factors before and have been able to fashion reasonable policies to rationalize their negative consequences. The Board is always contentious, intra-union solidarity has always been a struggle to build and maintain, and economic restructuring has been a continual process of change requiring considerable innovation to accommodate. I would assert that separately these factors have been manageable, perhaps even useful in some circumstances. In fact, we could probably imagine circumstances where the structural–legislative imperative of decentralization (to take only one factor) has been useful to unions. For instance, when a company has been limited by resources or by market opportunities to a limited set of locations, unions have been able to extract concessions which have then been used as leverage in negotiation with other similar companies.

But when these factors were combined or juxtaposed in the late 1970s and through the 1980s, they operated to reinforce one another, and reinforce the decline of unions. Corporations used local differences in labor–management relations as reference points in redesigning their production networks. Corporations have fought unions in representation elections in the hope that union solidarity would fragment under the pressure of their announced restructuring plans, and they have used the adjudication system against itself and unions by delaying and trivializing NLRB procedures.

The current crisis of organized labor is the product of inherited structure or rules of labor–management and recent events. Where the structural–legislative imperative of decentralization was once a source of power and community mobilization for unions it is now an opportunity for corporations to divide workers' loyalties. Where economic growth was once concentrated in industrial sectors, located in the heartland of the United States, the economic future of these industries depends upon wholesale rationalization of these regions. Where employment growth reinforced the power of industrial unions in communities, the dependence of the American labor movement on these sectors and communities has become its Achilles' heel. And, where the institutions of adjudication once provided the administrative structure for union organizing, their ability to respond to the vital issues of economic and geographical restructuring has been confounded by internal adjudicative incoherence, the result of treating the NLRB and the courts as law-making bodies rather than as forums for decision making.

In these circumstances, it is little wonder that industrial unions appear so powerless and incapable of responding to recent events. They grew as their industries grew, protected by widening networks of affiliated local unions. The decentralization imperative was accommodated by coordinated bargaining, referencing the strongest local unions. Corporate restructuring was accommodated by new plants, rarely the abandonment of old plants. While relatively successful in winning representation in these new plants (often located in the South), industrial unions did not have to win these plants as long as they retained representation in the old plants. Decisions of the NLRB could be circumvented by local agreements with management, or the issues themselves settled in grievance arbitration before appearing before the NLRB. Accommodation within an expanding economic environment made the difficulties of any one factor less significant. In these ways, unions survived and prospered. However, incremental accommodation did not equip unions to deal with the juxtaposition of these factors in the rapidly changing economic realities of the late 1970s and the 1980s.

Contested explanations of crisis

My argument that the recent crisis of organized labor is the result of the juxtaposition of three factors at an unfortunate point in time depends upon a couple of theoretical assumptions about economic events and processes. Most importantly, I assume that these three factors have operated semi-autonomously for many years. That is, I assume that the structural–legislative imperatives of decentralization, the structure and restructuring of the economy, and adjudication of labor–management disputes had enough autonomy to operate without colliding in ways that would have paralyzed the system of labor–management relations. By implication it is also assumed that the current crisis of organized labor is different than other problems that unions have faced and dealt with over the past fifty years.

Can institutions and events operate semi-autonomously as I imagine? What has to be assumed to make this plausible? There are, I think, three crucial assumptions. First, I assume that the economic system is less than perfectly integrated, so that there are sectors and places that have a separate (if not independent) life and character. This simply means that the spatial economy operates in disequilibrium rather than equilibrium – incremental changes of union policy in response to economic events can be accommodated within local circumstances. Second, I assume that the regulatory apparatus (the NLRB and the courts) have an administrative life of their own, consistent with the structure of the economy or at least not totally counter to the needs of the economic agents. Either the regulatory apparatus was unimportant, or it could be accommodated without radically changing economic behavior. Third, I assume that events can have major significance, although in ways which are typically unanticipated (see Clark 1986b and cf. Storper 1988).

The current crisis of organized labor is the result of recent economic events that have threatened unions' accommodation to each of the three factors – the design of labor–management relations, customary ways of accommodating economic change, and the regulation of labor–management disputes.

Compared to others' interpretation of the recent decline of organized labor, my approach is both more comprehensive and less ambitious. For example, I have noted many times that Weiler (1983) believes reform of NLRB election procedures and methods of adjudication would make a substantial difference to unions' success rates in representation elections. Likewise, Goldfield (1987) believes that the interpretation of federal labor law and its administration are responsible for the decline of organized labor. Both writers believe that a change in the law would change the environment faced by unions. There is no doubt in my mind that regulation of employers' behavior is critical if representation elections are to be meaningful. In this regard, I tend to agree with Weiler that the representation process needs to be streamlined, and that employers who deliberately subvert the election process ought to be penalized far more severely than is currently the case. And, it should be apparent from chapter 8 that I tend to agree with Goldfield (though not for his reasons) that the NLRB's integrity is substantially compromised.

It is also assumed by many theorists that state RTW legislation inhibits union organizing (see Farber 1984a). The argument advanced in support of this thesis typically goes as follows. First it is assumed that state RTW laws make an appreciable difference to the relative powers of labor and management. RTW legislation is assumed to favor management over labor in all manner of issues, from individuals' rights during representation campaigns through to what can be expected of unions and workers if unions win the right to represent workers. In most instances there is a strong correlation between low rates of state unionization and the existence of state RTW legislation. Second, it is assumed that even if RTW laws are generally not enforced, they are important as public symbols of private power, especially the rights of management over labor (see Moore and Newman 1975). As a consequence many labor supporters would like to see Section 14(b) of the National Labor Relations Act repealed (see chapter 10).[7]

Could changes in legislative and policy environments make an appreciable difference to unions' future? At the state level, repeal of RTW legislation could change the balance of power between management and the power of organized labor in representation elections and on the shop floor. At the federal level, repeal of Section 14(b) of the Taft–Hartley Act would effectively nationalize labor law, if not labor practices.[8] The message of such a repeal would be twofold. First, it would signal the acceptability of unions as legitimate worker representatives, and second, repeal would radically improve their effectiveness in collective bargaining. Internal discipline would be more predictable and the results of bargaining more directly attributable to the power of unions.[9] Still, I am skeptical of this happening in the near future. RTW legislation is, for many states, an economic development policy. And, at the national level, we saw how the labor law reform campaign of 1977 failed to win sufficient support in the Democrat-controlled Senate after passing the House (chapter 10).

Allowing for other factors such as unit size, local economic conditions, industry, and the like I argued that the RTW legislation has been an important strategic variable for corporations in their dealings with unions, as illustrated in the case study of chapter 3. More empirically (see chapters 5 through 7), although the direction of its effect has varied over time, it appears that RTW legislation may have reinforced declining union electoral fortunes during the most recent recession year (1982). In the attempt to predict the outcomes of union representation elections the RTW variable was also found to be important. The implication is that even if the economy expands, and unions contest more representation elections, the RTW effect will remain a substantial impediment to union success.

What of the significance of economic explanations of the decline of organized labor? Here, I think many writers are substantially mistaken about the nature of the environment in which unions operate. This is especially true of aggregate cyclical models like that championed by Ashenfelter and Pencavel (1969). Throughout the early chapters of this book, I attempted to show how these kinds of models misrepresent the representation electoral process and ignore the vital importance of local factors. More plausible are recent studies by Dickens and Leonard (1985) and Dickens et al. (1985) that emphasize the various components of declining membership – structural, cyclical, national, and local.

Unions' electoral performance varies with the business cycle, against the business cycle depending upon the union and the industry, and according to the year. It might be imagined that as the economy expands and employment grows industrial unions will contest more elections and win proportionally more of those elections. There is some evidence for this in chapter 5. Like Dickens and Leonard, I believe that a strong economy is unlikely to restore these unions' electoral success rates to levels experienced in the early 1970s. In this respect, Ashenfelter and Pencavel's model does not do justice to the temporal complexity of economic events and their changing relationship(s) to union growth and decline. But Dickens and others have still to explain how and why these components have changed in significance in recent years, and how structural change in particular affects the local electoral performance of unions. While it is useful as an accounting device to separate cyclical and structural factors, in fact I believe that this book demonstrated that these factors are often closely inter-related.

Another approach is to explain the crisis of organized labor by the policies of unions themselves. Getman (1986) suggested that many unions have lost the ability to organize the unorganized. He believes that most unions are unable to respond to local issues in ways that reach potential union members. Farber (1987) argues that unions no longer understand workers' aspirations, a point indirectly acknowledged by the AFL–CIO (1985). At issue here is the functional performance of unions as organizations. Both writers make useful observations, and there is anecdotal evidence that the industrial unions are particularly inept in organizing younger workers. And yet, unions face some significant barriers to improving their electoral effectiveness, barriers that indicate that it is often very difficult to respond to electoral needs. Just consider the electoral performance of the UAW and IBEW in relation to the issue of the size of their electoral units.

Most of the UAW's units are relatively large, certainly greater than 100. Larger units are easier to service and economically more efficient. But, smaller units are often better for electoral success. For the UAW, smaller unit sizes imply more homogeneous workers. Not only are they likely to perform similar work tasks, but they may also be socially more homogeneous (by age, ethnicity, race, and sex). Given that unions have to convince workers that union representation will improve their working lives, the more homogeneous a unit, the more likely workers will have common interests. The more heterogeneous a unit, the more likely management consultants will be able to rally dissidents against the union. By virtue of its functional specialization, the IBEW has very small units (nine workers or fewer) and fewer problems with defining the appropriate unit of the local firm as the basis of unions' claims to represent certain workers. In this sense, reaching out to potential members is more than an issue of "responsiveness"; the local and industrial settings of different unions may structurally affect unions' success at mobilizing potential members.

We could go on to review others' opinions on many different issues. But, I doubt that repeal of RTW legislation and reform of NLRB procedures would by themselves make a substantial difference to unions' electoral fortunes. Similarly, I doubt that tighter regulation of corporate restructuring programs by themselves – plant closing legislation, for example – would make a substantial difference to unions' solidarity. And, I doubt that removal of local discretion in the formation of labor–management practices could radically turn the path of organized labor. In this sense, I doubt the efficacy of a single explanation of the crisis of organized labor; this is what I mean by suggesting that my interpretation of the crisis is less ambitious than others'. At the same time, I believe their explanations may make an important contribution to a more comprehensive understanding of the crisis of organized labor.

If there are no unions, no communities

Based on the previous discussion and the material presented in the chapters of this book, I am pessimistic about the future of organized labor in the United States. This does not mean that I believe there will be no unions; rather I tend to think that organized labor will be a smaller and politically less significant part of American society. While industrial unions may play a significant role in their respective industries, this role is unlikely to maintain the political presence they have had in national policy making for the past fifty years. And, as I have indicated above, I do not see how clerical and white-collar unions will be able to make up the difference – I am not confident that they will attract massive numbers of new members, nor will they be able to replace industrial unions in the legislative arena.

Industrial unions will be of less and less significance for a variety of reasons. First, these industries are much smaller, and may be smaller still, in absolute terms and in terms of their share of total United States' employment. Second, given the political pressures accompanying restructuring, unions' leadership has had to become more conservative than before. Dissension in the UAW and other similar unions over the geographical allocation of the economic costs of restructuring is such that union leadership has had to become more focused on managing internal political dissent than leading national political issues. Third, smaller industrial unions, limited financial resources, and conservative management could easily translate into a less able and certainly less ambitious union movement.

For these reasons alone, industrial unions will be less important than ever before.

This scenario assumes (implicitly) a reasonably competitive industrial sector; competitive enough to withstand overseas competition. However limited this scenario may be it is, nevertheless, relatively optimistic. There are some commentators who argue that the United States' industries may practically collapse in the face of overwhelming foreign competition.[10] If this happens, organized labor will be a mere shadow of its former self. The International Trade Institute (1987) of the Japan Foreign Trade Council Inc. recently published a very pessimistic report on the prospects for US industry. The Institute was established in 1981, and has the support of the Japanese government, industry organizations, and the Ministry of International Trade and Industry (MITI).[11]

The Institute identified three fundamental deficiencies in the US economy. First, it suggested that post-war recovery of Japan and Europe, coupled with the 1970s oil crises, inevitably reduced the relative significance of the US economy in world commodity production. With the relative decline of manufacturing and rapid expansion of the service sector, the US economy was not competitive in world trade. Second, in dominating world markets for many years, American corporations effectively disseminated the basic technology of large-scale production abroad. However, their ability to innovate once other countries were able to compete has been quite limited. According to the Institute, American corporate management have been ineffective, and worse, have operated with adversary labor relations. As a consequence, American corporations have been subject to drastic competition in mass production industries burdened by out-dated technology, poor production methods, high wages, and low labor productivity.

In combination, corporate ineffectiveness and the economic growth of other nations was bound to affect US competitiveness. However, the Institute went further and argued that US industry has not only failed in the international arena, but has failed to serve the growing regions of its domestic market. That is, the West and the South are increasingly served by foreign producers exporting to these growing markets or producing in these markets, whereas domestic producers have failed to reorganize production, distribution, and sales adequately to serve these markets. Essentially, the US market has become internally spatially fractured. By sub-dividing the market by region, and allowing foreign competitors a large share of these growing markets, US trade problems with Japan, Asia, and Latin America have been exacerbated. If the US is not competitive internationally (by product and productivity) and "sells" portions of its own internal market overseas, only massive devaluation of the dollar could stabilize trading relations between the US and the rest of the world.

Thus the "hollowing-out" of American industry may take two forms: replacement of domestic manufacturing capacity by overseas plants of US multinationals and foreign producers and the balkanization of the domestic market into regional spheres of influence served by offshore producers. By this worst case scenario, all that may be left of the traditional unionized manufacturing sectors will be a fragment located in the Midwest serving a local (albeit large) market, buffeted by massive competition in the East, West, and South. By this scenario, the industrial unions will likely lose whatever representation they have in the South, and will find greater difficulty in penetrating employers in the Pacific regions, especially California. Reconfiguration of regional markets, non-American producers, and new forms of labor relations in plants owned by foreign producers at a time when unions are most fragile may conspire to block them from access to even their traditional centers of influence.

The worst case scenario implies a broken, irrelevant union movement. Union representation will be just a local phenomenon, isolated in a region (the Midwest) of the US. What will happen to communities if this occurs? Here, I think American communities face an uncertain future. Whereas unions tended to protect communities in the north and central regions of the US by virtue of their policies of coordinated collective bargaining and noncompetition between plants, collapse of an effective union movement may prompt a degree of competition between communities of extraordinary proportions. In such a world, local incomes, employment, and jobs would be directly at risk. In such a world, neither unions nor communities would be able to protect workers. In such a world, any chance for collective action would be effectively silenced as the possibility of collective action becomes (if it has not already) a crucial variable in firms' location decision making.

Exhausted ideals

Compared to Europe, Canada, Australia, and New Zealand, unions have never been particularly strong in the United States. And in recent years, their disenchantment with the laws and institutions governing American labor–management relations seems to have become endemic. Lane Kirkland, president of the AFL–CIO, has argued that the labor movement might be better off without the National Labor Relations Act and the National Labor Relations Board. According to Kirkland, the NLRA is an impediment standing in the way of new forms of cooperative relationships between organized labor and management. Others believe that federal labor laws institutionalize and narrow the antagonistic interests of labor and management at a time when these same laws ought to facilitate joint collaboration (see Fischer 1986a). As we have seen, labor's spokespersons also argue that the appeal procedures of the NLRB are so complicated and legalistic that unions may be more effective in organizing workers if they pursue direct confrontation tactics rather than continuing to work through the Board.

During the Reagan administration, employers' lobbying organizations tended to be less critical of federal labor laws and institutions than organized labor. Even so, there have been persistent, albeit muted, criticisms of the NLRA, especially in relation to the legal problems of rationalizing collaborative labor–management agreements within the terms of the Act. So, for example, Roger Smith (chairman of GM) has been a scathing critic of the NLRB's procedures, which have been used by opponents of the Saturn Project in their attempts to overturn the agreement (especially the National Right-To-Work Committee). In previous Democrat administrations employer organizations often objected to what they perceived to be the pro-union decisions of the NLRB. At one level, current union dissatisfaction with the NLRA and the NLRB reflects a partisan interest in the opinions of the Board which exists whatever the political composition of the Board.

It is also possible, moreover, that the 1977 campaign for labor law reform made dialogue on the logic and utility of federal labor law impossible between organized labor and employers' lobbying groups. Failure of labor law reform and the apparent anti-union stance of the Reagan administration encouraged factions within organized labor to assume a combative and antagonistic stance against those who would suggest changes in federal labor law. And, given the success of employers' lobbying groups and their Senate allies in derailing labor law reform, it is not surprising that subsequent arguments by these groups for revisions in federal labor law have been viewed by labor with such suspicion. There seems to be little chance of changing federal labor law in the near future; events during the 1977 campaign and subsequent actions by the Reagan administration and the NLRB have effectively created a stalemate in federal labor policy. As predicted by D. Quinn Mills (1979), business leaders' reactions to labor reform have "cast a long shadow" over federal labor–management relations policy.

The political economy of American labor law, and juxtaposition of the three factors contributing to the crisis of organized labor in the late 1980s – structural–legislative imperatives, economic restructuring, and institutional incapacity – indicate the need for a concerted legislative response. A new legislative initiative is needed because I doubt that reinvigorating the NLRA, changing the policies and membership of the NLRB, and/or stringently enforcing key provisions of the NLRA will make a substantial difference to the climate of labor–management relations. It is too late to reverse what has now become customary behavior; events and accommodations to the juxtaposition of the three factors identified above have spawned a spiral of response and counter-response. To retreat to the regulatory environment of the early 1960s (one possible benchmark) would be practically impossible.

Not only would it be practically impossible to return to a more innocent era of the NLRA, but it is doubtful that the NLRA is now a plausible framework for labor–management relations. The questions raised in chapters 8 and 9 about the integrity of the NLRB should be reason enough to query the integrity of the whole. More generally, it seems that the regulatory system put in place in 1935 is not able to deliver on the promises made by President Roosevelt and others at the time of passage of the Wagner Act. The integrity of collective bargaining has been made a shambles by a variety of employers' tactics. By simply refusing to bargain, let alone relocating to avoid bargaining responsibilities, employers have become nonparticipants in a system that was originally conceived as vital to the economic welfare of the whole economy. Reversing Roosevelt's terms, the NLRA no longer assures "employees the right of collective bargaining," nor does it foster "employment contracts on a fair and equitable basis."[12]

The ideal of industrial democracy, championed by congressional leaders at the time of passage of the Act and subsequently given greater significance as the conventional interpretation of the Act was modified after 1945 (see Stone 1981), has also suffered an ignominious fate. The consequences of employer resistance to representation elections has been well noted in this book and by many other commentators. As well, the process has suffered from schisms and tensions evident in the wider political environment. In this sense, the ideal of industrial democracy has not been met; it has gone the way of partisan political election process – divided and fragmented by narrow interests, dominated by media consultants, and transformed by the campaign process. While this may have been inevitable, given the evolution of American party politics, the union representation process is nothing like the ideal. To imagine that the NLRA could be justified even now by reference to this ideal would seem impossible.

At the time of passage of the Wagner Act, many supporters hoped that the Act would provide unions with security and legitimacy in representing their members. It was also hoped that union security would help stabilize local wages and employment, and thus lead the whole economy in economic revival. Although there were warnings that the Wagner Act would "strike a damaging blow against national unions" and would "degenerate into an extension of the government–union idea, one union for each plant," these warnings were ignored.[13] Passage of the Taft–Hartley amendments reinforced the localization of the American union movement. In the 1980s, union membership and affiliation with International unions have become vital elements of dispute between employers and communities. Many corporations have come to imagine that union security stands in the way of economic restructuring – geographical restructuring is one consequence. Where a truly national union movement may have forced a different design of economic restructuring, the weakness of unions as national entities has allowed corporate flight, even blackmail of communities.

Thus, union security has become an empty promise. The underlying structure of labor law, which encouraged localization of labor–management relations, has become a fundamental disadvantage for unions and communities in their bargaining with employers. Indeed, the very geography of the union movement has made it vulnerable to the global reach of corporate capitalism.

For all these reasons, the promise and potential of the NLRA is now exhausted. It cannot be legitimated by reference to fair labor contracts, industrial democracy, or union security. These goals of the Wagner Act have been systematically violated over the past decades. What society must face is the exhaustion of an ideal, and the perversion of the current structure of decentralized labor–management relations.

Appendix 1   Variables and data sources

Variable	Description
*Election variables**	
AGAINST	Number of votes cast against union representation
WL	Win–loss record
ELIG	Employees in the designated bargaining unit who were eligible to vote under the NLRB rules at the time of the representation election
FOR	Number of votes cast in favor of union representation
PRIOR	Indicates a prior representation election (the previous year) in the company at the location of the current election
TYPE	Representation election type, defined by the NLRB: B = Board-ordered election; C = consent election; E = expedited election (under Section 8(b)(7)(C)); R = regional director ordered; S = stipulated
SIC	Two-digit Standard Industrial Classification of the economic activities of the plant in which the election was held
UNIT	Functional classification of eligible voters according to work tasks within the firm: A = industrial production and maintenance; C = craft(s); D = departmental; G = guards; T = truck drivers; W = office staff; Z = others not classified
Local economic variables†	
EMPLOY	Number of employees in the SIC of the election in the county during the year of the representation election
ESTAR	Number of business establishments in the county
ESTSIC	Number of business establishments in the SIC of the election in the county
LESS	Number of employers with nineteen or fewer employees in the county, in the year of the election
PAY	Annual payroll of all business establishments in the SIC and county of the election, in the year of the election
AVPAY	Average pay per employee in the SIC and county, in the year of the election
AVPRL	Average payroll per establishment in the SIC and county of the election, in the year of the election
AVSIZE	Average establishment size by employment of the county in which the election was held

Unionization variables‡
PCT   Percentage unionization of nonagricultural employment by state
RTW   Indicates the existence or otherwise of state right-to-work legislation
REGION   North includes non-RTW states such as Minnesota, Wisconsin, Illinois,
         Missouri, Indiana, Kentucky, Ohio, West Virginia, Pennsylvania,
         Maryland, Delaware, New York, New Jersey, Connecticut, Rhode
         Island, Massachusetts, Vermont, New Hampshire, and Maine. South –
         RTW includes the states of Virginia, North and South Carolina,
         Tennessee, Georgia, Alabama, Florida, Mississippi, Arkansas, Loui-
         siana, and Texas. South and West includes non-RTW states California,
         Oregon, Washington, Idaho, Montana, Colorado, New Mexico, and
         Oklahoma. West – RTW includes states Nevada, Arizona, and Wyo-
         ming. Central – RTW includes states North and South Dakota,
         Nebraska, Utah, Kansas, and Iowa

Sources: * National Labor Relations Board, various years, Election Reports
          † US Department of Commerce, various years, County Business Patterns.
          Note that in some instances these variables were transformed by calculat-
          ing percentage changes (P) over the previous two years
          ‡ Troy and Sheflin (1985)

Appendix 2 Cases cited

Amalgamated Clothing and Textile Workers Union v. NLRB, 736 F.2d 1559, 117 LRRM 2453 (1984)

Amoco Production Co., 262 NLRB 1240 (1982), 721 F.2d 150 (CA 5, 1983)

Anamag Limited, 284 NLRB no. 72 (1987)

Banas v. Matthews International Corp., 502 A.2d 637 (1985)

D. & N. Boening, Inc. v. Kirsch Beverages, 63 NY2d 449 (1984)

Bristol Textile Company, 277 NLRB 182 (1986)

Brockway Motor Trucks v. National Labor Relations Board, 582 F.2d 720 (3rd Cir., 1978)

Butler v. Negley House, 129 PLJ 250 (1981)

Century Air Freight Inc., 284 NLRB no. 85 (1987)

Clark Equipment Co., 278 NLRB 85 (1986)

Cook v. Heck's Inc., 342 SE.2d 453 (1986)

Duldulao v. St. Mary of Nazareth Hospital Center, no. 62737 Ill SupCt (1987)

Duplex Printing Press Co. v. Deering, 254 US 443 (1921)

Fall River Dyeing and Finishing Corp. v. National Labor Relations Board, no. 85-1208 US (1987)

Farrell v. Automobile Club of Michigan, no. 82916 Mich App. (1987)

Fibreboard Paper Products Corp. v. National Labor Relations Board et al., 397 US 203 (1964)

First National Maintenance Corp., 242 NLRB 462 (1979)

First National Maintenance Corp. v. National Labor Relations Board, 627 F.2d 596, 104 LRRM 2924 (CA 2, 1980), *reversed and remanded*, 452 US 666, 107 LRRM 2705 (1981)

Geary v. United States Steel Corp., 456 PA 163 (1974)

General Knit of California, Inc., 239 NLRB 619, 99 LRRM 1687 (1978)

General Shoe Corp., 77 NLRB 124, 21 LRRM 1337 (1948)

Grayson v. American Airlines Inc., no. 85-1105 (10th Cir., 1986)

Hollywood Ceramics Co., 140 NLRB 221, 51 LRRM 1600 (1962)

International Brotherhood of Electrical Workers, Local 501 v. National Labor Relations Board, 341 US 694 (1951)

International Harvester Company, 227 NLRB 85 (1977), *remanded* (9th Cir.) no. 77-1349 (1977), 236 NLRB 712 (1978), *enforced* 618 F.2d 85 (9th Cir. 1980)

Kari v. General Motors Corp., 79 Mich App. 93, 261 NW2d 222 (1977)

Kilpatrick v. Delaware County SPCA, 632 F. Supp. 542 (ED PA 1986)

Kinoshita v. Canadian Pacific Airlines Ltd., no. 11148 SupCt Hawaii (1986)

Loewe v. Lawler, 208 US 274 (1908)

Los Angeles Marine Hardware Co., a Division of Mission Marine Associates, Inc.,

235 NLRB 720 (1978), CCH NLRB no. 19215, *enforced* 602 F.2d 1302 (CA 9, 1979), 87 LC no. 11628

Meyers Industries, Inc., 268 NLRB 493, 115 LRRM 1025 (1984)

Michael's Markets of Canterbury, 274 NLRB 105 (1985)

Midland National Life Insurance Co., 263 NLRB 127, 110 LRRM 1489 (1982)

Milwaukee Spring Division of Illinois Coil Spring Co. (Milwaukee Spring I), 265 NLRB 206, 111 LRRM 1486 (1982), *remanded*, 718 F.2d 1102, 114 LRRM 2376 (CA 7, 1983)

Milwaukee Spring Division of Illinois Coil Spring Co. (Milwaukee Spring II), 268 NLRB 601, 115 LRRM 1065 (1984), *enforced*, 765 F.2d 175 (DC Cir., 1985)

National Labor Relations Board v. Denver Building and Construction Trades Council, 341 US 675, 28 LRRM 2108 (1951)

National Labor Relations Board v. Idab Inc., 770 F.2d 991 (1985)

National Labor Relations Board v. International Rice Milling Co., 341 US 665, 28 LRRM 2105 (1951)

National Labor Relations Board v. Wooster Division of Borg–Warner Corp., 356 US 342 (1958)

North Shore Bottling Co. v. Schmidt & Sons, Inc., 22 NY2d 171 (1968)

Novosel v. Sears, Roebuck & Co., 495 F.Supp. 344 (ED Mich 1980)

Robert S. Ohanian v. Avis Rent a Car System, Inc. (2nd Cir.), Docket nos. 85–7284 and 85–7330 (1985)

Otis Elevator, a Wholly Owned Subsidiary of United Technologies (Otis Elevator I), 255 NLRB 235, 106 LRRM 1343 (1981)

Otis Elevator, a Wholly Owned Subsidiary of United Technologies (Otis Elevator II), 269 NLRB 891, 115 LRRM 1281 (1984)

Otis Elevator, a Wholly Owned Subsidiary of United Technologies (Otis Elevator III), 283 NLRB no. 40 (1987)

Payne v. The Western & Atlantic Railroad Company et al, 81 Tenn. 507 (1884)

Perks v. Firestone Tire and Rubber Co., 611 F.2d 1363 (3d Cir., 1979)

Purolator Armoured, Inc. NLRB no. 84–5222 (1985)

Reuther v. Fowler and Williams Inc., 386 A.2d 119 (1978)

Schechter Poultry Corp. v. United States, 295 US 495 (1935)

Shopping Kart Food Mkts. Inc., 228 NLRB 1331, 94 LRRM 1705 (1977)

Steelworkers Local 2179 v. NLRB, no. 85–1841 (5th Cir., 1987)

Teamsters' Local No. 670, 275 NLRB no. 127 (1985)

United Food and Commercial Workers, Local 174 v. Hebrew National Kosher Foods, Inc., no. 86–7840 (2d Cir., 1987)

United States v. Darby, 312 US 100 (1941)

United States v. Enmons et al., 410 US 396 (1973)

US Ecology, Inc. v. National Labor Relations Board, nos. 85–7154 & 85–7259 (1985)

Weather Tamer, Inc. and Tuskegee Garment Corporation, 253 NLRB no. 36 (1980); *enforced in part, denied in part*, 676 F.2d 483 (1982)

Weiner v. McGraw Hill, Inc., 57 NY2d 458 (1982)

Notes

[1] Crisis of organized labor

1. Bain and Price (1980) provide detailed "profiles" on union membership in Western Europe, Australia, and Canada. Kassalow (1985) has a useful analysis of the future of US unionism.

2. Based upon the Continuous Population Survey (CPS) of the US Department of Labor, the January 1988 issue of *Employment and Earnings* indicated unionization was about 14 percent in 1987 (see also Farber 1987).

3. This discussion centers upon the performance of unions in the private sector, and in the industrial sectors in particular. There is evidence that suggests public-sector unionism has increased in recent years to about 36 percent of all government employment (unpublished data from the US Department of Labor, Washington DC).

4. See Samuelson (1983) for a recent recapitulation of the role of Von Thunen in the evolution of neoclassical economic theory, and Isard (1956) for a generalization of Weber's approach.

5. See Borts and Stein's (1964) seminal contribution.

6. See Clark (1981), Storper and Walker (1983), Massey (1984), Gregory and Urry (1985), Scott and Storper (1986), and Clark, Gertler, and Whiteman (1986) for introduction to, and development of, this research agenda.

7. A reader of a draft of this chapter remarked that surely commercial firms whose business it is to locate firms still use conventional location theory. But even in this area, there are firms using the new location theory to locate firms in communities with an appropriate labor climate. Labor climate is sometimes measured by the track record of local firms in union representation elections (where success is defined as defeating unions in representation elections). One major American location company has built a massive data base which provides a profile of union organizing at the local level over a long period of time.

8. In late 1987, the Teamsters' union rejoined the AFL–CIO.

9. See Bernstein's (1961) historical model, which was formalized by Ashenfelter and Pencavel (1969), who argued that national patterns of unionization could easily be explained by changes in inflation, employment, unemployment, and the union sentiment of Congress.

10. Public Act no. 198, 49 Stat. 449–457, quoted in National Labor Relations Board, *Legislative History of the National Labor Relations Act, 1935*, vol. II, p. 3269 (5 July 1935).

[2] Understanding union growth and decline

1. Brian Berry, Ben Fischer, Meric Gertler, Bennett Harrison, Everett Kassalow, and Edward Montgomery provided helpful comments on drafts of this chapter.

2. See Dunlop (1948) for a seminal contribution.

3. See also Elsheikh and Bain (1978) and the critical comments by Fiorito (1982).

4. In some instances, industrial unions were recognized by employers as legitimate bargaining agents for all their plants, regardless of location. While a common practice in the steel and aluminium industries in the 1950s, this "gentleman's" agreement broke down under the combined pressures of state-level anti-union legislation (right-to-work laws which prohibited closed shop agreements), and employers' management strategies which sought to create different institutional environments in different regions of the country.

5. In particular see Scoville (1971), Freeman and Medoff (1984), and Hirsch and Berger (1984), amongst many others.

6. Ch. 372, 1, 49 Stat. 449 (1935) and ch. 120, tit. 1, 101, 61 Stat. 136 (1947) respectively. Notice that it is commonly held that the Wagner Act made it easier for unions to organize, while the Taft–Hartley Act made it more difficult (Rees 1973). However, I would argue that compared to European countries, both Acts made it difficult to organize labor on a national scale. Indeed, this was recognized in debates over the Wagner Act in 1935. See, for example, the remarks of Representative Schneider on the Senate version of the Act (*Legislative History of the National Labor Relations Act*, vol. II, pp. 3228–3231). It is clear, though, that the Taft–Hartley Act was more restrictive than the Wagner Act.

7. But see recent research on state-level experiments with modified employment-at-will doctrines (see Murg and Scharman 1982 and Bierman and Youngblood 1984).

8. See also Dickens (1983) and Lawler (1984) on the increasing use of management consultants by employers during representation campaigns. They suggested that many of these consultants are utilizing "dirty" tricks in attempting to affect election outcomes. In using these tricks, they obviously have at least the tacit support of employers, if not openly expressed support.

9. This was one of the first academic attempts to formally analyze the patterns of the American labor movement. It was based on a course of lectures given by Hoxie to students at the University of Chicago in 1915.

10. See the essays in Leab (1985) for examples of local union struggles and attempts to build a national movement.

11. Compared to Dunlop (1948), Lester was quite critical of Hoxie's framework. Lester thought that Hoxie had failed to provide a "systematic theory of union evolution" (4). He also had little sympathy with Hoxie's dialectical method of explaining the evolution of unionism as a constant struggle between pairs of opposing forces. While acknowledging Hoxie's "interesting flashes of insight" (5), Lester belittled his achievements by misrepresenting Hoxie's methodological stance, concluding that "regrettably, Hoxie did not reconcile or elaborate his diverse views on union development" (5).

12. See the volume edited by Pratt and Zeckhauser (1985) for a detailed exposition of the economics of agents and principals. A crucial issue in this literature is the policing of agents, given the costs involved for principals in searching out the requisite information regarding the performance and interests of agents.

13. This point is also made by Lazear (1983:69–72) in his discussion of local wage and bargaining policies of unions.

[3] Communities and corporate location strategies

1. This chapter was originally prepared for presentation to the American–Bulgarian Conference on Regional Economic Development and Environmental Management, sponsored in part by the National Science Foundation. I would like to thank Ben Fischer, Everett Kassalow, Richard Florida, Mickey Lauria, and Jae-Hong Kim for comments on a draft. Ken Kovacs of the United Steelworkers of America provided helpful information about current legislation before Congress. All opinions remain, of course, my responsibility.

2. Podgursky estimated that around 11 million workers lost their jobs in the early years of this decade. Though nearly 65 percent of those workers subsequently found re-employment, fewer than 40 percent of those re-employed were able to find jobs that provided the same levels of benefits as their previous jobs.

3. See Roach (1987) for a discussion of the recent relative performance of the manufacturing and service sectors in job creation. He argues that job creation has slowed in the last year, largely because of "sluggish" growth in personal income. In contrast to the patterns of the last decade, manufacturing has again taken over from service sectors as the leading job-creating sector.

4. These findings are quite controversial. While no one disputes the evidence that the number of manufacturing blue-collar jobs has declined, some commentators argue that American manufacturing as a whole is still very competitive even if there has been a shift away from unionized firms and sectors to more technologically intensive sectors. Others argue that the data on which Bluestone and Harrison base their findings are inadequate or misleading, and yet others suggest that even if their findings are correct, these patterns are only temporary – it is supposed that the long-term decline in the numbers of working-age people will inevitably lead to higher wages in the future. Still other critics argue that Bluestone and Harrison are only ideologues even though Bluestone and Harrison note that the tendency towards income polarization has been apparent for many years, and was not concocted to embarrass the Reagan administration.

5. See for instance Clark (1986b, 1988a respectively) for analyses of the spatial ramifications of restructuring in the US auto and steel industries.

6. For example, during the 100th Congress, House Bill (HR) 1122 and Senate Bill (S) 538 (trade bills) provided for advance notification of plant closings, HR 281 and S 492 (double-breasting bills) sought to outlaw the common business practice of switching work from union to nonunion plants, and HR 1324, 2172, and S 1323 (pension bills) aimed to prohibit corporations from skimming assets from pension plans in order to finance acquisitions and take-overs.

7. See Northrup (1984) for a similar kind of argument about the virtues of a case study, though perhaps not as explicit as mine. Northrup analyzed the changing fortunes of the air traffic controllers' union (PATCO).

8. Mack Trucks also assembled trucks in Canada at a plant in Oakville, Ontario. No figures are available on levels of employment in that plant.

9. At the time of the announcement, Mack Trucks held land options in Georgia, North and South Carolina, Tennessee, and Virginia. All five are right-to-work states. Under Section 14(b) of the National Labor Relations Act (as amended, 29 USC 141–144, 151–187, 1982), state governments have the option to pass laws which provide workers the right not to join unions even if their unit is represented by a union. This provision was passed in 1947 through the Taft–Hartley Act, and outlaws closed-shop agreements (see Morris 1983, ch. 29 (IV), for more details). These same five states have very low rates of unionization, and have proved to be difficult states in which to win representation elections (Clark and Johnston 1987b).

10. By the first quarter of 1987, Mack Trucks was in fourth place with 13.4 percent of the domestic US truck market. Its share of the market had drastically fallen from 1980, and had even significantly fallen over the period 1985–87 (*Journal of Commerce and Commercial*, vol. 372, no. 26,458, 20 April 1987, pp. 1A, 6A).

11. The *Washington Post*, 16 December 1985, p. WB23.

12. The *Washington Post*, 17 January 1986, pp. A1, A26.

13. As of 30 January 1986, 1,800 production workers were employed in the Allentown plant, with another 2,000 workers on lay-off. Including managerial and clerical workers, Mack Trucks employed about 6,000 people in the area (*Daily Labor Report*, no. 20, 30 January 1986, pp. A4–A6).

14. The *New York Times*, 19 January 1986, p. K.

15. *Journal of Commerce and Commercial*, vol. 372, no. 26,508, 30 June 1987, p. 1.

16. *Journal of Commerce and Commercial*, vol. 373, nos. 26,533 and 26,535, 4–6 August 1987, pp. 2B, 4B.

17. *Journal of Commerce and Commercial*, vol. 373, nos. 26,538, 26,543, and 26,544, 11, 18, and 19 August 1987, p. 2B.

18. In a neoclassical world, economic adjustment is based upon the flexibility of prices. It is prices that represent demand and supply, and it is prices that are the essential market signals that ensure market coordination (Leijonhufvud 1981, ch. 7). To make this kind of model work, full information is assumed and uncertainty is relegated to a form of risk, as opposed to a temporally or spatially heterogeneous process. Rational expectations is the extreme form of this kind of model (Lucas 1981). In contrast, Keynesian models of economic adjustment depend upon quantity adjustment as the levers of economic change, in a world assumed to be incomplete in terms of information and knowledge of the economic process (Morishima 1984).

19. This kind of location theory is ahistorical, and nondynamic. No attempt is made by neoclassical location theorists to specify the path of spatial–temporal adjustment that single firms take, or the path of adjustment that the economy takes in the aggregate to reach equilibrium (see Clark, Gertler, and Whiteman 1986 for a critique and alternative theoretical stance).

20. This interpretation of the dispute was often presented in the media. For instance, a vice-president with the consulting company Booz, Allen and Hamilton suggested that Mack Trucks are "a high-cost producer"; they (the union) have "got to realize they're dealing with a company that doesn't have that many options" (*Journal of Commerce and Commercial*, vol. 373, no. 26,526, 24 July 1987, p. 2B).

21. By using the term "Machiavellian," I mean to imply that the corporation was, as

Strauss (1973:272) described the philosophy of political action associated with Niccolò Machiavelli, "guided exclusively by considerations of expediency, which uses all means, fair and foul, iron and poison, [to achieve] its ends."

22. In the introduction to his book Dunlop (1944) warned against the "imperialism" of economic theory, which insists that "all aspects of behavior, particularly any activity related to markets, can be explained by models with the usual economic variables" (5). Unfortunately, few analysts took him seriously, as a recent treatment of the topic has demonstrated (Hirsch and Addison 1986).

23. Lazear's model is innovative in a couple of ways. It is sensitive to the NLRB procedures by which workers elect to join unions, and to the possibility of different legislative regimes in different areas – like RTW legislation.

24. Representative Mead (D – New York) said during the debates over the passage of the Act that the Wagner Act "creates a democracy within industry which gives to our industrial workers the same general idea of freedom which the founding fathers conferred upon citizens of the United States" (79 Cong. Rec. 9710, 19 June 1935). This ideal has become the basis of one important interpretation of the substantive objective of the NLRA (see Stone 1981).

25. Lazear does not strictly deal with Locals and nationals as union organizations. Rather, they are used as devices representing different levels of the market for labor. For example, national "refers to the relevant labor market defined by the pool over which workers are perfect substitutes" (72). In these terms, Locals are sub-sets of the same, separated from the whole by national legislation, NLRB rules, custom, and the like, which results in "too much unionization" (70).

26. The *Washington Post*, 17 January 1986, pp. A1, A26.

27. The idea of a business climate or a manufacturing climate seems to have originated in consulting companies whose primary function has been to locate and relocate plants in different areas of the US. It refers to the local circumstances in which production takes place, what theorists might term externalities. As indicated by the consulting company Grant Thornton (1987:1), concern for local business climates implies "an attitude of constructive enquiry which emphasizes looking beyond the accounting records to the operations and environments that create the accounting entries."

28. See also Harrison (1984) for a study of the evolution of the New England economy that integrates the economic fortunes of the region with its changing business climate – as indicated by the strength of the union movement through to the role of unions at the shop floor.

29. Harrison and Kanter (1978) provide a critical assessment of the relative significance of business incentives in promoting local economic growth. Their conclusion was that "there is neither theoretical nor empirical support for the belief that interstate business incentive differentials make an important difference to the decisions of firms" to relocate, expand operations, or set up new plants (433–34).

30. The *Washington Post*, 17 January 1986, pp. A1, A26.

31. See Williams' (1987) commentary for an extended discussion of this methodological issue.

[4] Rationing jobs within the union, between communities

1. This chapter was made possible by the generous help of Howard Young. Thanks also to Ben Fischer, Everett Kassalow, Harry Katz, Bennett Harrison, and Robert Reich, and others who made useful comments on a draft. None of the above should be held responsible for the opinions expressed or the interpretation of events argued herein.

2. American Motors Corporation was bought by Chrysler Corporation in early 1987. In early 1988, Chrysler announced plans to close the Kenosha/AMC works, prompting a political furore in the city and the State of Wisconsin.

3. For an in-depth analysis of American international competitiveness, see the recent study by Zysman and Cohen (1987). These writers are pessimistic, to say the least, and suggest that the US economy is undergoing such a radical transformation that the place of the US in the world economy is in imminent danger. This theme is developed more generally in the volume edited by Obey and Sarbanes (1986).

4. Fischer (1986b:1), in a sympathetic review of the book, summarized Halberstam's method by noting that the author "digs deeply into the intrigue, pettiness, jealousies and human shortcomings of the vaunted captains of enterprise, ours as well as those of Japan. He does this through biographical accounts derived from interviews and research."

5. Compare with Bowles, Gordon, and Weisskopf (1983), who also argue that American business has become bureaucratic and unproductive. Their thesis, however, was based upon marxian analytics emphasizing structural problems of the American corporate system as part of the over-arching capitalist mode of production.

6. In the 1978 letter of agreement signed between the corporation and Locals 72 and 75, it was stated that the PHCS program would only "become effective when three or more bargaining units represented by the Union have ratified its terms" (quoted in the Decision of the Convention Appeals Committee, dated 27 November 1985, p. 2).

7. In fact, as late as November 1985, Locals 72 and 75 had 3,400 people on permanent lay-off (see Decision of the Convention Appeals Committee dated 27 November 1985, p. 4).

8. Prehearing brief of Local 72, UAW filed before Arbitrator Paul Glendon, 14 July 1986 (1).

9. Under the terms of the EIP, the corporation was to repay its employees over the period 1985 to 31 December 1988 unless it repaid its obligations earlier. No date was given for the expiration of the PHCS provision, although Local 75 believed that it would co-terminate with the EIP (see Memorandum brief on behalf of Local 75, UAW, dated 11 July 1986, p. 4). Neither Local 72 nor the International union subscribed to this view (see the Arbitration award for grievance no. 4373 by Paul Glendon, dated 5 September 1986, p. 14).

10. It was also thought at the time that the corporation would have moved a portion of Toledo's work (the XJ automotive platform) to Kenosha had Local 12 not agreed to the EIP/PHCS plan. The Convention Appeals Committee estimated that this would have resulted in 2,000 permanent lay-offs in Toledo (see Decision of the Convention Appeals Committee, dated 27 November 1985, p. 3).

11. According to the corporation, most employees hired under the terms of the PHCS program had between six and twelve years' seniority with AMC corporation. Some even had as much as twenty-seven years' seniority (Statement of American Motors Corporation, undated, pp. 5–6).

12. Memorandum and order no. C 85–8048 of the US District Court for the Northern District of Ohio, dated 29 November 1985. Of course, the issue of the injunction does not mean that the Court reached any judgment regarding the merits of Local 12's grievance with the company. It was sufficient to find that the grievance would "not be a futile endeavor" (Memorandum and order, p. 16).

13. Agency is defined in UAW regulations as "a fiduciary relationship which results from the manifestation of consent by one person to another that the other shall act on his behalf and subject to his control, and consent by the other to act so" (quoted by Local 12 in Prehearing brief, p. 14). Compare this definition with Pratt and Zeckhauser (1985).

14. Apparently an official of the corporation had promised Majerus in 1982 not to "bargain by setting one local union against another" (Arbitration award, grievance no. 4373, p. 14).

15. A related interpretation of working-class institutions has been made by Przeworski (1985), principally concerning the organization of European social democracies. His interest was in social democratic strategies of reform and revolution sensitive to the current conditions.

[5] Democracy in the guise of representation elections

1. The National Labor Relations Act, as amended, 29 USC 141–144, 151–187 (1982).

2. 74th Congress, Report #1259, Congressional Record, vol. 79, p. 9710.

3. The Labor Management Relations Act of 1947 (Public Law 101, 61 Stat. 136). See Johnston (1986) for further details.

4. National Labor Relations Board (1985:3269).

5. If more than 50 percent of those workers judged eligible to vote in an election vote for a union to represent them, then that union has the right to represent all workers in the designated unit. If 50 percent or fewer vote for union representation, then the union is deemed not to have won the right to represent any workers in the unit.

6. The year 1970 was one of relative economic decline, compared to the late 1960s. During the last quarter of 1970, the national economy reached its cyclical trough. From early 1971, it began to expand, but at a relatively slow rate. The year 1974 was characterized by relatively slow growth followed by a sharp unanticipated recession, with a trough in the first quarter of 1975. By 1978, however, the economy had expanded quite dramatically, reaching a peak in the last quarter of 1978. In contrast, 1982 was the year of the worst post-war recession, in fact a depression in many manufacturing centers around the country. Again, 1986 was a relatively prosperous year, even if prosperity was somewhat concentrated in the service sectors rather than manufacturing (Gordon 1980; *Economic report of the President* 1986).

7. It has been observed by Rogoff and Sibert (1986) that political science models of the electoral cycle do not account for rational expectations. Even Hibbs' (1985)

recent work retains the adaptive expectations framework. Of course, this does not mean that Hibbs' models are now irrelevant; there is considerable debate over the plausibility of rational expectations. Some theorists have argued that rational expectations is fundamentally ahistorical (Bausor 1983). Rogoff and Sibert have provided an alternative electoral-cycle model based upon an assumption of asymmetrical distribution of information between voters and government.

8. See Archer and Taylor (1981), Taylor and Johnston (1979), and Johnston (1986) for introduction to this literature.

9. See also C. Vann Woodward (1966) on the significance of southern "Jim Crow" laws at the turn of the twentieth century. These laws segregated the races in housing, education, and employment, and many other aspects of life.

10. They were concerned to evaluate Key's (1949) suggestion that southern voting laws are simply reflections of the local culture, rather than real barriers to participation.

11. See also the study by Mann and Wolfinger (1980:631), wherein they argued that the presidential effect on local congressional elections "is modest compared to the salience of ... local choices."

12. Shister's (1953) model can be allied with a new movement in political science (March and Olsen 1984) and geography (Clark and Dear 1984) described as the "new institutionalism".

13. Note that the data reported on unions' electoral performance may be slightly different than the unions' own data. For reasons of computational convenience, a small number of election results for each union were dropped from the data file.

14. Except for the yearly total number of elections for both unions (which is the twelve months' total), the data for 1986 reported in this chapter and throughout the next two chapters are derived from unpublished data made available by the National Labor Relations Board for the first eight months of 1986.

15. Schuerman (1983:ch. 8) provides a detailed exposition of the MANOVA methods used in Clark and Johnston (1987b). Most generally, a step-down test of means was used, with variation in win/loss as a function of local economic variables.

[6] Organizing strategies in the heartland and the South

1. Detailed comments on a previous version of this chapter were provided by Edward Montgomery and Neil Wrigley. The MB Fund provided partial financial support for data collection.

2. There have been a number of attempts in economics to reintroduce complexity into theorizing, arguing that the stripped-down versions of many phenomena are so simple as to be simplistic. See Hirschman (1985) on complex interpretations of individual motivations.

3. As Bok (1971) observed, American labor law is distinctive for its emphasis on decentralized labor relations. Stone (1981) suggested that the guiding principles behind this legal structure were liberal, mimicking electoral democracy.

4. Union power might be also represented by instrumental variables like union income, membership, or union assets. It could be claimed that corporations are

inherently more powerful than unions because (as agents of stockholders) they own property. While this is plausible as an abstract proposition, in bilateral circumstances corporations have been willing to forgo their unilateral power and enter into joint-partnership agreements. We must be careful not to idealize the power of corporations.

5. This definition of rationality is based upon Simon's (1985) conception of bounded rationality. He also termed bounded rationality "procedural rationality," as opposed to substantive rationality. The distinction appears to be premised on whether or not an agent has "objective" information about the situation. Procedural rationality assumes situations are interpreted, as opposed to objectively known.

6. Some members withdraw from the union by voting against union representation (see Freeman and Medoff 1984 on "exit, voice, and loyalty" strategies within unions). This is a very difficult strategy, given the importance of the union to the auto firms; withdrawal may leave unrepresented members at the mercy of otherwise indifferent company representatives. Canadian auto workers recently withdrew from the union to form their own independent bargaining entity. In doing so, they retained elements of cross-local solidarity, not available to single American Locals who chose to go it alone.

7. A similar observation has been made by Gunderson (1980) regarding the labor force participation decision – one either participates in the labor market, or one does not. The fact that some people participate by varying degrees (hours, days, etc.), does not obviate the initial choice. Amemiya (1981) and McFadden (1982) provide more examples and reviews of the estimation issues involved in empirically analyzing categorical relationships.

8. This means, of course, that we are willing to sacrifice some information so as to be consistent with individual choice behavior. A reader objected to this strategy, arguing that since we are concerned with aggregate outcomes (not individual behavior) we ought to use all the information (specifically the percentage vote for and against union representation). However, we would assert that even at the aggregate level, unions are fundamentally concerned with the dichotomous nature of representation elections. After all, they only gain members if they win the election.

9. Core industries for the IBEW included electrical and electronic equipment, communications, and electric, gas, and related services. For the UAW, core industries included fabricated metals, machinery, electrical and electronic equipment, and transportation.

10. In fact, since there may be quite diverse interpretations of common variables by localities, it may be found that there are no statistically significant systematic local effects. In instances where there are nationally oriented union organizing strategies which reach down to the local level, we might expect to find common variables statistically significant.

11. There was another related issue. If the dependent variable was a continuous variable like the percentage vote for union representation, it is possible that observations would be clustered in two areas: around the 40–45 percent mark as in the case of losing elections, and around the 55–60 percent mark as in winning elections. Any OLS regression model would then be relatively inefficient, as there would be few observations in the middle of the distribution (Fox 1985).

12. Notice that the Probit results are not particularly robust. That is, relatively few variables' parameters were found to be highly significant, and even those varied year to year in terms of their levels of significance. In addition, the overall performance of each model was quite weak, with low estimates of the log likelihood R squared.

13. So as to control for the effects of different situations in each year, those variables not considered directly were set to their relevant mean values. Mean values were derived for specific geographical and industrial contexts. For an overview of the technical issues involved in translating estimated parameter coefficients into probabilities, the reader is referred to Wrigley (1985).

14. All variables except the one in question were set to their region/industry means. The values of the variables in question were set so as to reflect areas which had experienced high rates of growth (25 percent) in their employment and enterprises over the previous couple of years.

[7] At the margin of the rules of the game

1. *Bristol Textile Company* (1986), summarized in *Daily Labor Report*, no. 19, 29 January 1986, p. A-1.

2. *Michael's Markets of Canterbury* (1985), reported in the *Daily Labor Report*, no. 63, 4 April 1985, p. A-10.

3. See, for example, the decision of the United States Court of Appeals, Eleventh Circuit in *NLRB v. Idab Inc.* (1985), reported in *Daily Labor Report*, no. 184, 23 September 1985, pp. D-1–D-5. There the Court followed the lead of the NLRB in not considering two challenged ballots because they were "insufficient in number to affect the outcome of the election."

4. According to Weiler (1983), a favorite employer tactic is the use of discriminatory discharges as a means of breaking up internal support for union representation. He suggested that about 10,000 workers were fired in 1980 for their involvement in representation campaigns.

5. Some employer spokesmen have implied that Weiler's understanding of the American system is so fundamentally flawed that his proposals ought to be summarily rejected (De Bernardo 1985). De Bernardo also cited criticisms of Weiler's position by federal circuit judge Robert Bork in *Clothing and Textile Workers v. NLRB* (1984). Judge Bork argued that Weiler's position was only supported by one article, and that his logic was faulty and highly partisan.

6. Until very recently, Weiler's argument concerning the Canadian option has been well received (even if his empirical claims have been severely attacked). The AFL–CIO Committee on the Evolution of Work (1985) used Canadian experience to argue for revision of NLRB's election rules. However, Huxley, Kettler, and Struthers (1986) have suggested that Canadian experience is not so relevant after all. The crucial difference between the countries according to Huxley et al is Canada's more adversarial and political labor movement. Given this basic difference, they doubt that revision of election rules with respect to Canadian standards would make a significant difference to the success rates of American unions.

7. In this respect, unions are assumed to be nonprofit organizations (as in fact they are treated by the federal government). There is very little in the way of evidence

regarding unions' spending habits in representation elections (Voos 1984). While we assume that unions make strategic decisions regarding the costs and returns of representation campaigns, it is not clear whether or not unions like the UAW and the IBEW have such explicitly articulated decision rules.

8. See for example, the decision of the Eleventh Circuit Court of Appeals in *Purolator Armoured, Inc.* v. *NLRB* (1985), reported in the *Daily Labor Report*, no. 157, 14 August 1985, pp. D-1–D-5.

9. See the decision of the US Ninth Circuit Court in *US Ecology, Inc.* v. *NLRB* (1985), reported in *Daily Labor Report*, no. 203, 21 October 1985, pp. D-1–D-4.

10. I recognize that these percentage differences rules are somewhat arbitrary, being wholly dependent upon the data at hand. Despite the significance of the category for the NLRB's decisions, the Board has not made any explicit ruling regarding its own definition of close elections. We could not retreat to an administrative or judicial definition. On the other hand, given that the Board is most often concerned with "close elections" involving a handful of workers we were justified in using a sliding scale which similarly results in relatively few workers in each size class of electoral unit.

11. Separate attempts to estimate an outcomes model – the probability of winning a close election – were fundamentally compromised by a basic problem. The relatively small number of close elections for each union and year was further reduced because of limited availability of local data for the independent variables. For example, the 21 close UAW elections in 1982 reduced to about 10 once we took into account missing data: far too few to estimate a Probit model reasonably. A close–non-close dichotomous Probit model for each union and year was not estimated because of the highly skewed distribution of events. That is, there were many more non-close elections than close ones. Cline (1985) suggested that under these circumstances it is difficult to maintain the statistical integrity of Logit and Probit models.

12. The only danger in using such a routine is if MARGIN is bimodally distributed – that is, with two clumps of observations either side of 50.1 percent. If that is the case, regression could be relatively statistically inefficient. So as to account for such a possibility, and incidentally estimate separate MARGIN models for labor and management, the dependent variable was split into two variables: VMARGIN and LMARGIN. The former referred to the margin of victory and the latter to the margin of loss (taking the perspective of the union). One advantage of this procedure is that the margin of loss need not have negative values. As a consequence the results are more readily comparable between VMARGIN and LMARGIN.

13. State right-to-work legislation has been interpreted by many commentators as a deliberate barrier against union organizing, and is highly correlated with (low) state levels of unionization. Stipulated elections (STIP) are management's preferred mode of election. This kind of election allows for direct appeal to the Board, and makes no concessions to the union regarding its representation status. The IBEW's CORE industries are electrical oriented, including communications and utilities. The UAW's CORE industries are, not surprisingly, auto related.

14. Sources of these data and their specific details are described in Clark and Johnston (1987b). Notice that these economic variables were transformed to

represent changes in those categories over the previous two years (indicated by a P before the variable name).

15. Note, not all the possible independent variables were included in estimating model (2). Selection was necessary so as to reduce high levels of cross-correlation between some of the level variables. Readers have asked whether or not there is strong cross-correlation between level variables like PEMPLOY and change variables like PAVPAY. The answer is no.

[8] Integrity of the National Labor Relations Board

1. President Roosevelt established the National Labor Board on 5 August 1933 under the terms of the National Industrial Recovery Act (Pub. L. 67 (ch. 90), 16 June 1933, 48 Stat. 195). As a successor to the National Labor Board, Roosevelt issued an executive order on 29 June 1934 to create a National Labor Relations Board under the provisions of the same Act. This Board existed for another year before being abandoned in the wake of the 27 May 1935 decision of the US Supreme Court in *Schechter Poultry Corp.* v. *United States*.

2. 79 Congressional Record, 10720, 8 July 1935.

3. But see Gould's (1984) comparison of Japanese with American labor law. Gould argued that the latter has much to learn from the former, especially in the areas of collective bargaining and the powers of the NLRB with respect to the virtues of union–management agreements.

4. See the forum sponsored by the Bureau of National Affairs on the NLRB at fifty, and especially the position papers by Beiber and Gold (representing organized labor) and De Bernardo and Trowbridge (representing management).

5. Clark, Gertler, and Whiteman (1986) and Scott (1980) provide useful critiques of this literature, focusing upon regional economic dynamics and the structure of the built environment (respectively).

6. The role of propaganda in representation elections, like the threat of a plant closing or relocation if a union were to win an election, has been a problematic issue for the NLRB. The Board retreated from an early idea, expressed in its decision in *General Shoe Corp.* (1948), that elections be held in circumstances as close as possible to "laboratory conditions." A weaker rule, developed in *Hollywood Ceramics Co.* (1962), that elections should only be set aside in circumstances of "substantial misrepresentation," has given way to a quite permissive rule that allows considerable latitude for misrepresentation and trickery. In *Shopping Kart Food Mkts. Inc.* (1977) the Board held that "employees . . . are capable of recognizing campaign propaganda for what it is and discounting it" (1313). After some debate within the NLRB, this rule was reaffirmed in *Midland National Life Insurance Co.* (1982).

7. Section 8(a) of the NLRA, 29 USC 158, wherein "it shall be an unfair labor practice for an employer – (1) to interfere with, restrain, or coerce employees . . . (2) to dominate or interfere with the formation or administration of any labor organization . . . (3) . . . to encourage or discourage membership in any labor organization . . . (4) to discharge or otherwise discriminate against an employee because he has filed charges . . . (5) to refuse to bargain collectively with the representatives of his employees . . . " Hedlund (1986) provides a useful overview

of the law, and an imaginative argument in favor of mandatory bargaining over the relocation of work.

8. The distance between Mahwah and East Hartford is about 200 miles, certainly too far to commute on a daily basis.

9. The bargaining unit was comprised of professional and technical employees of Otis Elevator's Engineering Division. The principal location of the bargaining unit was Mahwah, but it did represent a few employees at the Division's other facilities in Yonkers, New York and Harrison, New Jersey. See the Brief to the Administrative Law Judge on Behalf of the General Counsel, dated 13 April 1979, available from the Formal File of Case no. 22–CA–8507, National Labor Relations Board, Washington DC.

10. Form NLRB–501 (2–67), Case no. 22–CA–8507, filed 7 June 1978, available as an exhibit in the Formal File held at the National Labor Relations Board, Washington DC.

11. Complaint and Notice of Hearing, 27 July 1978, filed before the NLRB 22 Region, Newark, New Jersey. Available from the Formal File held at the National Labor Relations Board, Washington DC.

12. Letter of Robert M. Kushnir to NLRB Board members Fanning, Jenkins, and Zimmerman, 9 June 1982. Available from the Formal File of Case no. 22–CA–8507, National Labor Relations Board, Washington DC.

13. For a detailed discussion of the interaction between political control of the NLRB and its institutional responsibilities see Moe (1986).

14. 74th Congress, Sess. 1, ch. 372, 5 July 1935 (49 Stat. 449).

15. 79 Congressional Record, 8 July 1935, p. 10720.

16. *Ibid.*, p. 10720.

17. See generally *The failure of labor law – a betrayal of American workers*, House report 98–xx, 98th Congress, US House of Representatives.

18. 79 Congressional Record, 8 July 1935, p. 10720.

19. As reported in the *Daily Labor Report*, 13 April 1987, Bureau of National Affairs, Washington DC.

20. Compare with the recent decision of the US Court of Appeals for the Second Circuit in *United Food and Commercial Workers, Local 174* v. *Hebrew National Kosher Foods, Inc.* (1987). In this case, an instance where the employer refused to bargain over the effects of a plant relocation, the Court decided in favor of the union, arguing that the issue must be decided by the arbitrator. Essentially, the integrity of the previous contract between the union and the company was upheld, even though the contract had in fact expired.

[9] Options for restructuring the US economy

1. A version of this chapter was first presented at the conference on The Future of the Labor Movement in an Advanced Economy, Hubert Humphrey Institute of Public Affairs, the University of Minnesota. Comments and advice were received from members of the UAW, the NLRB, and participants in seminars at UCLA, Kentucky, and West Virginia. Ben Fischer, Shirley Clark, Irving Horowitz, Guy Peters, Royce Hanson, Brian Berry, and many others provided comments on various drafts.

2. Bluestone and Harrison (1985:D-15) noted "we appear to be moving in the direction of an economy dominated by low-wage jobs."

3. Grossman (1984) provides a useful analysis of the respective contributions of foreign competition, capital inefficiency, and high relative wages to the recent decline of the US steel industry. Compare with Clark (1988a).

4. See Mieszkowski (1985) for a general analysis of the regional consequences of the trade crisis. It must also be noted that at present, this crisis is quite localized to older heavy manufacturing industries and their communities. But, there is no reason to think that the growth of the service sector will not be affected by the decline of these industries.

5. For examples of management lawyers' defense of the Reagan NLRB see the commentary by Trowbridge (1985), where he likened the proper role of the NLRB to that of an umpire, and the argument of De Bernardo (1985), where he claimed that the Board had returned to its proper role, consistent with its "statutory authority."

6. Weiler (1983, 1984a,b) is particularly critical of the Board. He contends that the current labor law system poses a fundamental threat to the labor movement, and the labor relations system in general. Delays in case processing, less than timely reviews of management–labor disputes, inadequate policing of management anti-union activities, and the lack of adequate sanctions all contribute to Weiler's critique of the NLRB's adjudicative integrity. Some of his arguments have received support from Roomkin and Block (1981) (on delays in case processing), Karper (1982) (on the explosion of unfair labor practices), and Lawler (1984) (on the increasing influence of management consultants in union certification elections).

7. Kathy Kieger (1987) in commenting on the attitudes and opinions of the current Board said, in part, "I find in the cases discussed above an attitude of profound hostility and distrust toward collective self-governance by workers." Of some of the cases she reviews, she terms the Board's views in *Meyers Industries* (1984) "dishonest," its views in *Amoco Production Co.* (1983), "irrational," and its views in *Teamsters' Local No. 670* (1985) "false." Whether or not she is correct in these assessments is of little consequence. Her assessments indicate a profound distrust of the current Board on behalf of organized labor.

8. But see the recent decision of the Board in *Anamag Limited* (1987). There the Board made a first step towards legitimizing the status of work teams' coordinators as non-supervisory workers, eligible to join unions.

9. Herein is the rationale for the so-called Kaldor–Hicks compensation principle (see Clark 1983 for further details of this principle as applied to regulating the outcomes of economic policy in the urban context).

10. Justice is most often equated with equality. So, for example, Walzer (1983) begins his book with the word "equality." However, in my argument, justice is taken to represent both the theory of outcomes (who gets what, where, and when) – which might be termed distributive justice – and the theory of procedures (how outcomes are created) – which might be termed procedural justice. As will become clear, I believe that justice requires both elements if it is to have validity.

11. For an example of a procedural (or process-based) theory of justice and criticisms of this theory see respectively the recent book by Ely (1980) and the responses by Tribe (1980) and Tushnet (1980).

12. This is surely the kind of logic behind decisions in cases such as *Teamsters' Local No. 670* (1985), where the Board held that the union could not withhold union benefits from members who resigned from the union during the course of a strike. It should also be noted that concern for individuals' rights is embedded in the Taft–Hartley Act of 1947, as opposed to the original Wagner Act of 1935. The Board has chosen to emphasize one section of the NLRA, and in doing so has sought to narrow the scope of collective bargaining.

13. Those of us schooled in contemporary political philosophy would question even the theoretical integrity of EOO (see Clark 1985b).

14. See for details the *Daily Labor Report*, 29 July 1985, no. 145, 5 June 1986, no. 108, and a recent issue (vol. 19, no. 6) of *UAW Local 160 Tech. Engineer* (available from Warren, Michigan).

15. The UAW had been unable to organize the Nissan plant. In fact, the UAW has had tremendous difficulty in organizing foreign-owned auto plants in the United States. It also had to withdraw recently from its attempt to organize Honda's assembly plant in Marysville, Ohio.

16. Building Trades AFL–CIO, Morrison-Knudsen Company, Inc., and Saturn Corporation; NLRB Case nos. 26–CE–8 to 26–CA–11429. This suit was rejected by the NLRB.

17. The Foundation chairman was quoted as saying that the UAW–GM agreement is "a shocking example of big business and big labor teaming up to deny workers their rights under the law." He also said that the agreement has "illegally coerced workers to toe the union line," *Daily Labor Report*, 9 August 1985, p. A-8. It might also be the case that because the agreement makes union membership a desirable option for nonunion workers, the RTW lobby found this prospect worse than anything else they might formally complain about.

[10] Republicans, Democrats, and the southern veto

1. Thanks to Ray Denison, Victor Kamber, and Charles McDonald for their time and patience in answering queries about the past and future prospects for labor law reform. Charles Ciccone was particularly helpful in providing a critical perspective on both the history of labor law reform and this chapter. Many people made useful comments on previous versions, especially Ben Fischer, Ron Johnston, Everett Kassalow, and Seymour Martin Lipset. None of the above should be held accountable for the opinions expressed herein.

2. *The failure of labor law – a betrayal of American workers, House report* 98–xx, 98th Congress, US House of Representatives.

3. See Weiler's (1984b) testimony in hearings before the Subcommittee on Labor–Management Relations on "Has labor law failed?" In testimony before the Subcommittee at the same time, Richard Freeman (1984) was not as optimistic as Weiler, though even Freeman believed that the future of the labor movement depended upon major revisions to current labor laws.

4. National Labor Relations Act – 49 Stat. 449 (1935), as amended, 29 USC Sections 151–169 (1982).

5. Senator Orrin Hatch (R – Utah) introduced a bill to apply the Hobbs Act (Anti-Racketeering Law of 1954, 18 USC 1951, 1982) to union activities during strikes

and other forms of collective action. The Supreme Court had ruled in *United States* v. *Enmons et al.*, 410 US 396 (1973) that violence during strikes does not come under the Hobbs Act.

6. For a general overview of the New Deal era and its implications for national government and the development of state policy see Karl (1983). Other studies of related interest include Achenbaum's (1986) in-depth treatment of the creation and structure of the Social Security Administration during the 1930s, and Weir and Skocpol's (1985) comparison of state policy responses in Britain, Sweden, and the United States to the Great Depression of the 1930s. More generally, Skocpol (1980) and Skocpol and Finegold (1982) consider the roots of US New Deal policies in terms of neo-marxist theories of the state and the bureaucratic structure of state policies.

7. Fair Labor Standards Act – 29 USC 201 *et seq.* and 29 USC 251 *et seq.* as amended.

8. *United States* v. *Darby* (1941).

9. An important, but relatively neglected, aspect of New Deal initiatives concerns the important role of the states in fostering policy innovations. This was especially apparent in unemployment insurance introduced by Wisconsin (1932), New York and Massachusetts (1935), Ohio (1936), and Illinois (1937). Apart from the recent work of Amenta et al (1985), there is a tendency in the literature to imagine that the New Deal was solely a national political movement. In fact, many policies, unemployment insurance included, were the result of state-level political movements: witness the patchwork quilt of state unemployment policies (concentrated in the North and hardly in evidence in the South).

10. *Loewe* v. *Lawler* (1908).

11. See especially *Duplex Printing Press Co.* v. *Deering* (1921), wherein the Court construed the assumptions of the Sherman Act regarding the existence of unions to be unchanged by the Clayton Act.

12. Norris–LaGuardia Act – 47 Stat. 70 (1932), 29 USC Sections 101–115 (1982); Railway Labor Act – 44 Stat., part II, 577 (1926), as amended by 48 Stat. 1185 (1934), 49 Stat. 1189 (1936), *et seq.*, 45 USC Sections 151–188 (1982).

13. See Cox, Bok, and Gorman (1986:26).

14. Six states that had enacted RTW legislation in the late 1940s and 1950s had repealed those laws by early 1965. These states included Delaware, Hawaii, Indiana, Louisiana, Maine, and New Hampshire. More recently, Kansas repealed their RTW law in 1982 and Louisiana enacted RTW legislation in 1977. There was a concerted attempt in 1985/6 to pass another RTW law in New Hampshire. Despite the support of the Governor, it failed to pass the state legislature.

15. Quoted in the *Congressional Quarterly Weekly Report*, 14 May 1965, 930.

16. Quoted *ibid.*, 14 May 1965, 932.

17. *Ibid.*, 28 January 1966, 304.

18. *Senate Report*, no. 89–697, 89th Congress, US Senate, 1965.

19. The most comprehensive analysis of the attempts at labor reform during the Carter years is provided by Townley (1986).

20. In the *Electrical Workers* case the union picketed a construction project because a unionized general contractor sub-contracted the electrical work to a non-unionized employer. The Supreme Court agreed with the NLRB that the union

had violated Section 8(b) 4(A). The Court also agreed with the NLRB in the *Rice Milling* case. In that case the Board held that there had not been a violation of Section 8(b) 4(A) even though the union concerned had sought to induce two employees from a third-party employer to observe the picket lines. According to the Court, the crucial test of applicability of the Section had to do with the degree to which picketing was a "concerted activity." It was held that the pickets' discussion with the two employees was not a concerted activity against the third-party employer (see Gregory and Katz 1979:422–25).

21. It has been suggested by some commentators that Ford vetoed the bill so as to improve his chances against Ronald Reagan in the forthcoming (February 1975) Republican Primary election in New Hampshire. Whether or not this gesture made a difference to Ford's performance in that election is difficult to judge. During passage of the bill in the House, both of New Hampshire's Representatives (one Democrat, the other Republican) voted against the bill, and in the Senate New Hampshire's Senators voted along party lines for (Democrat) and against (Republican) the bill. Ford only just won the primary with 50.6 percent of the vote as against Ronald Reagan's 49.4 percent of the vote.

22. Quoted in *Congressional Quarterly Weekly Report*, 23 July 1977, 1536.

23. Those involved in lobbying on behalf of labor at the time believed that there were actually 59 in favor of cloture. Victor Kamber claims that if one more vote in favor of cloture had been found, Senator Long would have changed his negative vote to a positive one. On the other hand, it is not clear that all those in favor of cloture would have then maintained their position. It is also thought that there would have been enough votes to pass the measure once cloture had been achieved.

[11] Employment contracts without unions

1. Research assistance for this chapter was provided by Paul Mathes. Oren Root of Patrick Wall Esq. and Robert Ohanian were particularly helpful in providing information and sources regarding their case against Avis Rent a Car, Inc.

2. In the auto industry, obvious examples include the Honda and Nissan assembly plants. In the electronics industry, IBM and Westinghouse Corporation have each instituted strong employee participation programs in their nonunion plants. Typical of these corporations are detailed employee-rights manuals, covering all manner of issues from compensation through to discipline and hiring and firing procedures (see chapter 3 of Kochan, Katz, and McKersie 1986 for an overview).

3. See chapter 9 for a discussion of the Saturn Project, and Smith and Childs (1987) for a discussion of the NUMMI experience. Rosow (1986) provides a useful overview of management and union perspectives on the role of collaborative teams in the American workplace.

4. Stieber and Murray (1983) estimate that about 60 million United States workers are subject to employment-at-will, and that millions of workers are discharged every year without the right to due process. While there are no reliable data on the significance or patterns of arbitrary dismissal, it seems very prevalent amongst middle managers, and at the lowest tier of the nonunionized blue-collar work force.

5. See for example the Committee Report (1981) of the Committee on Labor and Employment Law of the Bar of the City of New York on the status of employment-at-will, and see a journalist's treatment of the same issue in Strasser (1986).

6. *Geary* v. *United States Steel Corp.* (1974), a comment made by Justice Roberts in dissent from the majority opinion affirming the relevance of employment-at-will (188).

7. Epstein (1985a) provides a detailed over-view of the relevant cases and literature concerning the historical evolution of the doctrine. Not surprisingly, at least in terms of the evolution of economic thought, Epstein treats employment-at-will as a form of contract similar to other notions of contract found in commercial partnerships.

8. The idea that employers' unfettered power might cripple the economy has returned in many different guises since Freeman's dissenting opinion in Payne. For instance, it is an essential argument in the preamble to the Wagner Act of 1935 (see Mills and Brown 1950 for a related interpretation) justifying limits upon the power of employers in their bargaining with organized labor. Indeed, one might interpret the Wagner Act as an attempt to balance the powers of the two sides of the employment relationship.

9. Fried (1980: 1858) described Atiyah's book as a "monumental work ... informed by a single coherent theme." This book dealt with the history of English common law relating to contract (commercial and employment).

10. Kramer (1984) provides a useful over-view of developments in Pennsylvania.

11. An important exemption common in many states is a "whistle-blower" exemption (see Malin 1983). That is, in many states employees are protected from discharge if they notify authorities of unsafe, illegal, or otherwise malevolent behavior of their employers. In fact, the *Geary* case in Pennsylvania was an important reference point for local reform of employment-at-will.

12. See for example *Farrell* v. *Automobile Club of Michigan* (1987) and *Duldulao* v. *St. Mary of Nazareth Hospital Center* (1987).

13. For an especially interesting example see *Kinoshita* v. *Canadian Pacific Airlines Ltd.* (1986), where the link between a potential union contract and stated company policies regarding job tenure and dismissal was made explicit by the state court.

14. See for example *Grayson* v. *American Airlines Inc.* (1986).

15. See Stieber (1986) for details of recent legislative developments in Michigan and California. Both states have considered requiring mediation and appeal procedures, mimicking grievance hearings typical of union settings.

16. For details see respectively *Novosel* v. *Sears, Roebuck & Co.* (1980) and *Kari* v. *General Motors Corp.* (1977).

17. *Ohanian* v. *Avis Rent a Car System* (1985: 6708).

18. See Note (1985) on the history of the statute of frauds. It was originally enacted by the English Parliament in 1677 as an attempt to prevent fraud in the enforcement and interpretation of oral promises. In part, it required that oral promises be evidenced by written documents.

19. Citing *D. & N. Boening, Inc.* v. *Kirsch Beverages* (1984).

20. Citing *North Shore Bottling Co.* v. *Schmidt & Sons, Inc.* (1968).

21. The court cited a similar instance where a person had been induced to leave his

current employer and take a position in another firm. In that case, like this case, promises were made to the employee that he would be treated in a manner consistent with the firm's procedures regarding just cause for dismissal (see *Weiner* v. *McGraw Hill, Inc.* (1982).

22. This position was not accepted by a dissenting judge. He argued that the oral promise was insufficient evidence, given the hostility of Ohanian and the general manager, who was supposed to have made the promise. Both were fired at the same time. According to the dissenting judge it was for these kinds of circumstances, where the authority or credibility of the issue depended upon oral promises made in circumstances not immediately available to the judiciary, that the statute of frauds was originally conceived.

[12] Unions and communities unarmed

1. LaCapra (1985) provides a useful perspective on the method of presentation followed in this book. While dealing mainly with historiography, he argued the case for recognizing the vital importance of the interplay of themes at a variety of levels. Indeed, he suggested that history could only be understood in all its complexity if these themes were given a central place in theoretical discourse. See his discussion of the origins of the factory system and its attendant regional differentiation (76).

2. By means of contrast compare Glymour (1985) and Leamer (1985) on the dilemmas of scientific method in the social sciences.

3. Many social scientists would argue that the totally encompassing conclusion is the only appropriate conclusion for general theorizing (see Trigg 1985: ch. 1). Some readers might want to reorder all the evidence into one argument that is integrative as opposed to dialectical or dialogical. As I suggested in chapter 1, this instinct to totalize ought to be resisted: it strips events and motives of their complexity and denies the uneasy tension between social structures.

4. Norris (1985: ch. 3) provides a good over-view of rhetorical strategy, from a philosophical point of view.

5. Based on up-dated figures from the US Department of Labor, *Employment and Earnings* file.

6. See the volumes edited by Scott and Storper (1986) and Peet (1987) for further evidence and discussion of this point.

7. Notice, though, that there is considerable debate over the question of causation. It can be shown that in many of those states with RTW legislation, their rates of unionization were very low even before the passage of RTW legislation. Some theorists have argued, then, that RTW legislation per se is not particularly important in unions' representation campaigns. The passage of RTW legislation may have had a temporary chilling effect, but over the long run RTW legislation reflects an anti-union culture (see Ellwood and Fine 1983).

8. President Lyndon Johnson in his State of the Union address of 24 January 1966 noted that repeal of Section 14(b) of the Taft–Hartley Act would "make the national labor policy uniform throughout the country" (quoted in *Congressional Quarterly Weekly Report*, 28 January 1966: 304).

9. A third, though not directly related, implication would be that firms would not be able to shelter behind some states' RTW legislation during representation

campaigns, and would find it increasingly difficult to avoid unions simply by relocating production.

10. See Bluestone and Harrison (1982), but compare with Lawrence (1984).

11. According to its charter, the purpose of the Institute is to contribute "to a sound and stable expansion of world trade" through research and the exchange of ideas. Its research has included studies for the maintenance of world free trade, the development of the Pacific region, and cooperative exchanges with US academics.

12. President Franklin D. Roosevelt, 79 Cong. Rec. 10720 (5 July 1935).

13. Representative Gildea (D – Pennsylvania), 79 Cong. Rec. 9731–9732 (19 June 1935).

Bibliography

Achenbaum, W. A. 1986. *Social security: visions and revisions*. Cambridge: Cambridge University Press

AFL–CIO Committee on the Evolution of Work. 1985. *The changing situation of workers and their unions*. Washington, DC: AFL–CIO

Amemiya, T. 1981. Qualitative response models: a survey. *J. Econ. Lit.*, 19: 1483–1536

Amenta, E., E. Clemens, J. Olsen, S. Parikh, and T. Skocpol. 1985. The political origins of unemployment insurance in five American states. Chicago: Mimeo. Center for the Study of Industrial Societies, University of Chicago

Anderson, J. 1979. Local union participation: a re-examination. *Indust. Rel.*, 18: 18–31

Anderson, J., G. Busman, and C. O'Reilly. 1982. The decertification process: evidence from California. *Indust. Rel.*, 21: 178–95

Archer, J. C. and P. J. Taylor. 1981. *Section and party: a political geography of American presidential elections from Andrew Jackson to Ronald Reagan*. London: Wiley

Ashenfelter, O. and J. Pencavel. 1969. American trade union growth: 1900–1960. *Q. J. Econ.*, 83: 434–48

Atiyah, P. 1979. *The rise and fall of freedom of contract*. Oxford: Oxford University Press

1981. *Promises, morals, and the law*. Oxford: Clarendon Press

1986. *Essays on contract*. Oxford: Clarendon Press

Atleson, J. 1983. *Values and assumptions in American labor law*. Amherst, Mass.: University of Massachusetts Press

Avery, R. B. and V. J. Hotz. 1985. *HotzTran: users' manual*. Old Greenwich, Conn.: CERA Consultants

Bain, G. S. and R. Price. 1980. *Profiles of union growth: a comparative statistical portrait of eight countries*. Oxford: Blackwell

Barkin, S. 1985. An agenda for the revision of the American industrial relations system. *Labor Law J.*, 36: 857–60

Bausor, R. 1983. The rational-expectations hypothesis and the epistemics of time. *Cambr. J. Econ.*, 7: 1–10

Beck, N. 1982. Parties, administrations, and American macro-economic outcomes. *Am. Pol. Sci. Rev.*, 76: 83–93

Becker, B. and R. Miller. 1981. Patterns and determinants of union growth in the hospital industry. *J. Labor Res.*, 2: 309–28

Becker, G. 1964. *Human capital: a theoretical and empirical analysis*. New York: Columbia University Press

Beiber, O. 1985. Forum. In *NLRB at 50: labor board at the crossroads. A BNA special report*. Washington, DC: Bureau of National Affairs. 5–6

Bell, D. 1953. The next American labor movement. *Fortune*, April: 120–23; 201–206

Bernstein, I. 1954. The growth of American unions. *Am. Econ. Rev.*, 54: 301–18
 1961. The growth of American unions, 1945–1960. *Labor Hist.*, 2: 131–57

Bierman, L. and S. Youngblood. 1984. Employment-at-will and the South Carolina experiment. *Indust. Rel. Law J.*, 7: 28–39

Blades, L. E. 1967. Employment-at-will v. individual freedom: on limiting the abusive exercise of employer power. *Col. Law Rev.*, 67: 1404–35

Block, R. and M. Roomkin. 1982. A preliminary analysis of the participation rate and margin of victory in the NLRB elections. In *Proceedings of the Thirty-Fourth Annual Winter Meeting*. Madison: Industrial Relations Research Association. 220–26

Bluestone, B. and B. Harrison. 1982. *The deindustrialization of America*. New York: Basic Books
 1984. Storm clouds on the horizon: labor market crisis and industrial policy. Reported in the *Daily Labor Report* as Report on labor market crisis and industrial policy. (21 May 1984) (no. 98): D-1–18
 1987. The increasing incidence of low-wage employment in the US. Mimeo. Cambridge, Mass.: Department of Urban Studies and Planning, MIT

Bok, D. 1971. Reflections on the distinctive character of American labor laws. *Harv. Law Rev.*, 84: 1394–1463

Borts, G. and J. Stein. 1964. *Economic growth in a free market*. New York: Columbia University Press

Bowles, S., D. Gordon, and T. Weisskopf. 1983. *Beyond the waste land: a democratic alternative to economic decline*. New York: Anchor Press/Doubleday

Bureau of Labor Standards. 1962. *Growth of labor law in the United States*. Washington, DC: US Department of Labor

Bureau of National Affairs, ed. 1985. *NLRB at 50: labor board at the crossroads. A BNA special report*. Washington, DC

Cavanagh, T. and J. L. Sundquist. 1985. The new two-party system. In *The new directions in American politics*, ed. J. Chubb and P. Peterson. Washington, DC: Brookings Institution. 33–67

Caves, R. 1980. The structure of industry. In *The American economy in transition*, ed. M. Feldstein. Chicago: University of Chicago Press. 501–45

Chafetz, I. and C. Fraser. 1979. Union decertification: an exploratory analysis. *Indust. Rel.*, 18: 59–69

Chubb, J. E. and P. Peterson, eds. 1985. *The new directions in American politics*. Washington, DC: Brookings Institution

Ciccone, C. 1974. The labor exemption in antitrust law. Background information and analysis of S. 2237, 93rd Congress: a bill applying the Sherman Anti-trust Act to labor organizations. Washington, DC: Congressional Research Service, Library of Congress

Claggett, W., W. Flanigan, and N. Zingale. 1984. Nationalization of the American electorate. *Am. Pol. Sci. Rev.*, 78: 77–91

Clark, G. L. 1981a. The employment relation and spatial division of labor: an hypothesis. *Ann. Assoc. of Am. Geogr.*, 71: 412–24

1981b. Law, the state, and the spatial integration of the United States. *Environ. Plann. A.*, 13: 1197–1232

1983. *Interregional migration, national policy, and social justice*. Totowa, NJ: Rowman and Allanheld

1985a. The spatial division of labor and wage and price controls of the Nixon administration. *Econ. Geog.*, 61: 113–28

1985b. *Judges and the cities: interpreting local autonomy*. Chicago: University of Chicago Press

1986a. Restructuring the US economy: the National Labor Relations Board, the Saturn Project, and economic justice. *Econ. Geog.*, 62: 289–306

1986b. The crisis of the midwest auto industry. In *Production, work, territory: the geographical anatomy of industrial capitalism*, ed. A. Scott and M. Storper. Hemel Hempstead, Herts. and Winchester, Mass.: Allen and Unwin

1986c. The geography of employment: a progress report. *Progr. Human Geog.*, 12: 416–26

1988a. Corporate restructuring in the US steel industry: adjustment strategies and local labor relations. In *America's new economic geography*, ed. J. Hughes and G. Sternlieb. New Brunswick, NJ: Center for Urban Policy Research, Rutgers University

1988b. A question of integrity: the National Labor Relations Board and the relocation of work. *Pol. Geog. Q.*, 7

1988c. The geography of law. In *The new models in human geography*, ed. R. Peet and N. Thrift. Hemel Hempstead, Herts. and Winchester, Mass.: Allen and Unwin

Clark, G. L. and M. Dear. 1984. *State apparatus: structures and language of legitimacy*. Hemel Hempstead, Herts. and Winchester, Mass.: Allen and Unwin

Clark, G. L., M. Gertler, and J. Whiteman. 1986. *Regional dynamics: studies in adjustment theory*. Hemel Hempstead, Herts. and Winchester, Mass.: Allen and Unwin

Clark, G. L. and K. Johnston. 1987a. The geography of US union elections 1: the crisis of US unions and a critical review of the literature. *Environ. and Plann. A*, 19: 33–57

1987b. The geography of US union elections 2: performance of the United Auto Workers union and the International Brotherhood of Electrical Workers union, 1970–82. *Environ. Plann. A*, 19: 153–72

1987c. The geography of US union elections 3: the context and structure of union electoral performance (the International Brotherhood of Electrical Workers union and the United Auto Workers union, 1970–82). *Environ. Plann. A*, 19: 289–311

1987d. The geography of US union elections 4: patterns of close elections and determinants of the margins of victory and loss (the International Brotherhood of Electrical Workers union and the United Auto Workers union, 1970–1982). *Environ. and Plann. A*, 19: 447–69

1987e. The geography of US union elections 5: reconceptualizing the theory of industrial unionism. *Environ. and Plann. A*, 19: 719–34

Cline, W. 1985. *International debt: systemic risk and policy response*. Cambridge, Mass.: Institute for International Economics and MIT Press

Comment. 1987. The spring has sprung: the fate of plant relocation as a mandatory subject of bargaining. *San Diego Law Rev.*, 24: 221–41

Committee Report. 1981. At-will employment and the problem of unjust dismissal. *Record of the Bar of the City of New York*, 36: 170–216

Congress of Industrial Organizations. 1955. *The case against right to work laws: why recent state legislation is a threat to sound industrial relations and economic progress.* Washington, DC: AFL–CIO

Connerton, R. J. 1987. Collective bargaining: a process under siege. In *American labor policy*, ed. C. Morris. Washington, DC: Bureau of National Affairs

Converse, P. 1966. The concept of the normal vote. In *Elections and the political order*, ed. A. Campbell. New York: Wiley. 9–39

Cooke, P. 1985. Class practices as regional markers: contribution to labor geography. In *Social relations and spatial structures*, ed. D. Gregory and J. Urry. London: Macmillan. 213–41

Cooke, W. 1983. The failure to negotiate first contracts: determinants and policy implications. *Indust. Labor Rel. Rev.*, 38: 163–94

Cooper, L. 1984. Authorization cards and union representation election outcome: an empirical assessment of the assumption underlying the Supreme Court's *Gissel* decision. *Northwestern U. Law Rev.*, 79: 87–141

Cox, A. 1954. Federalism in the law of labor relations. *Harv. Law Rev.*, 67: 1297–1348

Cox, A., D. Bok, and R. Gorman. 1986. *Cases and materials on labor law: statutory supplement.* 10th edn. Mineola, New York: Foundation Press

Cox, A. and J. Dunlop. 1950. Regulation of collective bargaining by the National Labor Relations Board. *Harv. Law Rev.*, 63: 389–432

Cyert, R. and D. Mowery, eds. 1987. *Technology and employment: innovation and growth in the US economy.* Washington, DC: National Academy Press

Daily Labor Report. 1986. Idaho right-to-work law kept alive as voters surprise labor pollsters. 6 November 1986 (no. 215). Washington, DC: Bureau of National Affairs. A-9–A-10

Davis, M. 1986. *Prisoners of the American dream.* London: Verso Press

De Bernardo, M. A. 1985. Forum. In *NLRB at 50: labor board at the crossroads. BNA special report.* Washington, DC: Bureau of National Affairs. 7–10

Dickens, W. T. 1983. The effect of company campaigns: *Law and Reality* once again. *Indust. Labor Rel. Rev.*, 36: 560–75

Dickens, W. T. and J. S. Leonard. 1985. Accounting for the decline in union membership, 1950–1980. *Indust. Labor Rel. Rev.*, 38: 323–34

Dickens, W. T., D. Wholey, and J. Robinson. 1985. Bargaining unit, union, industry, and locational correlates of union support in certification and decertification elections. Mimeo. Cambridge, Mass.: National Bureau of Economic Research

Downs, A. 1957. *An economic theory of democracy.* New York: Harper and Row

Dunlop, J. 1944. *Wage determination under trade unions.* New York: Augustus Kelley

1948. The development of labor organization: a theoretical framework. In *Insights into labor issues*, ed. R. A. Lester and J. Shister. New York: Macmillan. 163–93

1987. The legal framework of industrial relations. In *American labor policy*, ed. C. Morris. Washington, DC: Bureau of National Affairs

Dworkin, R. 1978. *Taking rights seriously*. Cambridge, Mass.: Harvard University Press

　　1981. What is equality? Part I, equality of welfare. Part II, equality of resources. *Phil. Public Aff.*, 10: 185–246; 10: 283–345

　　1985. *A matter of principle*. Cambridge, Mass.: Harvard University Press

　　1986. *Law's empire*. Cambridge, Mass.: Harvard University Press

Eakin, P. J. 1985. *Fictions in autobiography. Studies in the art of self-invention*. Princeton: Princeton University Press

Economic report of the President. 1986. Washington, DC: USGPO

Ellwood, D. and G. Fine. 1983. Effects of right-to-work laws on union organizing. Mimeo. Cambridge, Mass.: National Bureau of Economic Research

Elsheikh, F. and G. Bain. 1978. American trade union growth: an alternative model. *Indust. Rel.*, 17: 75–79

Ely, J. 1980. *Democracy and distrust: a theory of judicial review*. Cambridge, Mass.: Harvard University Press

Ephlin, D. 1986. United Auto Workers, pioneers in labor–management partnership. In *Teamwork: joint labor–management programs in America*, ed. J. Rosow. New York: Pergamon

Epstein, R. 1983. A common law critique of labor relations: a critique of the New Deal labor legislation. *Yale Law J.*, 92: 1357–1406

　　1985a. In defense of the contract at will. In *Labor law and the employment market: foundations and applications*, ed. R. Epstein and J. Paul. New Brunswick, NJ: Transaction Books. 3–38

　　1985b. Agency costs, employment contracts, and labor unions. In *Principals and agents: the structure of business*, ed. J. W. Pratt and R. Zeckhauser. Boston, Mass.: Harvard Business School. 127–48

Faith, R. L. and J. Reid. 1983. The labor union as its members' agent. In *Research in labor economics (supplement)*, ed. J. Reid. Greenwich, Conn.: JAI Press. 3–26

Farber, H. 1984a. Right-to-work laws and the extent of unionization. *J. Labor Econ.*, 2: 319–52

　　1984b. The analysis of union behavior. Mimeo. Cambridge, Mass.: National Bureau of Economic Research

　　1985. The extent of unionization in the United States. In *Challenges and choices facing American labor*, ed. T. Kochan. Cambridge, Mass.: MIT Press. 15–43

　　1987. The decline of unionization in the United States: what can be learned from recent experience? Mimeo. Cambridge, Mass.: National Bureau of Economic Research

Feinman, J. 1976. The development of the employment at will rule. *Am. J. Legal Hist.*, 20: 118–35

Finnis, J. 1987. On 'The critical legal studies movement.' In *Oxford essays in jurisprudence. Third series*, ed. J. Eekelaar and J. Bell. Oxford: Oxford University Press. 145–66

Fiorina, M. 1981. *Retrospective voting in American national elections*. New Haven: Yale University Press

Fiorito, J. 1982. American trade union growth: an alternative model. *Indust. Rel.*, 21: 123–27

Fiorito, J. and C. Greer. 1982. Determinants of US unionism: past research and future needs. *Indust. Rel.*, 21: 1–32

Fischer, B. 1986a. Keeping labor relations up with the times. Pittsburgh: Center for Labor Studies, Carnegie Mellon University

   1986b. Review of *The reckoning* by Halberstam. Mimeo. Pittsburgh: Center for Labor Studies, Carnegie Mellon University

Flanagan, R. 1987. *Labor relations and the litigation explosion.* Washington, DC: Brookings Institution

Fox, J. 1984. *Linear statistical models and related methods: with applications to social research.* New York: Wiley

Frankel, K. 1985. The Wagner Act after fifty years: where we are – a labor perspective. Mimeo. Pittsburgh: United Steelworkers of America

Freeman, R. 1984. Statement. In *Oversight hearings on the subject "Has labor law failed?" Part I.* Joint hearings before the subcommittee on Labor–Management Relations of the Committee on Education and Labor, 98th Congress, House of Representatives. Washington, DC: USGPO. 117–19, 127

   1985. The effect of the union wage differential on management opposition and union organizing success. Mimeo. Cambridge, Mass.: National Bureau of Economic Research.

Freeman, R. and J. Medoff. 1984. *What do unions do?* New York: Basic Books

Frieberg, B. and W. Dickens. 1985. The impact of the runaway office on union certification elections in clerical units. Mimeo. Cambridge, Mass.: National Bureau of Economic Research

Fried, C. 1980. Book review: *The rise and fall of freedom of contract* by P. S. Atiyah. *Harv. Law Rev.*, 93: 1858–68

   1981. *Contract as promise: a theory of contractual obligation.* Cambridge, Mass.: Harvard University Press

Getman, J. 1986. Ruminations on union organizing in the private sector. *Univ. Chicago Law Rev.*, 53: 45–77

Getman, J., S. Goldberg, and J. Herman. 1976. *Union representation elections: law and reality.* New York: Russell Sage Foundation

Gifford, C. 1986. *Directory of U.S. labor organizations, 1986–87 edition.* Washington, DC: Bureau of National Affairs

Glymour, C. 1985. Interpreting Leamer. *Econ. Phil.*, 1: 290–94

Gold, L. 1985. Forum. In *NLRB at 50: labor board at the crossroads. A BNA special report.* Washington, DC: Bureau of National Affairs. 7–10

Goldberg, S., J. Getman, and J. Brett. 1984. The relationship between free choice and labor board doctrine: differing empirical approaches. *Northwestern U. Law Rev.*, 79: 721–90

Goldfield, M. 1987. *The decline of organized labor in the United States.* Chicago: University of Chicago Press

Gordon, R. J. 1980. Postwar macroeconomics: the evolution of events and ideas. In *The American economy in transition*, ed. M. Feldstein. Chicago: University of Chicago Press. 101–82

Gould, W. B. 1982. *A primer on American labor law.* Cambridge, Mass.: MIT Press

   1984. *Japan's reshaping of American labor law.* Cambridge, Mass.: MIT Press

Grant Thornton. 1987. *The eighth annual study of general manufacturing climates of the forty-eight contiguous states of America.* Suite 1700, Prudential Plaza, Chicago, Ill. 60601

Gregory, C. and H. Katz. 1979. *Labor and the law.* 3rd edn. New York: Norton

Gregory, D. 1981. Alfred Weber and location theory. In *Geography, ideology, and social concern*, ed. D. R. Stoddard. Oxford: Basil Blackwell

Gregory, D. and J. Urry, eds. 1985. *Social relations and spatial structures*. London: Macmillan

Grossman, G. 1984. Imports as a cause of injury: the case of the US steel industry. Mimeo. Cambridge, Mass.: National Bureau of Economic Research

Grunwald, J. and K. Flamm, eds. 1985. *The global factory: foreign assembly and international trade*. Washington, DC: Brookings Institution

Gunderson, M. 1980. Probit and logit estimates of labor force participation. *Indus. Rel.*, 19: 216–20

Halberstam, D. 1986. *The reckoning*. New York: W. Morrow

Hamermesh, D. 1984. The costs of worker displacement. Mimeo. Cambridge, Mass.: National Bureau of Economic Research

Harper, A. J., S. Logothteis, and H. J. Datz, eds. 1985. *The developing labor law – first supplement*. Washington, DC: Bureau of National Affairs

Harrison, B. 1984a. Regional restructuring and 'good business climates': the economic transformation of New England since world war II. In *Sunbelt/ snowbelt*, ed. L. Sawers and W. Tabb. New York: Oxford University Press. 48–96

Harrison, B. 1984b. The international movement for prenotification of plant closures. *Indust. Rel.*, 23: 387–409

Harrison, B. and B. Bluestone. 1987. The dark side of labor market flexibility: falling wages and growing income inequality in America. Mimeo. Cambridge, Mass.: Department of Urban Studies and Planning, MIT

Harrison, B. and S. Kanter. 1978. The political economy of states' job-creation business incentives. *J. Am. Inst. Plan.* Oct.: 424–35

Hart, H. L. A. 1961. *The concept of law*. Oxford: Oxford University Press

Hedlund, J. 1986. Note: An economic case for mandatory bargaining over partial termination and plant relocation decisions. *Yale Law J.*, 95: 949–68

Heneman, H. and M. Sandver. 1983. Predicting the outcome of union certification elections: a review of the literature. *Indust. Labor Rel. Rev.*, 36: 537–59

Hibbs, D. A. 1977. Political parties and macroeconomic policy. *Am. Pol. Sci. Rev.*, 71: 1467–87

1985. Inflation, political support, and macroeconomic policy. In *The politics of inflation and economic stagnation*, ed. L. Lindberg and C. Maier. Washington, DC: Brookings Institution

Hill, R. C. 1986. Global factory and company town: the changing division of labor in the international automobile industry. In *Global restructuring and territorial development*, ed. J. Henderson and M. Castells. Beverly Hills: Sage

Hill, R. C. and C. Negrey. 1987. Deindustrialization in the great lakes. *Urb. Aff. Q.*, 22: 580–97.

Hirsch, B. and J. Addison. 1986. *The economic analysis of unions: new approaches and evidence*. Hemel Hempstead, Herts. and Winchester, Mass.: Allen and Unwin

Hirsch, B. and M. Berger. 1984. Union membership determination and industry characteristics. *Southern Econ. J.*, 50: 665–79

Hirschman, A. 1981. *Essays in trespassing: economics to politics and beyond*. Cambridge: Cambridge University Press

1985. Against parsimony: three easy ways of complicating some categories of economic discourse. *Econ. Phil.*, 1: 7–21

Hoxie, R. 1917. *Trade unionism in the United States*. New York: Appleton and Co

Hutchinson, A. C. and J. Wakefield. 1982. A hard look at 'hard cases': the nightmare of a noble dreamer. *Ox. J. Legal Stud.*, 2: 86–110

Huxley, C., D. Kettler, and J. Struthers. 1986. Is Canada's experience 'especially instructive'? In *Unions in transition: entering the second century*, ed. S. M. Lipset. San Francisco: Institute for Contemporary Studies Press. 113–32

Hyclak, T. 1982. Union–nonunion wage changes and voting trends in representation elections. In *Proceedings of the Thirty-Fourth Annual Winter Meeting*. Madison: Industrial Relations Research Association. 334–50

Hyde, A. 1983. The concept of legitimization in the sociology of law. *Wisc. Law Rev.*, 1983: 379–426

International Trade Institute. 1987. *Outlook and the problems of international trade and industry of the United States*. Tokyo: Japan Foreign Trade Council, Inc.

Irving, J. S. 1983. Plant relocations and transfers of work: the NLRB's 'inherently destructive' approach. *Labor Law J.*, 34: 549–62

Isard, W. 1956. *Location and space-economy*. Cambridge, Mass.: MIT Press

Jacoby, S. 1982. The duration of indefinite employment contracts in the United States and England: an historical analysis. *Comparative Labor Law*, 5: 85–128

Jevons, S. 1882. *The state in relation to labor*

Johnston, K. 1986. Judicial adjudication and the spatial structure of production: two decisions by the National Labor Relations Board. *Environ. Plann. A*, 18: 27–39

Johnston, R. J. 1982. The changing geography of voting in the United States: 1946–1980. *Trans. Inst. Br. Geogr.*, NS 7: 187–204

1986. Places, campaigns and votes. *Pol. Geog. Q.*, 5: S105–S118

Karl, B. 1983. *The uneasy state: The United States from 1915 to 1945*. Chicago: University of Chicago Press

Karper, M. D. 1982. Changes in the labor relations climate: the evidence from NLRB caseload. In *Proceedings of the 34th Annual Meeting*. Industrial Relations Research Association, Madison: University of Wisconsin. 360–65

Kassalow, E. 1985. Trade unionism: once more into the future. In *Proceedings of the 38th Annual Meeting*. Industrial Relations Research Association, Madison: University of Wisconsin. 1–13

1987. The unions' stake in high tech development. Working Paper 87–10. Pittsburgh: Center for Labor Studies, School of Urban and Public Affairs, Carnegie Mellon University

Katz, H. C. 1985. *Shifting gears: changing labor relations in the US automobile industry*. Cambridge, Mass.: MIT Press

Katznelson, I. and A. R. Zolberg, eds. 1986. *Working-class formation: nineteenth-century patterns in western Europe and the United States*. Princeton: Princeton University Press

Kennedy, D. 1976. Form and substance in private law adjudication. *Harv. Law Rev.*, 89: 1685–1778

Key, V. O. Jr. 1949. *Southern politics in state and nation*. New York: Knopf

Kiewiet, D. R. 1983. *Macro-economics and micro-politics: the electoral effects of economic issues*. Chicago: University of Chicago Press

Kinder, D. and D. R. Kiewiet. 1979. Economic discontent and political behavior: the role of personal grievances and collective economic judgments in congressional voting. *Am. J. Pol. Sci.*, 23: 495–527

1981. Sociotropic politics: the American case. *Br. J. Pol. Sci.*, 11: 129–61

Klare, K. 1978. Judicial deradicalization of the Wagner Act and the origins of modern legal consciousness. *Minn. Law Rev.*, 62: 265–340

1981. Labor law as ideology: toward a new historiography of collective bargaining law. *Indust. Rel. Law J.*, 4: 450–82

Kochan, T., ed. 1985. *Challenges and choices facing American labor*. Cambridge, Mass.: MIT Press

Kochan, T., H. C. Katz, and R. McKersie. 1986. *The transformation of American industrial relations*. New York: Basic Books

Kokkelenberg, E. and D. Sockell. 1985. Union membership in the United States, 1973–1981. *Indust. Labor Rel. Rev.*, 38: 497–543

Kolchin, M. and T. Hyclak. 1984. Participation in union activities: multivariate analysis. *J. Labor Res.*, 5: 255–61

Kornhauser, R. 1961. Some social determinants and consequences of union membership. *Labor Hist.*, 2: 30–61

Kramer, M. 1984. The role of federal courts in changing state law: the employment at will doctrine in Pennsylvania. *Univ. Penn. Law Rev.*, 133: 227–64

Krieger, K. 1987. Response to Professor Aaron's paper. In *American labor policy*, ed. C. Morris. Washington, DC: Bureau of National Affairs

LaCapra, D. 1985. *History and criticism*. Ithaca, NY: Cornell University Press

Lahne, H. and J. Kovner. 1955. Local union structure: formality and reality. *Indust. Labor Rel. Rev.*, 9: 24–31

Lauria, M. 1986. Toward a specification of the local state: state intervention strategies in response to a manufacturing plant closure. *Antipode*, 18: 39–65

Lawler, J. J. 1984. The influence of management consultants on the outcome of union certification elections. *Indust. Labor Rel. Rev.*, 38: 38–51

Lawrence, R. Z. 1984. *Can America compete?* Washington, DC: Brookings Institution

Lazear, E. 1983. A microeconomic theory of labor unions. In *Research in labor economics (supplement)*, ed. J. Reid. Greenwich, Conn.: JAI Press. 53–96

Leab, D. J., ed. 1985. *The labor history reader*. Champaign–Urbana, Illinois: University of Illinois Press

Leamer, E. 1985. Self-interpretation. *Econ. Phil.*, 1: 295–302

Leijonhufvud, A. 1981. *Information and coordination: essays in macroeconomic theory*. New York: Oxford University Press

Le Louran, J.-Y. 1980. Predicting union vote from worker attitudes and perceptions. In *Proceedings of the Thirty-Second Winter Meeting*. Madison: Industrial Relations Research Association. 72–82

Lester, R. 1958. *As unions mature: analysis of the evolution of American unionism*. Princeton: Princeton University Press

Lipset, S. M. 1985. The elections, the economy, and public opinion. *PS*, 18: 28–38

Lloyd, P. and P. Dicken. 1972. *Location in space: a theoretical approach to economic geography*. New York: Harper and Row

Lucas, R. 1981. *Studies in business-cycle theory*. Cambridge, Mass.: MIT Press

Lynch, L. and M. Sandver. 1984. Determinants of the decertification process:

evidence from employer initiated elections. Mimeo. Columbus, Ohio: Faculty of Management and Human Resources, Ohio State University

McCloskey, D. 1985. *The rhetoric of economics.* Madison, Wisc.: University of Wisconsin Press

McFadden, D. 1982. Qualitative response models. In *Advances in econometrics,* ed. W. Hildenbrand. Cambridge: Cambridge University Press. 1–37

McKenzie, R. B. 1984. *Fugitive industry: the economics and politics of deindustrialization.* Cambridge, Mass.: Ballinger

McMullin, E. 1984. A case for scientific realism. In *Scientific realism,* ed. J. Leplin. Los Angeles: University of California Press. 8–40

Malin, M. 1983. Protecting the whistleblower from retaliatory discharge. *Univ. Mich. J. Law Reform,* 16: 277–318

Mann, T. E. and R. Wolfinger. 1980. Candidates and parties in congressional elections. *Am. Pol. Sci. Rev.,* 74: 617–32

March, J. G. and J. Olsen. 1984. The new institutionalism: organizational factors in political life. *Am. Pol. Sci. Rev.,* 78: 734–49

Markusen, A. 1985. *Profit cycles, oligopoly, and regional development.* Cambridge, Mass.: MIT Press

Marshall, F. R. 1967. *Labor in the south.* Cambridge, Mass.: Harvard University Press

1987. The labor board's impact on employment, society, and the national economy. In *American labor policy,* ed. C. Morris. Washington, DC: Bureau of National Affairs

1987. *Unheard voices: labor and economic policy in a competitive world.* New York: Basic Books

Marston, S. 1988. Urbanization, industrialization, and the social creation of the space economy. *Urban Geog.* (forthcoming)

Massey, D. 1984. *Spatial divisions of labor: social structures and the geography of production.* London: Macmillan

Mieszkowski, P. 1985. The differential effect of the foreign trade deficit on regions of the United States. In *American domestic priorities: an economic appraisal,* ed. J. M. Quigley and D. L. Rubinfeld. Berkeley: University of California Press

Mills, D. Q. 1979. Flawed victory in labor law reform. *Harv. Bus. Rev.* (May/June): 92–102

Mills, H. A. and E. C. Brown. 1950. *From the Wagner Act to Taft–Hartley: a study of national labor policy and labor relations.* Chicago: University of Chicago Press

Mitchell, D. J. B. 1980. *Unions, wages and inflation.* Washington, DC: Brookings Institution

Moe, T. M. 1985. Control and feedback in economic regulation: the case of the NLRB. *Am. Pol. Sci. Rev.,* 79: 1094–1116

1986. Political control and professional autonomy: the institutional politics of the NLRB. Mimeo. Pittsburgh: Carnegie Conference on Political Economy, Carnegie Mellon University

Montgomery, D. 1987. *The fall of the house of labor: the workplace, the state, and American labor activism, 1865–1925.* Cambridge: Cambridge University Press

Moore, W. J. and R. J. Newman. 1975. On the prospects for American trade union growth: a cross-section analysis. *Rev. Econ. Stat.,* 57: 435–45

Moore, W. J., R. J. Newman, and R. W. Thomas. 1975. Determinants of the passage of right-to-work laws: an alternative interpretation. *J. Law Econ.*, 18: 197–211

Morishima, M. 1984. *The economics of industrial society*. Cambridge: Cambridge University Press

Morris, C., ed. 1982. *The developing labor law*. Washington, DC: Bureau of National Affairs

Morris, C. 1987a. The NLRB in the dog house – can an old board learn new tricks? *San Diego Law Rev.*, 24: 9–50

Morris, C., ed. 1987b. *American labor policy*. Washington, DC: Bureau of National Affairs

Murg, G. and C. Scharman. 1982. Employment at will: do the exceptions overwhelm the rule? *Boston Coll. Law Rev.*, 23: 329–84

Murphy, W. 1987. The representation process. In *American labor policy*, ed. C. Morris. Washington, DC: Bureau of National Affairs

National Labor Relations Board. Various years. *Annual report of the National Labor Relations Board*. Washington, DC: USGPO

Various years. *Election report*. Washington, DC: Division of Information, National Labor Relations Board

1935. *First annual report: fiscal year ended June 30, 1936*. Washington, DC: USGPO

1985. *Legislative history of the National Labor Relations Act, 1935*. 2 vols. Washington, DC: USGPO

Neumann, G. and E. Rissman. 1984. Where have all the union members gone? *J. Labor Econ.*, 2: 175–92

Norris, C. 1985. *Contest of faculties: philosophy and theory after deconstruction*. London: Methuen

Northrup, H. R. 1984. The rise and demise of PATCO. *Indust. Labor Rel. Rev.*, 37: 167–84

Note. 1974. Implied contract rights to job security. *Stan. Law Rev.*, 26: 335–69

1985. The statute of frauds as a bar to an action in tort for fraud. *Fordham Law Rev.*, 53: 1231–1292

Obey, D. and P. Sarbanes, eds. 1986. *The changing American economy*. New York: Blackwell

Palomba, N. A. and C. A. 1971. Right-to-work laws: a suggested economic rationale. *J. Law Econ.*, 14: 475–83

Parfit, D. 1984. *Reasons and persons*. Oxford: Oxford University Press

Peet, R. 1983. Relations of production and the relocation of US manufacturing industry since 1960. *Econ. Geog.*, 59: 112–43

Peet, R., ed. 1987. *International capitalism and industrial restructuring*. Hemel Hempstead, Herts. and Winchester, Mass.: Allen and Unwin

Piore, M. and C. Sabel. 1984. *The second industrial divide: possibilities for prosperity*. New York: Basic Books

Podgursky, M. 1987. Job displacement and labor market adjustment: evidence from the displaced worker survey. Mimeo. Amherst, Mass.: Department of Economics, University of Massachusetts

Porter, M., ed. 1986. *Competition in global industries*. Boston, Mass.: Harvard Business School

Posner, R. 1979. Utilitarianism, economics, and legal theory. *J. Legal Stud.*, 8: 103–40

1980. The ethical and political basis of the efficiency norm in common law adjudication. *Hofstra Law Rev.*, 8: 487–507

1981. *The economics of justice*. Cambridge, Mass.: Harvard University Press

1985. *The federal courts: crisis and reform*. Cambridge, Mass.: Harvard University Press

Pratt, J. W. and R. Zeckhauser, eds. 1985. *Principals and agents: the structure of business*. Boston, Mass.: Harvard Business School

Prosten, R. 1979. The rise in NLRB election delays: measuring business new resistance. *Monthly Labor Rev.*, February: 38–40

Przeworski, A. 1985. *Capitalism and social democracy*. Cambridge: Cambridge University Press

Rees, A. 1973. *The economics of trade unions*. Englewood Cliffs, NJ: Prentice-Hall

Reich, R. 1983. *The next American frontier*. New York: New York Times Books

Reid, J., ed. 1983. *Research in labor economics (supplement)*. Greenwich, Conn.: JAI Press

Reynolds, M. 1986. The case for ending the legal privileges and immunities of trade unions. In *Unions in transition: entering the second century*, ed. S. M. Lipset. San Francisco: Institute for Contemporary Studies. 221–38

Road, S. 1987. The great American job machine shifts gears. Special economic study. New York: Morgan Stanley

Roback, J. 1985. Southern labor law in the Jim Crow era: exploitative or competitive? In *Labor law and the employment market: foundations and applications*, ed. R. Epstein and J. Paul. New Brunswick, NJ: Transaction Books. 217–48

Roberts, H. 1986. *Roberts' dictionary of industrial relations*. 3rd edn. Washington, DC: Bureau of National Affairs

Rogoff, K. and A. Sibert. 1986. Elections and macroeconomic policy cycles. Mimeo. Cambridge, Mass.: National Bureau of Economic Research

Roomkin, M. and R. N. Block. 1981. Case processing time and the outcome of representation elections: some empirical evidence. *U. Ill. Law Rev.*, 1981: 75–97

Rosow, J., ed. 1986. *Teamwork: joint labor–management programs in America*. New York: Pergamon Press

Ross, A. 1948. *Trade union wage policy*. Berkeley: University of California Press

Rottenberg, S. 1956. On choice in labor markets. *Indust. Labor Rel. Rev.*, 9: 183–99

Rusk, J. and J. J. Stucker. 1978. The effects of the Southern system of election laws on voting participation. In *The history of American electoral behavior*, ed. J. Silbey, A. Bogue, and W. Flanigan. Princeton: Princeton University Press. 198–250

St. Antoine, T. J. 1987. The collective bargaining process. In *American labor policy*, ed. C. Morris. Washington, DC: Bureau of National Affairs

Samuelson, P. 1983. Thunen at two hundred. *J. Econ. Lit.*, 21: 1468–88

Sanderson, S., G. Williams, T. Ballenger, and B. J. L. Berry. 1987. Impacts of computer-aided manufacturing on offshore assembly and future manufacturing locations. *Reg. Stud.*, 21: 131–42

Sayer, A. 1984. *Method in social science: a realist approach*. London: Hutchinson

Schlossberg, S. and J. Scott. 1983. *Organizing and the law.* 3rd edn. Washington, DC: Bureau of National Affairs

Schlozman, K. and S. Verba. 1979. *Insult to injury: unemployment, class, and political response.* Cambridge, Mass.: Harvard University Press

Schmitter, P. and G. Lehmbruch, eds. 1979. *Trends toward corporatist intermediation.* Beverly Hills: Sage

Schuerman, J. 1983. *Multivariate analysis in the human services.* Boston: Kluwer/ Nijhoff Publishing

Scott, A. 1980. *The urban land nexus and the state.* London: Pion
  1985. Location processes, urbanization, and territorial development: an exploratory essay. *Environ. Plann. A*, 17: 479–501

Scott, A. and M. Storper, eds. 1986. *Production, work, territory: the geographical anatomy of industrial capitalism.* Hemel Hempstead, Herts. and Winchester, Mass.: Allen and Unwin

Scoville, J. 1971. Influences on unionization in the US in 1966. *Indust. Rel.*, 10: 354–63

Seeber, R. and W. Cooke. 1983. The decline in union success in NLRB representation elections. *Indust. Rel.*, 22: 34–44

Sen, A. 1987. The standard of living. In *The standard of living. The Tanner Lectures, Clare Hall, Cambridge 1985*, ed. G. Hawthorn. Cambridge: Cambridge University Press. 1–38

Shister, J. 1953. The logic of union growth. *J. Pol. Econ.*, 61: 413–33

Simon, H. 1985. Human nature in politics: the dialogue of psychology with political science. *Am. Pol. Sci. Rev.*, 79: 293–304

Skocpol, T. 1980. Political response to capitalist crisis: neomarxist theories of the state and the case of the New Deal. *Pol. Soc.*, 10: 155–201

Skocpol, T. and K. Finegold. 1982. Economic intervention and the early New Deal. *Pol. Sci. Q.*, 97: 255–78

Smith, D. 1981. *Industrial location.* 2nd edn. New York: Wiley

Smith, J. and W. Childs. 1987. Imported from America: cooperative labor relations at New United Motor Manufacturing, Inc. *Indust. Rel. Law J.*, 9: 70–81

Smith, L. 1983. The effect of right-to-work laws on the level of unionization in regional economies. Mimeo. Berea, Ohio: Department of Economics, Baldwin-Wallace College

Spencer, H. 1954 [1864]. *Social statics: the conditions essential to human happiness specified, and the first of them developed.* New York: Robert Schalkenback Foundation

Stieber, J. 1986. Recent developments in employment-at-will. Mimeo. Ann Arbor: University of Michigan Law School

Stieber, J. and M. Murray. 1983. Protection against unjust discharge: the need for a federal statute. *Univ. Mich. J. Law Reform*, 16: 319–42

Stone, K. 1981. The post-war paradigm in American labor law. *Yale Law J.*, 90: 1509–80

Storper, M. 1988. Big events, small structures, and the theory of economic geography. *Environ. Plann. A*, 20: 165–86

Storper, M. and R. Walker. 1983. The theory of labor and the theory of location. *Intern. J. Urban Reg. Res.*, 7: 1–41
  1984. The spatial division of labor: labor and the location of industries. In *Sunbelt/ snowbelt*, eds. L. Sawers and W. Tabb. New York: Oxford University Press. 19–47

Strasser, F. 1986. Employment-at-will: death of a doctrine? *Nat. Law J.*, Monday 20 January 1986:1, 6, and 7

Strauss, L. 1973. Niccolò Machiavelli. In *History of political philosophy*, ed. L. Strauss and J. Cropsey. 2nd edn. Chicago: University of Chicago Press. 271–92

Summers, C. W. 1983. Introduction. *Univ. Mich. J. Law Reform*, 16: 201–5

Taylor, C. 1985. *Philosophical papers 2: philosophy and the human sciences.* Cambridge: Cambridge University Press

Taylor, P. and R. J. Johnston. 1979. *Geography of elections.* Harmondsworth: Penguin

Tollefson, J. and J. Pichler. 1975. A comment on right-to-work laws: a suggested rationale. *J. Law Econ.*, 18: 193–96

Townley, B. 1986. *Labor law reform in US industrial relations.* Aldershot: Gower

Tribe, L. 1980. The puzzling persistence of process-based constitutional theories. *Yale Law J.*, 89: 1063–80

Trigg, R. 1985. *Understanding social science.* Oxford: Blackwell

Trowbridge, A. B. 1985. Forum. In *NLRB at 50: labor board at the crossroads. A BNA special report.* Washington, DC: Bureau of National Affairs. 5–7

Troy, L. and N. Sheflin. 1985. *Union sourcebook: membership, structure, finance directory.* West Orange, New Jersey: Industrial Relations Data Information Services

Tushnet, M. 1980. Darkness on the edge of town: the contributions of John Hart Ely to constitutional theory. *Yale Law J.*, 80: 1037–62

Unger, R. M. 1986. *The critical legal studies movement.* Cambridge, Mass.: Harvard University Press

Verba, S. and N. Nie. 1972. *Participation in America: political democracy and social equality.* New York: Harper and Row

Von Thunen, J. [1823] 1962. *The isolated state*, trans. P. Hall. London: Edward Arnold

Voos, P., 1984. Trends in union organizing expenditures, 1953–1977. *Indust. Labor Rel. Rev.*, 38: 52–63

Walker, R. A. 1985. Technological determination and determinism: industrial growth and location. In *High technology, space, and society*, ed. M. Castells. Beverly Hills: Sage. 226–64

Walzer, M. 1983. *Spheres of justice.* New York: Basic Books

Warde, A. 1985. Spatial change, politics and the division of labor. In *Social relations and spatial structures*, ed. D. Gregory and J. Urry. London: Macmillan. 190–212

Warren, A. 1986. Quality of work life at General Motors. In *Teamwork: joint labor–management programs in America*, ed. J. Rosow. New York: Pergamon

Wattenberg, M. P. 1984. *The decline of American political parties 1952–1980.* Cambridge, Mass.: Harvard University Press.

Weber, A. 1929. *Theory of the location of industries*, trans. C. J. Friedrich. Chicago: University of Chicago Press

Weiler, P. 1983. Promises to keep: securing workers' rights to self organization under the NLRA. *Harv. Law Rev.*, 96: 1769–1827

   1984a. Striking a new balance: freedom of contract and the prospects for union representation. *Harv. Law Rev.*, 98: 351–420

   1984b. Statement. In *Oversight hearings on the subject "Has labor law failed?" Part I.* Joint hearings before the Subcommittee on Labor–Management Relations of the Committee on Education and Labor, 98th Congress, House of Representatives. Washington, DC: USGPO. 119–27

Weir, M. and T. Skocpol. 1985. State structures and the possibilities of "Keynesian" responses to the great depression in Sweden, Britain, and the United States. In *Bringing the state back in*, ed. P. B. Evans, D. Rueschemeyer, and T. Skocpol. Cambridge: Cambridge University Press. 107–63

White, H. 1980. The value of narrativity in the representation of reality. *Crit. Inquiry*, 7: 5–28

Whittaker, W. G. and C. Ciccone. 1978. The Fair Labor Standards Act Amendments of 1977 (PL 95–151): discussion with historical background. Washington, DC: Congressional Research Service, Library of Congress

Wilcock, R. and I. Sobel. 1955. Secondary labor force mobility in four midwestern shoe towns. *Indust. Labor Rel. Rev.*, 8: 520–40

Williams, B. 1987. The standard of living: interests and capabilities. In *The standard of living. The Tanner Lectures, Clare Hall, Cambridge 1985*, ed. G. Hawthorn. Cambridge: Cambridge University Press. 94–102

Williams, R. 1985. *NLRB regulation of election conduct*. Revised edn. Philadelphia: Labor Relations and Public Policy Series, no. 8. Industrial Relations Unit, University of Pennsylvania

Williamson, O. 1975. *Markets and hierarchies*. New York: Free Press
1985. *The economic institutions of capitalism*. New York: Free Press

Wolfinger, R. and S. Rosenstone. 1980. *Who votes?* New Haven: Yale University Press

Woodward, C. V. 1966. *The strange career of Jim Crow*. 2nd edn. New York: Oxford University Press

Wrigley, N. 1985. *Categorical data analysis for geographers and environmental scientists*. London: Longmans

Yin, R. 1984. *Case study research: design and methods*. Beverly Hills: Sage Publications

Youngblood, S., W. Mobley, and A. DeNisi. 1982. Attitudes, perceptions, and intentions to vote in a union certification election: an empirical investigation. In *Proceedings of the Thirty-Fourth Annual Winter Meeting*. Madison: Industrial Relations Research Association. 244–57

Zolberg, A. R. 1986. How many exceptions? In *Working-class formation: nineteenth-century patterns in western Europe and the United States*, ed. I. Katznelson and A. R. Zolberg. Princeton: Princeton University Press

Zysman, J. and S. Cohen. 1987. *Manufacturing matters*. New York: Basic Books

Name index

Subject index